HUMAN RELATIONS FOR CAREER AND PERSONAL SUCCESS

FOURTH EDITION

HUMAN RELATIONS FOR CAREER AND PERSONAL SUCCESS

FOURTH EDITION

Andrew J. DuBrin
Rochester Institute of Technology

Prentice Hall
Englewood Cliffs, New Jersey 07632

Library of Congress Cataloging-in-Publication Data

DuBrin, Andrew J.
    Human relations for career and personal success / Andrew J.
DuBrin.—4th ed.
      p.   cm.
    Includes bibliographical references and indexes.
    ISBN 0-13-149584-4
    1. Success in business. 2. Organizational behavior.
    3. Psychology, Industrial. 4. Interpersonal relations. I. Title.
HF5386.D768 1996
650.1'3—dc20
                                            95-11971
                                                CIP

Manufacturing manager: *Ed O'Dougherty*
Acquisitions editor: *Elizabeth Sugg*
Director of Production and Manufacturing: *Bruce Johnson*
Editorial/production supervision: *Mary Carnis*
Cover and interior design: *HRS, Inc.*

 © 1996 by Prentice-Hall, Inc.
A Simon & Schuster Company
Englewood Cliffs, New Jersey 07632

ISBN 0-13-149584-4

Printed in the United States of America
10 9 8 7 6 5 4 3 2 1

Prentice-Hall International (UK) Limited, *London*
Prentice-Hall of Australia Pty. Limited, *Sydney*
Prentice-Hall Canada Inc., *Toronto*
Prentice-Hall Hispanoamericana, S.A., *Mexico*
Prentice-Hall of India Private Limited, *New Delhi*
Prentice-Hall of Japan, Inc., *Tokyo*
Simon & Schuster Asia Pte. Ltd., *Singapore*
Editora Prentice-Hall do Brasil, Ltda., *Rio de Janeiro*

To Rosemary,
the first of the new generation

CONTENTS

PART 2: DEALING EFFECTIVELY WITH PEOPLE

PART 3: DEVELOPING CAREER THRUST

PREFACE

The purpose of this book remains the same as that of previous editions: to show you how you can become more effective in your work and personal life through knowledge of and skill in human relations. Numerous case examples illustrate the application of such knowledge.

A major theme of this book is that success in work and success in personal life are related. Success on the job often leads to success in personal life, and success in personal life can lead to job success. You need to deal effectively with yourself and other people in order to progress in your career. Dealing effectively with people is also valuable in personal life. As a result, human relations continues to be an important part of the curriculum in many programs of study, including general business, office practices, secretarial studies, computer applications, data processing, sales training, programs such as auto service and equipment repair, and CAD/CAM (computer-assisted design/computer-assisted manufacturing).

One major audience for this book is students who will meet human relations problems on the job and in personal life. The text is designed for human relations courses taught in colleges, career schools, vocational-technical schools, and other postsecondary schools. Another major audience for this book is managerial, professional, and technical workers who are forging ahead in their careers.

ORGANIZATION OF THE BOOK

The text is divided into four parts, reflecting the major issues in human relations. Part 1 covers four aspects of understanding and managing yourself: Chapter 1 focuses on self-understanding and the interrelationship of career and personal success; Chapter 2 explains how to use goal setting and other methods of self-motivation to improve your chances for success; Chapter 3 explains the basics of solving problems and making decisions with an emphasis on creativity; Chapter 4 deals with achieving wellness by managing stress and burnout; and Chapter 5 focuses on dealing with personal problems such as substance abuse, counterproductive habits, and other forms of self-defeating behavior.

Part 2 examines the heart of human relations—dealing effectively with other people. The topics in Chapters 6 through 9 are, respectively, communicating with people, handling conflict with others and being assertive, getting along with your boss, and getting along with your co-workers and customers.

Part 3 provides information to help career-oriented people capitalize on their education, experience, talent, and ambition. The topics of Chapters 10 through 13 are: choosing a career and career switching, finding a suitable job, developing good work habits, and getting ahead in your career. Chapter 14 is about the related topics of developing self-confidence and becoming a leader.

Part 4, "Managing Your Personal Life," is divided into two chapters. Chapter 15 offers realistic advice on managing personal finances. Chapter 16 describes how to enhance social and family life, including how to find new friends and keep a personal relationship vibrant.

Human Relations for Career and Personal Success, Fourth Edition, is both a text and a workbook of experiential exercises, including role plays and self-examination quizzes related to the text. (An experiential exercise allows for learning by doing, along with guided instruction.) Each chapter contains one or more exercises and ends with a human relations case problem. The experiential exercises can all be completed during a class session. In addition, they emphasize human interaction and thinking and minimize paperwork.

 ## CHANGES IN THE FOURTH EDITION

The fourth edition reflects several major changes along with an updating and selective pruning of previous editions. Chapter 5, about dealing with personal problems is new, and the topics of conflict and being assertive have been combined into Chapter 7. Chapter 9 now includes getting along with both co-workers and customers. New topics include managing personal problems, customer service, achieving the quality attitude, appreciating cultural diversity, developing self-discipline, and overcoming self-defeating behavior. Several more complex cases and examples have been added, and 50 percent of the cases and examples are new.

 ## INSTRUCTOR'S MANUAL AND TEST BANK

The instructor's manual for this text contains over 750 test questions, chapter outline and lecture notes, answers to discussion questions and case problems, and comments about the exercises. Computerized test banks, known as the Prentice Hall Test Manager, also accompany the text. In addition, the manual includes step-by-step instruction for the use of Computer-Assisted Scenario Analysis (CASA).

CASA is a user-friendly way of using any word processing program with any computer to assist in analyzing cases. The student enters an existing case into the computer, and then analyzes it by answering the case questions in the text. Next, the student makes up a new scenario or adds a new twist to the case, and enters this scenario in **bold** into the case. The case questions are reanalyzed in light of this new scenario. Any changes in the answers are **printed in bold.** CASA gives the student experience in a creative application of word processing. Equally important, it helps students develop a "what-if" point of view in solving human relations problems.

INFORMATION ON SCANS REQUIREMENTS

In 1990, the Secretary's Commission on Achieving Necessary Skills (SCANS) was formed to encourage a high-performance economy characterized by high-skills, high-wage employment. To help achieve this goal, the Commission recommended that postsecondary schools teach five competencies and a three-part foundation of skills and personal qualities needed for job performance.

The competencies state that effective workers can productively use resources, interpersonal skills, information, systems, and technology. In addition, the foundation competence requires basic skills (such as reading, writing, and arithmetic), thinking skills (such as thinking creatively), and personal qualities (such as self-management and integrity).

Human Relations for Career and Personal Success provides information and exercises directly aimed at satisfying components of five of the above eight requirements (information, systems, and technology are ordinarily taught outside of a human relations curriculum). A guide to meeting the SCANS requirement is presented next.

COMPETENCIES: EFFECTIVE WORKERS CAN PRODUCTIVELY USE

- *Resources: allocating time, money, materials, space, and staff.* Chapter 12, about developing good work habits, deals directly with allocating time.

- *Interpersonal Skills: working on teams, teaching others, serving customers, leading, negotiating, and working well with people from culturally diverse backgrounds.* Chapter 9, about getting along with co-workers and customers, contains information about working on teams, helping teammates, and getting along well with people from culturally diverse backgrounds. Chapter 14, about developing self-confidence and becoming a leader, deals directly with leading. Chapter 7, about handling conflict and being assertive, deals directly with negotiation.

- *Basic Skills: reading, writing, arithmetic and mathematics, speaking and listening.* Chapter 6, about communicating with people, provides suggestions for improved writing, speaking, and listening.

- *Thinking Skills: thinking creatively, making decisions, solving problems, seeing things in the mind's eye, knowing how to learn, and reasoning.*   Chapter 3, about solving problems and making decisions, deals directly with creative thinking, decision making, and problem solving. "Seeing things in the mind's eye" comes under the topic of visualization, which is described in several contexts: stress reduction, overcoming self-defeating behavior, and developing self-confidence.

- *Personal Qualities: individual responsibility, self-esteem, sociability, self-management and integrity.*   Chapter 1, about human relations and yourself, deals extensively with the development of self-esteem. Chapter 9, about getting along with co-workers and customers, deals directly with sociability. Chapter 2 is about self-motivation and goal setting, and thus deals directly with self-management.

 ACKNOWLEDGMENTS

A book of this nature cannot be written and published without the cooperation of many people. My thanks go first to my editorial and production team at Prentice Hall Education, Career and Technology— Elizabeth Sugg, Mary Carnis, and Judy Casillo, along with Christine Furry of North Market Street Graphics. My outside reviewers of this and the previous editions provided many constructive suggestions for improving the book. By name they are:

    Mary D. Aun, DeVry Technical Institute

    Donna Ana Branch and H. Ralph Todd, Jr., American River College

    Hollis Chaleau Brown, Oakton Community College

    Sheri Bryant, DeKalb Technical Institute

    Win Chesney, St. Louis Community College

    Ruth Keller, Indiana Vo-Tech College

    Robert F. Pearse, Rochester Institute of Technology

    Bernice Rose, Computer Learning Center

    Pamela Simon, Baker College

Thanks also to my family members, friends, and acquaintances whose emotional support and encouragement assist my writing.

                                      Andrew J. DuBrin
                                      Rochester, New York

ABOUT THE AUTHOR

An accomplished author, Andrew J. DuBrin, Ph.D. brings to his work years of research experience in business psychology. His research has been reported in *Psychology Today, The Wall Street Journal* and over 100 national magazines and local newspapers. An active speaker, Dr. DuBrin has appeared as a guest on over 350 radio and television shows. He has published numerous articles, textbooks and well-publicized professional books. Dr. DuBrin received his Ph.D. from Michigan State University and is currently teaching management and organizational behavior at the Rochester Institute of Technology.

CHAPTER 1

HUMAN RELATIONS AND YOURSELF

Learning Objectives

After studying the information and doing the exercises in this chapter you should be able to:

- Explain the meaning of human relations.

- Pinpoint how work and personal life influence each other.

- Explain how the self-concept influences behavior.

- Summarize the consequences of high and low self-esteem, and how to enhance self-esteem.

- Be aware of the dangers of preoccupation with the self.

*B*ryant, a computer operator, works effectively with other people in computer operations. He is quiet, but sincere and hardworking. Bryant's job doesn't require much conversation because he is always caught up in running computers. Off the job, he is a loner. He would like to make friends, but he doesn't take the initiative to reach out to people. Bryant prefers work to personal life, largely because he deals better with people in a computer center than in a social setting.

Tony, an attendant, has difficulty dealing with people in a hospital. He resents the low wages he is making and sometimes takes it out on patients, nurses, other attendants, and physicians. Tony's supervisor wrote on his last performance evaluation that "Tony is too short with people to last very long with us." Off the job, Tony's personality becomes more positive. He can be mildly sarcastic at times, but his friends realize that Tony's sharpness is a small price to pay for his worthwhile friendship.

Linda, a restaurant manager, is a likable person who interacts well with people both on and off the job. Linda is only twenty years old, while several of the people who work for her are in their mid-twenties. As one of them puts it, "Who cares if Linda is young? The woman is a natural leader." Despite Linda's nontraditional working hours, she has many friends with whom she shares her free time. Her friends include day-shift people and night-shift people. They are particularly impressed with her smooth and confident manner and her ability to be a good listener at the same time.

The three people just described tell us something about the meaning of human relations. Bryant practices a limited type of human relations. He deals effectively with people primarily on the job. Tony is the opposite. He is effective with people primarily in social settings. Linda practices the type of human relations emphasized in this book—she is effective with people in both work and personal settings.

In the context used here, **human relations** is the art of using systematic knowledge about human behavior to improve personal, job, and career effectiveness. In other words, you can accomplish more in dealing with people in both personal and work life. You can do so by relying on guidelines developed by psychologists, counselors, and other human relations specialists.

This book presents a wide variety of suggestions and guidelines for improving your personal relationships both on and off the job. Most of them are based on systematic knowledge about human behavior. Our main concern, however, will be with the suggestions and guidelines themselves, not the methods by which these ideas were discovered.

HOW WORK AND PERSONAL LIFE INFLUENCE EACH OTHER

Most people reading this book will be doing so to improve their careers. Therefore, the book centers around relationships with people in a job setting. Keep in mind that human relationships in work and personal life have much in common. If we followed the cases of Bryant and Tony over an extended period of time, we would probably discover certain similarities in their relationships with people on and off the job. As Bryant continued to develop confidence in his role as a computer operator, he would slowly become more effective in handling people off the job. Impressed with his job skills, a few of his co-workers might begin to invite him to social gatherings. As Tony became increasingly bitter about his job, some of his bitterness would probably spill over into his personal relationships. His occasional sarcasm might turn into a steady flow of verbal abuse toward others.

A recent study based on a nationwide sample supports the close relationship between job satisfaction and life satisfaction. The study also found that both job satisfaction and life satisfaction influence each other. Life satisfaction significantly influenced job satisfaction, and job satisfaction significantly influenced life satisfaction. The relationship between job and life satisfaction is particularly strong at a given time in a person's life. However, being satisfied with your job today has a smaller effect on future life satisfaction.[1]

Work and personal life influence each other in a number of specific ways. First, the satisfactions you achieve on the job contribute to your general life satisfactions. Conversely, if you suffer from chronic job dissatisfaction, your life satisfaction will begin to decline. Career disappointments have been shown to cause marital relationships to suffer. Frustrated on the job, many people start feuding with their partners and other family members.

Second, an unsatisfying job can also affect physical health, primarily by creating stress and burnout. Intense job dissatisfaction may even lead to heart disease, ulcers, intestinal disorders, and skin problems. People who have high job satisfaction even tend to live longer than those who suffer from prolonged job dissatisfaction.[2] Finding the right type of job may thus add years to a person's life.

Third, the quality of your relationships with people in work and personal life influence each other. If you experience intense conflict in your family, you might be so upset that you will be unable to form good relationships with co-workers. Conversely, if you have a healthy, rewarding personal life, it will be easier for you to form good relationships on the job. People you meet on the job will find it pleasant to relate to a seemingly positive and untroubled person.

Personal relationships on the job also influence personal relationships off the job. Interacting harmoniously with co-workers can put one in a better mood for dealing with family and friends after hours. Crossing swords with employees and customers during working hours can make it difficult for you to feel comfortable and relaxed with people off the job.

Fourth, certain skills contribute to success in both work and personal life. For example, people who know how to deal effectively with others and get things accomplished on the job can use the same skills to enhance their personal lives. Similarly, people who are effective in dealing with friends and family members, and who can organize things, are likely to be effective supervisors.

Can you think of any other ways in which success in work and personal life are related to each other?

HUMAN RELATIONS BEGINS WITH SELF-UNDERSTANDING

Before you can understand other people very well, you must understand yourself. All readers of this book already know something about themselves. An important starting point in learning more about yourself is self-examination. Suppose that instead of being about human relations, this book were about dancing. The reader would obviously need to know what other dancers do right and wrong. But the basic principles of dancing cannot be fully grasped unless they are seen in relation to your own style of dancing. Watching a videotape of your dancing, for example, would be helpful. You might also ask other people for comments and suggestions about your dance movements.

Similarly, to achieve **self-understanding,** you must gather valid information about yourself. (Self-understanding refers to knowledge about oneself, particularly with respect to mental and emotional aspects.) Every time you read a self-help book, take a personality quiz, or receive an evaluation of your work from a manager or instructor, you are gaining some self-knowledge.

In achieving self-understanding, it is helpful to recognize that the **self** is a complex idea. It generally refers to a person's total being or individuality. However, a distinction is sometimes made between the self a person projects to the outside world, and the inner self. The **public self** is what the person is communicating about himself or herself, and what others actually perceive about the person. The **private self** is the actual person that one may be.[3] A similar distinction is made between the real and the ideal self. Many people think of themselves in terms of an ideal version of what they are really like. To avoid making continuous distinctions between the various selves throughout this text, we will use the term *self* to refer to an accurate representation of the individual.

Because an entire chapter is devoted to the self, it does not imply that the other chapters do not deal with the self. Most of this text is geared toward using human relations knowledge for self-development and self-improvement. Throughout the text you will find questionnaires designed to improve insight. The self-knowledge emphasized here deals with psychological (such as personality traits and thinking style) rather than physical characteristics (such as height and blood pressure).

Here we discuss six types of information that contribute to self-understanding.

1. General information about human behavior

2. Informal feedback from people

3. Feedback from superiors

4. Feedback from co-workers

5. Feedback from self-examination exercises

6. Insights gathered in psychotherapy and counseling

GENERAL INFORMATION ABOUT HUMAN BEHAVIOR

As you learn about people in general, you should also be gaining knowledge about yourself. Therefore, most of the information in this text is presented in a form that should be useful to you personally. Whenever general information is presented, it is your responsibility to relate such information to your particular situation. Chapter 7, for example, discusses some causes of conflicts in personal relationships. One such general cause is limited resources; that is, not everyone can have what he or she wants. See how this general principle applies to you. An example involving others is, "That's why I've been so angry with Melissa lately. She was the one given the promotion, while I'm stuck in the same old job."

In relating facts and observations about people in general to yourself, be careful not to misapply the information. Feedback from other people will help you avoid the pitfalls of introspection (looking into oneself).

INFORMAL FEEDBACK FROM PEOPLE

As just implied, **feedback** is information that tells you how well you have performed. You can sometimes obtain feedback from the spontaneous comments of others, or by asking them for feedback. A materials-handling specialist grew one notch in self-confidence when co-workers began to call him, "Lightning." He was given this name because of the rapidity with which he processes orders. His experience illustrates that a valuable source of information for self-understanding is what the significant people in your life think of you. Although feedback of this type might make you feel uncomfortable, when it is consistent, it accurately reflects how you are perceived by others.

With some ingenuity you can create informal feedback. (In this sense, the term *formal* refers to not being part of a company-sponsored program.) A student enrolled in a human relations course obtained valuable information about himself from a questionnaire he sent to fifteen people. His directions were:

I am hoping that you can help me with one of the most important assignments of my life. I want to obtain a candid picture of how I am seen by others—what they think are my strengths, weaknesses, good points, and bad points. Any other observations about me as an individual would also be welcome.

Write down your thoughts on the enclosed sheet of paper. The information that you provide me will help me develop a plan for personal improvement that I am writing for a course in human relations. Mail the form back to me in the enclosed envelope. It is not necessary for you to sign the form.

A few skeptics will argue that friends never give you a true picture of yourself, but rather say flattering things about you because they value your friendship. Experience has shown, however, that if you emphasize the importance of their opinions, most people will give you a few constructive suggestions. You also have to appear and be sincere. Since not everyone's comments will be helpful, you may have to sample many people.

FEEDBACK FROM SUPERIORS

Virtually all employers provide employees with formal and/or informal feedback on their performance. A formal method of feedback is called a *performance appraisal*. During a performance appraisal your superior will convey to you what he or she thinks you are doing well and not so well. These observations become a permanent part of your personnel record. Informal feedback occurs when a superior discusses your job performance with you but does not record these observations.

MANY PEOPLE HAVE AN ACADEMIC SELF-CONCEPT
AND A NONACADEMIC SELF-CONCEPT

The feedback obtained from superiors in this way can help you learn about yourself. For instance, if two different bosses say that you are a creative problem solver, you might conclude that you are creative. If several bosses told you that you are too impatient with other people, you might conclude that you are impatient.

Given that work life consumes so much of a working adult's time, it becomes a valuable source of information about the self. Many people, in fact, establish much of their identity from their occupations. Next time you are at a social gathering, ask a person "What do you do?" Most likely, the person will respond in terms of an occupation or a company affiliation. It is a rare person in our culture who responds, "I sleep, I eat, I watch television, and I talk to friends."

FEEDBACK FROM CO-WORKERS

A growing practice in organizations is **peer evaluations,** a system in which co-workers contribute to an evaluation of a person's job performance. Although co-workers under this system do not have total responsibility for evaluating each other, their input is taken seriously. The amount of a worker's salary increase could thus be affected by peer judgments about his or her performance. The results of peer evaluations can also be used as feedback for learning about yourself. Assume that co-workers agree on several of your strengths and needs for improvement. You can conclude that you are generally perceived that way by others who work closely with you.

Customer service technicians (people who service and repair photocopying machines) at Xerox Corporation use an elaborate system of peer evaluations. A group of peers indicates whether a particular aspect of job performance or behavior is a strength or a *developmental opportunity*. A developmental opportunity is a positive way of stating that a person has a weakness. The five factors rated by peers are shown in Exhibit 1-1. The initials under "Peer Evaluations" are those of the co-workers who are doing the evaluations. The person being rated thus knows who to thank (or kick) for the feedback.

In addition to indicating whether a job factor is a strength or an opportunity, raters can supply comments and developmental suggestions. For example, CJ made the following written comment about Leslie Fantasia: "Missed 50 percent of our work group meetings. Attend work group member training and review our work group meeting ground rules."

FEEDBACK FROM SELF-EXAMINATION EXERCISES

Many self-help books, including this one, contain questionnaires that you fill out by yourself, for yourself. The information that you pick up from these questionnaires often provides valuable clues to your preferences, values, and personal traits. Such self-examination questionnaires should not be confused with the scientifically researched test you might take in a counseling center or guidance department, or when applying for a job.

EXHIBIT 1-1

PEER EVALUATION OF CUSTOMER SERVICE TECHNICIAN

PERSON EVALUATED: Leslie Fantasia

Skill Categories and Expected Behaviors	Peer Evaluations for Each Category and Behavior					
	TR	JP	CK	JT	CJ	ML
Customer Care						
Takes ownership for customer problems	O	S	S	S	S	S
Follows through on customer commitments	S	S	S	S	S	S
Technical Knowledge and Skill						
Engages in continuous learning to update technical skills	O	S	S	S	S	O
Corrects problems on the first visit	O	O	S	S	S	S
Work Group Support						
Actively participates in work group meetings	S	S	S	S	O	S
Backs up other work group members by taking calls in other areas	S	O	O	S	S	S
Minimal absence	S	O	S	S	O	S
Finance Management						
Adhere to work group parts expense process	S	S	S	O	S	S
Pass truck audits	S	S	S	O	S	S

NOTE: S refers to a strength, O refers to developmental opportunity.

The amount of useful information gained from self-examination questionnaires depends on your candor. Since no outside judge is involved in these self-help quizzes, candor is usually not a problem. An exception is that we all have certain blind spots. Most people, for example, believe that they have considerably above-average skills in dealing with people.

As a starting point in conducting self-examination exercises, do the self-awareness adjective list presented in Self-Examination Exercise 1-1. You will be asked to complete two other self-examination questionnaires in this chapter. The Self-Disclosure Survey estimates whether you are open or closed with others. The Self-Knowledge Questionnaire presented at the end of the chapter is a comprehensive survey of yourself. It provides a sound basis for profiting from much of the information in this book.

SELF-EXAMINATION EXERCISE 1-1:

Self-Awareness Adjective List

Read through the following list and circle the ten adjectives that you think best describe you. You have now formed a brief self-description—for example, aggressive, ambitious, bold, courageous, extroverted, friendly, greedy, skillful, tenacious, and zestful. Next, discuss your list with a friend. Your friend should be encouraged to discuss his or her list with you. This exchange should result in feedback that will help you determine the accuracy of your self-perceptions.

It is helpful to discuss the adjective lists of various people in a group setting. Each group member thus has an opportunity to obtain feedback from a greater number of people.

able	foolish	malicious	proud	simple
accepting	frank	manipulative	questioning	sinful
adaptable	free	materialistic	quiet	skillful
aggressive	friendly	maternal	radical	sly
ambitious	genial	mature	rational	sociable
annoying	gentle	merry	rationalizing	spontaneous
anxious	giving	modest	reactionary	stable
authoritative	greedy	mystical	realistic	strained
belligerent	gruff	naive	reasonable	strong
bitter	guilty	narcissistic	reassuring	stubborn
bold	gullible	negative	rebellious	sympathetic
calm	happy	nervous	reflective	taciturn
carefree	hard	neurotic	regretful	tactful
careless	helpful	noisy	rejecting	temperamental
caring	helpless	normal	relaxed	tenacious
certain	honorable	objective	reliable	tender
cheerful	hostile	oblivious	religious	tense
clever	idealistic	observant	remote	thoughtful
cold	imaginative	obsessive	resentful	tough
complex	immature	organized	reserved	trusting
confident	impressionable	original	resolute	trustworthy
conforming	inconsiderate	overburdened	respectful	unassuming
controlled	independent	overconfident	responsible	unaware
courageous	ingenious	overconforming	responsive	uncertain
cranky	innovative	overemotional	retentive	unconcerned
critical	insensitive	overprotecting	rigid	uncontrolled
cynical	insincere	passive	sarcastic	understanding
demanding	intelligent	paternal	satisfied	unpredictable
dependable	introverted	patient	scientific	unreasonable
dependent	intuitive	perceptive	searching	unstructured
derogatory	irresponsible	perfectionist	self-accepting	useful
dignified	irritable	persuasive	self-actualizing	vain
disciplined	jealous	petty	self-assertive	vapid
docile	jovial	playful	self-aware	visionary

(Continued)

dogged	juvenile	pleasant	self-conscious	vulnerable
domineering	kind	pompous	self-effacing	warm
dreamy	knowledgeable	powerful	self-indulgent	willful
dutiful	lazy	pragmatic	selfish	wise
effervescent	learned	precise	self-righteous	wishful
efficient	lewd	pretending	sensible	withdrawn
elusive	liberal	pretentious	sensitive	witty
energetic	lively	principled	sentimental	worried
extroverted	logical	progressive	serious	youthful
fair	loving	protective	silly	zestful
fearful				

SOURCE: Reprinted with permission from David W. Johnson, *Human Relations and Your Career* (Englewood Cliffs, N.J.: Prentice-Hall, 1978), p. 230.

INSIGHTS GATHERED IN PSYCHOTHERAPY AND COUNSELING

Many people seek self-understanding through discussions with a psychotherapist or other professional counselor. **Psychotherapy** is a method of overcoming emotional problems through discussion with a mental health professional. However, many people enter into psychotherapy with the primary intention of gaining insight into themselves. A representative area of insight would be for the therapist to help the client detect patterns of self-defeating and self-destructive behavior. For example, some people unconsciously do something to ruin a personal relationship or perform poorly on the job just when things are going well. The therapist might point out this self-defeating pattern of behavior. Self-insight of this kind often—but not always—leads to useful changes in behavior.

YOUR SELF-CONCEPT: WHAT YOU THINK OF YOU

Another aspect of self-understanding is your **self-concept,** or what you think of you and who you think you are. A successful person—one who is achieving his or her goals in work or personal life—usually has a positive self-concept. In contrast, an unsuccessful person often has a negative self-concept. Such differences in self-concept can have a profound influence on your career.[3] If you see yourself as a successful person, you will tend to engage in activities that will help you prove yourself right. Similarly, if you have a limited view of yourself, you will tend to engage in activities that prove yourself right. For example, you may often look for convenient ways to prevent yourself from succeeding.

Self-concepts are based largely on what others have said about us. If enough people tell you that you are "terrific," after a while you will have the self-concept of a terrific person. When people tell you that you are not a worthwhile person, after a while your self-concept will become that of a not worthwhile person. People who say "I'm OK" are expressing a positive self-concept. People who say "I'm not OK" have a negative self-concept.

Another important fact about the self-concept is that it usually has several components. Many people, for example, have an academic self-concept and a nonacademic self-concept.[4] One person might feel proud and confident in a classroom yet quite humble and shaky on the job. Another person might feel unsure and uneasy in the classroom yet proud and confident on the job. Following the same logic, a person's self-concept with respect to personal life may differ from his or her career self-concept.

THE SELF-CONCEPT AND SELF-CONFIDENCE

A strong self-concept leads to self-confidence, which has many important implications for job performance. People who are confident in themselves are more effective in leadership and sales positions. Self-confident workers are also more likely to set higher goals for themselves, and persist in trying to reach their goals.[5]

Why some people develop strong self-concepts and self-confidence while others have weak self-concepts and self-confidence is not entirely known. One contributing factor may be inherited talents and abilities. Assume that a person quickly learns how to perform key tasks in life such as walking, talking, swimming, running, reading, writing, computing, and driving a car. This person is likely to be more self-confident than a person who struggled to learn these skills.

Another contributing factor to a positive self-concept and self-confidence is lifelong feedback from others (as mentioned above). If, as a youngster, your parents, siblings, and playmates consistently told you that you were competent, you would probably develop a strong self-concept. However, some people might find you to be conceited.

YOUR BODY IMAGE AS PART OF YOUR SELF-CONCEPT

Our discussion of the self-concept so far has emphasized mental traits and characteristics. Your **body image,** or your perception of your body, also contributes to your self-concept.[6] The current emphasis on physical fitness stems largely from a desire on the part of people to be physically fit and healthy. It is also apparent that being physically fit contributes to a positive self-concept, and being physically unfit can contribute to a negative self-concept. The relationship between the self-concept and physical fitness also works the other way: If your self-concept is positive it may push you toward physical fitness. Conversely, if you have a negative self-concept you may allow yourself to become physically unfit.

A distorted body image can result in such severe problems as anorexia nervosa. Anorexic people have such an intense fear of obesity that they undereat to the point of malnutrition and illness. About 5 percent of these people die from their disorder. Having a positive body image is obviously important for personal life. Some people, for example, who are dissatisfied with their bodies will not engage in sports or attend activities where too much of their bodies is revealed. Also, having a positive body image helps one be more confident in making new friends.

A positive body image can also be important for work life. Employees who have a positive body image are likely to feel confident performing jobs that require customer contact, such as sales work. Many business firms today expect their managers to appear physically fit and to present a vigorous, healthy appearance. Managers with these qualities would generally have positive body images.

SELF-ESTEEM: THE KEY TO A GOOD SELF-CONCEPT

Although the various approaches to discussing the self may seem confusing, all of them strongly influence your life. A particularly important role is played by **self-esteem,** the sense of feeling worthwhile and the pride that comes from a sense of self-worth. Self-esteem is a major part of the self-concept. People with positive self-esteem have a deep-down, inside-the-self feeling of their own worth.[7] Consequently they develop a positive self-concept and do not find it necessary to put down or discriminate against others. In contrast, the person with low self-esteem (one who is self-rejecting) tends to reject many other people. You know you have high self-esteem when:

- You are excited about starting your day.
- You are handed a challenging assignment by your boss or instructor and you dive in with confidence.
- You speak up, set limits, and say no without anxiety.
- You don't make excuses for your mistakes.
- Someone else's bad mood doesn't affect your good mood.
- You don't care how much money someone else makes.
- You think for yourself.
- Hard work exhilarates you.[8]

We look next at the consequences and improvement of self-esteem. Also, as you study other information throughout this book, ask yourself, "How can this help me improve my self-esteem?"

CONSEQUENCES OF SELF-ESTEEM

One of the major consequences of high self-esteem is good mental health. People with high self-esteem feel good about themselves and have a positive outlook on life. The job consequences of self-esteem are also considerable. Workers with high self-esteem develop and maintain favorable work attitudes and perform at a high level. These positive consequences take place because such attitudes and behavior are consistent with the personal belief that they are competent individuals. Furthermore, research has shown that high-self-esteem individuals value reaching work goals more than do low-self-esteem individuals.[9]

The supervisor of paralegal assistants in a large law firm had a revealing comment to make about the importance of self-esteem in the office. "I think the major influence on whether a paralegal does a good job is his or her amount of self-esteem. The gals and fellows with high self-esteem regard every report they write as a reflection of their personality. A paralegal with high self-esteem does high-quality work. The few paralegals we get with low self-esteem just don't care if they make mistakes."

A major consequence of low self-esteem is poor mental health. People with low self-esteem are often depressed, and many people who appear to have "paranoid personalities" are suffering from low self-esteem. A store manager who continually accused store associates of talking behind his back finally said to a mental health counselor, "Face it, I think I'm almost worthless, so I think people have negative things to say about me."

School children with low self-esteem are more likely to be delinquents. These same students generally have a poor relationship with teachers and parents.[10] Workers with low self-esteem often develop and maintain unfavorable work attitudes and perform below average. These negative behaviors are consistent with the self-belief that they are people of low competence.[11]

IMPROVING YOUR SELF-ESTEEM

Improving self-esteem is a lifelong process because self-esteem is related to the success of your interactions with people. Following are four approaches to enhancing self-esteem that are related to how self-esteem develops.

Self-Disclosure and Self-Esteem

One method of increasing your self-esteem is to engage in the right amount of **self-disclosure,** the process of revealing your inner self to others. Self-disclosure assists self-acceptance because revealing more of oneself allows more for others to accept. As acceptance by others increases, so does self-esteem. Conversely, if you keep yourself hidden from others there is little opportunity to be accepted by them.

Nevertheless, you must be careful of excessive self-disclosure. Many people feel uneasy if another person is too self-revealing. The overly candid person thus risks rejection. For instance, if you communicate all your negative feelings and doubts to another person, that person may become annoyed and pull away from you.

Self-Examination Exercise 1-2 presents a questionnaire to assist you in assessing your level of self-disclosure. A person with a high degree of self-disclosure is open, while a person with a low degree of self-disclosure is closed.

SELF-EXAMINATION EXERCISE 1-2:

The Self-Disclosure Questionnaire

Directions

The following quiz may indicate how much of yourself you reveal to others. Think about the person closest to you, whether he or she is a spouse, parent, or close friend. Using the list of responses provided, review the questions and select the number of the response that best describes you.

1. I have not mentioned anything about this.

2. I have talked about this to some degree.

3. I have confided this to a large degree.

4. I have disclosed practically all there is to know about this.

Quiz

_____ **1.** Traits I am ashamed of, such as jealousy, daydreaming, and procrastination

_____ **2.** Pet peeves or prejudices about others

_____ **3.** Facts about my love life, including details about flirting, dating, and sexual activity

_____ **4.** Things I have done or said to others that I feel guilty about

_____ **5.** What it takes to make me extremely angry

_____ **6.** My feelings about my attractiveness and sex appeal, and my insecurities about how my romantic interests perceive me

_____ **7.** Aspects of myself I wish I could improve, such as my physique, mental abilities, and shyness

_____ **8.** What I worry about most, such as illness, job loss, and death

_____ **9.** Impulses I fear will get out of control if I "let go," such as drinking, gambling, sex, and anger

_____ **10.** My very deepest sensitivities, dreams, and goals

Scoring and Interpretation: To tally your score, add the numbers that correspond with the answers you gave to the quiz questions.

10 to 17 points: You are a closed person. You may feel satisfied with the level of intimacy you have established with others, but it's likely you would benefit from sharing your feelings more openly. Doing so allows others to give you feedback on your feelings and goals, helping you to get a clearer picture of yourself. Begin to change your style by making small disclosures at first. Perhaps it will be easier to start by talking about your goals.

18 to 28 points: You are average on self-disclosure and have a good balance between your private self and your openness.

(Continued)

29 to 40 points: You are a very open type of person, but beware. Sometimes indiscriminately revealing too much can be a sign of personal insecurity, guilt, or the need for acceptance by others. If others take advantage of you, look down on you, or feel uncomfortable with you, you may be telling more than the listener wants or cares to handle.

SOURCE: Reprinted with permission from Salvatore Didato, "Self-Disclosure Isn't Easy But It's Necessary to Bring People Together." Copyrighted feature appearing in newspapers.

AWARENESS OF STRENGTHS AND SELF-ESTEEM

Another method of improving your self-esteem is to develop an appreciation of your strengths and accomplishments. Research with over sixty executives has shown that their self-concept becomes more positive after one month of practicing this exercise for a few minutes every day.[12] A good starting point is to list your strengths and accomplishments on paper. This list is likely to be more impressive than you expected. The list of strengths and accomplishments requested in the Self-Knowledge Questionnaire presented later can be used for building self-esteem.

You can sometimes develop an appreciation of your strengths by participating in a group exercise designed for such purposes. A group of about seven people meet to form a support group. All group members first spend about ten minutes answering the question, "What are my three strongest points, attributes, or skills?" After each group member has recorded his or her three strengths, that person discusses them with the other group members.

Each group member then comments on the list. Other group members sometimes add to your list of strengths or reinforce what you have to say. Sometimes you may find disagreement. One member told the group: "I'm handsome, intelligent, reliable, athletic, self-confident, and very moral. I also have a good sense of humor." Another group member retorted, "And I might add that you're unbearably conceited."

Minimize Settings and Interactions That Detract from Your Feelings of Competence

Most of us have situations in work and personal life that make us feel less than our best. If you can minimize exposure to those situations, you will have fewer feelings of incompetence. The problem with feeling incompetent is that it lowers one's self-esteem. An office supervisor said she detested company picnics, most of all because she was forced into playing softball. At her own admission she had less aptitude for athletics than any able-bodied person she knew. In addition, she felt uncomfortable with the small-talk characteristic of picnics. To minimize discomfort the woman attended only those picnics she thought were absolutely necessary. Instead of playing on the softball team, she volunteered to be the equipment manager.

A problem with avoiding all situations in which you feel lowly competent is that it might prevent you from acquiring needed skills. Also, it boosts your self-confidence to become comfortable in a previously uncomfortable situation.

Talk and Socialize Frequently with People Who Boost Your Self-Esteem

Psychologist Barbara Ilardie says that the people who can raise your self-esteem are usually those with high self-esteem themselves. They are the people who give honest feedback because they respect others and themselves. Such high-self-esteem individuals should not be confused with yes-people who agree with others just to be liked. The point is that you typically receive more from strong people than weak ones. Weak people will flatter you but will not give you the honest feedback you need to build self-esteem.

A sports analogy is in order. Playing an individual sport such as tennis against players much weaker than yourself will give you a short-term ego boost. Yet if you do not play against opponents who represent a real challenge, you will not enhance your self-esteem enough to win tough matches yet to come. Similarly, surround yourself on the job with talented, independent-minded people who can challenge you. By so doing you will develop your confidence and self-esteem.[13]

POTENTIAL DISADVANTAGES OF PREOCCUPATION WITH THE SELF

We have emphasized the importance of understanding the self as a starting point in developing good human relations skills. Much of this chapter was also devoted to the importance of developing self-esteem. Despite the soundness of this advice, a person must also guard against becoming too caught up in the self. A recent study of the self proposes that the modern individual is burdened with a too-weighty self. For many people, the self has too many components, aspiration levels, and hard-to-meet expectations.[14]

Too much attention with the self can lead a person to be self-centered, self-conscious, and uninterested in other people and the outside world. You have met people who include in almost every conversation a statement about their health, and whether they feel hot or cold. The same people are likely to inform others when they are fatigued, even when nobody asked.

Preoccupation with the self can lead to unattainable aspirations. As a consequence of not attaining these aspirations, the person develops a negative self-evaluation. According to one theory, these negative self-evaluations prompt the person to escape the self. The path chosen to escape the self is often alcoholism, drug abuse, and craze eating (bulimia).[15] More will be said about personal problems in Chapter 5.

The right balance is to be concerned about yourself, your self-esteem, and your personal growth yet still focus on the world outside of you.

Focusing on the outside world can ultimately strengthen the self, because you develop skills and interests that will enhance your self-esteem. Kenny, a supervisor of electronics technicians, explains how his outside interests helped him achieve high self-esteem:

> I used to worry a lot about myself. I used to obsess over the fact that many people my age earned more money and owned better cars. I also used to worry too much about my appearance. Sometimes I would weigh myself several times a day, always hoping that I had shed a pound or two.
>
> It hit me one day that I had the most fun when I could get outside myself and not think so much about me. I then plunged myself further into my hobby of producing home videos. After shooting a scene, such as a trip to New York, I would edit the tape to make the production smooth. I showed my edited tapes to a few friends. Before long, many friends and acquaintances were calling me for help in editing their tapes. My reputation as a video expert spread. I felt great about myself that my hobby enabled me to help others.

 ## HOW THIS BOOK CAN HELP YOU

A person who carefully studies the information in this book and incorporates its suggestions into his or her way of doing things should derive the five benefits discussed next. Knowledge itself, however, is not a guarantee of success. Since people differ greatly in learning ability, personality, and life circumstances, some will get more out of this book than will others.

You may, for example, be getting along well with co-workers or customers so that the chapter on this topic is unnecessary from your viewpoint. Or you may be so shy at this stage of your life that you are at present unable to capitalize on some of the tips for being assertive with people. You might have to work doubly hard to reap benefit from that particular chapter.

The major benefits this book provides are:

1. *It should help make you aware of valid information about human relations.* To feel comfortable with other people and to make a favorable impression (both on and off the job) one needs to understand how people think and act. This book will provide you with some basic knowledge about interpersonal relationships such as the meaning of emotional security, openness, and nonverbal messages. You will even learn about such things as mimicking another person's body movements in order to improve rapport with that person.

2. *It should help you develop skills in dealing with people.* Anyone who aspires toward high-level jobs or an enriched social life needs to be able to communicate with others, resolve conflict, and behave in a confident manner. Relating well to diverse cultural groups is also an asset. Studying information about such topics in this book, coupled with trying them out in practice, should help you develop such interpersonal skills.

3. *This book should help you cope with job problems.* Almost everyone who holds a job inevitably runs into human relations problems. Reading about these problems and suggestions for coping with them could save you considerable inner turmoil. Among the job survival skills that you will learn about in the following chapters are how to cope with job stress and how to overcome what seems to be an overwhelming workload.

4. *You should learn how to cope with personal problems.* We all have problems. An important difference between the effective and ineffective person is that the effective person knows how to manage them. Among the problems this book will help you cope with are shyness, finding a job when you are unemployed, overcoming low self-confidence, and working your way out of debt.

5. *You should learn how to capitalize on opportunities.* Many readers of this book will someday spend part of their working time taking advantage of opportunities rather than solving daily problems. Every career-minded person needs a few breakthrough experiences in order to make his or her life more rewarding. Toward this end, the book discusses how to get ahead in your career and how to become a leader.

 ## SUMMARY

Human relations is the art and practice of using systematic knowledge about human behavior to improve personal, job, and career effectiveness.

Work and personal life often influence each other in several ways. A high level of job satisfaction tends to spill over to one's personal life. Conversely, an unsatisfactory personal life could lead to negative job attitudes. Another close tie between work and personal life is that one's job can affect physical and mental health. Severely negative job conditions may lead to a serious stress disorder, such as heart disease.

The quality of relationships with people in work and personal life influence each other. Also, certain skills (such as the ability to listen) contribute to success in work and personal life.

To be effective in human relationships, you must first understand yourself. Six methods for gaining self-understanding are: (1) acquire general information about human behavior and apply it to yourself; (2) obtain informal feedback from people; (3) obtain feedback from superiors; (4) obtain feedback from co-workers; (5) obtain feedback from self-examination exercises; (6) gather insights in psychotherapy and counseling.

An important aspect of self-understanding is your self-concept, or what you think of you and who you think you are. The self-concept is based largely on what others have said about us. A strong self-concept leads to self-confidence, which is a basic requirement for being successful as a leader or in sales.

Natural abilities contribute to a person's self-concept and level of self-confidence. Your body image, or your perception of your body, also contributes to your self-concept. A positive body image can help you in both your work and personal life because it enhances your self-confidence.

Self-esteem is a major part of the self-concept. People with high self-esteem have a deep-down, inside-the-self feeling of their own worth. One of the major consequences of high self-esteem is good mental health. High self-esteem also leads to job satisfaction and good job performance.

A major consequence of low self-esteem is poor mental health. School children with low self-esteem are more likely to be delinquents. Workers with low self-esteem often develop and maintain unfavorable work attitudes and perform below expectations.

Self-esteem can be increased by disclosing more of yourself to others. Developing an appreciation of your strengths and accomplishments also contributes to self-esteem. Minimize settings and interactions that detract from your feelings of competence. Talk and socialize frequently with people who boost your self-esteem.

Despite the importance of self-understanding, guard against becoming too caught up in the self. Too much attention with the self can lead a person to be self-centered, self-conscious, and uninterested in other people and the outside world. Another problem is that failure to attain aspirations can lead to negative self-evaluation. The negative evaluation may lead to escapist behavior such as alcoholism.

Questions and Activities

1. Why is it difficult for a person with poor human relations skills to succeed in business?

2. How important are human relations skills in an era of high technology in the workplace?

3. Many companies and government agencies now provide child-care facilities for children of employees. What does this employment practice tell you about the relationship between work and personal life?

4. How do some people attempt to combine work and personal life?

5. Give an example from your own experience of how work life influences personal life and vice versa.

6. Who can a person turn to as the most reliable source of feedback about himself or herself?

7. Of the six sources of information about the self described in this chapter, which one do you think is likely to be the most accurate? Why?

8. What factors are likely to change a person's level of self-esteem over the course of his or her life?

9. How would you interpret this adage? "A person can lower your self-esteem only if you give him or her permission."

10. Interview a person whom you perceive to have a successful career. Ask that person to describe his or her self-concept. Be prepared to discuss your findings in class.

A HUMAN RELATIONS CASE PROBLEM: THE OFFICE CLOWN

Jack Conway, the director of customer service at First Federal Bank, called a Saturday morning meeting. The purpose of the meeting was to conduct a lengthy problem-solving session about improving the bank's telemarketing program. (Telemarketing involves attracting new customers by calling them at home.) By 9 A.M. everybody scheduled to attend was present, except Sara Mandarin. At 9:05, in walked Sara, wearing a beanie with two springlike antennae extending from the base. The antennae bobbed up and down as Sara moved toward the conference table.

"OK, Sara," said Jack. "Join us at the table and please take off your beanie. We all appreciated the humor, but it's time to get back to work."

With a deadpan expression, Sara replied, "Sorry Jack, I couldn't possibly take off my beanie. It's my thinking cap." With her expression changed to a smile, Sara said, "OK, the meeting can begin. I'm here to be a source of inspiration to you all."

During the beverage and food break at 10:30, Sara went into an exaggerated impersonation of the bank president. In a haughty and overdignified tone, Sara said, "Members of our wonderful financial institution, I'm so glad you have voluntarily given up your Saturday morning to help make our great institution even greater.

"It is obvious that you take exceptional pride in providing outstanding customer service. It fills my heart with delight to know that we have such dedicated team members here at First Federal. Your true rewards will come from the smiles you will receive from your wonderful customers.

"I am so happy to share this exciting moment with all you members of our warm and friendly First Federal family."

Jack, who watched Sara's presentation, said, "OK, tone it down, Sara. It's time to get back to work. Besides that, I think you've created enough disruption for the morning. I wish you would put as much energy into your work as you do into your disruptions. Your performance has left much to be desired this year. I sometimes get the impression that you don't take your job seriously."

"Sorry about that," replied Sara. "I was just trying to lighten things up a bit."

QUESTIONS

1. What hints about Sara's self-concept do you find in this case?

2. How might Sara's behavior and job performance be tied to her self-esteem?

3. If you think that Sara has a self-esteem problem, what advice would you give her to raise her self-esteem?

A HUMAN RELATIONS SELF-EXAMINATION EXERCISE: THE SELF-KNOWLEDGE QUESTIONNAIRE

Directions

Complete the following questionnaire for your personal use. You might wish to make up a worksheet before putting your comments in final form.

I. Education
1. How far have I gone in school?
2. What is my major field of interest?
3. Which are (or have been) my best subjects?
4. Which are (or have been) my poorest subjects?
5. What further educational plans do I have? Why?
6. What extracurricular activities have I participated in?
7. Which ones did I enjoy? Why?

II. Work Experience
8. What jobs have I held since age sixteen?
9. What aspect of these jobs did I enjoy? Why?
10. What aspect of these jobs did I dislike? Why?
11. What were my three biggest accomplishments on the job?
12. What kind of employee am (was) I?
13. What compliments did I receive from my managers, co-workers, or customers?
14. What criticisms or suggestions did I receive?
15. What would be an ideal job for me?

III. Attitudes Toward People
16. The kind of people I get along best with are _____.
17. The kind of people I clash with are _____.
18. How many close friends do I have? What is it I like about each one?
19. Would I prefer working mostly with men or women? Why?
20. How much contact with other people do I need?
21. My arguments with other people are mostly about _____.

IV. Attitudes Toward Myself
22. What are my strengths?
23. What are my weaknesses or opportunities for improvement?
24. What do I think of me?
25. What do I worry about most?
26. What is my biggest problem?
27. What things in life do I dislike?
28. What have I accomplished in life so far?
29. Has this been enough accomplishment?
30. So far, what has been the happiest period of my life? Why?
31. What gives me satisfaction in life?
32. In what ways do I make life miserable for myself?
33. What motivates me?

(Continued)

V. How Others See Me
    34. What is the best compliment my spouse (or a good friend) has paid me?
    35. In what ways would my spouse (or a good friend) like me to change?
    36. What do my friends like best about me?
    37. What do my friends dislike about me?

VI. Hobbies, Interests, Sports
    38. What activities, hobbies, interests, sports, and so forth do I actively participate in?
    39. Which one of these do I really get excited about? Why?

VII. My Future
    40. What are my plans for further education and training?
    41. What positions would I like to hold within the next five years?
    42. What are my career goals beyond five years?
    43. Where would I like to be at the peak of my career?
    44. What activities and interests would I like to pursue in the future?
    45. What goals do I have relating to friends, family, and marriage?

Additional Thoughts

1. What other questions should have been asked of you on the Self-Knowledge Questionnaire?

2. To what use can you put all or part of this information?

3. What impact did completing this questionnaire have on your self-understanding?

A HUMAN RELATIONS ROLE PLAY: SELF-DISCLOSURE

In a role play, you assume the role of the person described in a scenario. In this and other role plays presented in this book, it may be your responsibility to add details to the brief sketches provided. Unlike an actor or actress, you will have to improvise beyond the bare essentials of the script presented by the author. Or your instructor may modify the role play to provide you with additional details.

In this role play, two co-workers are having lunch together. One student plays the role of an employee who is eager to disclose as much as possible about his or her inner self. Similarly, this employee would like the luncheon partner to be self-disclosing.

Another student plays the role of the second employee. This person is much more closed than open but nevertheless does not necessarily dislike allowing the luncheon companion to open up to him or her.

Those students not in the role play should make observations of the role players, and later use these observations as a basis for class discussion. The class discussion may include comments about the effectiveness of the role players.

REFERENCES

[1]Timothy A. Judge and Shinichiro Watanabe, "Another Look at the Job Satisfaction-Life Satisfaction Relationship," *Journal of Applied Psychology,* December 1993, pp. 939–948.

[2]An early study on this now well-accepted finding is E. Palmore, "Predicting Longevity: A Follow-up Controlling for Age," *The Gerontologist,* Winter 1969, pp. 247–50.

[3]C. R. Snyder, "So Many Selves," *Contemporary Psychology,* January 1988, p. 77.

[4]John Hattie, *Self-Concept* (Hillsdale, N.J.: Erlbaum, 1992).

[5]Marilyn E. Gist, "Self-Efficacy: Implications for Organizational Behavior and Human Resource Management," *Academy of Management Review,* July 1987, pp. 472–85.

[6]Thomas F. Cash, Barbara A. Winstead, and Louis H. Janda, "Your Body, Yourself," *Psychology Today,* July 1985, pp. 22–26.

[7]Wolf J. Rinke, "Maximizing Management Potential by Building Self-Esteem," *Management Solutions,* March 1988, p. 11.

[8]"Self-Esteem and Peak Performance: How to Improve Your Attitude, Productivity, and Satisfaction on the Job," *CareerTrack* brochure, 1994.

[9]Jon L. Pierce, Donald G. Gardner, Larry L. Cummings, and Randall B. Dunman, "Organization-Based Self-Esteem: Construct Definition, Measurement, and Validation," *Academy of Management Journal,* September 1989, p. 623.

[10]Lila L. Prigge and Charles M. Ray, Social and Personality Development," in *The Hidden Curriculum (National Business Education Yearbook, No. 30),* 1992, p. 145.

[11]Pierce, Gardner, Cummings, and Dunham, "Organization-Based Self-Esteem," p. 623.

[12]Daniel L. Araoz, "The Manager's Self-Concept," *Human Resources Forum,* July 1989, p. 4.

[13]"Self-Esteem: You'll Need It to Succeed," *Executive Strategies,* September 1993, p. 12.

[14]Roy F. Baumeister, *Escaping the Self: Alcoholism, Spirituality, Masochism, and Other Flights from the Burden of Selfhood* (New York: Basic Books, 1991).

[15]Ibid.

ADDITIONAL READING

Ashford, Susan J., and Tsui, Anne S. "Self-Regulation for Managerial Effectiveness: The Role of Active Feedback Seeking." *Academy of Management Journal,* June 1991, pp. 251–280.

Brockner, Joel. *Self-Esteem at Work: Research, Theory, and Practice.* Lexington, Mass.: Lexington Books, 1986.

Canfield, John V. *The Looking-Glass Self: An Examination of Self-Awareness.* New York: Praeger, 1990.

Erez, Mirian, and Earley, Christopher. *Culture, Self-Identity, and Work.* London: Oxford University Press, 1993.

Hermans, Hubert J. M., Kempen, Harry J. G., and van Loon, Rens J. P. "The Dialogical Self: Beyond Individualism and Rationalism." *American Psychologist,* January 1992, pp. 23–33.

Hillman, Carolynn. " 'Caress' Yourself: The 6 Keys to Self-Esteem." *New Woman,* June 1992, pp. 54–57.

London, Manuel, and Wohlers, Arthur J. "Agreement Between Subordinate and Self-Ratings in Upward Feedback." *Personnel Psychology,* Summer 1991, pp. 375–390.

Smith, Michael Lee. "Give Feedback, Not Criticism." *Supervisory Management,* February 1993, p. 2.

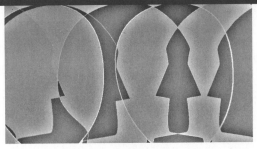

SELF-MOTIVATION AND GOAL SETTING

Learning Objectives

After studying the information and doing the exercises in this chapter you should be able to:

■ Explain how needs and motives influence motivation.

■ Identify several needs and motives that could be propelling you into action.

■ Pinpoint how the hierarchy of needs could explain your behavior.

■ Explain why and how goals contribute to self-motivation.

■ Describe how to set effective goals.

■ Specify the problems sometimes created by goals.

You have to be motivated to achieve success in work and personal life. Unless you direct your energies toward specific goals, such as improving your productivity or meeting a new friend, you will accomplish very little. A knowledge of motivation and goal setting as applied to yourself can therefore pay substantial dividends in improving the quality of your life. Being well motivated is also necessary for career survival. Today

most organizations insist on high productivity and quality from managers, professionals, and technicians. Assuming you have the necessary skills, training, and equipment, being well motivated will enable you to achieve high productivity and quality.

Knowledge about motivation and goal setting is also important when attempting to influence others to get things accomplished. Motivating others, for example, is a major requirement of a manager's job.

HOW NEEDS AND MOTIVES INFLUENCE MOTIVATION

According to a widely accepted explanation of human behavior, people have needs and motives that propel them toward achieving certain goals. Needs and motives are closely related. A **need** is an internal striving or urge to do something, such as a need to drink when thirsty. It can be regarded as a biological or psychological requirement. Because the person is deprived in some way (such as not having enough fluid in the body), the person is motivated to take action toward a goal. In this case the goal might be simply getting something to drink.

A **motive** is an inner drive that moves a person to do something. The motive is usually based on a need or desire, and results in the intention to attain an appropriate goal. Because needs and motives are so closely related, the two terms are often used interchangeably. For example, "recognition need" and "recognition motive" refer to the same thing.

THE NEED THEORY OF MOTIVATION

The central idea behind need theory is that unsatisfied needs motivate us until they become satisfied. When people are dissatisfied or anxious about their present status or performance, they will try to reduce this anxiety.[1] This need cycle is shown in Figure 2-1. Assume that you have a strong need or motive to achieve recognition. As a result, you experience tension that drives you to find some way of being recognized on the job. The action you take is to apply for a position as the team leader of your group. You reason that being appointed as team leader would provide ample recognition, particularly if the team performs well.

You are appointed to the position, and for now your need for recognition is at least partially satisfied as you receive compliments from your co-workers and friends. Once you receive this partial satisfaction, two things typically happen. Either you will soon require a stronger dose of recognition, or you will begin to concentrate on another need or motive, such as achievement.

In either case, the need cycle will repeat itself. You might seek another form of recognition, or satisfaction of your need for power. For example, you might apply for a position as department manager or open your own business. Ideally, in this situation your boss would give you more responsibility. This could lead to more satisfaction of your recognition need and to some satisfaction of your need for achievement. (The needs mentioned so far, and others, are defined next.)

IMPORTANT NEEDS AND MOTIVES PEOPLE ATTEMPT TO SATISFY

Work and personal life offer the opportunity to satisfy dozens of needs and motives. In this and the following section, we describe important needs that propel people into action. As you read these needs and motives, relate them to yourself. For example, ask yourself, "Am I a power-seeking person?"

Figure 2-1 The Need Cycle

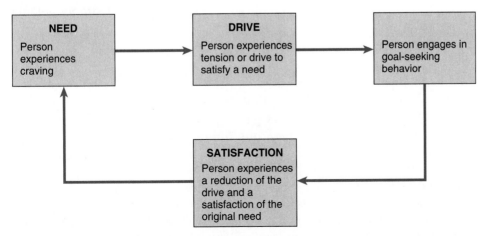

Achievement. People with a strong achievement need find joy in accomplishment for its own sake. The achievement motive or need is especially important for self-employed people and employees occupying high-level managerial positions.[2] The achievement need can be satisfied by such activities as building things from the ground up or by completing a major project.

Power. People with a high power need feel compelled to control resources, such as other people and money. Successful executives typically have a high power motive, and exhibit three dominant characteristics: (1) They act with vigor and determination to exert their power; (2) they invest much time in thinking about ways to alter the behavior and thinking of others; and (3) they care about their personal standing with those around them.[3] The power need can be satisfied through occupying a high-level position or by becoming a highly influential person. Or you can name skyscrapers and hotels after yourself, following the lead of Donald Trump.

Affiliation. People with a strong affiliation need seek out close relationships with others and tend to be loyal as friends or employees. The affiliation motive is met directly through belonging to the "office gang," a term of endearment implying that your co-workers are an important part of your life. Many people prefer working in groups to individual effort because of the opportunity the former provides for socializing with others.

Recognition. People with a strong need for recognition want to be acknowledged for their contribution and efforts. The need for recognition is so pervasive that many companies have formal recognition programs in which outstanding or long-time employees receive gifts, plaques, and jewelry inscribed with the company logo. The recognition motive can be satisfied through means such as winning contests, receiving awards, and seeing one's name in print.

Dominance. People with a strong need for dominance want to influence others toward their way of thinking, often by forceful methods. People driven by a dominance motive often take over in meetings, volunteer to be leaders, and are good at the hard sell. A need for dominance could therefore be satisfied by taking control over any situation in which you are placed.

Order. People with a strong need for order have the urge to put things in order. They also want to achieve arrangement, balance, neatness, and precision. The order motive can be quickly satisfied by cleaning and organizing one's work or living space. Occupations offering the opportunity to satisfy the order motive almost every day include accountant, computer programmer, and paralegal assistant.

Thrill Seeking. People with a strong thrill-seeking motive crave constant excitement, and are driven to a life of stimulation and risk taking.[4] The thrill-seeking motive can be satisfied through performing such dangerous feats as setting explosives, capping an oil well, and controlling a radiation leak. Introducing a new product in a highly competitive environment is another way of satisfying the thrill-seeking motive. A case history of on-the-job thrill seeking is presented in Exhibit 2-1. How might a person satisfy a need for thrill seeking off the job?

EXHIBIT 2-1

AN OCCUPATIONAL THRILL SEEKER: REPO MAN JAY CAVANAUGH

Jay Cavanaugh, age twenty-three, is the manager of Tri City Auto Recovery. As an automobile repossessor, or repo man, Cavanaugh is a modern-day bounty hunter in a credit-hungry world. He lurks in the small print of a car loan agreement, appearing when borrowers fail to live up to their end of the deal.

He has a seemingly insatiable appetite for risk, and he is a smooth talker who can extricate himself from the most difficult situations. He lives for the close calls. Cavanaugh repossesses cars, trucks, tractors, mobile homes, even computer equipment for banks and other lenders who prefer not to do the dirty work themselves. Once he assembled a crew of ten men to repossess nearly sixty pieces of heavy equipment at a construction site, working all night to clean the place out.

"Any time you go after a car, your blood starts to really go," he says. "Just the excitement of popping in a car in the middle of the night. Seeing how fast you can do it."

Adds George Taylor, a friendly, talkative man who has been apprenticing under Cavanaugh for the past year: "I feel like a thrill seeker. There is always a challenge, and you never know what you're going to come up against."

Take the Chrysler LeBaron that sits about ten feet from the front door of a house on Daisy Street. It is closer to morning than to night. There is only the faintest trace of a moon, and a street light that is too far away to be of any use to Cavanaugh. He leaves his pickup truck idling in the street as he moves slowly toward the LeBaron, whose owner has fallen behind in his payments.

Cavanaugh scrapes an inch of snow from the left front corner of the windshield to check the last six digits of the car's vehicle identification number. He could be arrested if he takes the wrong car. But the LeBaron is the car he wants. Two hours earlier, he used codes from the bank and from Chrysler to make a key for the car. The key, if it works, eliminates the need for a tow truck, which is used by most recovery companies but eschewed by Cavanaugh.

"This is it," he whispers as the key slips into the door. He slides into the soft, maroon interior and pushes the key into the ignition. It turns over quickly, and Cavanaugh smiles. The car then roars out of the driveway to a fenced-in lot where Tri City has its office. The car will be stored there until the bank claims it, either to sell at auction or return to the borrower when he makes good on his payments.

Taylor follows in Cavanaugh's pickup. This repossession took all of two minutes, but it is not always so easy. Cavanaugh does not always have the keys. When he doesn't he turns to a variety of tools to pick or pop the ignition.

Cavanaugh considers it a personal challenge to do a car quickly. Repo men often discuss their night's work, he says, comparing the numbers of cars they repossess and the difficulty of the jobs. A good repo man might make five or six repossessions on a busy evening, and do background work on the next night's targets. Cavanaugh's personal record is nine vehicles in a twenty-four hour span.

"You're always reaching for more in this business," he says. "A quicker job, more cars in a night. We're always trying to find something to make the game a little better."

SOURCE: Steve Mills, "The Night Stalker," *Upstate Magazine*, February 19, 1989, pp. 4–6. Excerpted with permission.

MASLOW'S NEED HIERARCHY

The best known categorization of needs is **Maslow's need hierarchy.** At the same time, it is the most widely used explanation of human motivation. According to psychologist Abraham H. Maslow, people strive to satisfy the following groups of needs in step-by-step order:

1. *Physiological needs* refer to bodily needs, such as the requirements for food, water, shelter, and sleep.
2. *Safety needs* refer to actual physical safety and to a feeling of being safe from both physical and emotional injury.
3. *Social needs* are essentially love or belonging needs. Unlike the two previous levels of needs, they center around a person's interaction with other people.
4. *Esteem needs* represent an individual's demands to be seen as a person of worth by others—and to himself or herself.
5. *Self-actualizing needs* are the highest levels of needs, including the needs for self-fulfillment and personal development.[5]

A diagram of the need hierarchy is presented in Figure 2-2. Notice the distinction between higher-level and lower-level needs. With few exceptions, higher-level needs are more difficult to satisfy. A person's needs for affiliation might be satisfied by being a member of a friendly work group. Yet to satisfy self-actualization needs, such as self-fulfillment, a person might have to develop an outstanding reputation in his or her company.

The need hierarchy implies that most people think of finding a job as a way of obtaining the necessities of life. Once these are obtained, a person may think of achieving friendship, self-esteem, and self-fulfillment on the

Figure 2-2   Maslow's Need Hierarchy

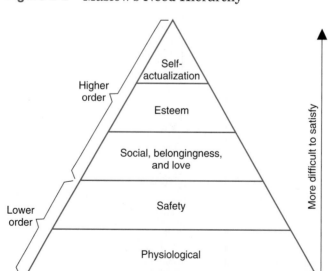

job. When a person is generally satisfied at one level, the person looks for satisfaction at a higher level. As Maslow describes it, a person is a "perpetually wanting animal." Very few people are totally satisfied with their lot in life, even the rich and famous.

The Extent of Need Satisfaction. Not everybody can have as much need satisfaction as he or she wishes. Maslow estimated that the typical adult satisfies about 85 percent of physiological needs; 70 percent of safety and security needs; 50 percent of belongingness, social, and love needs; 40 percent of esteem needs; and 10 percent of self-actualization needs.[6]

The extent of need satisfaction is influenced by a person's job. Some construction jobs, for example, involve dangerous work in severe climates, thus frustrating both physiological and safety needs. Ordinarily there is much more opportunity for approaching self-actualization when a person occupies a prominent position, such as a top executive or famous performer. However, a person with low potential could approach self-actualization by occupying a lesser position.

Need Theory and Self-Motivation. How do Maslow's needs and the other needs described in this chapter relate to self-motivation? First you have to ask yourself, "Which needs do I really want to satisfy?" After answering the question honestly, concentrate your efforts on an activity that will most likely satisfy that need. For instance, if you are hungry for power, strive to become a high-level manager or a business owner. If you crave self-esteem, focus your efforts on work and social activities that are well regarded by others. The point is that you will put forth substantial effort if you think the goal you attain will satisfy an important need.

GOALS AND MOTIVATION

A writer about success says, "All truly successful men or women I have met or read about have one thing in common. At some point in their lives, they sat down and wrote out their goals. The first great key to success begins with you, a piece of paper, and a pencil."[7] This statement indicates why goal setting is so important. A **goal** is an event, circumstance, object, or condition a person strives to attain. A goal thus reflects your desire or intention to regulate your actions. Here we look at two related topics: (1) the advantages of goals and (2) the underlying reasons why they are motivational.

ADVANTAGES OF GOALS

Goal setting is well accepted as a motivational tool. Substantial research indicates that setting specific, reasonably difficult goals improves performance.[8] Goals are useful for several reasons. First, when we guide our lives with goals, we tend to focus our efforts in a consistent direction. Without goals, our efforts may become scattered in many directions. We may keep trying, but we will go nowhere unless we happen to receive more than our share of luck.

Second, goal setting increases our chances for success, particularly because success can be defined as the achievement of a goal. The goals we set for accomplishing a task can serve as a standard to indicate when we have done a satisfactory job. A sales representative might set a goal of selling $300,000 worth of merchandise for the year. By November she might close a deal that places her total sales at $310,000. With a sigh of relief she can then say, "I've done well this year."

Third, goals serve as self-motivators and energizers. People who set goals tend to be motivated because they are confident that their energy is being invested in something worthwhile. Aside from helping you become more motivated and productive, setting goals can help you achieve personal satisfaction. Most people derive a sense of satisfaction from attaining a goal that is meaningful to them. The sales representative mentioned above probably achieved this sense of satisfaction when she surpassed her quota.

COGNITIVE AND NEUROLOGICAL REASONS WHY GOALS ARE EFFECTIVE

The advantages of goals just described provide some explanation of why goals help motivate people. Yet to fully understand the contribution of goals, it is important to dig further. Digging further refers here to uncovering the cognitive (or mental) and neurological reasons for the contribution of goals to motivation.

One cognitive explanation of the effectiveness of goals states they are not motivational by themselves. Rather, the discrepancy between what individuals have and what they aspire to achieve creates dissatisfaction. (The need cycle described earlier also deals with such discrepancies between a person's ideal and actual state.) The self-dissatisfaction serves as an incentive. People respond to reduce the discrepancy. A positive self-evaluation results from achieving the goal.[9]

An example will help clarify this cognitive explanation of why goals are motivational. Bob might be working as telemarketer (a person who sells over the phone). He sets a goal of being promoted to an outside sales position where he can call on customers and earn a bigger commission. Having set this goal, he is now dissatisfied with the discrepancy between his present job and being an outside sales representative. Bob's dissatisfaction prompts him to work extra hard to perform well as a telemarketer. Because of this, his manager might offer him a promotion.

The motivational effects of goal setting also have a neurological (nervous system) explanation. A building block for this explanation is that many of our actions are influenced by an arousal mechanism. The strength of the arousal moves along a continuum from a low point during sleep to a high point of frantic effort or excitement. (Have you ever observed a sports fan watch his or her team win the "big game" at the buzzer?) The state of being aroused is associated with activity in the sympathetic nervous system. The sympathetic nervous system readies the body for action. It also governs the amount of energy and effort available for performing a task.[10]

Arousal is linked to goals because setting a goal often arouses the sympathetic nervous system to action. Assume that on Monday, paralegal assistant Carla establishes the goal of preparing the paperwork for fifteen house closings. The goal is a stretch for Carla, but not impossible. Her nervous system will be activated to gear up for the task. By having extra energy to meet these demands, Carla will in essence be well motivated. A problem, however, is that if the task is too demanding, the goal may produce overarousal. As a result, the person may be too "hyper" to perform well and will back away from getting the task accomplished.

Before studying more about goals, do Self-Examination Exercise 2-1. It gives you an opportunity to think through your readiness to accept goals as part of your life.

GOAL SETTING ON THE JOB

If you are already well into your career, you have probably been asked to set goals or objectives on the job. Virtually all modern organizations have come to accept the value of goal setting in producing the results they want to achieve. One extreme example is Cyprus Semiconductor Conductor Corporation, where all 1,400 employees have goals. Every week they set their goals and commit to achieving them by a particular date. The goals are entered into a computer database, and the employees report whether they have achieved prior goals. Company management considers the goals to be a guide to the future and a record of past accomplishments. In any given week, 6,000 goals in the database come due.[11]

In most goal-setting programs executives at the top of the organization are supposed to plan for the future by setting goals such as "Improve profits 10 percent this year." Employees at the bottom of the organization are supposed to go along with such broad goals by setting more specific goals. An example is "I will decrease damaged merchandise by 10 percent this year. I will accomplish this by making sure that our shelving is adequate for our needs."

An interesting aspect of goal-setting programs on the job is that they lead you to pursue goals set by both your employer and yourself. The firm or company establishes certain goals that are absolutely essential to staying in business. A bank, for example, might impose the following goal on the tellers: "Shortages and overages of cash must be kept within 2 percent of transactions each week." The tellers will thus work extra hard to be sure that they do not give customers too much or too little money. Similarly, the top management of a hospital might impose the following goal (or objective) on all ward personnel: "All prescription drugs must be accounted for with 100 percent accuracy."

You participate in the goal-setting process by designing goals to fit into the overall mission of the firm. As a teller in the bank mentioned above, you might set a personal goal of this nature: "During rush periods, and when I feel fatigued, I will double-count all the money that I handle." In some goal-setting programs, employees are requested to set goals that will

SELF-EXAMINATION EXERCISE 2-1:

Are You Ready for Goal Setting?

Answer each of the following questions spontaneously and candidly. As with all self-help quizzes, if you try to answer the question in a way that will put you in a favorable light, you will miss some potentially valuable diagnostic information. For each question answer 1 for strongly disagree, 2 for disagree, 3 for a neutral attitude, 4 for agree, and 5 for strongly agree.

1. I almost always know what day of the month it is. _____

2. I regularly prepare "to do" lists. _____

3. I make good use of my "to do" lists. _____

4. I can tell you almost precisely how many times I engaged in my favorite sport or hobby this year. _____

5. I keep close tabs on the win and lose record of my favorite athletic team. _____

6. I have a reasonably accurate idea of the different income tax brackets. _____

7. I use a budget to control my personal expenses. _____

8. I know how much money I want to be making in five years. _____

9. I know what position I want to hold in five years. _____

10. Careful planning is required to accomplish anything of value. _____

Total _____

Scoring and Interpretation: Add up your point score. If your score is 40 points or higher, you are probably already convinced of the value of goal setting. If your score is between 20 and 39 points, you are in the middle range of readiness to incorporate goal setting into your life. You probably need to study more about goal setting to capitalize on its value. If your score is between 10 and 19 points, you are far from ready to accept goal setting. Carefully review the information about the advantages of goal setting mentioned previously. Until you change your attitudes about the contribution of goals to your life, you will not become an active goal setter and planner.

lead to their personal improvement. An auditor for the state set this goal for herself: "Within the next twelve months, I will enroll in and complete a supervisory training course in a local college." This woman aspired toward becoming a supervisor.

A sample set of work goals is shown in Figure 2-3. The service and repair shop supervisor who set these objectives took into account the requirements of his boss and the automobile dealership. Even if you set goals by yourself, they must still take into account the needs of your employer. As you read through the goals listed in Figure 2-3, see if they conform to the suggestions made in the section "Guidelines for Goal Setting."

PERSONAL GOAL SETTING

Personal goals are important in their own right. If you want to lead a rewarding personal life, your chances of doing so increase if you plan it. Personal goals heavily influence the formulation of career goals as well. For this reason it is worthwhile to set personal goals in conjunction with career goals. Ideally, they should be integrated. Two examples follow.

- A young man may have a strong interest in visiting museums, shopping at retail stores, dancing at night clubs, and dining at a variety of restaurants. One personal goal he might formulate is to have enough money for this lifestyle and to live in an area where it would be available. His occupational goals should then include developing job skills that are needed in large cities. The same young man may set a personal goal of dating a large number of women for many years into the future. His career planning might then focus on obtaining employment in a geographic location such as Washington, D.C., where there are many more single women than men.

Figure 2-3 Memo Form Used in Automobile Dealership for Statement of Goals

---

JOB TITLE AND BRIEF JOB DESCRIPTION

Manager, Service Department:
Responsible for supervision of service department of automobile dealership. Responsible for staffing service department with appropriate personnel and for quality of service to customers. Work closely with owner of dealership to discuss unusual customer problems. Handle customer complaints about mechanical problems of cars purchased at dealership.

Objectives for Scott Gilley

1. By December 31 of this year, decrease by 10 percent customer demands for rework.
2. Hire two general mechanics within forty-five days.
3. Hire two body specialists within forty-five days.
4. Decrease by 30 percent the number of repairs returned by customers for rework.
5. Reduce by 10 percent the discrepancy between estimates and actual bills to customers.

- A woman might develop a preference early in life for the outdoors, particularly for hunting, fishing, and camping. She might also be interested in raising a large family. Part of her career planning should include developing skills that are in demand in rural areas where her preferences are easier to satisfy than in a city. When she learns that many manufacturing facilities have been developed in rural and semirural areas, her career planning might then include the goal of developing job skills that are in demand in a factory or mill. Computer skills, of course, are in demand everywhere. Another alternative for her would be to develop technical and professional skills that would enable her to find a manufacturing job. For instance, she might seek a job as a manufacturing technician.

Types of Personal Goals

Personal goals can be subdivided into those relating to social and family life, hobbies and interests, physical and mental health, and finances. An example or two of each type follows:

Social and family: "By age thirty I would like to have a spouse and two children"; "have my own apartment by age twenty-three."

Hobbies and interests: "Become a black belt in karate by age twenty-eight"; "qualify as a downhill ski instructor by age twenty-one."

Physical and mental health: "Be able to run four miles without stopping or panting for breath by April 15 of next year"; "get my dermatitis under control within six months from now"; "maintain normal blood pressure for the indefinite future."

Financial: "Within the next four years be earning $40,000 per year, adjusted for inflation"; "build my money market fund account into a total value of at least $20,000 within five years."

The exhibits accompanying this discussion will give you an opportunity to set both work and personal goals. Ideally, reading this chapter and doing the exercises in it will start you on a lifelong process of using goals to help you plan your life. But before you can capitalize on the benefits of goal setting, you need a method for translating goals into action.

Action Plans to Support Goals

An **action plan** describes how you are going to reach your goal. The major reason you need an action plan for most goals is that without a method for achieving what you want, the goal is likely to slip by. Few people ever prepare a road map or plan that will lead them to their goal. Exhibit 2-2 illustrates how to go about this task.

Many people who would like to write a book have asked me how to go about it. My answer is to begin small. See if you can get a letter to the editor published in a newspaper. Then you might try writing an article for the school newspaper. After you have accomplished that, branch out into articles for magazines. This advice is essentially an action plan for building your competence in writing step by step so that you will eventually be able to achieve your long-range goal of writing a book. In the same way, if your goal were to build your own log cabin, part of your action plan would be to learn how to operate a buzz saw, to read a handbook on log-cabin building, to learn how to operate a tractor, and so forth.

RECOGNIZING WHEN YOU NEED AN ACTION PLAN

Some goals are so difficult to reach that your action plan might encompass hundreds of separate activities. You would then have to develop separate action plans for each step of the way. If your goal is to lead a rewarding and satisfying career, the techniques presented in this book can help you formulate many of your action plans. Among these skill-building techniques are assertiveness, resolving conflict, developing good work habits, and managing your money wisely.

Some immediate goals do not really require an action plan. A mere statement of the goal may point to an obvious action plan. If your goal were to start painting your room, it would not be necessary to draw up a formal action plan such as: "Go to hardware store, purchase paint, brush, and rollers; borrow ladder and drop cloth from Ken; put furniture in center of room"; and so on. Nor do you need an action plan to begin your running program for today. Simply put on the appropriate attire and get moving. Don't stop until you've reached your immediate goal of whatever distance you have decided is appropriate for your physical condition.

EXHIBIT 2-2

GOAL-SETTING AND ACTION PLAN WORKSHEET

The purpose of this activity is to help you gain some experience in setting both work and personal goals and action plans to accompany them. Before writing down your actual goals, consult both Figure 2-3 and the section, "Guidelines for Goal Setting." For each of the following level of goals, set a work goal, personal goal, and a brief action plan for each goal. If you are not currently employed, set up hypothetical goals and action plans for a future job. Or use goals and action plans that would have been appropriate for some job you held in the past.

Long–Range Goals (Beyond Five Years)

Work: _____
    Action plan: _____
Personal: _____
    Action plan: _____

Medium–Range Goals (Two to five years)

Work: _____
    Action plan: _____
Personal: _____
    Action plan: _____

GUIDELINES FOR GOAL SETTING

Goal setting is an art in the sense that some people do a better job of goal setting than others. The following paragraphs provide suggestions on setting effective goals—those that lead to achieving what you hoped to achieve.

Formulate Specific Goals. A goal such as "To attain success" is too vague to serve as a guide to daily action. A more useful goal would be to state specifically what you mean by success and when you expect to achieve it. For example, "I want to be the manager of customer service at a telephone company by January 1, 2001."

Formulate Concise Goals. A useful goal can usually be expressed in a short, punchy statement. An example: "Decrease input errors in bank statements so that customer complaints are decreased by 25 percent by September 30 of this year." People new to goal setting typically commit the error of formulating lengthy, rambling goal statements. These lengthy goals involve so many different activities that they fail to serve as specific guides to action.

Describe What You Would Actually Be Doing if You Reached Your Goal.
An effective goal specifies the behavior that results after the goal is achieved. A nonspecific goal for a sales representative would be "become a more effective salesperson." A more useful goal would be "increase the percent of leads I turn into actual sales." The meaning of a "more effective salesperson" is specified in the second goal (a higher conversion rate for leads).

Similarly, if your goal is to "get into good shape," you need to specify what signifies "good shape." It could mean such things as "weigh between 195 and 205 pounds," "run a mile in less than seven minutes," or "decrease the amount of time lost from work due to illness."

Exhibit 2-3 offers advice to managers about this important principle of describing what you would be doing if you reached your goals. Workers often lack a clear understanding of when they have reached their goals.

Use Past Performance as a Guide.   A good starting point in setting goals is to set them based on what you have achieved in the past. Past behavior gives a guide to capabilities. This information becomes a foundation for defining ordinary and reasonable levels, barring any unforeseen changes or events. For example, your current grade point average is a good basis for setting goals for a future grade point average.

EXHIBIT 2-3

YOU MUST KNOW YOUR OBJECTIVES

"Improve morale." "Teamwork." "Add two new staff members." "Purchase five personal computers." "Get everyone trained." "Get the new system installed."

These are the answers managers often given when they are asked, "What are the key objectives of your department?" says Gerald Graham, a management consultant and business school dean at Wichita State University. According to Graham, morale, teamwork, and two additional staff members may be important, but they are not necessarily key objectives. Appropriate objectives should represent outcomes desired or production quotas sought.

The product may be reports, services to other departments, information, analyses, responses to customers, as well as products or services to the consumer. Some examples of key objectives include: "Produce accurate financial reports by the fifth day of the month," or "accurately conduct an average of 1,000 lab tests a week," or "ship 95 percent of our orders within 24 hours."

To identify appropriate objectives, answer the question, "Why was the department created?" Then assign measures to the answer. Key objectives can be stated in terms of quantity, quality, and cost, such as, "We need to deliver twelve monthly reports by the fifth day of each month with no mistakes and stay within budget."

Further, all department members should know exactly what the two or three key objectives are, and managers should agree on them.[12]

Set Realistic Goals. A **realistic goal** is one that represents the right amount of challenge for the person pursuing the goal. On the one hand, easy goals are not very motivational—they may not spring you into action. On the other hand, goals that are too far beyond your capabilities may lead to frustration and despair because there is a good chance you will fail to reach them.[13] The extent to which a goal is realistic depends upon a person's capabilities. An easy goal for an experienced person might be a realistic goal for a beginner.

Set Goals for Different Time Periods. As just implied, goals are best set for different time periods, such as daily, short-range, medium-range, and long-range. Daily goals are essentially a "to do" list. Short-range goals cover the period from approximately one week to one year into the future. Finding a new job, for example, is typically a short-range goal. Medium-range goals relate to events that will take place within approximately two to five years. They concern such things as the type of education or training you plan to undertake and the next step in your career.

Long-range goals refer to events taking place five years into the future and beyond. As such they relate to the overall lifestyle you wish to achieve, including the type of work and family situation you hope to have. Although every person should have a general idea of a desirable lifestyle, long-range goals should be flexible. You might, for example, plan to stay single until age forty. But while on vacation next summer you might just happen to meet the right partner for you.

Include Some Fantasy in Your Personal Goal Setting. Breakthrough goals greatly enlarge your horizons. Fantasy goals take you one step further. Such fantasies can bridge the gap between personal and career goal setting. A fantasy goal would be difficult to attain at any stage in your life. Fantasy goals also reflect your vision of the ideal type of life you would like to lead. They help you dream the impossible dream. However difficult to attain, *some* people do eventually live out their wildest dreams.

Here is a sampling of fantasy goals found in the career reports of students in a career development course:

> "I'd like to become a big tycoon by owning about ten office buildings in Manhattan, along with the San Francisco Forty-Niners and the Boston Red Sox."

> "I hope to become a freelance photographer for major news magazines. My specialty would be shooting civil unrest and border wars."

> "I hope to become a millionaire philanthropist, and have a high school named after me in a poor neighborhood."

Aside from being exciting to pursue, fantasy goals are important for another reason. Research suggests that your fantasy life can help with personal adjustment and overcoming stress. A well-developed fantasy can result in a pleasurable state of physical and mental relaxation. Furthermore, fantasy goals can help you cope with an unpleasant current situation by giving you hope for the future.[14]

Specify What Is Going to Be Accomplished, Who Is Going to Accomplish It, When It Is Going to Be Accomplished, and How It Is Going to Be Accomplished. A comprehensive suggestion for effective goal setting is to specify the "what," "who," "when," and "how" of your goal. This suggestion includes many of the previous points about the characteristics of an effective goal. Here is a work goal that meets these requirements: "The VCR sales manager will increase the number of sales by 40 percent within fifteen months by selling to dealers with satisfactory credit records. Returns and nonpayments will be subtracted from the total number of sales."

Specifying that sales must be made to qualified dealers and that returns and nonpayments will not be counted focuses on the "how." It implies that sales should not be increased by pushing the VCRs on unqualified dealers who have low volume or are poor credit risks.

Review Your Goals from Time to Time. A sophisticated goal setter realizes that all goals are temporary to some extent. In time one particular goal may lose its relevance for you, and therefore may no longer motivate you. At one time in your life you may be committed to earning an income in the top 10 percent of the population. Along the way toward achieving that goal, some other more relevant goal may develop. You might decide that the satisfactions of being self-employed are more important than earning a particular amount of money. You might therefore open an antique store with the simple financial goal of "meeting my expenses."

Exhibit 2-4 gives class members an opportunity to improve their goal-setting skills.

EXHIBIT 2-4

GOAL SHARING AND FEEDBACK

Each person selects one work and one personal goal from Exhibit 2-3 that he or she would be willing to share with other members of the class. In turn, every class member presents those two goals to the rest of the class exactly as they are stated on the worksheet. Other class members have the opportunity of providing feedback to the person sharing his or her goals. Here are a few types of errors commonly made in goal setting that you should avoid:

1. Is the goal much too lengthy and complicated? Is it really a number of goals, rather than one specific goal?

2. Is the goal so vague that the person will be hard-pressed to know if he or she has reached the goal? (Such as, "I intend to become a good worker.")

3. Is the action plan specific enough to serve as a useful path for reaching that goal?

4. Does the goal sound sincere? (Admittedly, this is a highly subjective judgment on your part.)

PROBLEMS SOMETIMES CREATED BY GOALS

Despite the many positive features of goal setting, the process is not flawless. As one human relations student said, "I have never taken goal setting too seriously. I like to live my life spontaneously. It's fun never really knowing what the future will bring. Fate is my ally." Two major criticism of goals will be discussed next.

GOALS SOMETIMES CREATE INFLEXIBILITY

In some instances people become so focused on reaching particular goals that they cannot react to emergencies, or they fail to grasp real opportunities. Many sales representatives neglect to invest time in cultivating a prospective customer simply because of the pressure to achieve a specific sales quota.

Short-range goals sometimes backfire for another reason. Long-term negative consequences are sometimes ignored for the sake of short-range gain. The argument has been advanced, for example, that saving the taxpayer money by cutting back on youth programs could in some cases incur more expense in the long run. Some of the young people no longer enrolled in the youth program might turn to crime. It can cost society as much as $40,000 a year to imprison one convicted criminal.

Goals can become an obsession in another way. Sensing that reaching goals is the only thing the company cares about, an employee might neglect other important aspects of the job. Assume that a sales associate in a furniture store earns most of his money through sales commissions. In order to maximize pay, he might concentrate on selling fast-moving merchandise such as inexpensive rolltop desks. At the same time he might neglect trying to sell slower-moving items such as deluxe bedroom sets. Some students find themselves facing a similar situation when taking a course. They might be tempted to concentrate their efforts on the details they think will appear on a forthcoming test and neglect to review other aspects of the course.

GOALS CAN INTERFERE WITH RELAXATION

A preoccupation with goals makes it difficult to relax. Instead of improving one's life, goals then become a source of stress. In the words of one purchasing agent, "Ever since I caught on to goal setting as a way of life, I feel as if I'm a basketball player racing from one end of the court to another. Even worse, nobody ever calls a time out." If the person is already under pressure, taking on another goal may be overwhelming.[15]

Despite the problems that can arise in goal setting, goals are valuable tools for managing your work and personal life. Used with common sense, and according to the ideas presented in this chapter, they could have a major, positive impact on your life.

ADDITIONAL TECHNIQUES FOR SELF-MOTIVATION

Many people never achieve satisfying careers and never realize their potential because of low motivation. They believe they could perform better but admit, "I'm just not a go-getter" or "my motivation is low." Earlier we described how identifying your most important needs could enhance motivation. Here we describe six additional techniques for self-motivation.

1. Set goals for yourself.

2. Attempt to find self-determining work.

3. Get feedback on your performance.

4. Apply behavior modification to yourself.

5. Improve your skills relevant to your job.

6. Raise your level of self-expectation.

Set Goals for Yourself.   As shown throughout this chapter, goal setting is one of the most important techniques for self-motivation. If you set long-range goals and back them up with a series of smaller goals set for shorter time spans, your motivation will increase. Assume you knew that once you had passed a real estate broker's licensing exam you would be guaranteed a lucrative job as a commercial real estate broker. You would have two clearly defined goals: attaining the new position and passing your exam. If the position were important to you, you would be strongly motivated to pass the exam. Your longer-range goal of having a satisfying career would lead you to set daily goals such as, "Study for the broker exam for two hours today."

Attempt to Find Self-Determining Work. Self-determining work allows the person performing the task some choice in initiating and regulating his or her own actions.[16] Exerting such control over one's work (being self-determining) enhances motivation. An extreme form of self-determining work would occur when an employee says to the employer, "These are the projects I have decided to work on this week." A more realistic form of self-determination would occur when an employee is given leeway in deciding how to get certain assignments accomplished, and in what sequence to get them done. To the extent that you can find self-determining work, your motivation is likely to increase.

Get Feedback on Your Performance.   Few people can sustain a high level of motivation without receiving information about how well they are doing. Even if you find your work to be challenging and exciting, you will need feedback. One reason feedback is valuable is that it acts as a reward. If you learn that your efforts achieved a worthwhile purpose, you will feel encouraged. For example, if a graphics display you designed was well received by company officials, you would probably want to prepare another graphics display.

Apply Behavior Modification to Yourself.   **Behavior modification** is a system of motivating people that emphasizes rewarding them for doing the right things and punishing them for doing the wrong things. In recent years, behavior modification has been used by many people to change their own behavior. Specific purposes include overcoming eating disorders, tobacco addiction, nail biting, and procrastination.

To boost your own motivation through behavior modification you would have to first decide what specific motivated actions you want to increase (such as working thirty minutes longer each day). Second, you would have to decide on a suitable set of rewards and punishments. You may choose to use rewards only, since rewards are generally better motivators than punishments.

Improve Your Skills Relevant to Your Goals.   The **expectancy theory of motivation** states that people will be motivated if they believe that their efforts will lead to desired outcomes. According to this theory, people hold back effort when they are not confident that their efforts will lead to accomplishments. For example, some people are hesitant to attempt to operate a new piece of software because they suspect they will flounder. One way to increase their effort (motivation) toward learning the software would be to give them step-by-step training, thus increasing their skills.

Expectancy theory has an important implication for self-motivation. Seek adequate training to ensure that you have the requisite abilities and skills to perform your work. The training might be provided by the employer, or on your own through a course or self-study. Appropriate training gives you more confidence that you can perform the work. The training also increases your feelings of self-efficacy (as described in Chapter 1).[17] By recognizing your ability to mobilize your own resources to succeed, your self-confidence for the task will be elevated.

Raise Your Level of Self-Expectation.   A final strategy for increasing your level of motivation is to simply expect more of yourself. If you raise your level of self-expectation, you are likely to achieve more. Because you expect to succeed, you do succeed. The net effect is the same as if you had increased your level of motivation.

The technical term for improving your performance through raising your own expectations is the **Galatea effect.** In one experiment, for example, the self-expectations of subjects was raised in brief interviews with an organizational psychologist. The psychologist told the subjects they had high potential to succeed in the undertaking they were about to begin (a problem-solving task). The subjects who received the positive information about their potential did better than those subjects who did not receive such encouragement.[18]

High self-expectations and a positive mental attitude take a long time to develop. However, they are critically important for becoming a well-motivated person in a variety of situations.

SUMMARY

Self-motivation is important for achieving success in work and personal life. A well-accepted explanation of human behavior is that people have needs and motives propelling them toward achieving certain goals. The central idea behind need theory is that unsatisfied needs motivate us until they become satisfied. After satisfaction of one need, the person usually pursues satisfaction of another, higher need.

Work and personal life offer the opportunity to satisfy many different needs and motives. Among the more important needs and motives are achievement, power, affiliation, recognition, dominance, and order. The need for thrill seeking is also important for some people.

According to Maslow's need hierarchy, people have an internal need pushing them on toward self-actualization. However, needs are arranged into a five-step ladder. Before higher-level needs are activated, certain lower-level needs must be satisfied. In ascending order, the groups of needs are physiological, safety, social, esteem, and self-actualization (such as self-fulfillment).

Need theory helps in self-motivation. First identify which needs you want to satisfy, and then focus your efforts on an activity that will satisfy that need.

A goal is an event, circumstance, object, or condition a person strives to attain. Goals are valuable because they (1) focus effort in a consistent direction, (2) improve one's chances for success, and (3) improve motivation and satisfaction.

One explanation for the contribution of goals is that they create a discrepancy between what individuals have and what they aspire to achieve. Self-dissatisfaction with this discrepancy serves as an incentive to achieve. Goals are also said to create a state of arousal which readies people for accomplishment.

Goal setting is widely used on the job. Goals set by employees at lower levels in an organization are supposed to contribute to goals set at the top. Frequently, individual employees are asked to participate in goal setting by contributing ideas of their own.

Goal setting in personal life can contribute to life satisfaction. For maximum advantage, personal goals should be integrated with career goals. Areas of life in which personal goals may be set include (1) social and family, (2) hobbies and interests, (3) physical and mental health, and (4) financial.

Effective goals are specific and concise. You should describe what you would actually be doing if you reached your goal. Past performance should be used as a guide, and goals should be realistically challenging. Set goals for different time periods, and include some fantasy in your personal goal setting. Too much focus on goals can lead to missed opportunities. People may also neglect other aspects of the job because they are not included in the goals. Goals can also interfere with relaxation.

Key techniques of self-motivation include: (1) set goals for yourself; (2) engage in self-determining work; (3) get feedback on your performance; (4) apply behavior modification to yourself; (5) improve your skills relevant to your job; and (6) raise your level of self-expectation.

Questions and Activities

1. How would the need theory of motivation explain the fact that shortly after being promoted many people begin thinking about their next possible promotion?

2. How might a strong need for power be satisfied off the job?

3. How might having a strong need for affiliation retard a person's career advancement?

4. Identify any self-actualized person you know, and explain why you think that person is self-actualized.

5. How might esteem needs be satisfied through a person's career?

6. Explain whether setting a goal has ever placed you in a state of arousal.

7. Describe a potential risk of allowing workers to set all their own goals without input by management.

8. Books about career success have been criticized for encouraging almost everybody to shoot for the top. What is wrong, statistically and psychologically, with everyone shooting for the top?

9. How can a person be an ardent goal setter yet get around the potential problem of goals interfering with his or her relaxation?

10. Ask a manager if his or her organization uses goal setting. If the answer is affirmative, ask for details about the goal-setting system. Be prepared to discuss your findings in class.

REFERENCES

[1]Bill G. Gooch and Betty McDowell, "Use Anxiety to Motivate," *Personnel Journal,* April 1988, p. 54.

[2]David C. McClelland, *The Achieving Society* (New York: Van Nostrand Reinhold, 1961).

[3]David C. McClelland and Richard Boyatzis, "Leadership Motive Pattern and Long-term Success in Management," *Journal of Applied Psychology,* December 1982, p. 737.

[4]Research cited in John Leo, "Looking for a Life of Thrills," *Time,* April 15, 1985, pp. 92–93; Marvin Zuckerman, "The Search for High Sensation," *Psychology Today,* February 1978, pp. 38–40, 43, 46, 96–99.

A HUMAN RELATIONS CASE PROBLEM: HOW TO KEEP GOING

Barbara Harris faced a career setback when the fashion store she worked for was bought by a nationwide firm and converted into a subsidiary. The new owner's initial move was to replace existing management with their own people. Because of this, Barbara was on the verge of losing her job as assistant manager. Harris explains what happened:

"One week after I graduated with a degree in fashion merchandising, I obtained a job as a sales associate in a local retail outlet. Within a year I was promoted to assistant manager, and business was quite good. Three months after I was promoted, we were informed that a new company was buying the store. We were told not to worry about our jobs being disturbed.

"What we didn't know was that our job security was not guaranteed by the terms of the sales agreement between the companies. Upon acquiring our store, the new owners decided to move its own people into key positions. You can imagine the chaos that hit when we were told our jobs had been virtually eliminated with the stroke of a pen!

"The day the new company representative came to give us exit interviews we were told that the sales associates would be let go but that Julie (the store manager) and I would be able to work as sales associates. We were told that if we worked up to their standards, we might be reappointed as assistant managers in the future. Julie considered the offer to be a slap in the face after seven years in the business. She submitted her resignation that day. Who could blame her?

"I told them I'd like the weekend to consider my options and would give them my decision the following Monday morning. I spent Friday and Saturday fuming about the callous way we were all treated. By Sunday I got down to serious business, trying to understand what these changes meant to my career. I came to the conclusion that, because it was still early in my career, I had nothing to lose by accepting the company's offer. My one stipulation was that I be hired as a management trainee with the same pay and benefits as before.

"As I explained to the representative that Monday, I had a degree and nearly two years of merchandising experience. My experience included supervisory experience over sales associates. I felt I was overqualified for an associate's position. I knew I had much information to offer regarding local customer attitudes, behavior, likes and dislikes, and preferred lifestyles.

"I can't believe how bold I was. I told that man I had no qualms about learning another style of management and that working for his company could only add to my career develop-

(Continued)

ment. I wanted the chance to broaden my experience base. I could think of no reason why the company and I couldn't enjoy a mutually beneficial association.

"I couldn't believe my nerve, and I guess he couldn't either. I was hired that day as a manager trainee. I have to confess, I never thought my pitch would work. But you never know until you try. It's five years later and I am now the assistant regional manager for this chain. My boss is that same manager who was sent to reorganize the outlet I originally worked in."

QUESTIONS

1. What evidence can you find in this case that Barbara Harris is well motivated?

2. Identify several of Harris's strongest needs, and justify your answer.

3. What evidence do you find that Barbara Harris engaged in goal setting?

[5]The original statement of this famous explanation of human motivation is Abraham H. Maslow, "A Theory of Human Motivation," *Psychological Review,* July 1943, pp. 370–96. See also Maslow, *Motivation and Personality* (New York: Harper & Row, 1954).

[6]James L. Gibson, John M. Ivancevich, and James H. Donnelly, Jr. *Organizations: Behavior, Structure, Processes,* sixth ed. (Plano, Tex. Irwin, 1988), p. 111.

[7]"Getting There: 1983 *Success* Magazine Goal-Setting Guide," *Success!,* January 1983, p. A10.

[8]Patrick M. Wright, "Operationalization of Goal Difficulty as a Moderator of the Goal Difficulty–Performance Relationship," *Journal of Applied Psychology,* June 1990, p. 227.

[9]P. Christopher Earley and Terri R. Lituchy, "Delineating Goals and Efficacy: A Test of Three Models," *Journal of Applied Psychology,* February 1991, pp. 81–82.

[10]Ian R. Gellatly and John P. Meyer, "The Effects of Goal Difficulty on Physiological Arousal, Cognition, and Task Performance," *Journal of Applied Psychology,* October 1992, p. 695.

[11]T. J. Rodgers, "No Excuses Management," *Harvard Business Review,* July–August 1990, p. 87.

[12]Adapted from "News to Use on the Workplace: You Must Know Your Objectives," Rochester, N.Y. *Democrat and Chronicle,* December 16, 1993, p. 8B.

[13]William B. Werther Jr., "Workshops Aid in Goal Setting," *Personnel Journal,* November 1989, p. 34.

[14]Stephen Sprinkel, "Not Having Fantasies Can Be Hazardous to Your Health, Counselor Says," Gannett News Service, April 10, 1982.

A HUMAN RELATIONS EXERCISE: ARE YOU RESISTING THE PURSUIT OF GOALS?

Despite the benefits of goals, some people still resist them. The problem does not seem to lie in setting goals. Resistance comes about in *pursuing* them. Think through some of the reasons described below for not conscientiously pursuing goals. Check the ones that apply to you.

_____ 1. If I achieve my goals, people will expect me to attain many more goals.

_____ 2. It's burdensome to me to think that I will have to spend the rest of my life pursuing goals.

_____ 3. I really hate to try and then fail.

_____ 4. I would be embarrassed if friends knew I was pursuing something that flopped.

_____ 5. What most people consider to be goals are really cultural standards imposed upon us.

_____ 6. I dislike my life being programmed by goals.

_____ 7. I think I'm too talented to bother with having to set goals.

_____ 8. I enjoy my freedom too much to be contained by goals.

_____ 9. It's hard to believe that goals are really that useful.

_____ 10. I've gotten along fine up to this point in my life without having paid much attention to goals.

Turning the Situation Around. The first step is to admit that you indeed have a problem. The more statements that apply to you, the bigger your problem with resisting goals. But with self-awareness comes change. Keeping your problem in back of your mind will serve as a daily reminder to take some constructive action each day about pursuing your goals.

The second step is to review the advantages of goals, as described in this chapter. Mull them over and think through which ones would probably be the most relevant for you. For instance, you might say, "Goals would increase my chances for success, and that's what I need."

Finally, review the goals you have set for yourself. Which of these goals are the most meaningful? Pursue the most meaningful ones first. Many instances of failure to pursue goals can be attributed to not believing that the goal is relevant. If this is true, see if the goal can be modified to make it more relevant. The key to success is to pursue goals to which you are truly committed.

[15]P. Christopher Earley, Terry Connolly, and Goran Ekegran, "Goals, Strategy Development, and Task Performance: Some Limits to the Efficacy of Goal Setting," *Journal of Applied Psychology,* February 1989, p. 24.

[16]Edward L. Deci, James P. Connell, and Richard M. Ryan, "Self-Determination in a Work Organization," *Journal of Applied Psychology,* August 1989, p. 580.

[17]Earley and Lituchy, "Delineating Goal Effects," p. 96.

[18]Dov Eden and Joseph Kinnar, "Modeling Galatea: Boosting Self-Efficacy to Increase Volunteering," *Journal of Applied Psychology,* December 1991, pp. 770–780.

ADDITIONAL READING

Barrick, Murray K., Mount, Michael K., and Strauss, Judy P. "Conscientiousness and Performance of Sales Representatives: Tests of the Mediating Effects of Goal Setting." *Journal of Applied Psychology,* October 1993, pp. 715–722.

Chesny, Amelia A., and Locke, Edwin A. "Relationships Among Goal Difficulty, Business Strategies, and Performance on a Complex Management Simulation Task." *Academy of Management Journal,* June 1991, pp. 400–424.

Grensing, Lin. *Motivating Today's Workforce.* Vancouver, British Columbia: Self-Counsel Press, 1991.

Mahoney, Thomas, and Deckhop, John R. "Y'Gotta Believe: Lessons from American vs. Japanese-Run Factories." *Organizational Dynamics,* Spring 1993, pp. 27–38.

Schwisow, C. Ronald. "Tools for Your Motivational Campaign." *HRMagazine,* November 1991, pp. 63–64.

Troy, Kathryn. "Recognize Quality Achievement with Noncash Awards." *Personnel Journal,* October 1993, pp. 111–117.

Tubbs, Mark E., and Ekeberg, Steven E. "The Role of Intentions in Work Motivation: Implications for Goal-Setting Theory and Research." *Academy of Management Review,* January 1991, pp. 180–199.

Wilson, Susan R. *Goal Setting.* New York: AMACOM, 1993.

CHAPTER 3

SOLVING PROBLEMS AND MAKING DECISIONS

Learning Objectives

After studying the information and doing the exercises in this chapter you should be able to:

- Understand how personal characteristics influence the ability to solve problems and make decisions.

- Explain the four major decision-making styles as defined by the Meyers-Briggs Type Indicator.

- Summarize the characteristics of creative people.

- Describe various ways of improving your creativity.

- Solve problems and make decisions more effectively.

With one month to go until graduation from career school, Jenny was having Sunday dinner with her parents. Her dad said, "Jenny, I hope you've made up your mind by now. Your mom and I want you take over as office manager of our printing business. We need you. With the excellent training you've received in office procedures and office automation, you're a natural for the job. Besides that, why would any

rational person walk away from a good job in a family business?"

Jenny felt a surge of emotion. She now faced a major problem. Her parent's proposal placed an obstacle in her path to leading the type of life she wanted for now. She wanted to move to Florida where she and her boyfriend would both look for jobs. Jenny thought to herself, "If I say yes to my folks, that will mean that I will be pinned down here in North Dakota. Rick [her boyfriend] will think I don't love him because I won't move to Florida.

"If I say no to my folks, I will make Rick happy. And I'll also fill a dream of moving to the South. Yet I'll run the risk of hurting my parents. I'll also be walking away from a high-paying, interesting job. Who knows what position I'll find in Florida?

"I have to commit myself one way or another. I can't evade the issue any longer."

As Jenny's situation illustrates, problem solving and decision making are closely related. You have a problem to solve when an obstacle blocks the path you want to take. Worded in another way, a **problem** is a gap between what exists and what you want to exist. Jenny would like to please her parents, yet she wishes to move to Florida after graduation. If she does not join the family business she will displease her parents—an unwanted state of affairs. If she does join the family business her desire to move to Florida will be frustrated, and she will displease Rick.

Decision making means selecting one alternative from the various alternative solutions or courses of action that can be pursued. Jenny can say *yes, no,* or *maybe* to her parents. Or perhaps she can choose the rude alternative solution of evading the question. Being faced with a problem forces you to make a decision. Decision making takes place after you recognize that a problem exists.

The general purpose of this chapter is to help you become a more effective problem solver when working individually or in groups. Whether you are solving problems by yourself or as part of a group, most of the principles apply equally well. Most of the information in this chapter is designed to help you make unique and/or major decisions. Before reading more about problem solving, we recommend that you take the quiz in Self-Examination Exercise 3-1. It is designed for you to take stock of your present problem-solving tendencies.

PERSONAL CHARACTERISTICS THAT INFLUENCE YOUR PROBLEM-SOLVING ABILITY

As the quiz indicates, not everybody is equally adept at solving problems. Many personal characteristics and traits influence the type of problem solver and decision maker you are now or are capable of becoming. Fortunately, some personal characteristics that influence your decision-making ability can be improved through conscious effort. For instance, if you make bad decisions because you have limited information, you can take steps to become a more knowledgeable person. Most of the personal characteristics described next can be strengthened through the appropriate education, training, and self-discipline.

FLEXIBILITY VERSUS RIGIDITY

Some people are successful problem solvers and decision makers because they approach every problem with a fresh outlook. They are able to avoid developing rigid viewpoints. It has been said that uncreative people are those who suffer from a "hardening of the categories." If you can overcome the traditional way of thinking about things, you can solve some very difficult problems, as illustrated in the following situation:

> A motorcyclist was doing at least fifty miles an hour on a country road. He hit a wet, sandy spot on the road and went into a skid. As he worked his way out of the skid he left the road and veered into what he thought was a meadow. Unfortunately, the meadow turned out to be an optical illusion. It was really the top of a group of trees. The cyclist and his cycle tumbled down a ravine. His main injury proved to be a broken leg. Unable to walk, he could not make a temporary brace for himself with tree branches. His solution was to tie one leg to the other with his belt and drag himself to a clearing. He was sighted by a passerby two hours later. The motorcycle rider's flexibility in defining what can serve as a make-do cast perhaps saved his life.

The example just presented illustrates intellectual flexibility. An informal test of the flexibility of your attitudes is this puzzling situation: A doctor and his son are involved in a head-on automobile collision. The doctor is killed and his son is severely injured. When the boy is brought into the operating room, the surgeon says in anguish, "I can't operate on this boy. He is my son." How is this possible?[2]

SELF-EXAMINATION EXERCISE 3-1:

Problem-Solving Quiz

Indicate if the following statements are true or false about you. Then read on for the scoring and an explanation:

_____ **1.** Most problems solve themselves in one way or another.

_____ **2.** I'm known to be a perfectionist when it comes to solving problems.

_____ **3.** It's usually true that the first answer that comes to mind is the one to follow.

_____ **4.** I often shelve vexing problems and hope that they will go away.

_____ **5.** I often become rattled by tough problems.

_____ **6.** I often let others make decisions for me.

_____ **7.** I would prefer a job where I didn't have the burden of making decisions.

_____ **8.** I've never been able to judge how well I did on an exam.

_____ **9.** It's hard for me to admit that a solution of mine isn't working out well.

_____ **10.** It's hard to accept a solution from someone who is younger than I am or below my professional level.

Scoring All items in the quiz are examples of pitfalls common to poor problem solvers. Give yourself one point for each item you answered true. Then consider the following interpretations:

   0 to 3 points: You have a solid approach to solving problems. You are the person to ask when a good solution to a problem is needed.

   4 to 6 points: You are an average problem solver. Some conflicts you find easy to solve, but others are more difficult.

   7 to 10 points: You are weak as a problem solver. You rely too heavily upon your assumptions instead of examining the facts. Try to be more open-minded and flexible about solutions.[1]

Explanation Many people fall into problem-solving traps. Many of us have strong tendencies to deny that problems even exist in our daily lives. This is wishful thinking, and items 1 and 4 give such examples. Another trap in problem solving is to fall into a rigid mental set. This one-sided outlook hampers our flexibility to arrive at good solutions. More will be said about overcoming rigid mental sets at several places in this chapter. Problem-solving ability cannot be improved without improving mental flexibility.

INTELLIGENCE, EDUCATION, AND EXPERIENCE

In general, if you are intelligent, well educated, and well experienced you will make better decisions than people without these attributes. Intelligence helps because, by definition, intelligence denotes the ability to solve problems. Education improves the problem-solving and decision-making process because it gives you a background of principles and facts to rely on.

Experience facilitates decision making because good decisions tend to be made by people who have already faced similar situations in the past. This is one of the many reasons why experienced people command higher salaries. All things being equal, would you prefer to take your medical problem to an experienced or inexperienced specialist?

DECISIVENESS

Some people are ill-suited to solving problems and making decisions because they are fearful of committing themselves to any given course of action. "Gee, I'm not sure, what do you think?" is their typical response to a decision forced upon them. If you are indecisive, this characteristic will have to be modified if you are to become a success in your field. A scientist has to take a stand on which research project to pursue. A manager has to decide which person to hire. And a photographer has to decide which setting is best for the subject. As the old saying goes, at some point "you have to fish or cut bait."

SELF-CONFIDENCE AND RISK TAKING

Effective decision makers are confident of the courses of action they choose. They recognize that making a major decision involves some risk, yet are reasonably confident that they can make a good decision. An example is George Fisher, the top executive at Eastman Kodak, and formerly the president of Motorola Incorporated. He faced considerable criticism when he made the decision for Motorola to forge ahead into the cellular telephone and pager business. Fisher reflects back on his decision, and compares it to his decision to push Kodak forward into the photo CD business.

> You saw what happened in the cellular paging business. "Who wants a pager?" There are 30 million pagers out there now. "Who wants a cellular telephone? You want to talk to somebody while you're driving? You've got to be crazy." Let me tell you what. It's a wonderful business. You have to do the same sort of thinking in imaging.
> Photo CD is going to be, and is already becoming, a world standard. And there are a lot of naysayers who would have shot at my head way prematurely, and they would have shot cellular telephone. I [Motorola] was losing $50 million to $70 million a year on cellular telephones for several years and a lot of the wise people of the financial world were saying "Why are you doing that? That's stupid. You're never going to get that thing up." Let me tell you, it's a $5 billion dollar business today, and that was in less than 10 years.[3]

High self-confidence and a risk-taking attitude are assets to a decision maker, as exemplified by Fisher. Yet being too self-confident can lead to needless risks and a decision-making error. Overconfidence usually results from approaching a problem from a limited perspective. People tend to see the world through their own perspective and think that their viewpoint is the correct and only one. In reality, their view of reality is but one perspective. A man invested his total inheritance into an auto detailing (total cleaning) service because he assumed most people shared the importance he attached to an immaculate car. He also assumed people would be willing to pay approximately $95 to have their car "detailed." Unfortunately, not enough customers showed up to pay his operating expenses.

To avoid the error of overconfidence, seek other perspectives on a problem before making your decision.[4] Seek input from people with different interests and backgrounds. The man just referred to might have spoken to people who are not so concerned about auto cleanliness.

CONCENTRATION

Mental concentration is an important contributor to making good decisions. Many people who solve problems poorly do so because they are too distracted to immerse themselves in the problem at hand. In contrast, effective problem solvers often achieve the **flow experience**—total absorption in one's work. When flow occurs, things seem to go just right. The person feels alive and fully attentive to what he or she is doing. As a by-product of the flow experience, a good solution to a problem may surface.

INTUITION

Effective decision makers do not rely on careful analysis alone. Instead, they also use their **intuition,** a method of arriving at a conclusion by a quick judgment or "gut feel." Considerable attention has been drawn to the importance of intuition in managerial decision making. Managers must still analyze problems systematically. Yet they also need to be able to respond to situations rapidly. Developing intuition requires development over many years of experience and training.

To use intuition to your advantage, you have to know when to rely on facts and figures and when to rely on intuitive skills. Intuition is often required when the facts and figures in a situation still leave you with uncertainty. One way of sharpening your intuition is to keep an idea journal. Whenever an insight comes to you, record it on paper or electronically. If you notice that you shut off these insights without carefully processing them, you will know that you must learn to give them more careful thought.[5]

EMOTIONAL FACTORS

Problem solving and decision making are not entirely rational processes. Instead, emotion plays a key role in all stages of decision making. Have you ever decided to blow off a day instead of studying for an exam, although the facts in the situation suggest that you stay home and study? Intellect, reason, and emotion enter into most decisions. Even when decisions appear to be based almost entirely on hard data, *which* data are included in making the decision is influenced by emotion and feeling.

It is not necessarily wrong to be influenced by your emotions, but you should try to recognize when you are not being rational. You might say to yourself, for example, "Is this home-entertainment center really worth going into debt for? Or am I buying it just to impress my friends?"

Fear of making the wrong decision is another significant emotional factor that influences decision making. Each time you make a decision you run the risk that someone will disagree with you or not like your decision. (Remember George Fisher the business executive?) A person who is too fearful will hesitate to make important decisions. Keep in mind that you will never please everyone, so use facts and intuition to make the best possible decision.[6]

PROBLEM-SOLVING STYLES

A well-documented observation is that people go about solving problems in various ways. You may have observed, for example, that some people are more analytical and systematic while others are more intuitive. The most widely used method of classifying problem-solving styles is the Meyers-Briggs Type Indicator (MBTI).[7] A key aspect of the MBTI is to understand how people gather and evaluate information to solve problems.

To solve problems it is necessary to gather information. Styles of gathering information range from sensation to intuition. **Sensation-type individuals** prefer routine and order. They search for precise details when gathering information to solve a problem. These people would prefer to work with established facts rather than to search for new possibilities. **Intuitive-type individuals** prefer an overall perspective—the big picture. Such people enjoy solving new problems. In addition, they dislike routine and would prefer to look for possibilities rather than work with facts.

When shopping for an automobile a sensation-type individual would want to gather a large number of facts about such matters as miles per gallon, provisions of the warranty, finance charges, and resale value. In contrast, the intuitive-type individual would be more concerned about the overall style of the car and how proud he or she would be as the owner.

The evaluation aspect of problem solving involves judging how to deal with information after it has been collected. Styles of information evaluation range from an emphasis on feeling to an emphasis on thinking. **Feeling-type individuals** have a need to conform, and they attempt to adapt to the wishes of others. Because of these tendencies, they try to avoid problems that might result in disagreements. **Thinking-type individuals** rely on reason and intellect to deal with problems. They downplay emotion in problem solving and decision making.

Assume that the manager asks group members their opinion on an idea for a new product. Feeling-type people in the group are likely to look for the good in the proposal and express approval for the new project.

Thinking-type group members are likely to be more independent in their evaluation of the new product idea. As a result, they will express their opinion even if it is not what the manager wants to hear. (The people who told George Fisher that pagers and cellular phones had no future might have been thinking-type individuals.)

The two dimensions of information gathering and evaluation are combined to produce a four-way classification of problem-solving styles, as shown in Exhibit 3-1. The four styles are (1) sensation-thinking, (2) sensation-feeling, (3) intuitive-thinking, and (4) intuitive-feeling. Listed below each type are examples of occupations well suited for people of that particular type.

If you take the Meyers-Briggs Type Indicator, often available in career centers, you will discover your type. You can also study these four types, and make a tentative judgment as to your problem-solving style. Recognizing your problem-solving style can help you identify work that you are likely to perform well. For example, a person with an intuitive-feeling style is likely to be skillful in resolving customer complaints. The same person might not be well suited by temperament to bookkeeping.

PROBLEM-SOLVING AND DECISION-MAKING STEPS

Whatever complex problem you face, it is best to use the standard problem-solving and decision-making steps as a guide. These steps are similar

---

EXHIBIT 3-1

FOUR PROBLEM-SOLVING STYLES AND WORK MATCHUP[8]

Sensation-Thinking: decisive, dependable, alert to details
  Accounting and bookkeeping
  Computer programming
  Manufacturing technology

Intuitive-Thinking: creative, progressive, perceptive
  Design of systems
  Law, paralegal work
  Middle manager

Sensation-Feeling: pragmatic, analytical, methodical, and conscientious
  Supervision
  Selling
  Negotiating

Intuitive-Feeling: colorful, people person, helpful
  Customer service
  Business communications
  Human resources

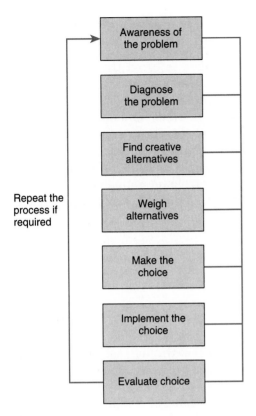

Figure 3-1 Decision-Making Steps

to the systematic approach used in the scientific method. Although based on the scientific method, the decision-making steps presented here do not exclude the role of intuition. Rather, finding creative alternatives to your problem is actually at the heart of the method. Figure 3-1 summarizes the steps involved in problem solving and decision making. It is based on the assumption that decision making should take place in an orderly flow of steps.

AWARENESS OF THE PROBLEM

Problem solving and decision making begin when somebody is aware that a problem exists. In most decision-making situations, problems are given to another person. Jenny was presented with the problem of what to do with her parent's proposal. At other times, people create their own problems to solve, or they find problems. When one man decided that there were too many potholes in the streets of his town, he campaigned for the town supervisor to take decisive action on his problems.

After you have identified the problem, recognize that it may represent an important opportunity. Paul Hawken, a company founder and author, says that a mess is a pile of opportunities.[9] For example, if you are bothered enough by a problem facing your company, you might volunteer to be the person in charge of overcoming the problem.

DIAGNOSE THE PROBLEM

Problems should be diagnosed and clarified before any action is taken because they are not always what they seem to be on the surface. Some may be more complicated than suspected, or may even be the wrong problem you need to solve in a particular situation. The person who found the potholes was thinking about treating the symptoms and not the real problem. Although it certainly would be advisable for the town to patch its potholes, the best solution is to attend to the cause of potholes. The town would never be able to change the weather conditions, of course, but it could strengthen all new pavement. One petroleum company, for example, has developed a webbing that dramatically reduces potholes when placed beneath the surface of a street.

FIND CREATIVE ALTERNATIVES

Here creativity and imagination enter into problem solving and decision making. Successful decision makers have the ability to think of different alternatives. The person who pushes to find one more alternative to a problem is often the person who finds a breakthrough solution. Consider the man who enrolled in a college 1,000 miles from his home. Excited about the prospects of attending this college, he had one pressing problem. "How do I go about moving my stuff down to the college? I would just hate the hassle of shipping the goods, picking them up at the railroad station, taking taxis, and looking for housing on foot."

The nonstandard (creative) solution he came up with was to rent a car, using his father's credit card, with permission. In this way the man had a pleasant trip to the campus, felt like an important person, carried all the gear he wanted to, and readily found suitable housing. His rental car alternative was a good buy considering the cost of plane fare, shipment of goods, and taxi fare. Creativity plays such an important role in decision making that it will be discussed again in the next two major sections of this chapter.

WEIGH ALTERNATIVES

This stage refers simply to examining the pros and cons of the various alternatives in the previous stages. In a major decision, each alternative would have to be given serious consideration. In practice, weighing alternatives often means jotting down the key good and bad points of each possible choice. Part of Jenny's list might read something like this:

ALTERNATIVE 1: AGREE TO ENTER FAMILY BUSINESS

On the plus side, I would have a high-paying secure job. My parents would be forever grateful to me, and I would avoid a family feud. I could also save money for Rick and I to get married someday.

On the negative side, I would miss out on fulfilling my dreams of moving to Florida. Even worse, my relationship with Rick might go down the tubes. It's hard to keep a relationship alive long distance.

A source of error when weighing alternatives is to rely too much on the first information you receive. The information anchors some people to their first alternative, thereby overshadowing data and impressions that come later.[10] Anchoring can be somewhat minimized by remembering that decision making is incomplete until many alternatives have been explored.

MAKE THE CHOICE

The essence of decision making is selecting the right course of action to follow. You have to choose an alternative, even if it is not to go ahead with a new plan of action. For instance, after conducting a job campaign you could decide *not* to change jobs. Experienced business executives have often criticized well-educated young people for their lack of decisiveness. Instead of coming to a decision, the young people are accused of over-analyzing a problem. Do you suffer from "analysis paralysis," or do you make up your mind after a reasonable amount of thought?

In choosing an alternative, it is helpful to remember that most problems really have multiple solutions. You therefore do not have to be overly concerned with finding the only correct answer to your problem. For instance, there might be several effective ways of reducing the costs of running a department.

IMPLEMENT THE CHOICE

After you decide which course of action to take, you have to put the choice into effect. Some decisions are more difficult to implement than others. Decisions made by top management, for example, are sometimes so difficult to implement that they have to be reversed. An executive announced a new policy that all employees would be restricted to forty-five-minute lunch breaks. Few employees took the edict seriously, and they continued to spend about sixty minutes at lunch. The executive gave up and reconsidered the decision in terms of its effect on morale.

EVALUATE THE CHOICE

The decision-making sequence is not complete until the decision has been evaluated. Evaluation may take a considerable period of time because the results of your decision are not always immediately apparent. Suppose you receive two job offers. It might take several months to a year to judge whether you are satisfied with the job you accepted. It would be necessary to look at the factors you think are most important in a job. Among them might be: "Is there opportunity for advancement?" "Are the people here friendly?" "Is the work interesting?" Evaluating your choice would be further complicated by the difficulty of determining how you might have fared in the job you didn't accept. Now and then you might obtain some information to suggest what that alternative held in store for you, as did a woman who turned down a job offer with a new and promising company. She questioned that decision until she read one morning a year later that the company had gone into bankruptcy.

What happens when your evaluation of a decision is negative? You go back to the drawing board, as the line and arrow on the left-hand side of Figure 3-1 indicates. Since your first decision was not a good one, you are faced with another problem situation.

A helpful decision-making aid is to visualize what you would do if the alternative you chose proved to be dreadful—the **worst-case scenario.** Suppose, for example, you choose a job that proves to be unsuited to your talents. Would you resign as soon as your mistake became apparent, or would you sweat it out for a year in order to show some employment stability? Or would you retain the job while starting to look around for a more suitable job? Developing a worst-case scenario helps prevent you from becoming overwhelmed by a bad decision.

USING A COMPUTER TO IMPROVE YOUR DECISION MAKING

Computers are now being used to assist people go through the decision-making steps just described. One major computerized aid to decision making is the use of computers to gather relevant data. Data gathering is greatly simplified by means of computerized files called databases. A **database** is a systematic way of storing files for future retrieval. An example of a database would be a list of all employers in a given geographic area that offer work-study (or cooperative education) programs.

A modern development in computer-assisted decision making is software that actually helps you reach valid alternative solutions to your problem. **Decision-making software** is any computer program that helps the decision maker work through the problem-solving and decision-making steps. In addition, the program asks you questions about such things as your values, priorities, and the importance you attach to such factors as price and quality.

The decision-making process used in these programs is referred to as *intuitive*, rather than *systematic*, because the programs rely more on human judgment than on heavy quantitative analysis. The intent of these programs is to improve the quality of decisions rather than to just make computations or generate data. A decision-making program might help a store owner to decide whether to open a new branch in a mall, downtown, or as a free-standing store in a shopping center.

To begin developing your skills in making major decisions, do the exercise in Exhibit 3-2. You will receive additional practice in using the problem-solving method in the end-of-chapter case, "A Bad Day at Citron Beverages."

CREATIVITY IN DECISION MAKING

Creativity is helpful at any stage of decision making, but is essential for recognizing problems, analyzing them, and searching for creative alternatives. Simply put, **creativity** is the ability to develop good ideas that can be put into action. If you have above-average creativity you will be more adept at solving problems in both work and personal life. Our discussion of creativity consists of four topics: measuring your creative potential, the characteristics of creative people, the conditions necessary for creativity, and improving your creativity.

MEASURING YOUR CREATIVE POTENTIAL

One way to gain an understanding of creativity is to try out exercises used to measure creative potential, such as those presented in Self-Examination Exercises 3-2 and 3-3. Do not be overly encouraged or dejected by any results you achieve on these exercises. They are designed to give only preliminary insights into whether your thought processes are similar to those of creative individuals.

The two exercises just presented measure creativity based on verbal ability. Creativity can also be expressed in terms of manipulating objects and shapes. The exercise presented in Exhibit 3-3 demonstrates how visualizing objects and shapes is important for creative problem solving. In

EXHIBIT 3-2

USING THE PROBLEM-SOLVING PROCESS

Imagine that you have received $500,000 in cash with the gift taxes already paid. The only stipulation is that you will have to use the money to establish some sort of enterprise, either a business or a charitable foundation. Solve this problem, using the worksheet provided below. Describe what thoughts you have or what actions you will take for each step of problem-solving and decision making.

I. *Awareness of the problem:* Have you found your own problem or was it given to you?

II. *Diagnose the problem:* What is the true decision that you are facing? What is your underlying problem?

III. *Find creative alternatives:* Think of the many alternatives facing you. Let your imagination flow and be creative.

IV. *Weigh alternatives:* Weigh the pros and cons of each of your sensible alternatives.

Alternatives	Advantages	Disadvantages
1.		
2.		
3.		
4.		
5.		

V. *Make the choice:* Based on your analysis in step IV, choose the best alternative.

VI. *Implement the choice:* Outline your action plan for converting your chosen alternative into action.

VII. *Evaluate the choice:* Do the best you can here by speculating how you will know if the decision you reached was a good one.

SELF-EXAMINATION EXERCISE 3-2:

Creative Personality Test

The following test will help you determine if certain aspects of your personality are similar to those of a creative individual. Since our test is for illustrative and research purposes, proceed with caution in mind. This is not a standardized psychological instrument. Such tests are not reprinted in general books.

Directions

Answer each of the following statements as "mostly true" or "mostly false." We are looking for general trends; therefore, do not be concerned if you answer true if they are not entirely true and false if they are not entirely false.

		Mostly True	*Mostly False*
1.	Novels are a waste of time. If you want to read, read nonfiction books.		
2.	You have to admit, some crooks are very clever.		
3.	People consider me to be a fastidious dresser. I despise looking shaggy.		
4.	I am a person of very strong convictions. What's right is right; what's wrong is wrong.		
5.	It doesn't bother me when my boss hands me vague instructions.		
6.	Business before pleasure is a hard and fast rule in my life.		
7.	Taking a different route to work is fun, even if it takes longer.		
8.	Rules and regulations should not be taken too seriously. Most rules can be broken under unusual circumstances.		
9.	Playing with a new idea is fun even if it doesn't benefit me in the end.		
10.	People say that I have an excellent sense of humor.		
11.	Writers should try to avoid using unusual words and word combinations.		
12.	Detective work would have some appeal to me.		
13.	Crazy people have no good ideas.		
14.	Why write letters to friends when there are so many clever greeting cards available in the stores today?		
15.	Pleasing myself means more to me than pleasing others.		
16.	If you dig long enough, you will find the true answer to most questions.		

(Continued)

Scoring the Test: The answer in the creative direction for each question is as follows:

1. Mostly False	7. Mostly True	13. Mostly False
2. Mostly True	8. Mostly True	14. Mostly False
3. Mostly False	9. Mostly True	15. Mostly True
4. Mostly False	10. Mostly True	16. Mostly False
5. Mostly True	11. Mostly False	
6. Mostly False	12. Mostly True	

Give yourself a plus one for each answer you gave that agreed with the keyed answers.

How Do You Interpret Your Score? A score of 12 or more suggests that your personality and attitudes are similar to those of a creative person. A score of 5 or less suggests that your personality is dissimilar to that of a creative person. You are probably more of a conformist (and somewhat categorical) in your thinking, at least at this point in your life. Don't be discouraged. Most people can become more creative.

SELF-EXAMINATION EXERCISE 3-3:

Rhyme and Reason[11]

A noted creativity expert says that exercises in rhyming release creative energy; they stir imagination into action. While doing the following exercises remember that rhyme is frequently a matter of sound and does not have to involve similar or identical spelling. This exercise deals with light and frivolous emotions.

After each "definition," write two rhyming words to which it refers.

Examples

1.	Large hog	Big	pig
2.	Television	Boob	tube
3.	Cooperative female	Game	dame

Now Try These

1. Happy father _____ _____
2. False pain _____ _____
3. Formed like a simian _____ _____
4. Highest-ranking police worker _____ _____
5. Voyage by a large boat _____ _____
6. Corpulent feline _____ _____
7. Melancholy fellow _____ _____
8. Clever beginning _____ _____
9. Heavy and unbroken slumber _____ _____
10. Crazy custom _____ _____
11. Lengthy melody _____ _____
12. Weak man _____ _____

(Continued)

13. Instruction at the seashore _____ _____
14. Criticism lacking in effectiveness _____ _____
15. A person who murders for pleasurable excitement _____ _____
16. Musical stringed instrument with full, rich sounds _____ _____
17. Courageous person who is owned as property by another _____ _____
18. Mature complaint _____ _____
19. Strange hair growing on the lower part of a man's face _____ _____
20. Drooping marine crustacean _____ _____
21. A man, short in height, accompanying a woman. _____ _____

Answers and Interpretation: The more of these rhymes you were able to come up with, the higher your creative potential. You would also need an advanced vocabulary to score very high (for instance, what is a "simian" or a "crustacean"?). Ten or more correct rhymes would tend to show outstanding creative potential, at least in the verbal area. Here are the answers:

1. Glad dad	8. Smart start	15. Thriller killer
2. Fake ache	9. Deep sleep	16. Mellow cello
3. Ape shape	10. Mad fad	17. Brave slave
4. Top cop	11. Long song	18. Ripe gripe
5. Ship trip	12. Frail male	19. Weird beard
6. Fat cat	13. Beach teach	20. Limp shrimp
7. Sad lad	14. Weak critique	21. Short escort

If you can think of a sensible substitute for any of these answers, give yourself a bonus point. For example, for number 21, how about a four-foot-eight date?

EXHIBIT 3-3

THE NINE-DOT PROBLEM

Connect the dots by drawing only four straight lines. Do not retrace any lines, and do not lift your pencil from the paper.

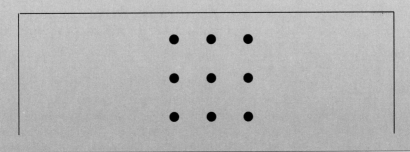

order to solve this problem you need insight into the correct solution. Persistence alone will not lead to the correct solution. (The solution may be found on the last page of this chapter.)

CHARACTERISTICS OF CREATIVE WORKERS

Creative workers tend to have different intellectual and personality characteristics from their less creative counterparts. In general, creative people are more mentally flexible than others, which allows them to overcome the traditional way of looking at problems. This flexibility often shows up in practical jokes and other forms of playfulness. Laurie, a computer whiz, knew that Sergio, one of her co-workers, had been working for a month on an inventory project. Laurie decided to play a high-tech joke on Sergio. One day when he booted his computer, a message flashed across the screen: "Sorry Sergio, your files have been dumped by the Great Computer Virus." After a five-second pause, another message flashed: "Sorry to frighten you Sergio. Everything is back to normal now. Press return to continue." Later that morning, Laurie confessed her prank. Sergio said he went through five seconds of agony, but had a good laugh when he realized that he was the victim of a practical joke.

The characteristics of creative workers can be grouped into four broad areas: knowledge, intellectual abilities, personality, and social habits and upbringing.[12]

Knowledge

Creative thinking requires a broad background of information, including facts and observations. Knowledge supplies the building blocks for generating and combining ideas. This is particularly true because some experts say that creativity always comes down to combining things in a new and different way. For example, a fax machine is a combination of a telephone and a photocopier.

Intellectual Abilities

In general, creative workers tend to be bright rather than brilliant. Extraordinarily high intelligence is not required to be creative. Yet creative people are good at generating alternative solutions to problems in a short period of time. Creative people also maintain a youthful curiosity throughout their lives. And the curiosity is not centered on just their own field of expertise. Instead, their range of interests encompasses many areas of knowledge, and they generate enthusiasm toward almost any puzzling problem. It has also been observed that creative people are open and responsive to feelings and emotions in the world around them.

Personality

The emotional and other nonintellectual aspects of a person heavily influence creative problem solving. Creative people tend to have a positive self-image without being blindly self-confident. Because they are self-confident, creative people are able to cope with criticism of their ideas. Creative people have the ability to tolerate the isolation necessary for developing ideas. Talking to others is a good source of ideas. Yet at some point the creative problem solver has to work alone and concentrate.

Creative people are frequently nonconformists, and do not need strong approval from the group. Many creative problem solvers are thrill seekers who find developing imaginative solutions to problems to be a source of thrills. Creative people are also persistent, which is especially important for seeing that a new idea is implemented. Selling a creative idea to the right people requires considerable follow-up. Creative people enjoy dealing with uncertainty and chaos. A creative person, for example, would enjoy the challenge of taking over a customer service department that was way behind schedule and ineffective. Less creative people become frustrated quickly when their job is unclear and disorder exists.

Social Habits and Upbringing

Contrary to their stereotype, most creative people are not introverted loners or nerds. Many creative people enjoy interacting with people and exchanging ideas. The majority of creative adults lacked a smooth and predictable childhood environment. Family upheavals caused by financial problems, family feuds, and divorce are common occurrences. During their childhood, many people who became creative adults sought escape from family turmoil by pursuing ideas.

THE CONDITIONS NECESSARY FOR CREATIVITY

Creativity is not just a random occurrence. For creativity to occur, ability, internal motivation, and certain mental activities are needed.[13] These necessary conditions are not surprising considering our discussion of creativity up to this point. *Ability* is the knowledge in the area in which the individual works, combined with the skills to process information to produce a useful, novel solution. A mind disciplined through study is therefore a major contributor to creativity.

Internal (or *intrinsic*) *motivation* is a fascination with the task. Even if you have the potential, you are unlikely to be creative unless you intensely enjoy the work. Creative people are usually wrapped up in their work.

For creativity to occur, the person must engage in certain cognitive (or mental) activities. Most of these cognitive activities are included in the decision-making steps outlined in Figure 3-1. For example, to be creative the individual must define the problem, gather information, and evaluate the solution. Added to these cognitive activities is unconscious thinking about the problem. If you are seriously interested in solving a problem, the unconscious thinking may take place automatically.

In addition to these conditions for creativity, an environmental need must stimulate the setting of a goal. (To quote an old adage, "Necessity is the mother of invention.") For example, a customer service representative might be confronted with the problem of processing more complaints without lowering the quality of service. No standard solution is available. The representative then sets a goal of handling more complaints in a given period of time while still paying careful attention to each complaint.

IMPROVING YOUR CREATIVITY

Because of the importance of creative problem solving, many techniques have been developed to improve creativity. Let us look at both specific techniques and general strategies for becoming more creative. The goal of these experiences is to think like a creative problem solver. Such a person lets his or her imagination wander. He or she ventures beyond the constraints that limit most people.

OVERCOME TRADITIONAL MENTAL SETS

An important consequence of becoming more intellectually flexible is that you can overcome a **traditional mental set,** a fixed way of thinking about objects and activities. Overcoming traditional mental sets is important because the major block to creativity is perceiving things in a traditional way. All creative examples presented so far in this chapter involved this process.

According to traditional thinking, business firms have the right to develop their own 800 numbers. The restrictions, of course, are that nobody else has the number and that the letter combination chosen is not offensive. You would think that if AT&T wanted to use the number (800) COLLECT it would be free to do so. You might also think that an automobile manufacturer might be able to claim rights to the number (800) MINIVAN.

A creative individual challenged traditional thinking about who has the rights to use which 800 numbers. His firm scouted for interesting and potentially useful 800 numbers that had meaningful spellings. He then secured the rights to them. As a result, AT&T has to pay him a royalty if the company wants to use (800) COLLECT. Does a salt company have the right to use (800) EAT SALT?

An effective way of overcoming a traditional mental set is to challenge the status quo. If you want to develop an idea that will impress your boss, or turn around an industry, you must use your imagination. Question the old standby that things have always been done in a particular way. To make the information superhighway possible, many old standby assumptions had to be questioned. Among them were that (1) the only way to obtain videos for home use is to bring a videocassette into the home, and (2) only telephone cables can be used to transmit digital information.

DISCIPLINE YOURSELF TO THINK LATERALLY

A major challenge in developing creative thinking skills is to learn how to think laterally in addition to vertically. **Vertical thinking** is an analytical, logical, process that results in few answers. The vertical thinker is looking for the one best solution to a problem, much like solving an equation in algebra. In contrast, **lateral thinking** spreads out to find many different alternative solutions to a problem. In short, critical thinking is vertical and creative thinking is lateral.

A vertical thinker might say, "I must find a part-time job to supplement my income. My income is not matching my expenses." The lateral thinker might say, "I need more money. Let me think of the various ways of earning more money. I can find a second job, get promoted where I am working, cut my expenses, run a small business out of my home. . . ."

To learn to think laterally, you have to develop the mental set that every problem has multiple alternative solutions. Do not leave the problem until you have sketched out multiple alternatives. Use a pencil or pen and paper or a computer screen, but do not walk away from your problem until you have thought of multiple alternatives.

CONDUCT BRAINSTORMING SESSIONS

The best-known method of improving creativity is **brainstorming,** a technique by which group members think of multiple solutions to a problem. Using brainstorming, a group of six people might sit around a table generating new ideas for a product. During the idea-generating part of brainstorming, potential solutions are not criticized or evaluated in any way. In this way spontaneity is encouraged. The original device for programming VCRs by simply punching one number was a product of brainstorming. The product retails for about $75. It is designed for people who are unable or unwilling to learn how to program a VCR. Rules for brainstorming are presented in Exhibit 3-4. Brainstorming has many variations, including an electronic approach, creative twosomes, and brainwriting.

Electronic Brainstorming

In electronic brainstorming, group members simultaneously enter their suggestions into a computer. The ideas are distributed to the screens of other group members. Although the group members do not talk to each other, they are still able to build on each other's ideas and combine ideas.

Electronic brainstorming helps overcome certain problems encountered in traditional brainstorming. Shyness, domination by one or two members, and participants who loaf tend to be less troublesome than in face-to-face situations. An experiment indicated that, with large groups, electronic brainstorming produces more useful ideas than the usual type.[15]

Creative Twosomes

Some of the advantages of brainstorming can be achieved by thinking through a challenging problem with a partner. As Michael Le Boeuf observes, creative twosomes are a favorite of the music business (for example, Rogers and Hammerstein). Many researchers work in twosomes. Part of the creative-twosome technique is to audiotape your problem-solving session. After exhausting your ideas, return and listen to your tape together. Listening to previous ideas helps spur new thoughts. The next

---

EXHIBIT 3-4

RULES AND GUIDELINES FOR BRAINSTORMING

1. Use groups of about five to seven people.

2. Encourage the spontaneous expression of ideas. All suggestions are welcome, even if they are outlandish or outrageous. The least workable ideas can be edited out when the idea-generation phase is completed.

3. Quantity and variety are very important. The greater the number of ideas, the greater the likelihood of a breakthrough idea.

4. Encourage combination and improvement of ideas. This process is referred to as "piggybacking" or "hitchhiking."

5. One person serves as the secretary and records the ideas, perhaps posting them on a chalkboard.

6. In many instances, it pays to select a moderator who helps keep the session on track. The moderator can prevent one or two members from dominating the meeting. If the moderator takes notes, a secretary is not needed.

7. Do not overstructure by following any of the above rules too rigidly. Brainstorming is a spontaneous process.

8. To broaden idea generation, think about how a characteristic of something might be if it were modified: how something might be if it were larger or more frequent; if it were smaller or less frequent; of if something else could be used instead.[14]

---

time you face a creative assignment, try teaming up with a compatible partner and a tape recorder.[16]

Brainwriting

In many situations brainstorming by yourself produces as many or more useful ideas as does brainstorming in groups. **Brainwriting,** or solo brainstorming, is arriving at creative ideas by jotting them down yourself. The creativity-improvement techniques discussed so far will help you to develop the mental flexibility necessary for brainstorming. After you have loosened up your mental processes, you will be ready to tackle your most vexing problems. Self-discipline is very important for brainwriting because some people have a tendency to postpone something as challenging as thinking alone.

An important requirement of brainwriting is that you set aside a regular time (and perhaps place) for generating ideas. The ideas discovered in the process of routine activities can be counted as bonus time. Even five minutes a day is much more time than most people are accustomed to spend thinking creatively about job problems. Give yourself a quota with a time deadline.

BORROW CREATIVE IDEAS

Copying the successful ideas of others is a legitimate form of creativity. Be careful, however, to give appropriate credit. Knowing when and which ideas to borrow from other people can help you behave as if you were an imaginative person. Creative ideas can be borrowed through such methods as:

Speaking to friends, relatives, classmates, and co-workers

Reading newspapers, newsmagazines, trade magazines, textbooks, nonfiction books, and novels

Watching television and listening to radio programs

Subscribing to computerized information services (very expensive but worth it to many ambitious people)

Business firms borrow ideas from each other regularly as part of quality improvement. The process is referred to as *benchmarking* because another firm's product, service, or process is used as a standard of excellence. Benchmarking involves representatives from one company visiting another to observe firsthand the practices of another company. The company visited is usually not a direct competitor. It is considered unethical to visit a competitor company for the purpose of appropriating ideas.

It is difficult to capitalize on your creative ideas unless you keep a careful record of them. A creative idea entrusted to memory may be forgotten under the pressures of everyday living. An important new idea kept on your list of daily errands or duties may become lost. Because creative ideas carry considerable weight in propelling your career forward, they deserve to be recorded in a separate notebook, such as a daily planner.

ENTER EMPLOYEE SUGGESTION PROGRAMS AND CONTESTS

A natural way of practicing creative thinking is to enter an employee suggestion program. The purpose of these programs is to encourage workers to contribute new ideas designed to perform work more efficiently or save the company money. Usually the employee receives a percentage of the savings resulting from the suggestion. Outstanding suggestions can pay off handsomely. An Eastman Kodak employee received $50,000 for his suggestions on how to improve the drying of photographic paper.

A committee is established to evaluate submissions to the program and to make awards. Both the financial rewards and the prestige associated with having an idea accepted and implemented foster creativity.

Entering various types of contests can also help you enhance your verbal creativity. Many contests are offered as part of sales promotion, such as explaining in twenty-five words or less why you like a particular product. In recent years several athletic teams have held contests among fans to select a new name for a mascot. The problem is that many mascot names are considered offensive to Native Americans and Native Canadians. Whether or not you win a prize in a contest, you will have had one more opportunity to practice creative thinking.

PLAY THE ROLES OF EXPLORER, ARTIST, JUDGE, AND LAWYER

A method for improving creativity has been proposed that incorporates many of the suggestions already made. The method calls for you to adopt four roles in your thinking.[17]

First, be an explorer. Speak to people in different fields and get ideas that you can use. For example, if you are a telecommunications specialist, speak to salespeople and manufacturing specialists.

Second, be an artist by stretching your imagination. Strive to spend about 5 percent of your day asking "what if" questions. For example, a sales manager at a fresh-fish distributor might ask, "What if some new research suggests that eating fish causes intestinal cancer in humans?" Also, remember to challenge the commonly perceived rules in your field. For example, a bank manager challenged why customers needed their canceled checks returned each month. This questioning led to some banks not returning canceled checks unless the customer paid an additional fee for the service. (As a compromise, some banks send customers photocopies of about ten checks on one page.)

Third, know when to be a judge. After developing some wild ideas, at some point you have to evaluate them. Do not be so critical that you discourage your own imaginative thinking. However, be critical enough to prevent attempting to implement weak ideas.

Fourth, achieve results with your creative thinking by playing the role of a lawyer. Negotiate and find ways to implement your ideas within your field or place of work. The explorer, artist, and judge stages of creative thought might take only a short time to develop a creative idea. Yet you may spend months or even years getting your brainstorm implemented. For example, it took a long time for the developer of the electronic pager to finally get the product manufactured and distributed on a large scale.

SUMMARY

Problem solving occurs when you try to remove an obstacle that is blocking a path you want to take, or when you try to close the gap between what exists and what you want to exist. Decision making takes place after you encounter a problem. It refers to selecting one alternative from the various courses of action that can be pursued.

One of the major pitfalls in solving problems is to have a rigid mental set. This one-sided outlook hampers our flexibility to arrive at good solutions. Most creativity-building exercises are aimed at helping people become more flexible thinkers.

Many traits and characteristics influence the type of problem solver you are now or are capable of becoming. Among them are (1) flexibility versus rigidity, (2) intelligence, education, and experience, (3) decisiveness, (4) self-confidence and risk taking, (5) concentration, (6) intuition, and (7) emotional factors.

The Meyers-Briggs Type Indicator is a widely used method of problem-solving styles. Information gathering is divided into two main types. Sensation-type individuals prefer routine and order. Intuitive-type individuals prefer an overall perspective. Information evaluation is also divided into two types. Feeling-type individuals have a need to conform. Thinking-type individuals rely on reason and intellect to deal with problems. The two dimensions of information gathering and evaluation are combined to produce a four-way classification of problem-solving styles. Recognizing your problem-solving style can help you identify work you are likely to perform well. (See Exhibit 3-2.)

The decision-making process outlined in this chapter uses both the scientific method and intuition for making decisions in response to problems. Decision making follows an orderly flow of events:

1. You are aware of a problem or create one of your own.

2. You diagnose the problem.

3. You find creative alternatives.

4. You weigh the alternatives.

5. You make the choice.

6. You implement the choice.

7. You evaluate whether you have made a sound choice. If your choice was unsound, you are faced with a new problem and the cycle repeats itself.

Computers can be used to improve problem solving and decision making. Data gathering is greatly simplified by means of computerized files called databases. Decision-making software helps one work through the problem-solving and decision-making steps, but it relies heavily on intuition.

Creativity is the ability to develop good ideas that can be put into action. Being creative helps you in both work and personal life. Creative workers tend to have different intellectual and personality characteristics than their less creative counterparts. In general, creative people are more mentally flexible than others, which allows them to overcome the traditional way of looking at problems.

Creative thinking requires a broad background of information, including facts and observations. Creative workers tend to be bright rather than brilliant. The emotional and other nonintellectual aspects of a person heavily influence creative problem solving. For example, creative people are frequently nonconformists and thrill seekers. Creative people tend not to be loners, but many experienced troubled family situations during childhood.

For creativity to occur, ability, internal motivation, and certain cognitive activities are needed. Among the cognitive activities are going through the problem-solving process and unconscious thinking about the problem. An environmental need must also be present to stimulate the setting of a creativity goal.

Methods of improving your creativity include (1) overcoming traditional mental sets, (2) disciplining yourself to think laterally (instead of only vertically), (3) conducting brainstorming sessions, (4) borrowing creative ideas, (5) entering employee suggestion programs and contests, and (6) playing the roles of explorer, artist, judge, and lawyer.

Brainstorming has many variations, including electronic brainstorming in which people enter ideas into a computer. Creative twosomes involve interaction with a partner, and brain writing is solo brainstorming.

Questions and Activities

1. How would you know if another person were a "rigid thinker"?

2. Why do so many instructors in so many fields claim that their courses help people become better problem solvers?

3. In what way is your current program of study contributing to your ability to solve problems and make decisions?

4. Why does concentration improve problem solving?

5. How can having good intuition help you on the job and in your career?

6. Which of the four problem-solving styles shown in Exhibit 3-1 would you prefer to be characteristic of your boss? Explain your reasoning.

7. Give two examples of decisions you have faced, or will face, that justify running through the problem-solving and decision-making steps.

8. Think of the most creative person you know. Describe his or her personal characteristics and compare them to the characteristics of creative people presented in this chapter.

9. Ask an experienced manager or professional how important creative thinking has been in her or his career. Report back to class with your findings.

10. After studying about creativity, one person said: "Creativity won't do me any good. I have a routine job." How would you respond to this person?

A HUMAN RELATIONS CASE PROBLEM: A BAD DAY AT CITRON BEVERAGES

Julia Anderson worked as the production manager at Citron Beverages, a manufacturer of lemon-flavored soft drinks. She looked forward to another fast-paced workday this Monday morning. Although Citron was not a major player in the vast soft-drink market, it had a solid group of loyal customers in the Northwest United States and Canada. A warm spell had increased demand for its top seller, Citron Power. However, production was able to keep up with demand.

At 9:15 A.M., Ramesh Sharma, a production supervisor, rushed into Anderson's office. "We've got to talk, Julia," said Ramesh with a worried look on his face. Anderson motioned for Sharma to sit down.

"Something awful may have happened on the production line," said Ramesh. "One of the maintenance workers said he found an empty container of lemon-scented liquid cleaner next to a production vat. He's worried that somebody may have dumped the cleaner into the vat as a joke or as sabotage.

"I had one of the quality control technicians test the vat for impurities. Her tests were inconclusive. We use so much artificial lemon flavoring in Citron Power, anyway, that it makes the testing more difficult."

"Oh how terrible," said Julia, "You mean to say a vat of Citron Power syrup might have been contaminated with liquid cleanser?"

"We don't know for sure. But it seems too late to do much about it now. We've already bottled and canned several hundred cases of Citron Power from the batch of syrup in question. Besides that, one bottle of liquid cleaner in one vat of Citron Power syrup might not be detectable to the consumer."

"Ramesh, I question your judgment. All it takes is one foamy-mouthed Citron drinker to lodge a complaint. Then the place will fall apart."

"Julia, keep in mind that if we attempt to recall any possible contaminated shipment the company will really fall apart."

"Okay Ramesh. Let me just think this problem through for ten minutes or so."

QUESTIONS

1. Why is this case problem included in a chapter on problem solving and decision making?

2. Which problem-solving style would be best suited to dealing with the dilemma faced by Anderson and Sharma?

3. Offer Julia a creative suggestion.

(Continued)

A HUMAN RELATIONS EXPERIEN-TIAL EXERCISE: BRAINSTORMING VERSUS BRAINWRITING

One-half the class will organize into brainstorming groups to develop alternative solutions to the problem described below. The other half of the class will develop alternative solutions to the same problem through brainwriting. The results achieved by the two methods can then be compared. For example, was it brainstorming or brainwriting that produced the most apparently useful suggestions?

A problem for which many useful alternative solutions are sought is the water crisis faced by industry. Water is becoming scarcer in supply and more costly. To help solve this problem, members of the brainstorming groups as well as the individual brainwriters will arrive at water-saving suggestions for business and industry. After spending about ten minutes on the task, the groups and individuals make a two-minute presentation of their suggestions. By listening to the other class members' suggestions, students can gauge their originality.

Although other groups or individuals may have presented a suggestion similar to yours, present it anyway. Your presentation gives others a chance to learn which ideas are more obvious.

REFERENCES

[1]This exercise is reprinted and adapted with permission from the files of Salvatore Didato, "A Mind-Set Can Impede Our Problem-Solving Abilities."

[2]The surgeon is the boy's mother.

[3]Adapted from "Focusing on the Customer," interview with George Fisher, Rochester, N.Y., *Democrat and Chronicle,* February 16, 1994, p. 7A.

[4]Orlando Behling and Norman L. Eckel, "Making Sense Out of Intuition," *Academy of Management Executive,* February 1991, p. 46.

[5]"When to Go with Your Intuition," *Working Smart,* May 27, 1991, pp. 1–2.

[6]Eleanor Davidson, "Overcoming the Fear of Decision Making," *Supervisory Management,* October 1991, p. 12.

[7]The Meyers Briggs Type Indicator (MBTI) is published by Consulting Psychological Press, Inc., Palo Alto, CA 94306; David A. Whetton and Kim S. Cameron, *Developing Management Skills,* 2d ed. (New York: Harper Collins, 1991), p. 66.

[8]Adapted from John R. Schermerhorn, Jr., James G. Hunt, and Richard N. Osborn, *Managing Organizational Behavior,* 5th ed. (New York: John Wiley & Sons, 1994), p. 119.

[9]"More on Problem Solving," *Personal Report for the Executive,* December 1, 1987, p. 4.

[10]"Decision-Making Flaws," p. 6.

[11]Reprinted with permission from Eugene Raudsepp with George P. Hough, Jr., *Creative Growth Games* (New York: Harcourt Brace Jovanovich, 1977).

[12]Richard W. Woodman, John E. Sawyer, and Ricky W. Griffin, "Toward a Theory of Organizational Creativity," *The Academy of Management Review,* April 1993, pp. 293–321; Robert R. Godfrey, "Tapping Employee's Creativity," *Supervisory Management,* February 1986, pp. 17–18; Frank Farley, "The Big T in Personality," *Psychology Today,* May 1986, p. 48.

[13]Christina E. Shalley, "Effects of Productivity Goals, Creativity Goals, and Personal Discretion on Individual Creativity," *Journal of Applied Psychology,* April 1991, pp. 179–180.

[14]"Better Brainstorming," *Working Smart,* February 1994, p. 8.

[15]R. Brente Gallupe et al., "Electronic Brainstorming and Group Size," *Academy of Management Journal,* June 1992, pp. 350–369.

[16]"The Two-Person Technique," *The Pryor Report,* July 1992, p. 1; Michael LeBoeuf, *Imaginineering: How to Profit from Your Creative Powers* (New York: Berkeley Books, 1985).

[17]"Be a Creative Problem Solver," *Executive Strategies,* June 6, 1989, pp. 1–2.

ADDITIONAL READING

Blohowiak, Donald W. *Mavericks! How to Lead Your Staff to Think Like Einstein, Create Like da Vinci and Invent Like Edison.* Burr Ridge, Ill.: Business One Irwin, 1992.

DeBono, Edward. *Serious Creativity.* New York: Harper Business, 1992.

Ganster, Daniel C., Williams, Steve, and Poppler, Paul. "Does Training in Problem Solving Improve the Quality of Group Decisions?" *Journal of Applied Psychology,* June 1991, pp. 479–483.

Harkleroad, David H. "Competitive Intelligence: A New Benchmarking Tool." *Management Review,* October 1992, pp. 26–29.

Johnson, Spencer. *Yes or No: The Guide to Better Decisions—A Story.* New York: HarperBusiness, 1992.

Sinnott, Jan D. (ed.). *Everyday Problem Solving: Theory and Applications.* New York: Praeger, 1989.

Solomon, Charlene Marmer. "Creativity Training." *Personnel Journal,* May, 1990, pp. 64–71.

Swann, Don. "Decisions, Decisions: First, Get the Facts." *Management Review,* April 1993, pp. 58–61.

Van Gundy, Arthur B. *Idea Power: Techniques and Resources to Unleash the Creativity in Your Organization.* New York: AMACOM, 1992.

von Oech, Roger. *Whack on the Side of the Head.* New York: Warner Books, 1990.

*T*o be successful in a competitive business world it is not enough simply to cope with job pressures and overcome health problems. You also have to feel and be at your best. Similarly, treating and curing physical and mental health problems is still important, but considerable emphasis is now being placed on preventing illness and staying well. Well people are not simply those who are not sick. Instead, they are vibrant, relatively

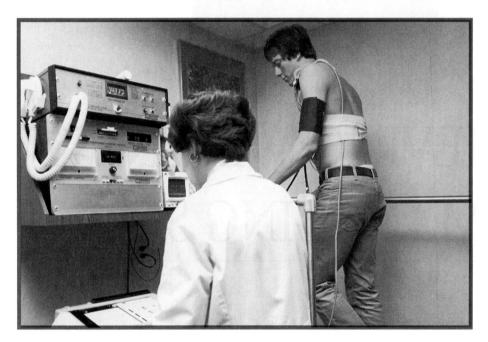

happy, and able to cope with life's problems. **Wellness** is thus a formalized approach to preventive health care. By promoting health, company wellness programs help prevent employees from developing physical and mental problems often associated with excessive job pressures.

One of the primary challenges in achieving wellness is to understand and manage stress. As the term is currently used, **stress** is an internal reaction to any force that threatens to disturb a person's equilibrium. The internal reaction usually takes the form of emotional discomfort. Notice that in general use the term *stress* typically refers to the stimulus or force that creates the problem.[1]

A **stressor** is the external or internal force that brings about the stress. The fact that something is dangerous, challenging, or disturbing in any way makes it a stressor. Your perception of an event or thought influences whether or not a given event is stressful. Your confidence in your ability to handle difficult situations also influences the amount of stress you experience. Most people find speaking in front of an audience to be a stressor; yet some experienced speakers regard the event as "no sweat." These people have learned how to handle the challenges involved in giving a talk.

Despite the importance of a person's size-up of an event, there are certain universal stressors. Almost everybody on a passenger plane experiences heavy stress when told to prepare for a crash landing. Can you think of a few other universal stressors?

In this chapter we describe the achievement of wellness and managing work stress. In the next chapter we continue with a stress-related topic: coping with personal problems.

STRATEGIES FOR ACHIEVING WELLNESS

According to Dot Yandle, the high cost of health care is causing people to listen more carefully to ideas many psychologists and medical professionals have proposed for years. An increasing number of people believe that we can live longer, healthier lives if we choose to do so. An important principle of behavioral medicine is now widely accepted—that the body and mind must work together for a healthy lifestyle.[2] Consider also that lifestyle decisions contribute to seven of the ten principal causes of mortality. And about half of the deaths resulting from these causes could be prevented by changes in behavior.[3] A person who smokes two packs of cigarettes per day, eats mostly fatty food and sweets, drinks a liter of wine per day, and leads a sedentary life has a below-average life expectancy. Note that all of these life-threatening activities are under the person's control.

In this section we describe achieving wellness through exercise, diet, competence, resilience, and a health-prone personality. Another key component of achieving wellness—stress management—is described later.

EXERCISING PROPERLY

The right amount and type of physical exercise contributes substantially to wellness. To achieve wellness it is important to select an exercise program that is physically challenging but that does not lead to overexertion and muscle injury. Competitive sports, if taken too seriously, can actually increase a person's stress level. The most beneficial exercises are classified as aerobic, because they make you breathe faster and raise your heart rate.

Most of a person's exercise requirements can be met through everyday techniques such as walking or running upstairs, vigorous housework, yard work, or walking several miles per day. Avoid the remote control for your television; getting up to change the channel can burn off a few calories! Another exercise freebie is to park your car in a remote spot in the parking lot. The exercise you receive from walking to and from your car is an investment in your wellness.

The physical benefits of exercise include: increased respiratory capacity; increased muscle tone; reduced risk of heart disease; improved circulation; reduced cholesterol level; increased energy; increased rate of metabolism; reduced body weight and improved fat metabolism; and slowed-down aging process.

The mental benefits of exercise are also plentiful. A major benefit is the euphoria that often occurs when morphinelike brain chemicals called *endorphins* are released into the body. The same experience is referred to as "runner's high." Other mental benefits of exercise include: increased self-confidence; improved body image and self-esteem; improved mental functioning, alertness, and efficiency; release of accumulated tensions; and relief from mild depression.[4]

Maintaining a Healthy Diet

Eating nutritious foods is valuable for mental as well as physical health. To illustrate, many nutritionists and physicians believe that eating fatty foods, such as red meat, contributes to colon cancer. Improper diet, such as consuming less than 1,300 calories per day, can weaken you physically. In turn, you become more susceptible to stress.

The subject of proper diet has been debated continually. Advice abounds on what to eat and what not to eat. Some of this information is confusing and contradictory, partly because not enough is known about nutrition to identify an ideal diet for each individual. For example, many people can point to an eighty-five-year-old relative who has been eating the wrong food (and perhaps consuming considerable alcohol) most of his or her life. The implication is that if this person has violated sensible habits of nutrition and has lived so long, how important can good diet be?

The food requirements for wellness differ depending on age, sex, body size, physical activity, and other conditions such as pregnancy and illness. A workable dietary strategy is to follow the guidelines for choosing and preparing food developed by the U.S. Department of Agriculture,[5] as shown in Figure 4-1. At each successive layer of the pyramid, a food group should be eaten less frequently.

At the base of the pyramid are grains (bread, cereal, rice, and pasta) which should comprise six to eleven servings per day. At the next level are fruits and vegetables of which we should consume from two to five servings per day. At the next-narrower level of the pyramid are found two groups of

Figure 4-1 The Food Guide Pyramid: A Guide to Daily Food Choices

SOURCE: U.S. Department of Agriculture, 1992.

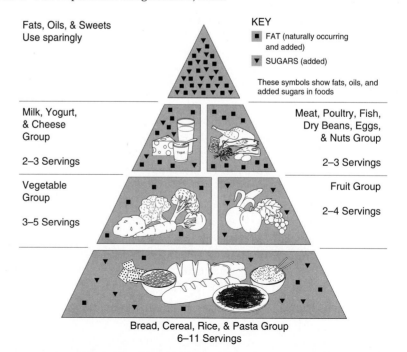

food of which we should eat only about two to three servings per day. One group is milk, yogurt, and cheese. The other is meat, poultry, fish, dry beans, eggs, and nuts. At the top of the pyramid are foods low in nutritional value, such as fats, oils, and sweets. It is recommended that these foods be eaten sparingly. Pizza, meat sausage, and milk shakes should therefore be an occasional treat, not a daily event.

The Department of Agriculture also recommends that if you drink alcoholic beverages, do so in moderation. Alcoholic beverages are high in calories and low in nutrients. Heavy drinkers, especially those who also smoke, frequently develop nutritional deficiencies. They also develop more serious diseases such as cirrhosis of the liver and certain types of cancer. This is partly true because of the loss of appetite, poor food intake, and impaired absorption of nutrients. One or two standard-size drinks per day appear to cause no harm in normal, healthy, nonpregnant adults. Some medical specialists believe that moderate doses of alcohol help prevent heart disease by preventing arteries from becoming clogged with fatty deposits.

The above dietary guidelines are intended only for populations with food habits similar to those of people in the United States. Also, the guidelines are for people who are already healthy and do not require special diets because of diseases or conditions that interfere with normal nutritional requirements. No guidelines can guarantee health and well-being. Health depends on many things, including heredity, lifestyle, personality traits, mental health, attitudes, and the environment, in addition to diet. However, good eating habits based on moderation and variety keep you healthy and even improve your health.

Developing Competence

Emory L. Cowen, a major contributor to the wellness movement, says that **competence** is an important part of wellness. Competence refers to both job skills and social skills, including the ability to solve problems and control anger. The presence of these skills has been shown to be related to wellness, and their absence to poor adaptation to one's environment. Although acquiring such capabilities is a lifelong undertaking, Cowen recommends that childhood is the best time to lay the groundwork for competency.[6] If you are a well-rounded person who has performed satisfactorily in school and on the job, and you have a variety of friends, you have probably achieved competency.

The importance of competence in developing wellness illustrates how different wellness strategies produce similar results. Developing competence improves self-confidence and self-esteem. Physical exercise also contributes to enhancements in self-confidence and self-esteem.

Developing Resilience

The ability to overcome setback is an important characteristic of successful people. It therefore follows that **resilience,** the ability to withstand pressure and emerge stronger for it, is a strategy for achieving wellness.[7] Most people at times in their lives experience threats to their wellness. Among these threats are death of a loved one, having a fire in one's home, a family breakup, or a job loss. Recovering from such major problems helps a person retain wellness and become even more well in the long term. Learning how to manage stress, as described later, is an important part of developing resilience. The story of Laura Baker, a confident person, illustrates the type of resilience needed to achieve wellness. She describes a problem she faced and how she dealt with it:

> Three years ago I hit a low point in my life. The company I worked for was involved in a scandal about paying kickbacks to a few school and city administrators in exchange for several major contracts. I wasn't directly involved in offering the kickbacks, but I was the sales representative on one of the unethically handled accounts. As you can imagine, I got tarred with the same brush.
>
> About the same time, my boyfriend was arrested for selling cocaine to stockbrokers in his office. In a two-week period I faced unemployment and the necessity to either help my boyfriend through his turmoil or leave him. At first I thought the world was caving in on me, but then I realized I was still a good person. I admit I should have been more perceptive about the wrongdoings of my firm and my boyfriend. Yet I had done nothing wrong.
>
> I had the self-confidence to face the world in a positive way. I told prospective employers that they could check on my story. I didn't offer kickbacks to anyone. My only error on the job was having too much trust in my employer. Based on my good sales record, I did find a comparable job. I also decided to help my boyfriend though his rough times. So what if a few people thought I was too forgiving? I have enough confidence in myself to stick with my own inclinations.

A key contributor to becoming resilient is to develop **psychological hardiness.** A psychologically hardy individual tends to profit from a stressful situation instead of developing negative symptoms. Psychologically hardy people are committed to the various parts of their lives, such as being devoted to work and parenting. The same people also feel a greater sense of control over events in their lives.[8] You will recall how Laura Baker took charge despite facing two major problems. Psychologically hardy people also see change as more of a challenge than a threat.

People with a hardy attitude take the major problems in life in stride. When they encounter a stressful event they are likely to consider it interesting, and they believe they can influence the outcome. Furthermore, they see major challenges as an opportunity for personal development.

Developing a Health-Prone Personality

Tentative evidence has been gathered that people can be taught to develop a personality that helps ward off cancer and heart disease. In one study, people prone to cancer and heart disease were taught to express their emotions more readily, and to cope with stress. The training was a step-by-step form of mental healing called *behavior therapy*. Equally important, the physically ill people were taught to become less emotionally dependent on others and to be more self-reliant.

The results from the behavior training were astonishing. Fifty of the people with cancer-prone personalities received training and fifty did not. Many more people died of cancer (and of other causes) in the no-therapy group than in the therapy group. Thirteen years later, forty-five people who received therapy were still alive. Only nineteen in the no-therapy group were still alive. Similar encouraging results were achieved in studies conducted by other psychologists and researchers.[9]

The implication of these studies is that a person might be able to develop a well personality by becoming more emotionally expressive and self-reliant. Even if these behaviors did not prolong life, the person's enjoyment of life would increase. If you are already emotionally expressive and self-reliant, no changes need to be made.

Exhibit 4-1 will help you further appreciate the scope of the wellness movement. The information illustrates what companies are doing to help their employees achieve wellness.

THE PHYSIOLOGY AND CONSEQUENCES OF STRESS

An important aspect of learning about stress is to understand its underlying physiology and its consequences to the person. The physiological changes taking place within the body are almost identical for both positive and negative stressors. Riding a roller coaster, falling in love, or being fired, for example, make you feel about the same inside. The experience of stress helps activate hormones that prepare the body to fight or run when faced with a challenge. This battle against the stressor is referred to as the **fight-or-flight response.** (The "response" is really a conflict because one is forced to choose between struggling with the stressor or fleeing from the scene.) It helps you deal with emergencies.

An updating of the fight-or-flight response explains that when faced with stress the brain acts much like a thermostat. When outside conditions deviate from an ideal point, the thermostat sends a signal to the furnace to increase heat or air conditioning. The brain senses stress as damage to well-being and therefore sends out a signal to the body to cope. The purpose of coping is to modify the discrepancy between the ideal (low-stress) and actual (high-stress) conditions.[10] The brain is thus a self-regulating system that helps us cope with stressors.

The activation of hormones when the body has to cope with a stressor produces a short-term physiological reaction. Among the most familiar reactions are an increase in heart rate, blood pressure, blood glucose, and blood clotting. To help you recognize these symptoms, try to recall the internal bodily sensations the last time you were almost in an automobile accident or heard some wonderful news. Less familiar changes are a redirection of the blood flow toward the brain and large muscle groups and a release of stored fluids from places throughout the body into the bloodstream.

If stress is continuous and accompanied by these short-term physiological changes, annoying and life-threatening conditions can occur. A

EXHIBIT 4-1

SONY PROMOTES WELLNESS

Several years ago executives at Sony Corporation of America were concerned about rapidly rising health costs. So they decided to closely examine the health care claims of their 12,000 employees. A study of three years of claims revealed a disturbing trend. About half of the costs were for illnesses and accidents that could have been prevented or modified through changes in behavior. Based on this finding, the company embarked upon an Employee Wellness Campaign designed to raise the health consciousness of its employees.

Sony initiated improved coverage for preventive care and wellness programs, including (1) annual blood screening for such health indices as cholesterol levels and blood-sugar levels, and (2) paying up to 80 percent of the cost of completing a smoking cessation program.

Sony took another step to involve employees in the idea of wellness and participating in preventive health care. Each employee was mailed an audiocassette on wellness. Called "Sony's Flex Steps to Good Health: Lend Us Your Ear," the tape gives tips and facts on leading a healthy lifestyle. The tape uses a game-show format called *Health Quest,* and leads listeners through a series of health categories: exercise, nutrition, cancer prevention, smoking, safety, stress, and children's health.

Under the nutrition topic, for example, a panel of contestants is presented with the answer: "A high level of this substance in the diet contributes to elevated blood cholesterol." A contestant gives the question, "What is saturated fat?" Next, the game-show host elaborates for the audience: "A diet high in saturated fat—the kind found in most meat and whole-milk dairy products—can boost cholesterol. Heredity also plays a role." A brief discussion of Sony's preventive care coverage and the importance of testing cholesterol levels follows.

Sony management believes that their Employee Wellness Campaign will stabilize the cost of health care insurance. More importantly, management believes that employees who take care of themselves properly are going to become more useful to the company. The initiatives are designed to produce a more healthy, productive group of employees in the long run.

SOURCE: Adapted with permission from Joyce E. Santora, "Sony Promotes Wellness to Stabilize Health Care Costs," *Personnel Journal,* September 1992, pp. 40–44.

stressful life event usually leads to a high cholesterol level (of the unhealthy type) and high blood pressure. Other conditions associated with stress are cardiac disease, migraine headaches, ulcers, allergies, skin disorders, and cancer. To make matters worse, stress can hamper the immune system, thus increasing the severity of many diseases and disorders. For example, people whose stress level is high recover more slowly from colds and injuries, and are more susceptible to sexually transmitted diseases.

THE BENEFICIAL CONSEQUENCES OF STRESS

Despite all the problems just mentioned, stress also plays a positive role in our lives. The right amount of stress prepares us for meeting difficult challenges and spurs us on to peak intellectual and physical performance. An optimum of stress exists for most people and most tasks.

In general, performance tends to be best under moderate amounts of stress. If the stress is too great, people become temporarily ineffective; they may freeze or choke. Under too little stress, people may become lethargic and inattentive. Figure 4-2 depicts the relationship between stress and performance. An exception to this relationship is that certain negative forms of stress are likely to lower performance even if the stress is moderate.[11] For example, the stress created by an intimidating boss or worrying about radiation poisoning—even in moderate amounts—will not improve performance.

The optimum amount and type of stress is a positive force that is the equivalent of finding excitement and challenge. Your ability to solve problems and deal with challenge is enhanced when the right amount of adrenaline flows in your blood to guide you toward peak performance. In fact, highly productive people are sometimes said to be hooked on adrenaline. Let us look at several of these beneficial consequences of encountering the right type and amount of stressors:

1. *Greater strength and physical coordination.*   Visualize yourself competing against another person in an individual activity such as tennis, ski racing, or chess. You will probably perform at your best if your opponent is at or above your level. It is difficult to perform well against too easy an opponent because the challenge is lacking.

2. *Increased motivation.*   How many students have you heard say, "I can't study unless I have an exam coming up" or "I never get started on a

Figure 4-2   The Relationship Between Stress and Job Performance

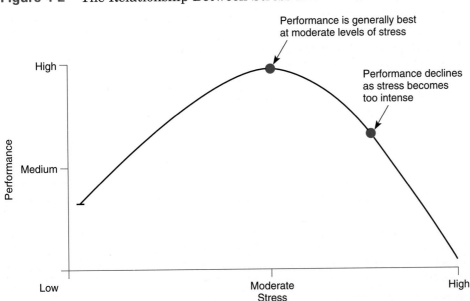

paper unless it's close to the deadline. I work best under pressure"? Self-motivated people, in contrast, are able to establish their own deadlines. They keep pressure on themselves by constantly establishing new goals.

3. *Better problem-solving ability and decision making.* Laboratory experiments have shown repeatedly that people solve problems more readily when pressure is moderate. The pressure might take the form of having to race with the clock. People solve problems less well when the time limits are too loose or too tight. Similarly, you might make the most satisfactory decision if you were given a week, rather than a day or a month, to find a new dwelling.

4. *Increased creativity.* In the same way as problem solving, creativity improves when people are placed under the right amount of stress. In the words of the old adage, "Necessity is the mother of invention." People tend to be creative when life circumstances demand creativity. Many creative approaches to reducing the cost of making a product come about only under the pressure of reduced business or severe inflation.

5. *Better use of time.* Have you ever noticed how much you can accomplish under pressure? One of the many reasons is that you are energized to the point of being a more efficient and productive machine. When the pressure diminishes, most people lapse into a mode of once again squandering time. Many people need to have pressure imposed on them by others to be really productive.

THE NEGATIVE CONSEQUENCES OF STRESS

Heavy doses of stress can lead to physical and psychological ailments, shorten life, and make you forgetful about everyday things. Several of these negative stress symptoms have already been mentioned in this chapter. Look at Self-Examination Exercise 4-1 to determine whether you might be experiencing too many negative consequences of stress. It is helpful to divide these consequences into six types of categories or symptoms:

1. *Negative emotions and feelings.* Among these are anxiety, aggression, apathy, depression, fatigue, frustration, guilt and shame, irritability and bad temper, moodiness, low self-esteem, nervousness, loneliness, and tension. You can almost always count on being tense when placed under stress.

2. *Negative behavior.* A wide variety of negative behaviors are linked to excessive stress. Among the more frequent are emotional outbursts, nervous laughter, restlessness, trembling, stuttering or other speech difficulties, nervous ticks, and increased use of cigarettes, alcohol, and illegal drugs.

3. *Intellectual problems.* Thinking can be impaired under too much negative stress. Among the problems are inability to make decisions and concentrate, frequent forgetfulness, oversensitivity to criticism, mental blocks, and poor judgment.

4. *Adverse physiological symptoms.* Negative physiological conditions include increased blood glucose level, dilation (widening) of the pupils, difficulty in breathing, hot and cold spells, lump in the throat, numbness and tingling in parts of the limbs, poorer vision and hearing, and need for frequent elimination.

SELF-EXAMINATION EXERCISE 4-1:

How Much Stress Are You Facing?

Here's a brief questionnaire to roughly estimate if you are experiencing too many negative consequences of stress (or too much distress). Apply each question to the past six months of your life. Answer each question Mostly Yes or Mostly No.

	Mostly Yes	*Mostly No*
1. Have you been feeling uncomfortably tense lately?	____	____
2. Are you engaged in frequent arguments with people close to you?	____	____
3. Is your life very unsatisfactory?	____	____
4. Do you have trouble sleeping?	____	____
5. Do you feel lethargic about life?	____	____
6. Do many people annoy or irritate you?	____	____
7. Do you have constant cravings for candy and other sweets?	____	____
8. Is your cigarette or alcohol consumption way up?	____	____
9. Are you becoming addicted to soft drinks or coffee?	____	____
10. Do you find it difficult to concentrate on your work?	____	____
11. Do you frequently grind your teeth?	____	____
12. Are you increasingly forgetful about little things like mailing a letter?	____	____
13. Are you increasingly forgetful about big things like appointments and major errands?	____	____
14. Are you making far too many trips to the lavatory?	____	____
15. Have people commented lately that you do not look well?	____	____
16. Do you get into verbal fights with other people too frequently?	____	____
17. Have you been involved in more than one physical fight lately?	____	____
18. Do you have more than your share of tension headaches?	____	____
19. Do you feel nauseated much too often?	____	____
20. Do you feel light-headed or dizzy almost every day?	____	____
21. Do you have churning sensations in your stomach far too often?	____	____
22. Are you in a big hurry all the time?	____	____
23. Are far too many things bothering you these days?	____	____
24. Do you frequently feel tired and exhausted for no particular reason?	____	____
25. Do you have difficulty shaking colds or other infections?	____	____

Scoring: The following guidelines are of value only if you answered the questions sincerely:

0–7: Mostly Yes answers: You seem to be experiencing a normal amount of stress.

8–17: Mostly Yes answers: Your stress level seems high. Become involved in some kind of stress management activity, such as the activities described later in this chapter.

18–25: Mostly Yes answers: Your stress level appears much too high. Seek the help of a mental health professional or visit your family doctor (or do both).

5. *Burnout.* An extreme negative response to stress is **burnout,** a condition of emotional, mental, and physical exhaustion along with cynicism in response to long-term job stressors. Burnout is a unique type of stress syndrome that comes about as a final stage of an adverse reaction to job stress.[12] Burnout was originally observed primarily among people-helpers such as nurses, social workers, and police officers. It then became apparent that people in almost any occupation could develop burnout. Students can also experience burnout because studying is hard work. Conscientiousness and perfectionism contribute to burnout. People who strive for perfection stand a good chance of becoming disappointed about not achieving everything.

6. *Problems for employers.* Employers also suffer when employees experience too much stress. The problems include increased absenteeism, lowered productivity, disputes between management and labor, high accident rates, high turnover and tardiness, bickering among employees and supervisors, and increased medical costs.

SOURCES OF STRESS IN PERSONAL LIFE

Almost any form of frustration, disappointment, setback, inconvenience, or crisis in your personal life can cause stress. The different sources of stress encountered in personal life are described as follows: significant life changes in general; everyday annoyances; social and family problems; physical and mental health problems; financial problems; and school-related problems.

Significant Life Change

A general stressor that encompasses both work and personal life is having to cope with significant change. A pioneering series of studies on stressful life events was conducted by Thomas Holmes and Richard Rahe over a period of twenty-five years. Their research (and similar studies) showed repeatedly that the necessity of significant change in the life pattern of an individual created stress.

The research on life changes resulted in the assigning of scale values to the impact of changes in forty-two life events. These values, called **life-change units,** were taken to represent the average amount of social readjustment considered necessary to cope with a given change. The more significant the change one has to cope with in a short period of time, the greater the probability of experiencing a stress disorder. According to the Holmes-Rahe scale, the maximum negative change (death of a spouse) is assigned 100 points.[13] An example of a change in life that would produce modest stress for most people is a minor violation of the law (11 points). The life-change units assigned to a number of events are listed in Table 4-1.

Individual differences are important in understanding the stressful impact of life changes. The mean values listed in Table 4-1 do not hold true for everybody. For example, if a person were on parole, a minor violation of the law might have a value considerably higher than 11.

TABLE 4-1

STRESS IMPACT OF LIFE CHANGES AS MEASURED BY LIFE-CHANGE UNITS

Life Event	Mean Life-Change Units
Death of spouse	100
Divorce	73
Marital separation	65
Imprisonment	63
Death of close family member	63
Marriage	50
Fired from job	47
Marital reconciliation	45
Pregnancy	45
Retirement	45
Sexual difficulties	39
Gain of new family member	39
Major business readjustment	39
Death of close friend	37
Change to a different career	36
Buying a house	31
Trouble with in-laws	29
Beginning or ending formal schooling	26
Trouble with boss	23
Change in residence	20
Change in eating habits	15
Vacation	13
Minor violation of the law	11

SOURCES: Rabi S. Bhagat, "Effects of Stressful Life Events on Individual Performance and Work Adjustment Processes within Organizational Settings: A Research Model," *Academy of Management Review,* October 1983, pp. 660–71. The values reported in Bhagat are an updating of Thomas H. Holmes and Richard H. Rahe, "The Social Adjustment Rating Scale," *Journal of Psychosomatic Research,* 15, 1971, pp. 210–23.

Everyday Annoyances

Managing everyday annoyances can have a greater impact on your health than can major life catastrophes. Sweating the small stuff can hurt you more than dealing with the significant changes mentioned above, according to several studies.[14] Everyday annoyances that create stress for many people include concerns about weight, the health of a family member, inflation, home maintenance, overcrowded schedules, yard work and outside maintenance, taxes, crime, and physical appearance. Several of these hassles are discussed here as separate categories.

An important finding of these studies is that people who are able to cope well with daily hassles tend to have good health. They are resilient enough to tailor-make a coping strategy for each hassle they face, such as overcoming a billing error made by a credit-card company. Another method of coping with this general category of stress is to recognize that these annoyances happen to everybody. You are not being singled out for harassment; you are not a loser; it's just part of modern living.

Social and Family Problems

Friends and family are the main source of love and affection in your life. But they can also be the main source of stress. Most physical acts of violence are committed among friends and family members. One of the many reasons we encounter so much conflict with friends and family is that we are emotionally involved with them.

Physical and Mental Health Problems

Prolonged stress produces physical and mental health problems, and the reverse is also true. Physical and mental illness can act as stressors—the fact of being ill is stressful, as one man discovered when he developed a severe case of gingivitis (infection of the gums). One by one his teeth fell out until treatment finally halted the process. He found the situation so stressful that he made some errors on the job. If you receive a serious injury, that too can create stress. The stress from being hospitalized can be almost as severe to some patients as the stress from the illness or injury that brought them to the hospital.

Stress operates in a cycle: stress can bring about illness and injury; the illness and injury, in turn, serve as stressors themselves, thus exacerbating the discomfort. You must learn to break the cycle by using the appropriate method of stress management.

Financial Problems

A major life stressor is financial problems. Although you may not be obsessed with money, not having enough money to take care of what you consider the necessities of life can lead to anxiety and tension. If you do not have enough money to replace or repair a broken or faulty personal computer or automobile, the result can be stressful. Even worse, imagine the stress of being hounded by bill collectors. Lack of funds can also lead to embarrassment and humiliation (both stressors). A photography student once showed up on a field trip without a tripod for his camera. The instructor said, "What's the matter, can't you afford a tripod?" The student responded, "No, I can't afford one." Unthinkingly, several class members laughed at the financially troubled student.

School-Related Problems

The life of a student can be stressful. Among the stressors to cope with are exams in subjects you do not understand well, having to write papers on subjects unfamiliar to you, working your way through the complexities of registration, or having to deal with instructors who do not see things your way. Another source of severe stress for some students is having too many competing demands on their time. On most campuses you will find someone who works full-time, goes to school full-time, and has a family. This type of three-way pull often leads to marital problems. You do not have to be a middle-aged executive to develop ulcers!

 PERSONALITY FACTORS AND STRESS

Some people are more stress-prone than others because of factors within their personalities. Important examples are emotional insecurity and low self-confidence. If you worry a lot about making mistakes, any demanding task will create stress. Two well-studied personality factors predisposing people to stress are Type A behavior and a belief that much of their life is controlled by external forces.

Type A Behavior

People with **Type A behavior** characteristics have basic personalities that lead them into stressful situations. Type A behavior has two main components. One is a tendency to try to accomplish too many things in too little time. This leads the Type A individual to be impatient and demanding. The other component is free-floating hostility. Because of this combined sense of urgency and hostility, these people are irritated by trivial things. On the job, people with Type A behavior are aggressive and hardworking. Off the job, they keep themselves preoccupied with all kinds of errands to run and things to do.[15]

Type A personalities are more likely to experience cardiac disease and other stress-related illnesses at an early age. Recognize, however, that not every hardworking and impatient individual is prone to severe stress disorders. Hard chargers who like what they are doing—including many top executives—are remarkably healthy and outlive less competitive people.

The vast majority of people reading this book probably are Type B personalities—those who are easygoing and can relax readily. People who display Type B behavior rarely suffer from impatience or a sense of time urgency, nor are they excessively hostile.

Belief in External Locus of Control

If you believe that your fate is controlled more by external than internal forces, you are probably more susceptible to stress. People with an **external locus of control** believe that external forces control their fate. Conversely, people with an **internal locus of control** believe that fate is pretty much under their control.

The link between locus of control and stress works in this manner: If people believe they can control adverse forces, they are less prone to the stressor of worrying about them. For example, if you believed that you can always find a job, you will worry less about unemployment. At the same time, the person who believes in an internal locus of control experiences a higher level of job satisfaction. Work is less stressful and more satisfying when you perceive it to be under your control.

What about your locus of control? Do you believe it to be internal? Or is it external?

Negative Affectivity

A major contributor to being stress-prone is **negative affectivity,** a tendency to experience aversive (intensely disliked) emotional states. In more detail, negative affectivity is a predisposition to experience emotional stress that includes feelings of nervousness, tension, and worry. Furthermore, a person with negative affectivity is likely to experience emotional states such as anger, scorn, revulsion, guilt, self-dissatisfaction.[16] Such negative personalities seem to search for discrepancies between what they would like and what exists. Instead of attempting to solve problems, they look for them.

People with negative affectivity are often distressed even when working under conditions that co-workers perceive as interesting and challenging. In one company, a contest was announced that encouraged customer-contact workers to compete against each other in terms of improving customer service. An employee with a history of negative affectivity said: "Here we go again. We're already hustling like crazy to please customers. Now we're being asked to dream up even more schemes to make sure the customer is right. It's about time the company thought of ways to please employees as well as customers."

Sex Differences in Stress Symptoms

Related to personality factors are the contrasting ways the bodies of men and women respond to stress. A number of studies have investigated this issue, and the findings are sometimes contradictory. The most pronounced difference is that women show symptoms of low emotional well-being to a greater extent than men do. Men are more likely to suffer serious disorders as a consequence of stress.

More specifically, women suffer more than men do from migraines, arthritis, vision problems, and emotional discomfort. Men are more likely to suffer from coronary heart disease, cirrhosis of the liver, alcoholism, and suicide. In general, men are more prone to serious and incapacitating illness in response to stress. Women more often tend to suffer from less severe psychological problems. Also, men suffer more from chronic (long-term) problems, while women experience more acute (sudden onset) ones.[17]

Debra L. Nelson and James C. Quick offer additional ideas on sex differences in stress. The two researchers concluded that employed women experience more stress than either nonemployed women or men. The reason is that employed women face several unique stressors, including job discrimination and many conflicts between marriage and work.[18] These same stressors may be less true today than in the past because an increasing number of women are fully involved in business careers.

Other studies have questioned whether these sex differences in stress exist.[19] When differences in symptoms between men and women have been found, the results could be attributed to differences in ability to handle stress, rather than sex itself. For example, men may experience more severe stress symptoms than women because they handle stress differently.

SOURCES OF STRESS IN WORK LIFE

No job is without potential stressors for some people, and dozens of sources of stress on the job have been identified. Here we discuss six major job stressors you might encounter or might already have encountered, as listed in Figure 4-3.

Figure 4-3 Frequently Observed Job Stressors

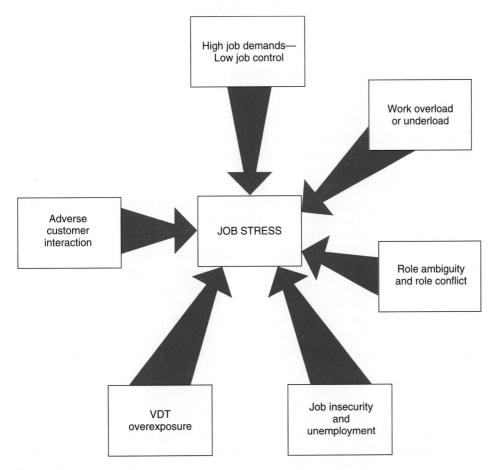

HIGH JOB DEMANDS—LOW JOB CONTROL

Many workers experience stress when they are faced with a heavy work load combined with limited ability to control key features of the job.[20] Among these features would be how many phone calls to handle, when to perform certain tasks, and how fast to perform the work. Imagine being required to write more reports than you thought you could handle, yet being unable to concentrate on them for more than a few minutes at a time. The impediments to your concentration might include demands from customers, co-workers, and your boss.

Why a combination of high demand and low control creates stress can be explained as follows: High job demands produce a state of arousal that is typically reflected in such responses as increased heart rate and flow of adrenaline. When the worker has low control the arousal cannot be properly channeled into a coping response. As a result, the physiological stress reaction is even larger and persists for a longer time.[21]

A service station mechanic suffered from migraine headaches. Asked by a health professional if he was experiencing job stress, the mechanic replied: "My job is killing me. Half the time we're shorthanded. That means while I'm doing repair work I also have to work the cash register. Sometimes I have to pump gas for the people who don't use self-serve. Every time the bell rings I have to stop what I'm doing. I can't do decent repair work when I'm being jerked around like this."

WORK OVERLOAD OR UNDERLOAD

As just described, having limited control over a heavy work load creates job stress. A heavy work load itself, however, can also be a stressor. **Role overload,** a burdensome work load, can create stress for a person in two ways. First, the person may become fatigued and thus be less able to tolerate annoyances and irritations. Think of how much easier it is to become provoked over a minor incident when you lack proper rest. Second, a person subject to unreasonable work demands may feel perpetually behind schedule, a situation that in itself creates an uncomfortable, stressful feeling.

A disruptive amount of stress can also occur when people experience **role underload,** or too little to do. Some people find role underload frustrating because it is a normal human desire to want to work toward self-fulfillment. Also, making a contribution on the job is one way of gaining self-respect. As with any facet of human behavior, there are exceptions. Some people find it relaxing not to have much to do on the job. One direct benefit is that it preserves their energy for family and leisure activities.

ROLE AMBIGUITY AND ROLE CONFLICT

Not being certain of what they should be doing is a stressor for many people. **Role ambiguity** is a condition in which the job holder receives confusing or poorly defined expectations. A typical complaint is "I'm not really sure I know what I'm supposed to be doing around here." You will recall, however, that creative people enjoy ambiguity because they can define problems for themselves when clear directions are lacking. Role ambiguity is related to job control. If you lack a clear picture of what you should be doing, it is difficult to get your job under control.

Role conflict refers to having to choose between two competing demands or expectations. Many workers receive conflicting demands from two or more managers. Imagine being told by your manager to give top priority to one project. You then receive a call from your manager's manager who tells you to drop everything and work on another project. It's often up to you to resolve such a conflict. If you don't you will experience stress.

JOB INSECURITY AND UNEMPLOYMENT

Workers have always worried about losing their jobs for reasons such as a business recession, automation, and making serious mistakes. In the last decade, however, workers at all levels have been very concerned about losing their jobs because of corporate downsizings. **Downsizing** (or *rightsizing*) is a method of reducing the number of employees to save money and improve efficiency.) A concern for many workers is that profitable companies sometimes downsize to further increase profits. When a company is going through downsizing, many workers worry whether they will be placed on the next list of people to be laid off. Worry of this type is a major stressor.

Unemployment itself creates more stress than job insecurity. Unemployed people have high rates of depression, spouse abuse, suicide, and homicide. The suicide rate for laid-off workers is thirty-five times the national average.[22] Conscientious people who are laid off become increasingly stressed out as the number of weeks without a job increases. The best antidote to worrying about losing your job is to perform well and have a portfolio of skills that are valuable to many employers.

VDT OVEREXPOSURE

Working with computers can lead to **VDT stress,** an adverse physical and psychological reaction to prolonged work at a video display terminal. The symptoms often reported by VDT workers include headaches; neck aches; fatigue; and hot, tired, watery eyes and blurred vision after long periods of operation. Adding to the impact of VDT stress is the controversy about whether prolonged exposure to computer monitors can contribute to miscarriages and birth defects. (The National Institute of Safety and Health concludes that VDTs *do not* emit unsafe levels of electromagnetic radiation—a possible contributor to miscarriages.)[23]

Another aspect of VDT-related stress is acquiring a repetitive-motion disorder as a consequence of prolonged keyboarding. The repetitive-motion disorder most frequently associated with keyboarding (and optical scanning) is **carpal tunnel syndrome.** The syndrome occurs when repetitive flexing and extension of the wrist causes the tendons to swell, thus trap-

A DISRUPTIVE AMOUNT OF STRESS CAN ALSO OCCUR
WHEN PEOPLE EXPERIENCE ROLE UNDERLOAD

ping and pinching the median nerve.[24] Carpal tunnel syndrome creates stress because of the pain and misery. The thoughts of having to permanently leave a job requiring keyboarding is another potential stressor.

Much of VDT stress, including repetitive-motion disorder, can be prevented by VDT operators taking frequent rest breaks and using a well-designed combination of the work table, chair, and video display terminal. Being comfortable while working prevents much physical strain.

ADVERSE CUSTOMER INTERACTION

Interviews conducted with ninety-three employees revealed that interactions with customers can be a major stressor. Stressful events frequently cited were customers losing control, using profanity, badgering employees, harassing employees, and lying. The employees interviewed said that these adverse interactions with customers negatively affected the quality of their work environment.[25] Part of the problem is that the sales associate often feels helpless when placed in conflict with a customer. The sales associate is told that "the customer is always right." Furthermore, the store manager usually sides with the customer in a dispute with the sales associate.

MANAGING STRESS

Because potentially harmful stressors surround us in work and personal life, virtually everybody needs a program of stress management in order to stay well. Stress management techniques are placed here into three categories: attacking the source of stress; getting close to people; and relaxation techniques.

Dealing with Stress by Attacking Its Source

Stress can be dealt with in the short range by indirect techniques such as exercise and relaxation. However, to manage stress in the long range and stay well you must also learn to deal directly with stressors. Several of these techniques are described in the next few paragraphs.

Eliminating or Modifying the Stressor.   The most potent method of managing stress is to eliminate the stressor giving you trouble. For example, if your job is your primary stressor, your stress level would be reduced if you found a more comfortable job. At other times, modifying the stressful situation can be equally helpful. Using the problem-solving method, you search for an alternative that will change the stressor. Here is a useful model to follow:

> A retailing executive repeatedly told her boss that she wanted to open a new branch of the business. He agreed with her, but took no action. Feeling rejected, frustrated, and stressed, she took another approach to the problem. She drew up the plans for opening a new branch, presented them to her boss, and informed him she was ready to move ahead. To the executive's surprise, he said, "Great! I was only hesitating to ask you to do this because I thought you were overworked."
>
> Everything worked out just as she wanted after she pursued the alternative of restating her plans in writing.[26]

Place the Stressful Situation in Perspective.   Stress comes about because of our perception of the situation. If you can alter your perception of a threatening situation, you are attacking the source. A potentially stressful situation can be put into perspective by asking, "What is the worst thing that could happen to me if I fail in this activity?"[27]

The answer to the above question is found by asking a series of questions, starting with the grimmest possibility. For instance, you are late with a report that is due this afternoon. Consider the following questions and answers:

- Will my reputation be damaged permanently? (*No.*)

- Will I get fired? (*No.*)

- Will I get reprimanded? (*Perhaps, but not for sure.*)

- Will my boss think less of me? (*Perhaps, but not for sure.*)

Only if the answer is yes to either of the first two questions is negative stress truly justified. The thought process just described allows stressful situations to be properly evaluated and kept in perspective. You therefore avoid the stress that comes from overreacting to a situation.

Gaining Control of the Situation.   As implied in the discussion of low job control, feeling that a bothersome situation is out of control is almost a universal stressor. A key method of stress management is therefore to attack the stressor by gaining control of the situation. A multipurpose way of gaining control is to improve your work habits and time management, as described in Chapter 12. By being "on top of things," you can make heavy work and school demands less stressful.

Keep a Hostility Log.   Hostility is a major stressor. You can partially modify this stressor by monitoring the amount of hostility you are experiencing. To keep a hostility log, first write down where and when you experienced hostile feelings, and what provoked them. Describe what you thought, what you did, and how you felt. For example, "Today, I was introduced as 'the guy from the purchasing department.' I felt that was a slight. I would have felt much better if I was introduced as, 'Glenn, our assistant buyer.' Status is very important to me."

After a week or ten days, look for patterns and frequent triggers of hostility. Ponder whether minor events sometimes provoked major reactions needlessly.[28] In Glenn's situation, he might reevaluate whether the informal introduction was really a put-down.

HANDLING STRESS BY GETTING CLOSE TO PEOPLE

An ideal way of managing stress is one that provides side benefits. Getting close to people falls into this category. You will reduce some of your tension and form healthy relationships with other human beings in the process. Closeness suggests getting in touch with your feelings or tuning into others. If you want to be close to someone else, and therefore reduce stress, you may have to first get close to yourself.

Getting Close to Yourself.   Solitude, perhaps taking the form of walking by oneself, can be tension reducing. Yet many people have difficulty in getting close to themselves. Part of the reason is that they find solitude uncomfortable. Psychoanalyst Herbert Freudenberger advises us that most people seem to be running away from rather than toward themselves. He writes:

> We run from ourselves every chance we get. Think about it. When did you last spend time by yourself, with yourself, doing something you enjoy? *With* yourself is the important thing to check, because much of the time we're alone we shut off our minds and feelings. We get involved in a television program or have a couple of drinks and fall asleep. We're not really there for ourselves in a related kind of way. We're merely alone. Being alone *with* yourself, however, means your senses are alive, your thoughts are keeping you company, you're sitting in that room or going to that art gallery with a person, not just an empty body. You're sharing an experience *with* yourself, and you're enjoying it.[29]

Getting Close to Others.   By getting close to others you build a **support system,** a group of people on whom you can rely for encouragement and comfort. The trusting relationship you have with these people is critically important. People you can go to with your problems include family members, friends, co-workers, and other students. In addition, some people in turmoil reach out to strangers to discuss personal problems. An effective way of developing a social support network is to become a good listener so others will reciprocate when you need to talk through your problems.

The usual method of reducing stress is to talk over your problems while the other person listens. Switching roles can also help reduce stress. Listening to other people will make you feel better because you have helped them. Another advantage to listening to the feelings and problems of others is that it helps you get close to them.

RELAXATION TECHNIQUES FOR HANDLING STRESS

"You ought to relax" is the advice family physicians, relatives, and friends have always offered the stressed individual. Stress experts today give us similar advice but also offer specific techniques. Here we describe five do-it-yourself techniques that can help you to relax, and consequently reduce stress and its accompanying tension. In addition, Exhibit 4-2 distills extensive knowledge about relaxation techniques into fourteen practical suggestions. Observe that several of these techniques are aimed at achieving wellness. Pick and choose from among these brief suggestions and those presented in more detail for dealing with stressors.

EXHIBIT 4-2

EVERYDAY SUGGESTIONS FOR RELAXATION

1. Take a nap when facing heavy pressures.

2. Have a good laugh (laughter is an excellent tension reducer).

3. Smile frequently every day.

4. Concentrate intensely on reading or a sport or hobby.

5. Breathe deeply, and between inhaling and exhaling tell yourself you can cope with the situation.

6. Have a quiet place at home and have a brief idle period there every day.

7. Take a leisurely vacation (even if only a weekend) during which virtually no time is programmed.

8. Finish something you have started, however small. Accomplishing almost anything reduces some stress.

9. Avoid drinking many caffeinated or alcoholic beverages. Try fruit juice or water instead.

10. Stop to smell the flowers, make friends with a preschool child or elderly person, or play with a kitten or puppy.

11. Strive to do a good job, but not a perfect job.

12. Work with your hands, doing a pleasant task.

13. Write down your angry thoughts on a piece of paper or record them on a computer instead of keeping them inside you.

14. Next time you are faced with a difficult situation ask yourself how your favorite cartoon character would handle it. (The chuckle you get from this activity might help you place your problem in proper perspective.)

Relaxation Response

A standard technique for reducing stress is to achieve the relaxation response. The **relaxation response** is a bodily reaction in which you experience a slower respiration and heart rate, lowered blood pressure, and lowered metabolism. The response can be brought about in several ways, including meditation, exercise, or prayer. By practicing the relaxation response you can counteract the fight-or-flight response associated with stress.

According to cardiologist Herbert Benson, four things are necessary to practice the relaxation response: a quiet environment, an object to focus on, a passive attitude, and a comfortable position. You are supposed to practice the relaxation response ten to twenty minutes, twice a day. To evoke the relaxation response, Dr. Benson advises you to close your eyes. Relax. Concentrate on one word or prayer. If other thoughts come to mind, be passive, and return to the repetition.[30]

Similar to any other relaxation technique, the relaxation response is harmless and works for most people. However, some very impatient people find it annoying to disrupt their busy day to meditate. Unfortunately, these may be the people who most urgently need to learn to relax.

Transcendental Meditation

An old but still widely practiced relaxation technique is **transcendental meditation** (TM), a mental technique for establishing a physiological state of deep rest. This technique was very popular in the 1960s, then declined somewhat in use, but has surged in popularity in recent years. Transcendental meditation is simple, natural, and easily learned. It consists of getting into a comfortable upright position, closing the eyes, and relaxing for fifteen to twenty minutes twice a day. The mind is allowed to drift, with no effort or control required. During transcendental meditation the mind focuses on what is known as a *mantra,* a sound assigned to the meditator by the teacher. The mantra takes the form of a relaxing sound, such as "om."

During transcendental mediation, the mind enjoys a settled state of inner wakefulness. At the same time, the body achieves a unique state of deep rest. The meditator shows distinct physiological changes, including a decrease in heart and respiratory rate and lower metabolism. Meditators frequently note that they feel more relaxed or less hurried than before they began to meditate.

Visualizing a Pleasant Experience

Perhaps the most effortless and enjoyable relaxation technique when under stress is to visualize a calm and pleasant experience. **Visualization** means to picture yourself doing something that you would like to do. Whatever fantasy suits your fancy will work, according to the advocates of this relaxation technique. Visualizations that work for some people include: trout fishing on a sunny day, floating on a cloud, caressing a baby, petting a kitten, and walking in the woods. Notice that all of these scenes are relaxing rather than exciting. What visualization would work for you?

Rehearsal of the Stressful Situation

Akin to visualization is the technique of rehearsing a stressful situation in your mind. Imagine that you face the difficult task of having to resign from one job in order to take a better one. You are tense, and your tension level increases as the day progresses. One approach to relaxing enough to handle this situation is to mentally rehearse this scenario. Most important, rehearse your opening line, which might be something like, "Mr. Gordon, I've asked to see you to discuss something very important," or "Mr. Gordon, the company has been very nice to me, but I've decided to make an important change in my life."

Muscle Monitoring

An important part of many stress-reduction programs is to learn to relax your muscles. Learn to literally loosen up and be less uptight. Muscle monitoring involves becoming aware that your muscles have tightened and then consciously relaxing them. If your jaw muscles are tightening up in a tense situation, you learn to relax your jaw enough to overcome the stress effects.

Try to determine whether muscle tautness occurs in association with some recurring event. Pay attention to the tautness of your muscles on those occasions. For example, you might experience a tightening of your neck muscles whenever it is the time of the month to pay your rent. Take a few moments to be aware of that muscle tension. After a while you will learn to relax when the last day of the month arrives and your rent (and other bills) are due.

SUMMARY

Wellness is a formalized approach to preventive health care. By promoting health, company wellness programs help prevent employees from developing physical and mental problems often associated with excessive job pressures.

Four strategies for achieving wellness were described in this chapter. First, the right amount and type of physical exercise contributes substantially to wellness. Second, maintaining a healthy diet is valuable for mental and physical health. The Food Guide Pyramid (Figure 4-1) contains many useful suggestions. Third, developing competence, including both job and social skills, helps us stay well. Fourth, being resilient is another wellness strategy. Psychological hardiness contributes to resiliency. Fifth, developing a health-prone personality (emotional expressiveness and self-reliance) helps us be well.

The body's battle against a stressor is the fight-or-flight response. Stress always involves physiological changes such as an increase in heart rate, blood cholesterol, and blood pressure. The right amount of stress can be beneficial. Performance tends to be best under moderate amounts of stress, yet certain negative forms of stress almost always decrease performance.

Almost any form of frustration, disappointment, setback, inconvenience, or crisis in your personal life can cause stress. The categories of situations that can produce stress include: significant life changes; everyday annoyances; social and family problems; sports; physical and mental health problems; financial problems; and school-related problems.

People with Type A behavior are impatient and demanding, and have free-floating hostility. They are rarely able to relax and frequently have heart attacks and other stress-related illnesses at an early age. The behavior of Type B personalities, the relaxers, is basically the opposite. Another personality factor related to stress is locus of control. If you believe that your fate is controlled more by external than internal forces, you are more susceptible to stress. Another major contributor to stress-proneness is negative affectivity (a predisposition to negative mental states).

Sex differences in stress symptoms have been frequently observed. In general, women show symptoms of low emotional well-being to a greater extent than do men. Men are more likely to suffer serious physical disorders as a consequence of stress.

Sources of job stress are quite varied. Among them are high job demands and low job control; work overload or underload; role ambiguity and role conflict; job insecurity and unemployment; VDT overexposure; and adverse customer interaction.

To successfully manage stress in the long range you have to deal with stressors directly. Four direct approaches are: eliminate the stressor; put the situation into proper perspective; gain control of the situation; and keep a hostility log.

Getting close to people is another useful strategy for managing stress. Closeness involves both getting close to yourself (such as enjoying solitude) and getting close to others in order to develop a support system. It can reduce your tension to discuss your problems with others.

Five relaxation techniques for reducing stress are: the relaxation response; transcendental meditation; visualizing a pleasant experience; rehearsal of the stressful situation; and muscle monitoring.

Questions and Activities

1. Why is employee wellness a concern of so many employers?

2. Some researchers have suggested that the term *challenge* be substituted for the term *stress*. What do you think of the merit of their suggestion?

3. How does a person know when one stressor he or she is facing is stronger than other stressors?

4. Looking at the stress impact of changes listed in Table 4-1, which two have the highest life-change units for you?

5. What stressors might earning a very high income help a person avoid?

6. Several case histories have revealed that people who win large cash prizes in government lotteries wind up suffering severe stress disorders. What's their problem?

7. How does carefully choosing a career help a person reduce stress?

8. Do career-school students tend to suffer from the stress of high job demands and low job control with respect to their schooling? Explain your reasoning.

9. If you were beginning to suffer from carpal tunnel syndrome, what requests might you make of your employer?

10. Get in touch with a person you consider to be much more relaxed than most people. Ask your contact which (if any) of the relaxation techniques listed in Exhibit 4-2 (and the surrounding text) he or she uses. Report your findings.

A HUMAN RELATIONS CASE PROBLEM: THE REAL ESTATE BLUES

After receiving an associate's degree in business administration, Jimmy Chang worked at a bank for five years. He began as an assistant in the mortgage department and was promoted to associate loan specialist three years later. Chang's job responsibilities centered around processing residential mortgage applications. The more Chang learned about mortgages, the more fascinated he became with the real estate business.

In addition to learning about mortgages and real estate on the job, Chang took several courses in banking and real estate. The bank managers who knew Chang were impressed with his dedication to the job and his interest in upgrading himself professionally. Chang received outstanding performance evaluations for three consecutive years. He was also well liked by his co-workers and clients.

Midway through his fourth year at the bank, Chang modified his career goals. He thought to himself, "I'm really into mortgages and real estate. I see this field as a long-time career. Yet I wonder if I'm in the right end of the business for me. Selling real estate might be more exciting than screening loan applications. If I were as successful in selling real estate as I am in making loans, I could triple my income."

Chang's many contacts in the real estate business made it easy for him to inquire about job opportunities. Three out of the four people he contacted encouraged Chang to explore the possibilities of becoming a real estate agent in their agency. The manager at one of the agencies said, "Jimmy, you would be a

(Continued)

natural in real estate sales. You know the business from the other side of the fence. You're a real pro, and we'd love to have you join us at Trans-National." Chang then enrolled in a real estate agent's course to prepare himself for a job switch six months later.

With some trepidation, Jimmy Chang resigned from his position at the bank. At his farewell party, he said, "My parents are from the old school. They told me that a person should never leave a secure job. I'm taking a risk, but I'm not leaving you entirely. I hope to refer my best clients to our bank for their mortgages. Remember to treat them well." (Laughter from the group.)

Armed with his recently acquired real estate license, Chang began his career shift with enthusiasm. Trans-National gave him a $1,000 per month advance against commissions. At the end of three months, Chang had earned only $500 in commissions despite long hours of hard work. He was also spending considerable money on gas and car washes as he drove prospective home buyers around town.

By the end of the third week on the job, Chang noticed he was having difficulty sleeping. He would wake up at night with disturbing thoughts about getting into deep financial trouble. He was particularly disturbed about having to borrow money from his parents to cover his weekly expenses. Chang thought to himself, "I'm using my credit card more than I ever wanted to. I'm even paying for gas and food with plastic. If I don't close some sales soon, I'll be headed toward a financial crisis. I thought a former banker should be able to manage his finances."

Chang had several meetings with Paula Madison, the owner of his Trans-National agency, to discuss how he could earn more money. "Jimmy," she said, "the way to earn money in this business is to get original listings. You have to find people who intend to sell their houses, and have them sign up with you as the principal agent."

Chang then formulated plans for getting some original listings by calling every homeowner he knew. After his first fifty calls, only one couple expressed an interest in selling their house. The owners were retired people who wanted about 35 percent more money for the house than its market value.

As Chang made his fifty-first phone call, he felt dizzy and nauseous. He reflected, "This is getting me sick. I hate bothering people. If a person wanted to sell a house, he or she would call a real estate firm. Why pester people?"

By ten each morning, Chang arrived at the office where he would work until seven in the evening. His day consisted of waiting for people to respond to newspaper ads placed by his agency. He then had his turn to pursue a promising lead. He would also make an occasional phone call to a prospect for an original listing.

(Continued)

Chang was becoming increasingly uncomfortable working in the office. He noticed he was beginning to nibble his nails, and he sweated under the arms much more than he had ever noticed before. Most disturbing of all to Chang was how his heart pounded when he compared his small commissions to his draw. When Chang read the newspaper or watched television, he noticed that he could hardly remember anything of what he read, heard, or saw.

Jimmy confided in his parents one night, "I'm getting sicker every day. The pressure of doing so poorly is getting to me. But I'm not a quitter."

Jimmy's mother responded, "We know you're not a quitter. Why don't you go back to the bank? They'll take you back. You were doing so well there. I hate to see what your job is doing to you."

Jimmy exhaled and said, "Folks, you'₋ me thinking. But I know I can work things out. I hate ᵗ n my career plans."

QUESTIONS

1. What sti⸻ ⸻cing?

2. What rec⸻ ⸻ke him feel well agai⸻

3. What care⸻

A HU⸻
THE⸻

Each class mem⸻ ⸻ıch techniques he or she uses to red⸻ ⸻ress. Class members then come to the front ⸻ ⸻ıvidually to make a brief presentation of their m⸻ ⸻ective stress-reduction technique. After the presentations are completed, class members analyze and interpret what they heard. Among the issues to explore are:

1. Which are the most popular stress-reduction techniques?

2. How do the stress-reduction techniques used by the class compare to those recommended by experts?

Welland resident takes first place

TRIBUNE STAFF

WELLAND

Welland resident Joe Vrbanek, a graduating student at RCC College of Technology, was a first-place winner at the college's sixth Technology Showcase held last week.

Vrbanek was a member of the team that developed and built two Smart Car Accessories: one is a rain detector which will raise any open windows when it starts raining and the second feature is distance sensors to tell drivers how close they are to adjacent cars in a situation such as parallel parking.

REFERENCES

[1]Steve M. Jex, Terry A. Beehr, and Cathlyn K. Roberts, "The Meaning of Occupational Stress Items to Survey Respondents," *Journal of Applied Psychology,* October 1992, p. 623.

[2]Dot Yandle, "Staying Well May Be Up to You," *Success Workshop Folio* (a supplement to *The Pryor Report Management Newsletter*), February 1994, pp. 2–3.

[3]Cary L. Cooper and Roy Pane (eds.), *Personality and Stress: Individual Differences in the Stress Process* (New York: John Wiley & Sons, 1991).

[4]Philip L. Rice, *Stress and Health: Principles and Practice for Coping and Wellness* (Monterey, Calif.: Brooks/Cole Publishing Company, 1987), pp. 353–54.

[5]*Dietary Guidelines for Americans,* 3d ed., U.S. Department of Agriculture, U.S. Department of Health and Human Services, 1990; updated with food pyramid, May 1992.

[6]Emory L. Cowen, "In Pursuit of Wellness," *American Psychologist,* April 1991, p. 406.

[7]Ibid.

[8]James M. Kouzes and Barry Z. Posner, *The Leadership Challenge: How to Get Extraordinary Things Done in Organizations* (San Francisco: Jossey-Bass, 1987), pp. 65–67; Suzanne C. Kobasa and Salvatore R. Maddi, *The Hardy Executive: Health Under Stress* (Chicago: Dorsey Professional Books/Dow Jones-Irwin, 1984), pp. 31–32.

[9]Hans J. Eysenck, "Health's Character," *Psychology Today,* December 1988, pp. 28–35.

[10]Jeffrey R. Edwards, "A Cybernetic Theory of Stress, Coping, and Well-Being in Organizations," *Academy of Management Review,* April 1992, p. 248.

[11]R. Douglas Allen, Michael A. Hitt, and Charles R. Greer, "Occupational Stress and Perceived Organizational Effectiveness: An Examination of Stress Level and Stress Type," *Personnel Psychology,* Summer 1982, pp. 359–70.

[12]Cynthia L. Cordes and Thomas W. Dougherty, "A Review and an Integration of Research on Job Burnout," *Academy of Management Review,* October 1993, pp. 621–656.

[13]Rabi S. Bhagat, "Effects of Stressful Life Events on Individual Performance and Work Adjustment Processes Within Organizational Settings: A Research Model," *Academy of Management Review,* October 1983, pp. 660–71.

[14]Michael E. Cavanagh, "What You Don't Know About Stress," *Personnel Journal,* July 1988, p. 55.

[15]Jeffrey R. Edwards, A. J. Baglioni, Jr., and Cary L. Cooper, "Examining the Relationships Among Self-Report Measures of the Type A Behavior Pattern: The Effects of Dimensionality, Measurement Error, and Differences in Underlying Constructs," *Journal of Applied Psychology,* August 1990, pp. 440–54; Ray H. Rosenman, *Type A Behavior and Your Heart* (New York: Fawcett, 1975).

[16]Peter Y. Chen and Paul E. Spector, "Negative Affectivity as the Underlying Cause of Correlations Between Stressors and Strains," *Journal of Applied Psychology,* June 1991, p. 398.

[17]Todd D. Jick and Linda F. Mitz, "Sex Differences in Work Stress," *Academy of Management Review,* July 1985, pp. 410–412.

[18]Debra L. Nelson and James C. Quick, "Professional Women: Are Distress and Disease Inevitable?" *Academy of Management Review,* April 1985, pp. 206–213.

[19]Joseph J. Martocchio and Anne M. O'Leary, "Sex Differences in Occupational Stress: A Meta-Analytic Review," *Journal of Applied Psychology,* June 1989, pp. 495–501.

[20]Marilyn L. Fox, Deborah J. Dwyer, and Daniel C. Ganster, "Effects of Stressful Job Demands and Control on Physiological and Attitudinal Outcomes in a Hospital Setting," *Academy of Management Journal,* April 1993, p. 290–291.

[21]Ibid., p. 290.

[22]"More Cuts . . . Deeper Cuts . . . and More Help for Employees," *HRfocus,* November 1993, p. 24.

[23]Norma R. Fritz, "VDTS: Reducing the Risk," *Personnel,* September 1988, pp. 4–5.

[24]Michael J. Lotito and Frances P. Alvarez, "Integrate Claims Management with ADA Compliance Strategy," *HRMagazine,* August 1993, p. 89.

[25]James D. Brodzinski, Robert P. Scherer, and Karen A. Goyer, "Workplace Stress: A Study of the Internal and External Pressures Placed on Employees," *Personnel Administrator,* July 1989, pp. 77–78.

[26]"Making Stress Work for You," *Executive Strategies,* October 3, 1989, p. 5.

[27]Philip Morgan and H. Kent Baker, "Building a Professional Image: Dealing with Job Stress," *Supervisory Management,* September 1985, p. 38.

[28]Redford Williams, *The Trusting Heart: Great News About Type A Behavior* (New York: Times Books, 1989).

[29]Herbert J. Freudenberger, *Burn Out: The High Cost of High Achievement* (Garden City, N.Y.: Anchor Press/Doubleday, 1980), p. 124.

[30]Herbert Benson (with William Proctor), *Beyond the Relaxation Response* (New York: Berkely Books, 1985), pp. 96–97.

ADDITIONAL READING

Beauvais, Laura L. "The Effects of Perceived Pressures on Managerial and Nonmanagerial Scientists and Engineers." *Journal of Business and Psychology,* spring 1992, pp. 333–347.

Brockner, Joel, et al. "Layoffs, Job Insecurity, and Survivors' Work Effort: Evidence of an Inverted-U Relationship." *Academy of Management Journal,* June 1992, pp. 413–25.

Cave, Douglas G. "Employees Are Paying for Poor Health Habits." *HRMagazine,* August 1992, pp. 52–54.

Edwards, Jeffrey R., and Van Harrison, R. "Job Demands and Worker Health: Three Dimensional Reexamination of the Relationship Between Person–Environment Fit and Strain." *Journal of Applied Psychology,* August 1993, pp. 628–648.

Leatz, Christine A. *Career Success/Personal Stress: How to Stay Healthy in a High-Stress Environment.* New York: McGraw-Hill, 1992.

Mason, Julie Cohen. "Healthy Equals Happy Plus Productive." *Management Review,* July 1992, pp. 33–37.

Newman, John. *How to Stay Cool, Calm & Collected When the Pressure's On: A Stress-Control Plan for Businesspeople.* New York: AMACOM, 1992.

Schaufeli, Wilmar B., Maslach, Christina, and Marek, Tadeusz (eds.) *Professional Burnout: Recent Developments in Theory and Research.* Bristol, Pa.: Taylor & Francis, 1993.

CHAPTER 5

DEALING WITH PERSONAL PROBLEMS

Learning Objectives

After studying the information and doing the exercises in this chapter you should be able to:

■ Recognize how self-defeating behavior contributes to personal problems.

■ Explain how alcohol and drug abuse interfere with career and personal success, and how to deal with these problems.

■ Describe how to deal with the loss of a relationship.

■ Recognize the career impact of absenteeism and tardiness.

■ Describe how depression and neurobiological disorders can lower job productivity.

■ Develop a strategy for overcoming personal problems.

*I*n the previous chapter we described methods of achieving wellness and managing stress. Another contributor to wellness and stress control is to effectively manage personal problems. Unless personal problems are kept under control, a person's chances of achieving career and personal success are greatly diminished. How many people have you

known or heard about who damaged their career or an important relationship because of personal problems?

Our approach to understanding and overcoming personal problems will be to first describe the self-defeating behavior in general, and how to reverse the trend. We then describe major forms of self-defeating behavior. Among them are alcohol abuse, substance abuse, family and financial problems, tardiness, and absenteeism. Finally, we describe two types of personal problems that are much less under a person's control: depression and neurobiological disorders. An example of a neurobiological disorder would be an attention deficit.

 ## SELF-DEFEATING BEHAVIOR

Many problems on the job and in personal life arise because of factors beyond our control. A boss may be intimidating and insensitive, an employer might lay you off, or a significant other might abruptly terminate your relationship. Many personal problems, nevertheless, arise because of **self-defeating behavior.** A person with self-defeating tendencies intentionally or unintentionally engages in activities or harbors attitudes that work against his or her best interest. A person who habitually is late for important meetings is engaging in self-defeating behavior. Dropping out of school for no reason other than being bored with studying is another of many possible examples. Let's examine several leading causes of self-defeating behavior, and how to reverse the pattern.

WHY PEOPLE ENGAGE IN SELF-DEFEATING BEHAVIOR

Many different forces lead people to work against their own best interests, often sabotaging their careers. The major cause of self-defeating behavior is a *loser life script.*[1] Early in life, our parents and other influential forces program our brains to act out certain life plans. These plans are known as *scripts.* People fortunate enough to have winner scripts consistently emerge victorious. When a tough assignment needs doing, they get the job done. For example, they figure out how to get a jammed computer program running again that baffles everybody else in the office.

In contrast, others have scripts that program them toward damaging their careers and falling short of their potential. Much of this damage paradoxically occurs just when things seem to be going well. A person might steal equipment from a company shortly after receiving an outstanding performance appraisal.

The simplest explanation for self-defeating behavior is that some people suffer from a personality that fosters defeat. People with a *self-defeating personality pattern* have three notable characteristics. First, they repeatedly fail at tasks they have the ability to perform. Second, they place themselves in very difficult situations and respond helplessly. Third, they typically refuse to take advantage of escape routes, such as accepting advice and counsel from a manager.[2]

Self-defeating beliefs put many people on the road to career self-sabotage. In this context, a self-defeating belief is an erroneous belief that creates the conditions for failure. For example, some people sabotage their job campaigns before even starting. They think to themselves: "I lack the right experience," "I'm not sharp enough," "I'm too old," "I'm too young," and so forth.

Fear of success is yet another contributor to career self-sabotage. People who fear success often procrastinate to the point of self-defeat. The same people worry that being successful will lead to such negative outcomes as an overwhelming work load or loss of friends. They also worry that success will bring about unrealistic expectations from others, such as winning a big suggestion award every year.

To examine your present tendencies toward self-defeating behavior take the self-sabotage quiz presented in Self-Awareness Exercise 5-1. Taking the quiz will help alert you to many self-imposed behaviors and attitudes that could potentially harm your career and personal life.

STRATEGIES AND TECHNIQUES FOR OVERCOMING AND PREVENTING SELF-DEFEATING BEHAVIOR

Overcoming self-defeating behavior requires hard work and patience. Here we present six widely applicable strategies for overcoming and preventing self-defeating behavior. Pick and choose among them to fit your particular circumstance and personal style.

SELF-AWARENESS EXERCISE 5-1:

The Self-Sabotage Questionnaire

Indicate how accurately each of the statements below describes or characterizes you, using a five-point scale: (0) very inaccurately, (1) inaccurately, (2) midway between inaccurately and accurately, (3) accurately, (4) very accurately. Consider discussing some of the questions with a family member, close friend, or work associate. Another person's feedback may prove helpful in providing accurate answers to some of the questions.

Answer

1. Other people have said that I am my worst enemy. _____

2. If I don't do a perfect job, I feel worthless. _____

3. I am my own harshest critic. _____

4. When engaged in a sport or other competitive activity, I find a way to blow a substantial lead right near the end. _____

5. When I make a mistake, I can usually identify another person to blame. _____

6. I have a sincere tendency to procrastinate. _____

7. I have trouble focusing on what is really important to me. _____

8. I have trouble taking criticism, even from friends. _____

9. My fear of seeming stupid often prevents me from asking questions or offering my opinion. _____

10. I tend to expect the worst in most situations. _____

11. Many times I have rejected people who treat me well. _____

12. When I have an important project to complete, I usually get sidetracked, and then miss the deadline. _____

13. I choose work assignments that lead to disappointments even when better options are clearly available. _____

14. I frequently misplace things, such as my keys, then get very angry at myself. _____

15. I am concerned that if I take on much more responsibility people will expect too much from me. _____

(Continued)

16. I avoid situations, such as competitive sports, where people can find out how good or bad I really am.   _____

17. People describe me as the "office clown."   _____

18. I have an insatiable demand for money and power.   _____

19. When negotiating with others, I hate to grant any concessions.   _____

20. I seek revenge for even the smallest hurts.   _____

21. I have an overwhelming ego.   _____

22. When I receive a compliment or other form of recognition, I usually feel I don't deserve it.   _____

23. To be honest, I choose to suffer.   _____

24. I regularly enter into conflict with people who try to help me.   _____

25. I'm a loser.   _____

                                        Total score   _____

Scoring and Interpretation: Add your answers to all the questions to obtain your total score. Your total score provides an approximate index of your tendencies toward being self-sabotaging or self-defeating. The higher your score, the more probable it is that you create conditions to bring about your own setbacks, disappointments, and failures. The lower your score, the less likely it is that you are a self-saboteur.

0–25: You appear to have very few tendencies toward self-sabotage. If this interpretation is supported by your own positive feelings toward your life and yourself, you are in good shape with respect to self-defeating behavior tendencies. However, stay alert to potential self-sabotaging tendencies that could develop at later stages in your life.

26–50: You may have some mild tendencies toward self-sabotage. It could be that you do things occasionally that defeat your own purposes. Review actions you have taken during the past six months to decide if any of them have been self-sabotaging.

51–75: You show signs of engaging in self-sabotage. You probably have thoughts, and carry out actions, that could be blocking you from achieving important work and personal goals. People with scores in this category characteristically engage in negative self-talk that lowers their self-confidence and makes them appear weak and indecisive to others. People in this range frequently experience another problem. They sometimes sabotage their chances of succeeding on a project just to prove that their negative self-assessment is correct. If you scored in this range, carefully study the suggestions offered in this chapter.

76–100: You most likely have a strong tendency toward self-sabotage. (Sometimes it is possible to obtain a high score on a test like this because you are going through an unusually stressful period in your life.) Study this chapter carefully and look for useful hints for removing self-imposed barriers to your success. Equally important, you might discuss your tendencies toward undermining your own achievements with a mental health professional.

Examine Your Script and Make the Necessary Changes.   Much importance has been attached to the influence of early-life programming in determining whether a person is predisposed to self-defeat. Note carefully the word *predisposed.* A person may be predisposed to snatch defeat from the jaws of victory, but that does not mean the predisposition makes defeat inevitable. It does mean that the person will have to work harder to overcome a tendency toward self-sabotage. A good starting point is to look for patterns in your setbacks:

- Did you blow up at people who have the authority to make the administrative decisions about your future?

- Did you get so tense during your last few command performances that you were unable to function effectively?

- Did you give up in the late stages of several projects, saying "I just can't get this done"?

Stop Blaming Others for Your Problems.   Blaming others for our problems contributes to self-defeating behavior and career self-sabotage.[3] Projecting blame onto others is self-defeating because doing so relieves you of most of the responsibility for your setback and failure. Consider this example: If someone blames favoritism for not receiving a promotion, he or she will not have to worry about becoming a stronger candidate for future promotions. Not to improve one's suitability for promotion is self-sabotaging. If you accept most of the blame for not being promoted, you are more likely to make the changes necessary to qualify in the future.

An underlying theme to the suggestions for preventing and overcoming self-defeating behavior is that we all need to engage in thoughts and actions that increase our personal control. This is precisely the reason that blaming others for our problems is self-sabotaging. By turning over control of your fate to forces outside yourself, you are holding them responsible for your problems.

Solicit Feedback on Your Actions.   Feedback is essential for monitoring whether you are sabotaging your career or personal life. A starting point is to listen carefully to any direct or indirect comments from your superiors, subordinates, co-workers, customers, and friends about how you are coming across to them. Consider the case of Bill, a technical writer.

> Bill heard three people in one week make comments about his appearance. It started innocently with, "Here, let me fix your collar." Next, an office assistant said, "Bill, are you coming down with something?" The third comment was, "You look pretty tired today. Have you been working extra hard?" Bill processed this feedback carefully. He used it as a signal that his steady late-night drinking episodes were adversely affecting his image. He then cut back his drinking enough to revert to his normal healthy appearance.

An assertive and thick-skinned person might try the technique described for soliciting feedback described in Chapter 1. Approach a sampling of people both on and off the job with this line of questioning: "I'm trying to develop myself personally. Can you think of anything I do or say that creates a bad impression in any way? Do not be afraid of offending me. Only people who know me can provide me with this kind of information."

Take notes to show how serious you are about the feedback. When someone provides any feedback at all, say, "Please continue, this is very useful." Try not to react defensively when you hear something negative. You asked for it, and the person is truly doing you a favor.

Learn to Profit from Criticism.   As the above example implies, learning to profit from criticism is necessary to benefit from feedback. Furthermore, to ignore valid criticism can be self-defeating. People who benefit from criticism are able to stand outside themselves while being criticized. It is as if they are watching the criticism from a distance and looking for its possible merits. People who take criticism personally experience anguish when receiving negative feedback. Here are several specific suggestions for benefiting from valid criticism.[4]

1. *See yourself at a distance.*   Place an imaginary plexiglass shield between you and the person being criticized. Attempt to be a detached observer looking for useful information.

2. *Ask for clarification and specifics.*   Ask politely for more details about the negative behavior in question, so you can change if change is warranted. If your boss is criticizing you for being rude with customers, you might respond: "I certainly don't want to be rude. Can you give me a couple of examples of how I was rude? I need your help in working on this problem." After asking questions you can better determine if the criticism is valid.

3. *Decide on a response.*   An important part of learning from criticism is to respond appropriately to the critic. Let the criticizer know what you agree with. Apologize for the undesirable behavior, such as saying, "I apologize for being rude to customers. I know what I can do differently now. I'll be more patient, so as not to appear rude." If the feedback was particularly useful in helping you overcome self-defeating behavior, thank the person for the constructive feedback.

Stop Denying the Existence of Problems. Many people sabotage their careers because they deny the existence of a problem and therefore do not take appropriate action. Denial takes place as a defensive maneuver against a painful reality. An example of a self-sabotaging form of denial is to ignore the importance of upgrading one's credentials despite overwhelming evidence that it is necessary. Some people never quite complete a degree program that has become an informal qualification for promotion. Consequently, they sabotage their chances of receiving a promotion for which they are otherwise qualified. Many people in recent years have damaged their chances for career progress by not upgrading their computer skills.

Visualize Self-Enhancing Behavior. Visualization is a primary method for achieving many different types of self-improvement. It is therefore an essential component of overcoming self-defeating behavior. To apply visualization, program yourself to overcome self-defeating actions and thoughts. Imagine yourself engaging in self-enhancing, winning actions and thoughts. Picture yourself achieving peak performance when good results count the most.

A starting point in learning how to use visualization for overcoming career self-sabotage is to identify the next job situation you will be facing that is similar to ones you have flubbed in the past. You then imagine yourself mentally and physically projected into that situation. Imagine what the room looks like, who will be there, and the confident expression you will have on your face. Visualization is akin to watching a video of yourself doing something right. An example:

> Matt, an actuary in a life insurance company, has an upcoming meeting with top management to discuss his analysis of how insurance rates should be changed to factor in the impact of AIDS on mortality rates. Based on past experience, Matt knows that he becomes flustered and too agreeable in high-level meetings about controversial topics (such as rate increases) Matt also knows that to behave in this way is self-defeating.
>
> As he prepares for the meeting, he visualizes himself calmly listening to challenges to his analysis. In response, he does not back off from his position, but smiles and presents his findings in more detail. Matt visualizes the people who challenged him changing their attitudes as he knowledgeably explains his case. By the end of the meeting Matt is warmly thanked for his recommendations on making rate changes to meet the incidence of AIDS in the population. The president congratulates him on how well he stood up to the challenges to his forecasts.

ALCOHOL ABUSE

At least 10 percent of the workforce at any given time experiences lowered job performance because of **substance abuse,** the overuse of any substance that enters the bloodstream. Substance abuse is usually associated with alcohol, illegal drugs, and prescription drugs. Yet it can also include the abuse of tobacco, coffee, soft drinks, nonnutritional food substances, and vaporous fluids such as rubber cement. For convenience, our discussion will focus on alcohol and drug problems separately. Recognize, however, that alcohol is commonly regarded as a drug.

HEALTH EFFECTS OF ALCOHOL ABUSE

A major concern about consuming large amounts of alcohol is that health may be adversely affected. What constitutes a large amount of alcohol depends on a person's size and tolerance level. For the average-size adult, more than four alcoholic beverages per day would be considered a large amount. Alcohol consumption leads to marked changes in behavior. Even low doses significantly impair the judgment and coordination required to drive an automobile safely, potentially leading to injury and death.

Moderate to high doses of alcohol cause marked impairment in higher mental functions. The brain damage that results can severely alter a person's ability to learn and remember information. Very high doses of alcohol cause respiratory depression and death. Heavy alcohol consumption over a prolonged period of time contributes to heart disease. (Consuming up to three alcoholic beverages a day, however, may help prevent heart disease by stimulating the heart and unclogging arteries.)

Long-term consumption of large quantities of alcohol, particularly when combined with poor nutrition, can lead to permanent damage to vital organs such as the brain and liver. Drinking large quantities of alcohol during pregnancy may result in newborns with fetal alcohol syndrome. These infants have irreversible physical abnormalities and mental retardation.

As with other drugs, repeated use of alcohol can lead to dependence. Abrupt cessation of alcohol consumption can produce withdrawal symptoms including severe anxiety, tremors, hallucinations, and convulsions. Severe withdrawal symptoms can be life threatening.

WORK AND PERSONAL LIFE CONSEQUENCES
OF ALCOHOL ABUSE

Heavy consumption of alcohol has many adverse consequences for a person's career and personal life. Heavy drinking will eventually being to interfere with work performance, resulting in some of the following behaviors[5]:

- Low productivity and quality of work

- Erratic performance

- Erratic and unusual behavior such as swearing at co-workers during a meeting

- Excessive tardiness and absenteeism

- Increased difficulty in working cooperatively with supervisors

- Increased difficulty in working cooperatively with co-workers
- Carelessness, negligence, or disinterest

Alcohol consumption is potentially disruptive to personal and family life. Even moderate doses of alcohol increase the incidents of a variety of aggressive acts, including partner and child abuse. Purchasing alcoholic beverages can lead to family problems because household bills may go unpaid. Many alcoholics lose friends because they are uncomfortable to be around when drinking. Sexual desire and performance often declines with heavy alcohol abuse. Many male drinkers suffer from impotency. Alcohol abuse often leads to divorce and other broken relationships.

OVERCOMING ALCOHOL ABUSE

A person's approach to overcoming alcohol abuse depends to some extent on whether he or she regards alcoholism as a disease or as maladaptive behavior. Regarding alcoholism as a disease is the majority viewpoint among mental health specialists and the general public. People who regard alcoholism as a disease are likely to seek medical or psychological help. To conquer alcoholism they would therefore seek help from physicians and counselors. Such help might consist of outpatient visits to mental health practitioners, often at clinics for substance abusers. People with severe alcoholism might volunteer to become an inpatient at a hospital specializing in the treatment of alcoholism.

Another viewpoint is to regard alcoholism as self-defeating behavior that is somewhat under a person's control. People who accept the *bad habit* view of alcohol abuse might seek professional assistance with their problem. Yet the thrust of their efforts to overcome alcoholism will be to discipline themselves to change their counterproductive ways. Looking upon alcoholism as maladaptive behavior runs contrary to groups such as Alcoholics Anonymous. Such groups label alcoholism as a sickness over which the victim has no control, and therefore insist on abstinence.[6] A person who believes that alcohol abuse is under his or her control could take the following precautions to prevent a major drinking problem[7]:

- Limit the consumption of alcoholic beverages to three on any given day, but average no more than two per day. Remember that in order of increasing strength, popular alcoholic beverages are ranked as follows: wine cooler, beer, wine, and whiskey. Whiskey should therefore be consumed in smaller quantities than the other three types of beverages.

- Abstain from alcoholic beverages for at least two consecutive days each week.

- Drink only standard-size beverages: one ounce of whiskey in a mixed drink; 12 ounces of beer; or 5 ounces of wine.

- Don't drink on an empty stomach.

- Drink slowly and intersperse alcoholic beverages with nonalcoholic beverages while at parties.

- When you have the urge for an alcoholic beverage, on occasion substitute a glass of fruit juice or water.

- Make friends with people whose social life does not revolve around drinking alcoholic beverages. Associate with responsible drinkers.

- Regard drinking before 6 P.M. as a personal taboo.

The above suggestions are useful because they assume that mature adults can enjoy moderate alcohol consumption without falling prey to alcohol abuse. The same suggestions can be used to convert problem drinking into relatively safe drinking. Implementing these suggestions requires considerable self-discipline, as do approaches to overcoming other forms of self-defeating behavior.

 # DRUG ABUSE

Another major personal problem many people face is drug abuse. The use of illegal drugs is often perceived more harshly than alcohol abuse because alcohol use is legal. Similarly, the abuse of prescription drugs is not considered as wrong as the abuse of illegal drugs. The health effects and personal life consequences of abusing both illegal and prescription drugs are similar to those of alcohol abuse. Self-Awareness Exercise 5-2 will help sensitize you to the many similarities of the behavior consequences of drug and alcohol abuse. Here we will summarize the effects of five major categories of drugs, and then describe how drug abusers can be helped.

USES AND EFFECTS OF CONTROLLED SUBSTANCES

The term *drug* refers to a variety of chemicals with different chemical compositions and effects. One individual might purchase heroin for recreational use, while another person might sniff paint thinner to achieve the same effect. The United States government has compiled a five-way classification of frequently used drugs.[8] Each of the five categories of drugs has different possible effects and different consequences for overdoses. Each category of drug has both illegal and legitimate uses. For example, stimulants include both crack and a drug with the trade name Dexedrine.

Narcotics

A **narcotic** is a drug that dulls the senses, facilitates sleep, and is addictive with long-term use. Well-known narcotics include opium, morphine, codeine, and heroin. The possible effects of narcotics include euphoria, drowsiness, and decreased breathing. A narcotic user may also experience constricted pupils and nausea. Overdosing on narcotics may lead to slow and shallow breathing, clammy skin, convulsions, and coma. Death is also possi-

SELF-AWARENESS EXERCISE 5-2:

Symptoms of Alcohol and Drug Abuse

People with alcohol or drug abuse problems are often poor judges of the extent of their problem. Nevertheless, it is helpful to use the symptoms mentioned below as a checklist to help identify an alcohol or drug problem you might be experiencing. Review the symptoms listed below and indicate whether each one applies to you.

Alcohol Abuse	Yes	No
Sudden decreases in my job performance	____	____
Decreases in my mental alertness	____	____
Many long lunch hours	____	____
Tardiness for work and social appointments	____	____
Wobbling instead of walking straight	____	____
Many absences from work or school	____	____
Comments by others that my speech is slurred	____	____
Frequent use of breath freshener	____	____
Frequent depressed moods	____	____
Trembling of my hands and body	____	____
Errors in judgment and concentration	____	____
Many financial problems because of my drinking	____	____
Comments by others that my eyes look sleepy	____	____
Much lost time due to physical illness	____	____
Elaborate alibis for not getting work done on the job or at home	____	____
Denying a drinking problem when I know I have one	____	____

Interpretation: If five or more of the above symptoms fit you, you may have a problem with alcohol abuse. Act on the remedial measures described previously.

Drug Abuse	Yes	No
Sudden decreases in my job performance	____	____
Decreases in my mental alertness	____	____
Hiding out on company premises	____	____
Many absences from work or school	____	____
My pupils appear dilated when I look in the mirror	____	____
Unusual bursts of energy and excitement	____	____

(Continued)

Drug Abuse	Yes	No
Prolonged and serious lethargy	____	____
States of apathy and elation I cannot explain	____	____
Errors in concentration and judgment	____	____
Many financial problems because of drug purchases	____	____
Comments by others that my eyes look sleepy	____	____
Frequent sniffing	____	____
People telling me that I look "out of it."	____	____
Elaborate alibis for not getting work done on the job or at home	____	____
Denying a drug problem when I know I have one	____	____

Interpretation: If five or more of the above symptoms fit you, you may have a problem with drug abuse. Act on the remedial measures described previously.

ble. People who use narcotics frequently do severe damage to their career and personal lives in the long run.

Depressants

A **depressant** is a drug that slows down vital body processes. Barbiturates are the best-known depressant (or sedative). Alcohol is also classified as a depressant. Heavy doses of depressants can lead to slurred speech and disorientation. A depressant user will show drunken behavior without the odor of alcohol. An overdose of depressants leads to shallow breathing, clammy skin, and dilated pupils. With extreme overdoses, the person may lapse into coma and then death.

Many anxious people are convinced they must take legally prescribed sedatives to calm down. The trade-off is the risk of lacking the mental alertness to perform at their peak. Frequent users of depressants make poor companions because they lack vitality.

Stimulants

The class of drugs known as **stimulants** produces feelings of optimism and high energy. Cocaine and amphetamines are the two best-known stimulants. Taking stimulants leads to increased alertness, excitation, and euphoria. The user will also experience increased pulse rate and blood pressure, insomnia, and loss of appetite. (Many diet pills are really stimulants.) Overdoses of stimulants lead to agitation, increased body temperature, hallucinations, convulsions, and possible death. Stimulant abusers are regarded by others as being "hyper," and may be too agitated to do high-quality work.

Hallucinogens

In small doses the class of drugs known as **hallucinogens** produce visual effects similar to hallucinations. Three well-known hallucinogens are LSD, mescaline, and peyote. Hallucinogens lead to illusions (misperceptions) and poor perception of time and distance. Overdoses of hallucinogens can produce "trip" episodes, psychosis (severe mental disorder), and possible death. While under the influence of a hallucinogen, a person is unfit for work. The bizarre behavior of hallucinogen abusers leads to a deterioration of their relationships with people.

Cannabis

The class of drugs known as **cannabis** are derived from the hemp plant and generally produce a state of mild euphoria. Marijuana and hashish are placed in the cannabis category. Cannabis use leads to euphoria, relaxed inhibitions, and increased appetite. The same drug may cause disorientation. Cannabis abuse may lead to fatigue, paranoia, and possible psychosis. Because marijuana is used as a cigarette, it may cause lung cancer and cardiovascular damage. Used in moderate doses, cannabis does much less damage to career and personal life than the other drugs described here.

GETTING HELP FOR DRUG ABUSE PROBLEMS

Drug abuse is so widespread that many forms of assistance are available for drug abusers. The comments made earlier in relation to alcohol abuse also apply to drug abuse. Drug abusers can seek help from physicians and from mental health specialists (some of whom are physicians). At the same time, the drug abuser may view his or her problem as a form of maladaptive behavior that can be controlled through concentrated effort. Assume, for example, a person says, "I simply cannot get through the day without an amphetamine pill. Life is too boring for me if I don't have an upper."

The antidote is for the person to say something to the following effect: "This week, I won't take an amphetamine on Monday. Next week, no amphetamine on Monday or Tuesday. I'll keep adding a day until I have gone an entire week drug-free." Self-management of this type can work for many people.

An avenue of help for an employed person with a drug abuse problem is the company employee assistance program. A major purpose of these programs is to help employees overcome personal problems that drain productivity. Typically, the assistance program coordinator refers the troubled employee to an outside treatment facility. Some larger organizations have their own treatment facilities located on or off company premises. The program is confidential, sometimes to the extent that the company does not know which employees have referred themselves for help.

Many of the problems dealt with by the employee assistance program involve forms of self-defeating behavior in addition to drug abuse. Among them are other forms of substance abuse, cigarette addiction, compulsive gambling, financial problems, and physical abuse of family members. Employees can also spend one or two sessions with the assistance counselor to talk about self-defeating behavior in general. If the counselor thinks multiple sessions are required, an appropriate referral is made.

Seeking help from an assistance counselor rather than going to a mental health practitioner on one's own has an important advantage. Employee assistance counselors work regularly with people whose personal problems are hurting job performance. Also, the company usually pays the entire fee.

COPING WITH THE LOSS OF A RELATIONSHIP

A major personal problem many people encounter is the loss of a valued personal relationship. The loss may take the form of separation, divorce, or a nonmarried couple splitting up. A more subtle loss is when a couple stays together, yet the intimacy in a relationship vanishes. Loneliness and conflict result from the lost intimacy. Chapter 16 presents ideas on maintaining and revitalizing relationships. Our attention here is directed toward specific suggestions for dealing with the loss of an important personal relationship.

When you are emotionally and romantically involved with another person, the loss of that relationship usually has a big impact. Even if you believe strongly that splitting up is in your best interests, the fact that you cared at one time about that person leads to some hurt. The major reason we need tactics for dealing with lost relationships is that many upsetting feelings surface in conjunction with the loss.

A newly unattached person might feel lonely, guilty, angry, or frightened. Your role in the disengagement will usually dictate which emotion surfaces. For instance, if you dumped your partner, you will probably experience guilt. If you were the person dumped, you would probably experience anger. If you survive a spouse, you might feel guilty about not having been nice enough to your partner during your years together.

A number of suggestions are presented below to help a person recover from a lost relationship.[9] Choose the tactics that seem to fit your personality and circumstances. As with the other personal problems described in this chapter, professional counseling may be helpful in making a recovery.

1. *Be thankful for the good in the relationship.*   An excellent starting point in recovering a broken relationship is to take stock of what went right when the two of you were together. Looking for the good in the relationship helps place the situation in proper perspective. It also helps prevent you from developing the counterproductive attitude that your time together was a total waste.

2. *Release some of your anger.*   You will find it is a good time to express anger over a lost relationship when self-confidence begins to return, nurtured by the support of friends and family. You might try such anger-releasing techniques as yelling about your problem or punching pillows.

3. *Find new outlets for spare time.*   Some of the energy you were investing in your partnership can now be invested in spare-time activities. This activity provides a healthy form of the defense mechanism called *compensation* or *substitution*.

4. *Get ample rest and relaxation.*   A broken relationship is a stressor. As a result, most people need rest and relaxation to help them overcome the emotional pain associated with the departure of a partner.

5. *Pamper yourself.*   Pampering involves finding little ways of doing nice things for yourself. These could take the form of buying yourself a new outfit, taking a weekend vacation, eating pizza at midnight, or getting a body massage.

6. *Use support groups.*   A well-documented antidote to a broken relationship can be found in support groups specifically designed to help people cope with recent separation or divorce. Parents without Partners is an example of such a group.

7. *Seek emotional support from individuals.*   Friends and relatives can also be an important source of emotional support to help you cope with postseparation blues. Be careful, however, not to let your loss of a relationship dominate conversations with friends to the point of boring them.

8. *Get out and go places.*   The oldest suggestion about recovering from a lost relationship is perhaps the most valid—keep active. While you are doing new things you tend to forget about your problems. Also, as you go places and do things, you increase your chances of making new friends. And new friends are the only true antidote to the loneliness of being unattached.

9. *Give yourself time to heal.*   The greater the hurt, the more time it will take to recover from the broken relationship. Recognizing this fact will help to curb your impatience over disentangling yourself emotionally from the former spouse or partner.

10. *Anticipate a positive outcome.*   While you are on the path toward rebuilding your social life, believe that things will get better. Also believe that all the emotional energy you have invested into splitting and healing will pay dividends. Self-fulfilling prophecies work to some extent in social relationships. If you believe you will make a satisfactory recovery from a broken relationship, your chances of doing so will increase. The underlying mechanism seems to be that if you believe in yourself, you exude a level of self-confidence that others find appealing.

ABSENTEEISM AND TARDINESS

Absenteeism and tardiness are the leading causes of employee discipline. Developing a poor record of attendance and punctuality is also a form of career self-sabotage. Employees who are habitually absent or late develop a poor reputation and receive negative employment references. It becomes difficult to find a good job with another employer after having established a poor record of attendance and punctuality. Maintaining good attendance and punctuality is more important than ever today because worldwide competition has forced many private organizations to trim costs. Governmental organizations are also under constant pressure to control costs. The person who is habitually absent or late therefore risks termination.

Here we will first look at data about absenteeism and tardiness standards. We then discuss how a person might overcome the problem of high absenteeism and tardiness.

RATES OF ABSENTEEISM AND TARDINESS

In school, standards of absenteeism are often established by an instructor or school policy. A student might be informed, for example, that missing more than six classes will result in being dropped from the course or failing. A national absenteeism average for manufacturing firms is five days of absenteeism per employee per year.[10] Considering that most employees work about 245 days per year, this means that about 2 percent absenteeism is average. Absenteeism rates for nonmanufacturing firms are slightly higher, about seven days per year.

Statistics for tardiness are more difficult to obtain than those for absenteeism. Some help is provided by a survey conducted by the Merchants and Manufacturing Association. The employers surveyed reported that six "tardies" during a twelve-month period usually results in a disciplinary warning. Fifteen instances of being late in a year is likely to result in termination.[11]

Employee handbooks typically emphasize the importance of good attendance and punctuality. The handbook for a division of Allen-Bradley Company, a manufacturing firm, explains its attendance policy in these words:

> It is important to the successful operation of the Motion Control Division that employees be at work each scheduled workday. Each employee is performing an important set of tasks or activities. Excessive and/or avoidable absenteeism places unfair burdens on co-workers and increases the company's cost of doing business by disruption of work schedules. Such absenteeism creates inefficiency and waste, delays, costly overtime, job pressures and customer complaints.
>
> —*Allen-Bradley Employee Handbook,* p. 1.

Notice that the handbook does not state an acceptable level of absenteeism. What do you think would be the possible negative consequence for a company of specifying the maximum number of acceptable absences?

HOW TO OVERCOME AVOIDABLE ABSENTEEISM AND TARDINESS

During a person's career, many unexpected situations arise in which it is necessary to be absent or late. Accidents, illnesses, severe family problems, and family deaths all may require time away from the job. A serious-minded worker should therefore strive to attain near-perfect attendance and punctuality when not faced with an emergency. Some suggestions follow to help a person develop the right mental set for achieving an excellent record of attendance and punctuality.

1. *Recognize that not to have excellent attendance and punctuality is self-defeating.*   For reasons already described, poor attendance and punctuality can lead to a poor reputation and job loss. Why self-handicap your chances for career success?

2. *Look upon your job as self-employment.*   Few people operating their own business will take a day off, or begin late, for no valid reason. The smaller the business, the better the attendance and punctuality, because so little help is available. You can therefore improve your attendance and punctuality by imagining that your area of responsibility is your own business.

3. *Regard your job responsibilities as important as those of the person in charge of opening the bank's doors in the morning.*   People in charge of opening banks, department stores, movie theaters, and other retail businesses have excellent records of attendance and punctuality. To do otherwise would create panic, especially in the case of the bank. To improve your attendance and punctuality, think of your responsibilities as being as important as opening the doors in the morning.

4. *Reward yourself for good attendance and punctuality and punish yourself for the opposite.*   Following the suggestions for self-motivation described in Chapter 2, modify your behavior in relation to attendance and punctuality. Treat yourself after six months of excellent attendance and punctuality. Punish yourself for a poor record. For example, if you miss one day of work for a flimsy reason, punish yourself by working all day on a national holiday.

5. *Think through carefully the consequences if all company employees were absent and late frequently.*   Some people argue that they are entitled to take the maximum number of sick days allowable under company policy. If everybody took the maximum number of sick days and were late as often as possible without incurring discipline, the company would suffer. Customer service would deteriorate, productivity would decrease, and more people would have to be hired just to cover for employee "no-shows." Less money might be available for salary increases and employee benefits. Even worse, the company might have to lay off employees because of low profits.

6. *Imagine being fired by two employers for poor attendance and punctuality.*   Being fired once for poor attendance and punctuality might adversely affect your career. Being fired twice for the same reason could place you at the bottom of the labor pool in terms of employability.

7. *Think of the consequences to co-workers if you are absent and late frequently.*   Being absent or late may hurt the company. The same behavior can adversely affect your relationships with co-workers. Co-workers become annoyed and irritated quickly when they have to cover for a negligent peer. The worker who is frequently absent and late runs the risk of losing the cooperation of co-workers when he or she needs assistance.

8. *Remember that unwarranted absenteeism and tardiness violates company policy.*   Some people with poor attendance and punctuality seem to ignore the reality that they are violating company policy—and that such behavior can lead to termination.

DEPRESSION AND NEUROBIOLOGICAL DISORDERS

Many employees perform poorly on the job because of reasons beyond their control. They would like to perform well, but disturbed emotions or brain malfunctioning interfere with handling some aspects of their job responsibilities well. To illustrate this problem, we describe two problems faced by many workers, depression and neurobiological disorders (defined later).

DEPRESSION

A widespread emotional disorder is **depression.** A depressed person has such difficulties as sadness, changes in appetite, sleeping difficulties, and a decrease in activities, interests, and energy. Approximately 16.5 Americans and Canadians will suffer depression serious enough during their lives to interfere with happiness and productivity.

Being depressed on the job creates many problems. Depression drains energy and reduces productivity and quality. The reduced effectiveness triggers a cycle of failure. As effectiveness decreases, the person's thinking, acting, and feeling become more damaged. As relationships with co-workers and job performance deteriorates, the person becomes more depressed.[12] Here is an example of how depression affects job behavior:

> A sales manager known for his exuberance and enthusiasm slowly began to withdraw from face-to-face contact with team members. During one team meeting the manager abruptly terminated the meeting, telling the group, "I'm just too emotionally drained to continue today." Soon he rarely communicated with others in the firm except through E-mail. At times he was observed just staring out the window. Reports of his unusual behavior soon reached his manager, who in turn urged the sales manager to visit a mental health professional. A combination of antidepressant drugs and psychotherapy helped the sales manager to overcome his problems enough to function satisfactorily on the job.

Self-Awareness Exercise 5-3 will help you better appreciate the symptoms of depression as they apply to the job. These symptoms are easier to recognize in another person than in oneself. Having more than a few of these symptoms is an indicator that treatment by a mental health professional is important. Many people who commit suicide are extremely depressed.

NEUROBIOLOGICAL DISORDERS

Personal problems on the job are sometimes the result of **neurobiological disorders,** a quirk in the chemistry or anatomy of the brain that creates a disability. The quirk is usually inherited, but could also be caused by a brain injury or poisoning, such as exposure to harmful vapors. The dis-

---

SELF-AWARENESS EXERCISE 5-3:

Symptoms of Depression on the Job

Employees suffering from depression often experience a combination of one or more of the following symptoms.

- Slow movement, drooped posture
- Deterioration in grooming, such as rumpled clothing, unkempt hair, neglected facial shaving
- Speaking only when spoken to
- Losing interest and pleasure in most things
- Crying on the job
- Frequent complaints of being tired
- Feeling sad regularly
- Taking unusually long to complete tasks
- Slow thinking and poor memory
- Attributing any personal successes to luck
- Increasing intensity and frequency of any of the above symptoms

SOURCE: John Lawrie, "Coping with Depression on the Job," *Supervisory Management,* June 1992, pp. 6–7; Canadian Mental Health Association, 1995.

---

abilities take the form of reduced ability to control one's behavior, movements, emotions, or thoughts.[13] If you experience sudden changes in your job behavior, a thorough neurological examination is strongly recommended. The most common neurobiological disorders on the job are described next. Depression, already described, is sometimes classified as a neurobiological disorder when it stems from chemical or anatomical factors.

Attention Deficit Disorder.   People with this disorder have difficulty concentrating that may be accompanied by hyperactivity. The person might therefore engage in a flurry of activity on the job, yet much of the activity might be wasted effort. Many difficulties in paying attention in school are attributed to attention deficit disorder.

Obsessive-Compulsive Disorder.   People with this disorder have uncontrollable and recurring thoughts or behavior relating to an unreasonable fear. A job example of obsessive-compulsive disorder would be a person who becomes obsessed with cleaning his or her work area. The person could be motivated by fear of being contaminated by impurities in the ventilation system.

Narcolepsy.   People with this disorder have uncontrollable sleepiness, even after receiving adequate sleep. A person with narcolepsy may fall asleep at the desk, or while driving a company vehicle or operating dangerous machinery.

Tourette Syndrome.   People suffering from this disorder experience uncontrollable movement or utterances, and often shout profanities at inappropriate times. A person with Tourette syndrome is often misinterpreted as consciously attempting to create a disturbance.

Although damaging to work performance, neurobiological disorders can be treated successfully. In addition to the proper medication, the person usually needs a supportive environment both at home and on the job. Most people with neurobiological disorders can function close to normally after appropriate medication is determined and they are taught how to cope with their symptoms.

Training individuals to understand their condition is an important part of the treatment. The person with Tourette syndrome, for example, should explain to co-workers that at times he or she may appear insulting and abusive. Furthermore, co-workers can be advised not to take such behavior seriously, and that the behavior is under medical control and may soon disappear entirely. Discussing a personal problem with co-workers may help to reduce their fears about your problem and lead to better understanding.

SUMMARY

Unless personal problems are kept under control, a person's chances of achieving career and personal success diminish. Many personal problems arise out of self-defeating behavior. The major cause of this behavior is a loser life script, a life plan of coming out a loser in important situations. Other causes of self-defeating behavior include a self-defeating personality pattern, self-defeating beliefs, and fear of success. Approaches to overcoming and preventing self-defeating behavior include:

1. Examine your script and make the necessary changes.

2. Stop blaming others for your problems.

3. Solicit feedback on your actions.

4. Learn to profit from criticism.

5. Stop denying the existence of problems.

6. Visualize self-enhancing behavior.

About 10 percent of workers have job performance problems attributed to some form of substance abuse. Alcohol abuse often adversely affects health. Moderate to high doses of alcohol cause marked impairment in mental functions. Alcohol consumption is associated with heart and liver disease and fetal alcohol syndrome. Very high doses of alcohol cause respiratory depression and death. Alcohol abuse adversely affects job performance and career success. Alcoholism can be treated as a disease or as maladaptive (counterproductive) behavior. Precautions can be taken to prevent alcohol abuse, such as not drinking during the day.

The health effects and personal life consequences of abusing both illegal and prescription drugs are similar to those of alcohol abuse. The various categories of drugs have different possible effects and different consequences for overdoses. The five drug categories are (1) narcotics, (2) depressants, (3) stimulants, (4) hallucinogens, and (5) cannabis. Many forms of professional help are available for drug abusers, yet self-management of the problem is also an important form of help. Employee assistance programs sponsored by employers can help with drug abuse problems.

A major personal problem many people encounter is the loss of a valued personal relationship. Suggestions for dealing with this problem include the following: (1) Be thankful for the good in the relationship. (2) Release some of your anger. (3) Get ample rest and relaxation. (4) Seek emotional support from individuals. (5) Get out and go places.

Absenteeism and tardiness are the leading causes of employee discipline, and thus can be a major personal problem. A national absenteeism average for manufacturing firms is five days per person per year. A survey showed that being late fifteen times in one year can often result in termination. People must develop the right mental set to achieve excellent attendance and punctuality. For example, a person might look upon the job as self-employment.

Many employees perform poorly on the job because they are depressed. Depression drains energy and reduces productivity and quality. As job performance deteriorates, the person becomes more depressed. Many job problems are also caused by neurobiological disorders, a quirk in the chemistry or anatomy of the brain that creates a disability. The disabilities take the form of reduced ability to control one's behavior, movements, emotions, or thoughts. Major neurobiological disorders are attention deficit disorder, obsessive-compulsive disorder, narcolepsy, and Tourette syndrome. These disorders can be treated with medication, but a supportive environment is also needed.

Questions and Activities

1. What is the difference between making a bad mistake once and self-defeating behavior?

2. Describe a person you know who appears to have a winner life script, and justify your reasoning.

3. How can a person tell if criticism of him or her is valid?

4. Most people obviously know that large amounts of alcohol are hazardous to health. Why then is alcohol abuse such a major problem throughout the world?

5. How can looking upon substance abuse as a bad habit help substance abusers overcome their problem?

A HUMAN RELATIONS CASE
PROBLEM: HIGH FLYING EDUARDO

Eduardo was an excellent college student at Penn State University. He majored in business administration and was the president of a student organization. With a wealthy family backing him, Eduardo drove a Corvette and took lavish vacations during school breaks. After graduation from college, Eduardo went on to receive a master's degree in international business at the Thunderbird School at the University of Arizona. He was heavily recruited by several major business corporations.

Eduardo accepted an attractive offer from a multinational company based in the United States that produced manufacturing control systems. His goal was someday to become the vice president of international marketing. As part of his management training program, Eduardo was given assignments in general accounting, auditing, credit, and sales. He was immediately placed on the company's fast track, reserved for new management recruits of exceptional promise.

After a three-year stint in company headquarters, Eduardo was promoted to marketing manager of the company's branch in Mexico City. During this assignment, Eduardo remained single and pursued the lifestyle of an affluent bachelor. After six months in Mexico City, reports began to trickle back to headquarters that Eduardo was having problems.

Eduardo's job performance was erratic, particularly with respect to getting field reports completed on time. He was also getting into disputes with local management about sales strategies. Eduardo's position was that the Mexico City branch relied too much on existing customers to increase business. He believed that new customers must be pursued more aggressively.

Eduardo entertained prospective customers lavishly, including taking them to bullfights. He especially enjoyed the bullfights because he was in training to become an amateur matador. Local management was also concerned that Eduardo was using his expense account to entertain too many women who could not influence sales.

Around 1:00 A.M. on a Tuesday, Eduardo drove a company car into a tree on the way back from a nightclub. He escaped with facial cuts and a severely sprained wrist, but his companion was killed. Police reports suggested that Eduardo was driving beyond a safe speed and, though not drunk, he had been drinking heavily. Headquarters responded by recalling Eduardo to the United States and reassigning him to a market research analyst position. Eduardo feels remorse about the accident, his family is angry at him, and he wonders how he will regain his career thrust.

(Continued)

QUESTIONS

1. What evidence of self-defeating behavior does Eduardo display?

2. Does Eduardo qualify as having an alcohol abuse problem?

3. How could Eduardo's problems have been prevented?

4. What should Eduardo do now to rebuild his career?

A HUMAN RELATIONS ROLE PLAY: HELPING A FALLEN HERO

One person assumes the role of one of Eduardo's work associates. Another person assumes the role of Eduardo. Troubled by recent events in his career, Eduardo comes to his work associate to discuss his problems. He is also seeking friendly advice on dealing with his problems. The work associate contacted by Eduardo is motivated to be helpful and constructive, and will offer whatever sensible advice he or she can give. The two role players spend about ten minutes in front of the class with their role play. Observers provide feedback as to how well the session accomplished its purpose.

6. Find a recent magazine or journal article about new developments in treating drug or alcohol abuse. Share the information with classmates.

7. Should employers be expected to help employees cope with broken relationships? Why or why not?

8. Some companies offer awards for good attendance. Why is this necessary from a motivational standpoint?

9. Do you think people who have poor attendance records in school will probably have poor attendance records on the job? Explain your reasoning.

10. What is the difference between having a depression disorder and being depressed over a terrible problem?

REFERENCES

[1]John Wareham, *Wareham's Way: Escaping the Judas Trap* (New York: Antheneum, 1983), p. 107.

[2]Thomas A. Widiger and Allen J. Frances, "Controversies Concerning the Self-Defeating Personality Disorder," in Rebecca C. Curtis (ed.), *Self-Defeating Behaviors* (New York: Plenum Press, 1989), p. 304.

[3]Seth Allcorn, "The Self-Protective Actions of Managers," *Supervisory Management,* January 1989, pp. 3–7.

[4]Connirae Andreas and Steve Andreas, *Heart of the Mind* (Moab, Utah: Real People Press, 1991).

[5]Jonathan A. Segal, "Alcoholic Employees and the Law," *HRMagazine,* December 1993, pp. 87–88.

[6]Michael E. Cavanagh, "Myths Surround Alcoholism," *Personnel Journal,* February 1990, pp. 112–121.

[7]Based mostly on Harriet B. Braiker, "What All Career Women Need to Know about Drinking," *Working Woman,* August 1989, p. 72.

[8]Based on information in the Drug-Free Workplace Act of 1988, and Drug-Free Schools and Communities Act of 1989.

[9]Andrew J. DuBrin, *Bouncing Back: How to Handle Setbacks in Your Work & Personal Life* (Englewood Cliffs, N.J.: Prentice Hall, 1982), pp. 85–102; Melba Colgrove, Harold H. Bloomfeld, and Peter McWilliams, *How to Survive the Loss of a Love* (New York: Bantam Books, 1976).

[10]Jeff Stinson, "Company Policy Attends to Chronic Absentees," *Personnel Journal,* August 1991, p. 82.

[11]Ibid., p. 84.

[12]John Lawrie, "Coping with Depression on the Job," *Supervisory Management,* June 1992, pp. 6–7.

[13]Peggy Stuart, "Tracing Workplace Problems to Hidden Disorders," *Personnel Journal,* June 1992, p. 84. Our discussion of neurobiological disorders is based on the Stuart article.

ADDITIONAL READING

DuBrin, Andrew J. *Your Own Worst Enemy: How to Overcome Career Self-Sabotage.* New York: AMACOM, 1992.

"Fewer People Fail as Workplace Drug Testing Increases." *HRfocus,* June 1993, p. 24.

Goff, J. Larry, and Goff, Patricia J. *Organizational Co-Dependence: Causes and Cures.* Niwot, Colo.: University Press of Colorado, 1991.

Gunsch, Dawn. "Training Prepares Workers for Drug Testing." *Personnel Journal,* May 1993, pp. 52–59.

Oliver, Bill. "How to Prevent Drug Abuse in Your Workplace." *HRMagazine,* December 1993, pp. 78–81.

Stuart, Peggy. "The Hidden Addiction." *Personnel Journal,* November 1991, pp. 103–108.

Wisman, Eric W. "Peer Pressure Curbs Drug Use." *Personnel Journal,* November 1990, pp. 29–30.

CHAPTER 6

COMMUNICATING WITH PEOPLE

Learning Objectives

After studying the information and doing the exercises in this chapter you should be able to:

■ Understand the importance of effective communication for your career and personal life.

■ Explain the basic communication process.

■ Identify and overcome many roadblocks to communication.

■ Become more aware of nonverbal messages.

■ Improve your sending and receiving of messages.

■ Enhance your skill in using the telephone and voice mail.

A large bank acquired the branch offices of another large bank. Information bulletins were mailed to account holders in the first bank by the acquiring bank. The portion of the bulletin dealing with direct deposit of pay into employee bank accounts read as follows:

> If you have Social Security or SSI payments directly deposited in your _____ checking account, this service will be *continued* by _____ Bank without any direct action on your part. All *other* types of direct deposit, such as direct deposit of payroll will be *discontinued* after close of business April 18, 1994. Please contact your employer to arrange for payments to be forwarded to your _____ Bank account.

In response to this written notice, hundreds of bank customers called the payroll departments of their employers asking a question to the effect, "How do I get my direct deposits to continue." A typical answer was, "The banks have told us nothing. When you find out what to do, let us know." When customers called the old bank they were informed that the new bank would be sending out new account numbers. Bank customers would then be required to pass this information along to their employers. Hundreds of phone calls later, most of the confusion had cleared away. Yet so many customers were irate about the mix-up that they switched to another bank.

As the above incident indicates, effective communication is necessary to avoid wasted time and effort. Communication is so vital that it has been described as the glue that holds organizations and families together. Most job foul-ups and marital tiffs are considered to be communication problems. **Communication,** as used here, is the sending and receiving of messages. Furthermore, to be successful in work or personal life, you usually have to be an effective communicator. You can't make friends or stand up against your enemies unless you can communicate with them. And you can't accomplish work through others unless you can send and receive messages effectively.

In this chapter we explain several important aspects of communication between and among people. A few sections of the chapter deal specifically with improving communication skills. As with other chapters in this text, however, explanation should also lead to skill improvement. If you understand the steps involved in getting a message across to another person, for example, you may be able to prevent many communication problems.

HOW COMMUNICATION TAKES PLACE

A convenient starting point in understanding how people communicate is to look at the steps involved in communicating a message. A diagram of how the process takes place is shown in Figure 6-1. The theme of the model is that two-way communication involves three major steps and that each step is subject to interference, or noise.[1] Assume that Crystal, a customer, wishes to inform Tony, a used-car sales representative, that she is willing to make an offer of $4,000 on a used car. The price tag on the car is $4,500.

Step 1: Encoding the Message. **Encoding** is the process of organizing ideas into a series of symbols, such as words and gestures, designed to communicate with the receiver. Word choice has a strong influence on communication effectiveness. The better a person's grasp of language, the easier it is for him or her to encode. Crystal says, "Tony, this car obviously is not in excellent condition, but I am willing to give you $4,000 for it."

Step 2: Transmission Over Communication Media. The message is sent via a communication medium, such as voice, telephone, paper, or electronic mail. It is important to select a medium that fits the message. It would be appropriate to use the spoken word to inform a co-worker that he swore under his breath at a customer. It would be inappropriate to send the same message through electronic mail. Many messages on and off the job are sent nonverbally, through the use of gestures and facial expressions. For example, a smile from a superior during a meeting is an effective way of communicating the message, "I agree with you." Crystal has chosen the oral medium to send her message.

Step 3: Decoding. In **decoding,** the receiver interprets the message and translates it into meaningful information. Decoding is the process of understanding a message. Barriers to communication are most likely to surface at the decoding step. People often interpret messages according to their psychological needs and motives. Tony wants to interpret Crystal's message that she is very eager to purchase this car. He may therefore listen attentively for more information demonstrating that she is interested in purchasing the car.

Figure 6-1 The Communication Process

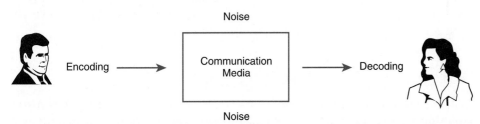

Decoding the message leads naturally to action—the receiver does something about the message. If the receiver acts in the manner the sender wants, the communication has been successful. If Tony says, "It's a deal," Crystal had a successful communication event.

Noise.   Many missteps can occur between encoding and decoding a message. **Noise,** or unwanted interference, can distort or block a message. If Crystal has an indecisive tone and raises her voice at the end of her statement, it could indicate she is not really serious about offering a maximum of $4,000 for the car.

NONVERBAL COMMUNICATION (SENDING AND RECEIVING SILENT MESSAGES)

So far we have been talking mostly about spoken communication. However, much of the communication among people includes nonspoken and nonwritten messages. These nonverbal signals are a critical part of everyday communication. As a case in point, *how* you say "Thank you" makes a big difference in the extent to which your sense of appreciation registers. In **nonverbal communication** we use our body, voice, or environment in numerous ways to help put a message across. Sometimes we are not aware how much our true feelings color our spoken message.

One problem of paying attention to nonverbal signals is that they can be taken too seriously. Just because some nonverbal signals (such as yawning or looking away from a person) might reflect a person's real feelings, not every signal can be reliably connected with a particular attitude. Jason may put his hand over his mouth because he is shocked. Lucille may put her hand over her mouth because she is trying to control her laughter about the message, and Ken may put his hand over his mouth as a signal that he is pondering the consequences of the message. Here we look at seven categories of nonverbal communication that are generally reliable indicators of a person's attitude and feelings.[2]

Environment or Setting

Where you choose to deliver your message indicates what you think of its importance. Assume that a neighbor invites you over for dinner to discuss something with you. You will think it is a more important topic under these circumstances than if it were brought up when the two of you met in the supermarket. Other important environmental cues include room color, temperature, lighting, and furniture arrangement. A person who sits behind an uncluttered large desk, for example, appears more powerful than a person who sits behind a small, cluttered desk.

Distance from the Other Person

How close you place your body relative to another person's also conveys meaning when you send a message. If, for instance, you want to convey a

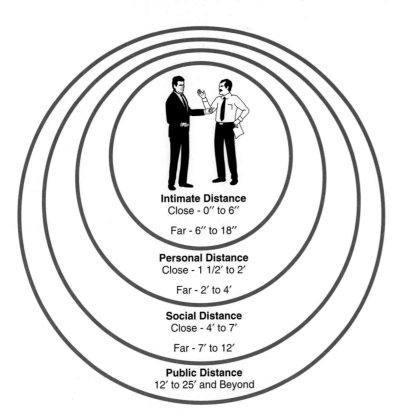

Intimate Distance
Close - 0″ to 6″

Far - 6″ to 18″

Personal Distance
Close - 1 1/2′ to 2′

Far - 2′ to 4′

Social Distance
Close - 4′ to 7′

Far - 7′ to 12′

Public Distance
12′ to 25′ and Beyond

Figure 6-2 Four Circles of Intimacy

positive attitude toward another person, get physically close to him or her. Putting your arm around someone to express interest and warmth is another obvious nonverbal signal. Cultural differences must be kept in mind in interpreting nonverbal cues. To illustrate, a French male is likely to stand closer to you than a British male, even if they had equally positive attitudes toward you. A set of useful guidelines has been developed for estimating how close to stand to another person (at least in many cultures).[3] They are described below and diagramed in Figure 6-2.

> *Social distance* covers from 4 to 8 feet and in general is reserved for interaction that is businesslike and impersonal. We usually maintain this amount of distance between ourselves and strangers such as retail sales associates and cab drivers.

> *Public distance* covers from 12 feet to the outer limit of being heard. This zone is typically used in speaking to an audience at a large meeting or in a classroom, but a few insensitive individuals might send ordinary messages by shouting across a room. The unstated message suggested by such an action is that the receiver of the message does not merit the effort of walking across the room.

People sometimes manipulate personal space in order to dominate a situation. A sales representative might move into the personal or intimate circle of a customer just to intimidate him or her. Many people become upset when you move into a closer circle than the situation calls for. They consider it an invasion of their personal space, or their "territorial rights." How would you feel if, while waiting in line at the post office, a complete stranger stood within 4 inches of your face?

POSTURE

Certain aspects of your posture communicate a message. Leaning toward another individual suggests that you are favorably disposed toward his or her message. Leaning backward communicates the opposite. Openness of the arms or legs serves as an indicator of liking or caring. In general, people establish closed postures (arms folded and legs crossed) when speaking to people they dislike. Standing up straight generally indicates high self-confidence. Stooping and slouching could mean a poor self-image. In any event, there is almost no disadvantage to standing up straight.

Related to posture are the nonverbal signals sent by standing versus sitting. Sitting down during a conversation is generally considered to be more intimate and informal than standing. If you do sit down while conversing, be sure to stand up when you wish the conversation to end. Standing up sends a message to the other person that it is time to leave. It also gives you the chance to be more attentive and polite in saying goodbye.[4]

GESTURES

An obvious form of body language is gestures. Hand gestures are universally recognized as conveying specific information to others. If you make frequent hand movements, you will generally communicate a positive attitude. If you use few gestures, you will convey dislike or disinterest. An important exception here is that some people wave their hands vigorously while arguing. Some of their hand movements reflect anger. Another example is that open-palm gestures toward the other person typically convey positive attitudes.

HEAD, FACE, AND EYE SIGNALS

"Here comes a live one," said one fellow to another at a sports bar. "I can tell she's interested in getting to know me. Just look into her eyes and at the expression on her face." The young man who spoke these words may have a valid point. When used in combination, the head, face, and eyes provide the clearest indications of attitudes toward other people. Lowering your head and peering over your glasses, for instance, is the nonverbal equivalent of the expression, "You're putting me on." As is well known, maintaining eye contact with another person improves communication with that person. In order to maintain eye contact, it is usually necessary to correspondingly move your head and face. Moving your head, face, and eyes away from another person is often interpreted as a defensive gesture or one suggesting a lack of self-confidence. Would you lend money to someone who didn't look at you directly?

The face is often used as a primary source of information about how we feel. We look for facial clues when we want to determine another person's attitude. You can often judge someone's current state of happiness by looking at his or her face. The expression "sourpuss" attests to this observation. Happiness, apprehension, anger, resentment, sadness, contempt, enthusiasm, and embarrassment are but a few of the emotions that can be expressed through the face.

Blinking is a specific eye movement that communicates meaningful messages. According to experiments conducted by John Stern, blinks are punctuation marks. People blink at psychologically important times. After they have listened to and understood a question, people typically take time out for a blink. People in control of a situation, such as pilot in control of an aircraft, are less likely to blink.[5] Many people use rapid blinking to send the message, "I have no idea what you are talking about."

VOICE QUALITY

More significance is often attached to the *way* something is said than to *what* is said. A forceful voice, which includes a consistent tone without vocalized pauses, connotes power and control. Closely related to voice tone are volume, pitch, and rate of speaking. Anger, boredom, and joy can often be interpreted from voice quality. Anger is noted when the person speaks loudly, with a high pitch, and fast rate. Boredom is indicated by a monotone. A tip-off to joy is when the person speaks loudly, with a high pitch, and fast rate. Joy is also indicated by loud volume.

Avoiding an annoying voice quality can make a positive impact on others. The research of voice coach Jeffrey Jacobbi provides some useful suggestions. He surveyed a nationwide sample of 1,000 men and women, and asked, "Which irritating or unpleasant voice annoys you the most?" The most irritating quality was a whining, complaining, or nagging tone. See Self-Examination Exercise 6-1 for more details on his findings.

Jacobbi notes that we are judged by the way we sound. He also notes that careers can be damaged by voice problems such as those indicated in the survey. Jacobbi continues: "We think about how we look and dress. And that gets most of the attention. But people judge our intelligence much more by how we sound than how we dress."[6]

PERSONAL APPEARANCE

Your external image plays an important role in communicating messages to others. Job seekers show recognition of this aspect of nonverbal communication when they carefully groom for a job interview. People pay more respect and grant more privileges to people they perceive as being well dressed and attractive. Furthermore, some research indicates that a favorable personal appearance leads to higher starting salaries and, later,

SELF-EXAMINATION EXERCISE 6-1:

Voice Quality Checkup

Jacobbi's study of voice quality (cited in the text) ranked voice quality, in decreasing order of annoyance, as follows:

- Whining, complaining, or nagging tone—44.0 percent
- High pitched, squeaky voice—15.9 percent
- Mumblers—11.1 percent
- Very fast talkers—4.9 percent
- Weak and wimpy voice—3.6 percent
- Flat, monotonous tone—3.5 percent
- Thick accent—2.4 percent

Ask yourself, and two other people familiar with your voice, if you have one or more of the above voice-quality problems. If your self-analysis and feedback from others does indicate a serious problem, get started on self-improvement. Tape your voice and attempt to modify the biggest problems. Another avenue of improvement is to consult with a speech coach or therapist.

salary increases.[7] The observations of an image consultant about the messages sent by personal appearances are presented in Exhibit 6-1.

ROADBLOCKS TO COMMUNICATION

Communication rarely proceeds as swiftly or as effectively as we would like. Many different factors filter our message on its way to the intended receiver. Have you ever tried to make a telephone call when moisture is entrapped in the underground cables? You hear more static than voice. In this section we will look at some of the human, rather than physical or mechanical, roadblocks to communication. If you are aware of their presence, you will be better able to overcome them.

Routine or neutral messages are the easiest to communicate. Communication roadblocks are most likely to occur when a message is complex, emotionally arousing, or clashes with the receiver's mental set. An emotionally arousing message would deal with such topics as a relationship between two people or money. A message that clashes with a receiver's mental set requires that person to change his or her familiar pattern of receiving messages. The next time you order a meal in a restaurant, order dessert first and an entrée second. The server will probably not "hear" your dessert order because it deviates from the normal ordering sequence.

LIMITED UNDERSTANDING OF PEOPLE

If you do not understand people very well, your communication effectiveness will be limited. To take a basic example, if you frame your message in terms of what can be done for you, you may be in trouble. It's much more effective to frame your message in terms of what you can do for the other person. Suppose a person in need of money wants to sell magazine subscriptions to a friend. Mentioning financial need is a very self-centered message. It could be made less self-centered:

Very self-centered: "You've got to buy a few subscriptions from me. I can't meet my credit card payments."

Less self-centered: "Would you be interested in subscribing to a few magazines that would bring you enjoyment and help you get ahead in your career? If your answer is yes, I can help you."

Guidelines for helping a person overcome a limited understanding of people are presented in Exhibit 6-2.

EXHIBIT 6-1

ADVICE FROM AN IMAGE CONSULTANT

Fingernails tell more about a person than the clothes he or she wears, says Paul Glick, an image consultant. "Fingernails are an indication of your ability to manage details. You must have noticed someone with very dirty glasses on, or one with bad breath, or one with dirty fingernails. They aren't fully there. You don't make the assessment consciously. But if someone is put together physically we can pretty well assume he or she is well adjusted."

Like it or not, says Glick, how you look is a statement about who you are socially and intellectually, so he advocates being concerned about presentation and making the best of what you have.

"Put a wardrobe together—the right shirts, blouses, ties, jackets, shapes of clothing, the right glasses, the right hairstyling, the right management of all your grooming aspects—so that it all can be done within an hour," said Glick.

"The right appearance is the one most appropriate for the context in which you will be presenting yourself. The right appearance might be jeans and a T-shirt. The right appearance could be a business suit. It's where you are going and whom you are going to be with."

SOURCE: Adapted with permission from Karol Stonger, "Stylist: Looks Are Not Necessarily Deceiving," Associated Press story, June 11, 1989.

ONE-WAY COMMUNICATION

Effective communication proceeds back and forth. An exchange of information or a transaction takes place between two or more people. Person A may send messages to person B to initiate communication, but B must react to A to complete the communication loop. One reason written messages (including electronic mail) fail to achieve their purpose is that the person who writes the message cannot be sure how it will be interpreted. One written message that is subject to many interpretations is "Your idea is of some interest to me." (How much is *some?*) Face-to-face communication helps to clarify meanings.

FALSE ASSUMPTIONS ABOUT THE RECEIVER

The assumptions you make about the receiver of your message may be false, thus serving as a communication roadblock. A parent might say to his or her child: "In order to be as successful as I am, you'll have to spend more time studying and less time partying." If the child continues with the same ratio of studying to partying, the parent will become upset. Perplexed, he or she might say silently, "I wonder why my child didn't listen to me."

The false assumption made by the message sender is, "My child wants to be as successful as I am." Furthermore, the parent assumed the child measured success in terms of job and salary. What false assumptions have you made lately when trying to communicate with another person?

EXHIBIT 6-2

A SHORT COURSE IN HUMAN RELATIONS

The *six* most important words are "I admit I made a mistake."
The *five* most important words are "You did a good job."
The *four* most important words are "What is your opinion?"
The *three* most important words are "If you please."
The *two* most important words are "Thank you."
The *one* most important word is "We."
The one *least* important word is "I."

Some people who first read this "short course" react to it negatively. Among their reservations are that "It is corny," "It's so obvious. Anybody with common sense knows that," or "Good for people in kindergarten." Yet if you put these seven rules into practice, you will find they do help overcome the communication roadblock called *limited understanding of people.* As one example, if you use "I" too frequently in your conversation, you will create communication roadblocks.

DIFFERENT INTERPRETATION OF WORDS (SEMANTICS)

Semantics is the study of the meaning and changes in the meaning of words. These different meanings can create roadblocks to communication. Often the problem is trivial and humorous; at other times, semantic problems can create substantial communication barriers. Consider first an example of trivial consequence:

> Two first-time visitors to Montreal, Quebec (a French-Canadian province) entered a restaurant for dinner. After looking over the menus, the husband suggested they order the shrimp cocktail *entrées*. He said to his wife, "A whole shrimp dinner for $9.95 Canadian is quite a deal. I guess it's because Montreal is a seaport." When the entrées arrived, the visitors were sadly disappointed because they were the size of an *appetizer*.
>
> The husband asked the server why the entrées were so small in Montreal. With a smile, the server replied: "You folks must be Americans. In French-speaking countries the entrée is the beginning of the meal, like the word enter. In the United States it's just the reverse, the entrée is the main meal. Are you now ready to order your main meal?"

Of greater consequence is the experience of a trainer of airplane pilots who inadvertently contributed to a crash. As a rookie pilot navigated down the runway, the trainer shouted, "Takeoff power." The pilot shut off the engine and skidded off the runway. What the trainer really meant was to *use* takeoff power—a surge of energy to lift the airplane off the ground. He was using takeoff as an *adjective,* not a *verb.*

Distortion of Information

A great problem in sending messages is that people receiving them often hear what they want to hear. Without malicious intent, people modify your message to bolster their self-esteem or improve their situation. An incident that occurred between Jennifer and her mother is fairly typical of this type of communication roadblock. Jennifer asked her mother if she might have a 35mm camera system for Christmas. Regarding the request as farfetched and beyond her means, Jennifer's mother replied, "Why should I buy you a camera system like that when you never even take pictures of your little brother with your present camera?"

Jennifer *heard* her mother say, "If you take pictures of your little brother, I would then buy you that camera system." Three weeks later Jennifer presented her mother with a surprise gift—a small album containing twenty photographs of her little brother. "Mom," said Jennifer, "Here's the album you ordered. Now let me tell you in more detail about that 35mm outfit you said you would get me for Christmas." Her mother replied, "I never said that. Where did you get that idea?"

The reason some people are so difficult to criticize or insult is that they ward off your message just as a duck wards water off its feathers. What messages of yours has someone not heard recently? Can you think of any messages that bounced off you lately?

Different Perspectives and Experiences (Where Are You Coming From?)

People perceive words and concepts differently because their experiences and vantage points differ. On the basis of their perception of what they have heard, many Hispanic children believe that the opening line of the "Star-Spangled Banner" is "José, can you see . . ." (note that few children have *seen* the national anthem in writing).

Young people with specialized training or education often encounter communication barriers in dealing with older workers. A minority of older workers think that young people are trying to introduce impractical and theoretical ideas. It takes time to break down this type of resistance to innovation and the application of current knowledge.

Emotions and Attitudes

Have you ever tried to communicate a message to another person while that person is emotionally aroused? Your message was probably distorted considerably. Another problem is that people tend to say things when emotionally aroused that they would not say when calm. Similarly, a person who has strong attitudes about a particular topic may become emotional when that topic is introduced. The underlying message here is try to avoid letting strong emotions and attitudes interfere with the sending or receiving of messages. If you are angry at someone, for example, you might miss the merit in what that person has to say. Calm down before proceeding with your discussion or attempting to resolve the conflict.

IMPROPER TIMING

Many messages do not get through to people because they are poorly timed. You have to know how to deliver a message, but you must also know *when* to deliver it. Sending a message when the receiver is distracted with other concerns or is rushing to get somewhere is a waste of time.[8] Furthermore, the receiver may become discouraged and therefore will not repeat the message later.

The art of timing messages suggests not to ask for a raise when your boss is in a bad mood, or to ask a new acquaintance for a date when he or she is preoccupied. On the other hand, do ask your boss for a raise when business has been good. And do ask someone for a date when you have just done something nice for that person and have been thanked.

 # BUILDING BRIDGES TO COMMUNICATION

With determination and awareness that communication roadblocks and barriers do exist, you can become a more effective communicator. It would be impossible to remove all barriers, but they can be minimized. The following techniques are helpful in building better bridges to communication.

1. Appeal to human needs.
2. Listen carefully and use empathy.
3. Use verbal and nonverbal feedback.
4. Repeat your message.
5. Communicate with feelings as well as facts.
6. Minimize defensive communication.
7. Combat information overload.
8. Use bias-free language and have bias-free attitudes.
9. Use mirroring to establish rapport.

APPEAL TO HUMAN NEEDS

People are most receptive to messages that promise to do something for them. In other words, if a message promises to satisfy a need that is less than fully satisfied, you are likely to listen. The hungry person who ordinarily does not hear low tones readily hears the whispered message, "How would you like a pizza with everything on it?" Somehow, I have always been able to communicate this message to my class: "Unfortunately the class will not meet a week from today." I wonder to which need I have been appealing.

Listen Carefully and Use Empathy

Because communication involves sending and receiving messages, effective listening helps overcome communication barriers. A later section of this chapter deals with improving your receiving of messages. For now, try this advice: "Both sender and receiver should be fully aware what the other person is trying to communicate and should concentrate on listening as if a summary of the remarks were going to be required."[9]

Another advantage of listening is that it allows for **empathy,** or understanding another person's point of view. If you know "where the other person is coming from," you will be a better receiver and sender of messages. Empathy does not necessarily mean that you sympathize with the other person. For example, you may understand why some people are forced to beg in the streets, but you may have very little sympathy for their plight.

A useful way of showing empathy is to accept the sender's figure of speech. By so doing, the sender feels understood and accepted. Also, if you reject the person's figure of speech by rewording it, the sender may become defensive. Many people use the figure of speech, "I'm stuck," when they cannot accomplish a task. You can facilitate smooth communication by a response such as, "What can I do to help you get unstuck?" If you respond with something like, "What can I do to help you think more clearly?," the person is forced to change mental channels, and may become defensive.[10]

Use Verbal and Nonverbal Feedback

Don't be a hit-and-run communicator. Such a person drops a message and leaves the scene before he or she is sure the message has been received as intended. Some of the teachers you have rated as outstanding have probably been those who ask the class if there are any questions, and also ask questions themselves.

Nonverbal feedback refers to the signs other than words that indicate whether or not your message has been delivered. A blank expression on the face of the receiver might indicate no comprehension. A disturbed, agitated expression might mean that the receiver's emotions are blocking the message.

Repeat Your Message

In general, you can overcome roadblocks to communication by repeating your message several times. It is usually advisable to say the same thing in different ways so as to avoid annoying the listener with straight repetition. In any case, your message may not have been understood in its first form. If there is too much repetition, however, people no longer listen to the message. They think they already understand the message.

Repetition, like any other means of overcoming communication roadblocks, does not work for all people. Many people who repeatedly hear the message "Drinking and driving do not mix" are not moved by it. It is helpful to use several methods of overcoming roadblocks or barriers to communication.

A generally effective way of repeating a message is to use more than one communication channel. For example, follow up a face-to-face discussion with a letter or telephone call or both. Your body can be another channel or medium to help impart your message. If you agree with someone about a spoken message, state your agreement and also shake hands over the agreement. Can you think of another channel by which to transmit a message?

COMMUNICATE FEELINGS AS WELL AS FACTS

When a person speaks, we too often listen to the facts and ignore the feelings. If feelings are ignored, the true meaning and intent of the message is likely to be missed, thus creating a communication barrier. Your boss might say to you, "You never seem to take work home." To clarify what your boss means by this statement, you might ask, "Is that good or bad?" Your boss's response will give you feedback on his or her feelings about getting all your work done during regular working hours.

When you send a message it is also helpful to express your feelings in addition to conveying facts. For example, "Our defects are up by 12 percent [fact], and I'm quite disappointed about those results [feelings]."

MINIMIZE DEFENSIVE COMMUNICATION

Distortion of information was described previously as a communication barrier. Such distortion can also be regarded as **defensive communication,** the tendency to receive messages in such a way that our self-esteem is protected. Defensive communication is also responsible for people sending messages to make themselves look good. For example, when criticized for achieving below-average sales, a store manager might shift the blame to the sales associates in her store.

Overcoming the barrier of defensive communication requires two steps. First, people have to acknowledge the existence of defensive communication. Second, they have to try not to be defensive when questioned or criticized. Such behavior is not easy because of **denial,** the suppression of information we find uncomfortable. For example, the store manager just cited would find it uncomfortable to think of herself as being responsible for below-average performance.

COMBAT INFORMATION OVERLOAD

A major communication barrier facing literate people today is **information** (or **communication**) **overload.** An extensive amount of potentially useful information comes to people from so many sources. Consequently, it is often difficult to decide which information should receive attention and which should be discarded. The problem is worsened when low-quality information is competing for your attention.[11] One example is receiving a lengthy letter informing you that you are one of 100 select people to receive a sweepstake prize. (All you need to do is send $19.95 to cover the shipping and handling costs for your valuable prize.)

A flood of information reaching a person acts as a communication barrier because people have a tendency to block out new information when their capacity to absorb information becomes taxed. Literally, their "circuits become overloaded," and they no longer respond to messages.

You can decrease the chances of suffering from communication overload by such measures as carefully organizing and sorting information before plunging ahead with reading. Speed reading may also help, provided you stop to read carefully the most relevant information. You can help prevent others from suffering from communication overload by being merciful in the frequency and length of your messages.

USE BIAS-FREE LANGUAGE AND HAVE BIAS-FREE ATTITUDES

An important implication of semantics is that certain words are interpreted by some people as signs of bias. A **bias** is a prejudgment about another person or group based on something other than fact.[12] The use of biased words is thus a form of discrimination. To avoid this type of discrimination, attempt to use bias-free language. An obvious example of a biased statement would be for a supervisor to say, "I need a real man for this job." The bias-free statement expressing the same thought would be, "I need a courageous person for this job."

Selecting bias-free terms is complex for several reasons. One problem is that terms preferred by specific groups to refer to themselves change frequently. For example, many black people now prefer to refer to themselves as "people of color" or "African Americans" rather than "black." Although the term "Hispanic" is still popular, many people of Latin American origin now prefer the term "Latino." Another problem is that some bias-free terms are technically incorrect. For instance, there is a substantial difference between being "blind" and being "visually impaired."

Table 6-1 presents a list of biased words and terms, along with their current, bias-free equivalent. Recognize, however, that you cannot please everybody. It is best to avoid terms that refer to people's race, religion, or physical status unless the information is needed for purposes of identification.

Using bias-free language is equivalent to being politically correct, or choosing words and terms carefully to avoid offending anyone. Some people are concerned that political correctness can go too far. A group called the British Political Correctness Police attempted to get the Gingerbread

TABLE 6-1

BIASED TERMS AND THEIR BIAS-FREE SUBSTITUTES

	Usually Perceived as Biased	**Usually Perceived as Bias-Free**
Gender-related	Girl (for adult)	Woman
	Boy (for adult)	Man
	Salesman, saleswoman	Sales representative
	Woman crane operator	Crane operator
	Hotel maid	Housekeeper
	Cleaning man	Custodian, cleaner
	Flag man, flag woman	Flagger
	Chairman, chairwoman	Chairperson, chair
Disabilities	Handicapped	Physically challenged or disabled
	Blind	Visually impaired
	Confined to a wheelchair	Uses a wheelchair
Race	Nonwhite	People of color, African American, Native American, Native Canadian, Asian, East Indian (from India)
	Whitey	White, white person, Caucasian
Nationality, ethnic background	Jewish person	Jew
	"Scottish in me"	"My frugality"
	Ethnic jokes	Jokes with nationality un-specified

Man changed to a gender neutral Gingerbread Person. A British association of master bakers refused to make the change. A spokesperson said that "Gingerbread men have been around in some shape or form since the seventeenth century. Why should we interfere with a name that everyone understands and accepts because of a few people who are obsessed with being politically correct?"[13]

Having bias-free attitudes requires the same type of open-mindedness as using bias-free language. Even if you cannot overcome your biases completely, at least be willing to look at situations in a new perspective. Images of men and women exemplify the importance of bias-free attitudes. In traditional (or biased) thinking, photographs of children on a female manager's desk mean that children come first. Similar photographs on a male manager's desk are likely to evoke the reaction, "It's nice to see that he cares about his family."

Another workplace bias is that people over age fifty are either unable or unwilling to learn about high technology. In reality, some older people have high aptitude for and strong interest in high technology. A club has been formed across the United States to accommodate the interests of "high-tech seniors." These are retired people who work with computers as a pastime. Many of these people send electronic messages to each other late into the night, and also develop new programs.

Bias-free attitudes improve communication because messages flow back and forth more freely when you have an open mind toward another person or group. For example, if you do not prejudge older people as disliking high technology you are more apt to listen to their opinions about software.

USE MIRRORING TO ESTABLISH RAPPORT

Another approach to overcoming communication barriers is to improve rapport with another person. A form of nonverbal communication called **mirroring** can be used to establish such rapport. To mirror someone is to subtly imitate that individual. The most successful mirroring technique for establishing rapport is to imitate another's breathing pattern. If you adjust your own breathing rate to someone else's, you will soon establish rapport with that person. Mirroring sometimes takes the form of imitating the boss in order to communicate better and win favor. Many job seekers now use mirroring to get in sync with the interviewer. Is this a technique you would be willing to try?

OVERCOMING CROSS-CULTURAL COMMUNICATION BARRIERS

Another potential communication barrier in the workplace is that communication takes place between and among people from different cultures. Personal life, too, is often more culturally diverse today than previously. Understanding how to react to cultural differences is important because the work force has become more culturally diverse in two major ways. More subgroups from within our own culture have been assimilated into the work force. In addition, there is increasing interaction with people from other countries.

Because of this diversity, many workers face the challenge of preventing and overcoming communication barriers created by differences in language and customs. Here we describe several strategies and specific tactics to help overcome cross-cultural communication barriers.

Be Sensitive to the Fact That Cross-Cultural Communication Barriers Exist. If you are aware of potential barriers, you will be ready to deal with them. When you are dealing with a person in the workplace with a different cultural background than yours, solicit feedback in order to minimize cross-cultural barriers to communication.

Use Straightforward Language and Speak Slowly and Clearly. When working with people who do not speak your language fluently, speak in an easy-to-understand manner. Minimize the use of idioms and analogies specific to your language. For example, in North America the term "over the hill" means outdated or past one's prime. A person from another culture may not understand this phrase, yet be hesitant to ask for clarification.

Speaking slowly is also important because even people who read and write a second language at an expert level may have difficulty catching the nuances of conversation. Facing the person from another culture directly also improves communication because your facial expressions and lips contribute to comprehension.

Observe Cultural Differences in Etiquette.   Violating rules of etiquette without explanation can erect immediate communication barriers. A major rule of etiquette is that in many countries people address each other by last name unless they have worked together for a long time. Letitia Baldrige recommends that you explain the difference in custom to prevent misunderstanding. Imagine this scenario in which you are working with a man from Germany, and you are speaking:

> Herr Schultz, in my country by now I would be calling you Heinrich and you would be calling me Charlie. Would you be comfortable with that? Because if you wouldn't, I would be glad to call you Herr Schultz until you tell me it's time to call you Heinrich.[14]

Be Sensitive to Differences in Nonverbal Communication.   Stay alert to the possibility that your nonverbal signal may be misinterpreted by a person from another culture. A problem happened to an engineer for a New Jersey company who was asked a question by a German co-worker. He responded OK by making a circle with his thumb and forefinger. The German worker stormed away because in his native country the same gesture is a personal insult.[15]

Do Not Be Diverted by Style, Accent, Grammar, or Personal Appearance. Although these superficial factors are all related to business success, they are difficult to interpret when judging a person from another culture. It is therefore better to judge the merits of the statement or behavior.[16] A brilliant individual from another culture may still be learning your language and thus make basic mistakes in speaking your language. He or she might also not have developed a sensitivity to dress style in your culture.

IMPROVING YOUR SENDING OF MESSAGES

The information already presented in this chapter will assist you in sending messages more effectively. If you can build better bridges to communication, for example, you will get more messages across to people. Here we are concerned with several specific suggestions for improving communication in four modes: face-to-face speaking, public speaking, nonverbal, and writing. Because most readers of this book have already studied speech and writing, the information below is intended as a brushup along with several new insights.

FACE-TO-FACE SPEAKING

Improving one's ability to express ideas in face-to-face encounters has a big potential payoff because most communication involves two people and other small groups. Among these situations are work-unit meetings, problem-solving discussion, and two-way conversations in general. Six practical suggestions, if carried out, should help improve your face-to-face speaking skills.

1. *Take the opportunity to speak in a meeting or class whenever it arises.* Volunteer comments in class and committee meetings, and capitalize on any chance to be the group leader. But avoid the extreme of monopolizing the time available for comments. When you make your presentations, generally include an anecdote. The vast majority of people think positively about anecdotes. Making effective use of anecdotes thus enhances your communication skills. (Examples of anecdotes are the stories about the OK sign and the Gingerbread Person.)

2. *Obtain feedback by listening to tape recordings, camcorder, or voice-mail renditions of your voice.* Eliminate or minimize vocalized pauses and repetitious phrases (such as "OK" or "you know" or "really") that detract from your communication effectiveness. Ask a knowledgeable friend for his or her opinion of your voice and speech.

3. *Use appropriate models to help you develop your speech.* An instructor, television talk-show host or commercial announcer, or manager in your company may have the type of voice and speech that fits your personality. The goal is not to imitate that person but to use him or her as an approximate guide to generally acceptable speech.

4. *Sprinkle your speech with colorful new vocabulary to add flavor and punch.* Consider these possibilities: A "Clydesdale" in traditional meaning is a breed of horse. The term now also refers to a good-looking young man who is dating an equally attractive young woman. A "McPaper" is a college term paper written at the last minute, and without much research or thought. (The point of reference is McDonald's, the fast-food restaurant.) To "gafiate" is to take a vacation (from the acronym for *get away from it all* in the first five letters).[17] Overuse of these words, however, will make you difficult to understand.

5. *Practice expressing the feelings behind your factual statements.* Feelings are important because they add to persuasiveness and help establish a relationship with the receiver of the message. An example of a factual statement is "You said you would ship my order by March 15. Three weeks later it is not here." A person who backed up the factual statement might say, "You said you would ship my order . . . here. I'm angry about what happened, and my feelings are hurt that you didn't follow through."

6. *Use proper grammar.* Although language standards change with time, there are still outer limits to what constitutes proper grammar. People who make grammatical errors in virtually every sentence tend to be perceived as lacking in intelligence. Furthermore, they do not project a professional image. Self-Examination Exercise 6-2 gives you an opportunity to briefly assess your grammar.

SELF-AWARENESS EXERCISE 6-2:

Does Your Grammar Make the Right Impression?

Test yourself on word usage—just one of our many workshop topics.

Circle the correct word(s) in parentheses.

1. You drive more slowly than (her, she).
2. It must be (we, us) who are to blame.
3. Let's keep this between you and (me, I).
4. (Who, Whom) would you prefer to complete the report?
5. We (use to, used to) file all our memos.
6. No one on the committee (has, have) enough time.
7. I was so tired I (laid, lay) down and went to sleep.
8. Can you (insure, assure) me the carpenter will arrive on time?
9. The schedule change had a positive (affect, effect) on me.
10. I propose we conduct our business with (he, him).

Answers: 1-she; 2-we; 3-me; 4-Whom; 5-used to; 6-has; 7-lay; 8-assure; 9-effect; 10-him

If you answered more than 8 correctly, your English skills are above average.

SOURCE: Reprinted with permission from a brochure for National Seminars Group, 6901 West 63rd Street, Shawnee Mission KS 66201-1349, undated.

PUBLIC SPEAKING

Few people in business are required to engage in frequent public speaking. Nevertheless, many people have at least some opportunity to make an occasional presentation in front of an audience. To perform well on such occasions keep in mind these suggestions from speech professionals.[18]

1. *Be prepared.*   A large part of self-confidence in speaking comes from being prepared. Give your audience information that fits their needs, and explain how you will be helping them.

2. *Stand up straight.*   Place your feet about a foot part so you look balanced and have a strong presence. Although you are standing up straight, move around if your presentation exceeds five minutes in length.

3. *Reduce vocalized pauses by learning to close your mouth between words.*   Pauses without sounds add to speech effectiveness.

4. *Recognize that nervousness is normal.*   Just before going on stage use a simple relaxation technique such as exhaling and inhaling several times, stretching your muscles, or taking a sip of water. As you walk up to the podium smile at the audience; both you and the audience will be more relaxed.

5. *Block out negative thoughts about performing poorly.* If you feel you are on the verge of panic, say to yourself "stop" several times.

6. *Establish eye contact and maintain it, moving from person to person.* You might begin by looking at a person directly in front of you, then shift to the left, then the right, then back to the middle of the room.

Nonverbal Communication

To improve your effectiveness in sending messages, it is important to support words with appropriate forms of nonverbal communication. (An understanding of nonverbal communication is also important for receiving messages.) The following suggestions should help you send nonverbal messages more effectively.

1. *Obtain feedback on your body language by asking others to comment on the gestures and facial expressions that you use in conversations.* Have a videotape prepared of you conferring with another individual. After studying your body language, attempt to eliminate those mannerisms and gestures that you think detract from your effectiveness (such as moving your knee from side to side when being interviewed).

2. *Learn to relax when communicating with others.* Take a deep breath and consciously allow your body muscles to loosen. The relaxation techniques discussed in Chapter 4 should be helpful here. A relaxed person makes it easier for other people to relax. Thus you are likely to elicit more useful information from other people when you are relaxed.

3. *Talk with conviction.* An enthusiastic tone of voice and an animated face are helpful in persuading others. Also, use hand and body gestures to supplement your speech—but don't overdo it. A good starting point is to use hand gestures to express enthusiasm. You can increase the persuasiveness of enthusiastic comments by shaking the other person's hand, nodding approval, smiling, or patting the person on the shoulder.

4. *Avoid using the same nonverbal gesture indiscriminately.* To illustrate, if you want to use nodding to convey approval, do not nod with approval even when you dislike what somebody else is saying. Also, do not pat everybody on the back. Nonverbal gestures used indiscriminately lose their communication effectiveness.

5. *Use role-playing to practice various forms of nonverbal communication.* A good starting point would be to practice selling your ideas about an important project or concept to another person. During your interchange, supplement your spoken messages with appropriate nonverbal cues such as posture, voice intonation, gestures, and so forth. Later, obtain the other person's perception of the effectiveness of your nonverbal behavior.

Written Communication

Written communication in the workplace has always been important. The widespread use of E-mail has heightened the requirement for writing competence because of its widespread use. Four suggestions for effective written communication are presented as a refresher. In addition, avoid the six common writing mistakes noted in Exhibit 6-3.

1. *Read a book about effective business report writing and attempt to implement the suggestions it offers.*[19]

2. *Regularly read material that is written in the style and format that would be useful to you in your career.* The *Wall Street Journal* and *Business Week* are useful models for most forms of job-related writing. Managerial and staff jobs require you to write brief, readily understand-

---

EXHIBIT 6-3

COMMON WRITING MISTAKES TO AVOID

Frank Edmund Smith, a professor of business writing, observes that any piece of writing sends at least two messages. The literal message is found in the words themselves and the other message is conveyed through unconscious signals. Writing sends information not only about the message but also about the writer. Some of these signals are obvious, such as the quality of paper used for letters or job résumés.

When it comes to matters of grammar, usage, and style, the kind of people who make it to the executive suite are often stricter than the most rigid grade school teacher. Executives expect high-quality written documents from their employees. Professor Smith has noticed several signals of the wrong sort that are sent regularly in business writing. He bases his conclusions on the thousands of pieces of business correspondence he has reviewed in recent years.

1. *Possessives and plurals.* Many people completely confuse possessives and plurals. The most common mix-up occurs between "its" (the possessive) and "it's" (the contraction of it is). In addition, every business writer who is concerned with accuracy will be quick to recognize the confusion that can result if the expression "the manager's position" is written as "the managers' position." The former refers to the position taken by one manager, while the second is the position taken by more than one manager.
2. *Collective nouns.* The possessive-plural confusion suggests another frequent error in business correspondence—treating collective nouns as plurals. An expression such as "The corporation has decided to move their headquarters," ignores the fact that a business is a single entity. The correct expression is, "The corporation has decided to move *its* headquarters."
3. *Double negatives.* Double negatives such as "I haven't seen nobody" are really positives. They cause no real confusion since nobody actually interprets a double negative as a positive. However, the use of a double negative says something negative about the writer.
4. *Homonyms.* An increasingly common misusage is the substitution of words that sound almost alike. But do we feel comfortable doing business with someone who does not know the difference between "insure" (to obtain financial protection against risk) and "ensure" (to make certain)?

(Continued)

5. *Right justification on the word processor.* Professor Smith believes that right margin justification (or "block writing") makes a letter or memo look cold, impersonal, and uninviting. Right margin justification is therefore best used for overdue payment letters and information about machine parts.

6. *Heavy reliance on the passive voice.* Writing experts advise using the active voice. The active voice consists of verbs that describe what is going on, what has happened, or what will happen. The first sentence of this paragraph expressed in the passive voice is, "The active voice is advised by writing experts." Avoid making the mistake, however, of using the active voice exclusively. Occasional use of the passive voice adds variety to your writing. The passive voice is also useful because it allows you to put the most important part of the message first, as follows: "Prescription drugs should be dispensed by medical professionals only." (Prescription drugs is the writer's key phrase here.)

Don't rely on even the best secretary to catch all of these mistakes. In fact, some of the above problems would not necessarily be spotted as "mistakes" except by the person for whom the message is intended.

SOURCE: Excerpted and paraphrased from Frank Edmund Smith, "Does Your Writing Send the Wrong Signals?" *Personnel Journal,* December 1985, pp. 28–30. Reprinted with permission of *Personnel Journal,* Costa Mesa, California; all rights reserved. Point 6 is from Donald Weiss, *How to Write Easily and Effectively,* The Successful Office Skills Series (New York: American Management Association, 1993), p. 7.

able memos and reports. If your goal is to become a competent technical report writer, continuously read technical reports in your specialty.

3. *Practice writing at every opportunity.* E-Mail and word processing provide natural opportunities to practice writing skills. Send yourself and friends messages by E-mail to supplement memo writing for job purposes. Successful writers constantly practice writing. If you do not write frequently you run the risk of getting out of "writing shape."

4. *Get feedback on your writing.* Ask a co-worker or classmate to critique a rough draft of your reports and memos. Offer to reciprocate. Editing other people's writing is a valuable way of improving your own. Feedback from a person with more writing experience and knowledge than you is particularly valuable. For instance, comments made by an instructor about a submitted paper are usually extremely useful.

IMPROVING YOUR RECEPTION OF MESSAGES

Many people are surprised to discover that they have developed the reputation of being "good communicators" simply because they are good at receiving messages. Yet receiving messages is a basic part of the communication process. Unless you receive messages as they were intended, you cannot properly perform your job or be a good social companion. To simplify matters, we have organized improving the reception of messages into three different skills: basic listening, paraphrasing, and summarization.

BASIC LISTENING

Your listening skills will improve if you follow several basic ideas and principles.[20] First, improve your concentration. Much is forgotten because a message was never received correctly in the first place. As the sender delivers a message, focus intently on what he or she is saying.

Second, hold your fire. A common barrier to effective listening is the habit of mentally preparing an answer while another person is speaking. Therefore, learn not to get too excited about the sender's point, pro or con, until you are sure you understood it. Do not make up your mind immediately whether the message sender is good or bad.

Third, listen for key ideas. Facts can serve as documentation for ideas of broader significance. When your boss tells you your reports are careless, he or she may also be telling you that you are careless in a number of ways. Simply polishing several reports will not cure the entire problem.

Fourth, resist external distractions. Aside from distractions taking place inside your head, external distractions also have to be resisted. While listening to the speaker, try to ignore the low-flying plane or that physically attractive person next to you. A good listener intuitively combats distractions. Unless you resist distractions, concentration is impaired.

Fifth, capitalize on thought speed. The average rate of speed for spoken English is 125 words per minute. We think, and therefore listen, at almost four times that speed. Be careful not to let your mind wander while you are waiting for the person's next thought. Instead, try to listen between the lines. Try to interpret the speaker's nonverbal communication. For instance, did the sender of the message look sincere when he or she said, "You're doing great"?

Sixth, listen for total meaning. As stated earlier, listen for feeling as well as fact. Suppose that your boss says, "I wonder if we're putting you under too much pressure?" Find out if the boss means that you look as though you are faltering under the pressure. Your boss might simply think that you have been carrying an unfair burden.

Finally, ask yourself if there is anything the other person is saying that could benefit you. Maintaining this perspective will enable you to benefit from most listening episodes.

PARAPHRASING

According to one human relations specialist, paraphrasing is the keystone to receiving messages. Restating in your own words what the sender says, feels, and means improves communication in a couple of ways:

> First it helps you avoid judging and evaluating. When you are restating, you are not passing judgment. Second, restating gives the sender direct feedback as to how well you understand the messages. If you do not fully understand, the sender can add messages until you do.[21]

You might feel awkward the first several times you paraphrase. Therefore, first try it with a person you feel comfortable with. With some practice, it will become a natural part of your communication skill kit. Here is an example of how you might use paraphrasing:

Other Person:	I'm getting ticked off at working so hard around here. I wish somebody else would pitch in and do a fair day's work.
You:	You're saying that you do more than your fair share of the tough work in our department.
Other Person:	You bet. Here's what I think we should be doing about it. . . .

SUMMARIZATION

The final basic message-receiving skill deals with summarizing what you heard from the other person during your communication session. When you summarize, you pull together, condense, and thereby clarify the main points communicated about the other person. It allows for further clarification on the part of the sender. Here are two basic summarization statements:

"Lynn, what I've heard you say during our meeting is that . . ."

"Les, as I understand you, your position is that . . ."

◼ IMPROVING TELEPHONE AND VOICE-MAIL COMMUNICATION SKILLS

Telephone and voice-mail communication skills are important for several reasons. Many businesses attract and hold onto customers because their representatives interact positively with people through the telephone and voice mail. Many other firms lose money, and nonprofit organizations irritate the public because their employees have poor telephone communication and voice-mail skills. Furthermore, a substantial amount of work among employees is conducted via telephone and voice mail.

Most of the previous comments about overcoming communication barriers, sending spoken messages, and receiving messages apply to telephone communications. A number of suggestions related specifically to improving telephone and voice-mail communications are also worth considering. The general goal of these suggestions is to help people who communicate by telephone sound courteous, cheerful, cooperative, and competent.[22]

1. When answering the telephone, give your name and department. Also, give the company name if the call is not a transfer from a main switching center.

2. When talking to customers or clients, address them by name, but not to the point of irritation.

3. Vary your voice tone and inflection in order to avoid sounding bored or uninterested in your job and the company.

4. Speak at a moderate pace of approximately 150 to 160 words per minute. A rapid pace conveys the impression of impatience, while a slow rate might suggest disinterest.

5. Smile while speaking on the phone—somehow a smile gets transmitted over the telephone wires or optic fibers!

6. If the caller does not identify himself or herself, ask "Who is calling, please?" Knowing the caller's name gives a human touch to the conversation.

7. Be particularly tactful in your choice of words because you cannot look at the caller's face to determine if he or she is irked by your phrases. For example, the statement, "I'll tell you once more" can sound even harsher over the phone than in person.

8. Use voice mail to minimize "telephone tag" rather than to increase it. If your greeting specifies when you will return, callers can choose to call again or to leave a message. When you leave a message, suggest a good time to return your call. Another way to minimize telephone tag is to assure the person you are calling that you will keep trying.

9. Place an informative and friendly greeting (outgoing message) on your voice mail (or answering machine). Used effectively, a voice-mail greeting will minimize the number of people irritated by not talking to a person. Here is a sample greeting that plays in about twenty seconds: "Hello, this is Tony Chavez in employee benefits. I'm on another call at the moment, but I'll get back to you soon if you leave a message at the beep. Please give me your name, telephone number, and the reason for calling. If you need to talk to someone personally right now, you can reach another benefits counselor by pressing 5. Thank you for calling."

10. When you respond to a voice-mail outgoing message, leave specific, relevant information. As in the suggestions for minimizing telephone tag, be specific about why you are calling and what you want from the person called. The probability of receiving a return call increases when you leave honest and useful information. If you are selling something or asking for a favor, be honest about your intent.

SUMMARY

Communication is the sending and receiving of messages. Therefore, almost anything that takes place in work and personal life involves communication. The steps involved in communication are encoding, transmission over a communication medium, and decoding.

Nonverbal communication, or silent messages, are important parts of everyday communication. Nonverbal communication includes: the environment or setting in which the message is sent; distance from the other person; posture; gestures; head, face, and eye signals; voice quality; and personal appearance.

Many potential roadblocks or barriers to communication exist. These roadblocks are most likely to occur when messages are complex, emotional, or clash with the receiver's mental set. Communication roadblocks include: limited understanding of people; one-way communication; false assumptions about the receiver; semantics; distortion of information; different perspectives and experiences; emotions and attitudes; and improper timing.

Strategies to overcome communication roadblocks include: appeal to human needs; listen carefully and use empathy; use verbal and nonverbal feedback; repeat your message; communicate feelings as well as facts; minimize defensive communication; combat information overload; use bias-free language and have bias-free attitudes; and use mirroring to establish rapport.

Strategies and tactics have been proposed to help overcome cross-cultural communication barriers. Be sensitive to their existence; use straightforward language and speak slowly and clearly; observe differences in etiquette; be aware of nonverbal differences; and do not be diverted by superficial factors.

To improve your face-to-face speaking, you should: practice at every opportunity; obtain feedback; use appropriate models; use some colorful vocabulary; practice expressing your feelings; and use proper grammar. Public speaking ability can be improved by being prepared, standing up straight, reducing vocalized pauses, recognizing that nervousness is normal, and establishing eye contact.

Nonverbal communication skills can be improved by obtaining feedback, relaxing when communicating, speaking with conviction, avoiding indiscriminate use of gestures, and role-playing.

Methods of improving written communication include: reading about effective writing; modeling good writing; and getting feedback. Also, avoid such common mistakes as confusing possessives and plurals, and over-reliance on the passive voice. Your receiving of messages can be improved by working on your basic listening skills, paraphrasing what people tell you, and summarization.

Improving telephone and voice-mail communication skills requires special attention. Telephone communicators should speak in such a manner as to sound courteous, cheerful, cooperative, and competent. Place an informative and friendly greeting on your voice-mail or answering machine. When you respond to a voice-mail message, leave specific, relevant information.

Questions and Activities

1. Why does it take so long to improve one's communication skills?

2. How can knowing the three major steps in communication help a person communicate more effectively?

3. Why is nonverbal communication so important for the effectiveness of a manager or sales representative?

4. Would you classify a handshake as a form of nonverbal communication? Explain your reasoning.

5. What barriers to communication typically exist in a classroom? What can be done to reduce these barriers?

6. Find an example of a cross-cultural barrier to communication by speaking to an informed person or by reading. Be prepared to report your findings to the class.

7. Identify at least five opportunities on which a person might capitalize to practice public speaking.

8. Why is a high level of face-to-face speaking skill very important for a successful business career?

9. What are several of the most common writing mistakes you have found among your friends and acquaintances?

10. During your next three work- or school-related phone calls, analyze what the people you speak to are doing right and wrong from the standpoint of telephone communication. Be prepared to report your findings to the class.

REFERENCES

[1]Our communication model is a condensation of a widely used model. An example of such a model is Robert E. Coffee, Curtis W. Cook, and Phillip L. Hunsaker, *Management and Organizational Behavior* (Burr Ridge, Ill.: Irwin, 1994), pp. 197–200.

[2]Walter D. St. John, "You Are What You Communicate," *Personnel Journal,* October 1985, pp. 40–43.

[3]Edward T. Hall, "Proxemics—A Study of Man's Spatial Relationships," in *Man's Image in Medicine and Anthropology* (New York: International Universities Press, 1963); Pauline E. Henderson, "Communication Without Words," *Personnel Journal,* January 1989, pp. 28–29.

[4]Merrill E. Douglass, "Standing Saves Time," *Executive Forum,* July 1989, p. 4.

[5]Research cited in Marco R. della Cava, "In the Blink of an Eye, Researcher Learns about Humans," Gannett News Service, May 7, 1988.

[6]Kathleen Driscoll, "Your Voice Can Make or Break You," Rochester New York, *Democrat and Chronicle,* August 26, 1993, p. 10B.

[7]Irene Hanson Frieze, Jospehine E. Olson, and June Russell, "Attractiveness and Business Success: Is It More Important for Women or Men?," paper presented at the Academy of Management, Washington D.C., August 1989.

[8]Daniel Araoz, "The Effective Boss," *Human Resources Forum,* November 1989, p. 4.

A HUMAN RELATIONS CASE PROBLEM: PROFESSIONALISM AT ABILENE HEALTH CENTER

Joan McKenzie, the health care administrator at Abilene Health Center (AHC), had become concerned about the casual behavior of nurses at the center. McKenzie observed that some of the RNs (registered nurses) and LPNs (licensed practical nurses) were dressing and acting in a manner that detracted from the professional image of the health center.

McKenzie set up a meeting to deal with what she perceived to be a problem of professionalism. At the outset of the meeting, McKenzie distributed an agenda that described the goals and objectives for the nursing staff. She instructed the people present to read the memo, and then said, "After you have digested the information, we will have a full group discussion of the issues raised." A copy of her memo follows

> *To:* All members of the AHC nursing staff
> *From:* Joan McKenzie, Health Care Administrator
> *Subject:* Professionalism

We are *professional* adults and must behave accordingly. Professionalism can be achieved by keeping the following goals and objectives in mind.

1. Provide comprehensive health care of high quality in a cost-effective manner which provides satisfaction to those who receive and those who deliver services.
2. Assist, guide, and direct each nurse to her or his highest potential. Help each nurse be the best she or he can be.
3. Maintain and improve respect, pride, and dignity for co-workers.

In order to resolve existing problems, please observe the following rules:

1. Cursing will not be tolerated.
2. Screaming, yelling, or raising your voice is not acceptable.
3. Calling others names is not acceptable.
4. Everybody is to be at work from 8 A.M. to noon, and 1 to 5 P.M. If there is a problem with leaving at noon or 5 P.M., please call your supervisor one hour before that time.
5. If you are sick, you should call AHC before 8 A.M. at 442-0483. Lori Fanuco will answer the telephone and take your message. If there is no answer, please keep trying.
6. When you are asked to float to an area, please stay in that area and work appropriately.
7. There will be no nail polishing in nurse's stations. Reading should be confined to nursing journals. Breaks must be taken in the break room.
8. As of May 1, the nursing staff is to wear white dresses or white pants or skirts with white or colored uniform-type tops. White nurse's shoes and sheer hose are also required. Name tags are to be worn by all employees at all times within AHC.
9. A policies and procedures manual will be available in each nurse's station in the future.

(Continued)

As the nursing staff finished reading the memo, Joan McKenzie looked around the room to see if she could gauge their reaction.

QUESTIONS

1. How effective is her memo from a communication standpoint?

2. What communication barriers might McKenzie be erecting?

3. What improvement in nonverbal communication is McKenzie seeking, as revealed by her memo?

4. How effective are the goals set forth in the memo (review Chapter 2)?

A HUMAN RELATIONS ROLE PLAY: DISCUSSING A CONTROVERSIAL MEMO

The role play is a follow-up to McKenzie's memo and meeting. One of the nurses at the meeting initiates a discussion of his or her reaction to the memo and its implications. The nurse feels that McKenzie is putting the nursing staff on the defensive by using accusatory and hostile language. McKenzie believes that her memo is a useful communication vehicle, and that the nurse is being too sensitive. One person plays the role of McKenzie, another person plays the role of the dissenting nurse. Several other people can play the role of other meeting participants who want to express how they feel about McKenzie's written message.

[9]G. James Francis and Gene Milbourn, Jr., *Human Behavior in the Work Environment: A Managerial Perspective* (Santa, Monica, Calif.: Goodyear, 1980), p. 230.

[10]Daniel Araoz, "Right-Brain Management (RBM): Part 2," *Human Resources Forum,* September 1989, p. 4.

[11]Rodger W. Griffeth, "Information Overload: A Test of the Inverted U Hypothesis with Hourly and Salaried Employees," *Academy of Management Best Papers Proceedings,* p. 234.

[12]Judy E. Pickens, "Terms of Equality: A Guide to Bias-Free Language," *Personnel Journal,* August 1985, p. 24. The basic idea for Table 6-1 stems from the same source.

[13]"Gingerbread Man on Run from 'Political Correctness Police' in Great Britain," Cox New Service, January 27, 1994.

[14]"Letitia Baldrige: Arbiter of Business Manners and Mores," *Management Review,* April 1992, p. 50.

[15]Roger E. Axtell, *Gestures: The Do's and Taboos of Body Language around the World* (New York: Wiley, 1991).

[16]David P. Tulin, "Enhance Your Multi-Cultural Communication Skills," *Managing Diversity,* vol. 1, 1992, p. 5.

[17]Sid Lerner and Gary S. Belkin, *Trash Cash, Fizzbos and Flatliners: A Dictionary of Today's Words* (New York: Houghton Mifflin, 1993).

*A*s long as you are willing to stand up for what you think are your rights, you will run into conflict in your work and personal life. Conflicts can take various forms, including such incidents as these:

- Your boss wants you to work from 11 A.M. to 7 P.M. but your lifestyle requires a nine-to-five schedule.

- Your significant other wants to become engaged now but you prefer to wait another year before making such a commitment.

Both situations illustrate the underlying nature of **conflict,** a condition that exists when two sets of demands, goals, or motives are incompatible. You cannot work both an eleven-to-seven and a nine-to-five schedule; and you cannot be engaged and not engaged at the same time. Such differences in demands often lead to a hostile or antagonistic relationship between two or more parties. A conflict can also be considered a dispute, feud, controversy, or private war!

Conflict is important to study because it is far more complex than it appears on the surface. Many delicate human feelings are involved when two people are in conflict. The noted counseling psychologist, Carl Rogers, observed that most conflict between people includes four elements. First, each side thinks he or she is right and the other side is wrong. Second, communication breaks down as people do not hear each other. Third, there are distortions in perceptions as both sides ignore evidence that does not fit their viewpoint. Fourth, people distrust each other.[1]

A major purpose of this chapter is to describe ways of resolving conflict so that a win-win solution is reached. Both sides should leave the conflict feeling that their needs have been satisfied without having had to resort to extreme behavior. Both parties get what they deserve, yet preserve the dignity and self-respect of the other side. Another purpose of this chapter is to explain assertiveness, because being assertive helps to prevent and resolve conflict.

WHY SO MUCH CONFLICT EXISTS

Many reasons exist for the widespread presence of conflict in all aspects of life. All of these reasons are related to the basic nature of conflict—the fact that not every person can have what he or she wants at the same time.

COMPETITION FOR LIMITED RESOURCES

A fundamental reason you might experience conflict with another person is that not everybody can get all the money, material, supplies, or human help they want. Conflict also ensues when employees are asked to compete for prizes such as bonuses based on individual effort or company-paid vacation trips. Because the number of awards is so limited, the competition becomes intense enough to be regarded as conflict. In some families, two or more children are pitted in conflict over the limited resources of money available for higher education.

Conflict stemming from limited resources has become prevalent as so many companies acquire others or decide to downsize. After one company takes over another, a decision is often made to eliminate a number of positions and to cut costs in other ways. People then squabble over which people should be entitled to hold onto their jobs, and whose budget should be cut. In this instance, the positions in question and the money available become limited resources.

PERSONAL DIFFERENCES AND PERSONALITY CLASHES

Various personality and cultural differences among people contribute to job conflict. Difference in age is one such factor. The generation gap can lead to conflict because members of one generation may not accept values of another. Cooperation is sometimes difficult to achieve between older and younger members of a department because older employees question the seriousness of purpose of the younger employees. Simultaneously, the younger workers may believe that the older workers are resistant to change and blindly loyal to the company.

Cultural diversity in the work force has increased the potential for conflict. William L. Ury, a negotiation expert, says "Conflict resolution is perhaps the key skill needed in a diverse work force."[2] When these conflicts are properly resolved, diversity lends strength to the organization because the various viewpoints make an important contribution to solving a problem.

Many disagreements on the job stem from the fact that some people simply dislike each other. A **personality clash** is thus an antagonistic relationship between two people based on differences in personal attributes, preferences, interests, values, and styles. People involved in a personality clash often have difficulty specifying why they dislike each other. The end result, however, is that they cannot maintain an amiable work relationship. A strange fact about personality clashes is that people who get along well may begin to clash after working together for a number of years. Many business partnerships fold because the two partners eventually clash.

DIFFERENCES IN GOALS

One middle-aged man is embroiled in frequent conflict with his daughter. Her goal is to "take life easy" by working at odd jobs and spending as much time as possible at the beach or at ski resorts. His goal is to have a daughter who will "make something of herself." Until they both modify their goals in each other's directions, they will stay in conflict over this issue. In general, when two groups differ considerably in their goals, the potential for conflict is high.

Conflict between instructor and students sometimes reflects a difference in goals. An instructor might look upon his or her course as a valuable contribution to each student's career. The instructor's goal is that students maximize their effort in study and classroom participation. The goal of some of the students may be to receive the maximum grade for the minimum amount of study and participation. When an examination question is based on a minor point made in supplementary reading, conflict occurs. If the students shared the goal of maximizing learning, they would not object to the question. If the instructor shared the goal of maximum grade for minimum effort, he or she might not have asked the question.

THE BUILDING OF STONE WALLS

The slow and steady growth of a conflict situation has been likened by Richard J. Mayer to the building of a stone wall. The seed of the conflict is usually a minor incident that is not dealt with openly. The minor incident is called a *pinch*. Next, the person pinched unconsciously gathers data to support his or her view of the situation because of a need to be right. Much of the data are subject to perceptual distortion (seeing things in a way that fits our needs). As a result, a wall of minor incidents is built. The incidents eventually become an insurmountable obstacle (or stone wall) for honest and candid interaction with the *pincher*.[3]

A typical pinch is when an employee fails to share credit for a good idea he or she received from a co-worker. The co-worker feels slighted and then looks for other incidents of the first person being dishonest. Communication breaks down between the two, and they are involved in frequent arguments. The employee who failed to share credit may be unaware of how or why the conflict began. If the pinched worker had confronted the issue early on, the conflict might not have festered.

Sexual Harassment

A substantial number of employees experience conflict because they are sexually harassed by a manager, co-worker, or customer. **Sexual harassment** is behavior of a sexual nature at work that is offensive to an individual and that interferes with a person's ability to perform the job. Harassment can include something as violent as rape or as subtle as making a sexually oriented comment about another person's body or appearance. Decorating the work area with pictures of nude people is another example of behavior that can be categorized as sexual harassment. The most frequent form of harassment involves men against women. Harassment also takes the form of women sexually harassing men, and same-sex people harassing each other.

Two types of sexual harassment are legally recognized. Both are violation of the Civil Rights Acts of 1964 and 1991. In quid pro quo sexual harassment, the individual suffers loss (or threatened loss) of a job benefit as a result of his or her response to a request for sexual favors. The demands of a harasser can be blatantly obvious or implied.

The other form of sexual harassment is hostile-environment harassment. Another person in the workplace creates an intimidating, hostile, or offensive working environment. No tangible loss has to be suffered under this form of sexual harassment. According to a 1993 U.S. Supreme Court ruling, the person does not have to suffer severe psychological injury for an act to be classified as harassing. So long as a "reasonable person" would be offended by the behavior in question, the act could be considered harassment.[4]

An employee who is continually subjected to sexually suggestive comments, lewd jokes, or requests for dates is a victim of hostile-environment harassment. When the offensive behavior stems from customers or vendors it is still harassment. Although the company cannot readily control the actions of customers or vendors, the company may still be liable for such harassment. According to several legal decisions, it is a company's job to take action to remedy harassment problems involving employees.[5]

Sexual harassment through creating an intimidating environment received worldwide attention in 1991. The occasion was the Congressional hearings to determine if Judge Clarence Thomas, a Supreme Court justice nominee, had sexually harassed a former employee, Professor Anita F. Hill. Although Congress subsequently approved Thomas as a Supreme Court justice, employers became more sensitive to the problem of sexual harassment. Employees apparently perceived the climate to be favorable for filing sexual harassment charges. In the quarter following the hearings, sexual harassment claims filed with the U.S. EEOC increased by 71 percent.

Sexual harassment creates conflict because the harassed person has to make a choice between two incompatible motives. One motive is to get ahead or at least keep the job. But to satisfy this motive, the person is forced to sacrifice the motive of holding on to his or her moral values or preferences. Exhibit 7-1 presents suggestions for dealing with sexual harassment.

EXHIBIT 7-1

HOW TO HANDLE OR PREVENT SEXUAL HARASSMENT

The potential or actual victim of sexual harassment is advised to use the methods and tactics described below to deal with the problem.

Formal Complaint Procedure

Organizations that have formal policies against sexual harassment typically use a complaint procedure that follows this format:

Whenever an employee believes that he or she has encountered sexual harassment, or if an employee is suspected to be the perpetrator of sexual harassment, the complainant should:

Report the incident to his or her immediate superior (if that person is not the harasser) or to the next-highest level of management if the supervisor *is* the harasser. The supervisor contacted is responsible for contacting the Affirmative Action officer immediately regarding each complaint.

The Affirmative Action officer will explain the investigative procedures (both informal and formal inquiries) to the complainant and any supervisor involved. All matters will be kept strictly confidential, including private conversations with all parties.

Dealing with the Problem on Your Own

The easiest way to deal with sexual harassment is to nip it in the bud. The first time it happens, respond with a statement of this type: "I won't tolerate this kind of talk." "I dislike sexually oriented jokes." "Keep your hands off me." Or just say "No" at the first hint of harassment.

Tell the actual or potential harasser, "You're practicing sexual harassment. If you don't stop I'm going to exercise my right to report you to management." Similarly, "I think I heard you right. Would you like to accompany me to the boss's office and repeat what you said to me?"

Another effective method of warding off harassment is to write the person a letter describing how negatively you feel about his or her behavior. Also insist that the offending actions stop immediately or you will take firmer action.

COMPETING WORK AND FAMILY DEMANDS

Balancing the demands of career and family life has become a major challenge facing today's workforce. The challenge is particularly intense for employees who are part of a two-wage earner family—a group that represents approximately one-half of the work force.[6] Attempting to meet work and family demands is a frequent source of conflict because the demands are often incompatible. Imagine having planned to attend your child's solo recital, and then being ordered at the last minute to work late because of an emergency.

The conflict over work versus family demands intensifies when the person is serious about both work and family responsibilities. The average professional working for an organization works approximately fifty-five hours per week, including five hours on weekends. Adhering to such a schedule almost inevitably results in some incompatible demands from work versus those from family members and friends. Conflict arises because the person wants to work sufficient hours to succeed on the job, yet still have enough time for personal life.

Employers have taken major steps in recent years to help employees balance the competing demands of work and family. These programs help reduce conflict that arises from competing work and family demands. A sampling of these programs are as follows:

1. *Flexible work schedules.*   Many employers allow employees to work flexible hours providing they work the full forty-hour schedule, and are present at certain core times. A related program is the compressed work-week whereby the person works forty hours in four days or less. Some employees prefer the compressed workweek because it gives them longer weekends with their families. (For many others, however, ten-hour work-days create family problems.)

Family leave programs allow employees to take extended time off work, without pay, in order to take care of family responsibilities. The employee's benefits continue while on leave, and the employee is guaranteed a job upon return. The leave applies to any combination of family and/or medical leaves. Twelve weeks of such leave is required by the U.S. Family Leave Bill of 1993. The bill applies to firms with fifty or more employees.

2. *Child-care and elder-care programs.*   Assistance in dealing with two categories of dependents, children and elderly parents, lies at the core of programs and policies to help employees balance the demands of work and family. According to one survey, 66 percent of major corporations offer child-care services to employees.[7] At one end of child-care assistance is a model nursery school such as the child-development center at Marriott Corp. headquarters. At the other end is simply a referral service that helps working parents find adequate child care. Many companies offer financial assistance for child care, including pretax expense accounts that allow employees to deduct child-care and elder-care expenses.

3. *Compassionate attitudes toward individual needs.*   An informal policy that facilitates balancing work and family demands is for the manager to decide what can be done to resolve individual conflicts. Yet the manager cannot make arrangements with employees that would violate company policy. Being sensitive to individual situations could involve such arrangements as allowing a person time off to deal with a personal crisis. After the crisis is resolved the employee makes up the lost time in small chunks of extra work time.

Do you think employers should be required to help employees resolve competing demands of work and family?

THE GOOD AND BAD SIDE OF CONFLICT

Conflict over significant issues is a source of stress. We usually do not suffer stress over minor conflicts such as having to choose between wearing one sweater or another. Since conflict is a source of stress, it can have both positive and negative consequences to the individual. Like stress in general, we need an optimum amount of conflict to keep us mentally and physically energetic.

You can probably recall an incident in your life when conflict proved to be beneficial in the long run. Perhaps you and your friend or spouse hammered out an agreement over how much freedom each one has in the relationship. Handled properly, moderate doses of conflict can be beneficial. Some of the benefits that might arise from conflict can be summarized around these key points:

1. *Talents and abilities may emerge in response to conflict.* When faced with a conflict, people often become more creative than they are in a tranquil situation. Assume that your employer told you that it would no longer pay for your advanced education unless you used the courses to improve your job performance. You would probably find ways to accomplish such an end.

2. *Conflict can help you feel better because it satisfies a number of psychological needs.* By nature, many people like a good fight. As a socially acceptable substitute for attacking others, you might be content to argue over a dispute on the job or at home.

3. *As an aftermath of conflict, the parties in conflict may become united.* Two adolescents engaged in a fistfight may emerge bloodied but good friends after the battle. And two warring supervisors may become more cooperative toward each other in the aftermath of confrontation.

4. *Conflict helps prevent people in the organization from agreeing too readily with each other, thus making some very poor decisions.* *Group-think* is the situation that occurs when group members strive so hard to get along that they fail to critically evaluate each other's ideas.

Despite the positive picture of conflict just painted, it can also have some detrimental consequences to the individual, the organization, and society. These harmful consequences of conflict make it important for people to learn how to resolve conflict:

1. *Prolonged conflict can be detrimental to some people's emotional and physical well-being.* As a type of stress, prolonged conflict can lead to such problems as heart disease and chronic intestinal disorders. U.S. President Lyndon B. Johnson suffered his first heart attack after an intense argument with a young newspaper reporter.

2. *People in conflict with each other often waste time and energy that could be put to useful purposes.* Instead of fighting all evening with your roommate, the two of you might fix up your place. Instead of writing angry E-mail messages back and forth, two department heads might better invest that time in thinking up ideas to save the company money.

3. *The aftermath of extreme conflict may have high financial and emotional costs.* Sabotage—such as ruining machinery—might be the financial consequence. At the same time, management may develop a permanent distrust of many people in the work force, although only a few of them are saboteurs.

4. *Too much conflict is fatiguing, even if it does not cause symptoms of emotional illness.* People who work in high-conflict jobs often feel spent when they return home from work. When the battle-worn individual has limited energy left over for family responsibilities, the result is more conflict. (For instance, "What do you mean you are too tired to go to the movies?" or "If your job is killing your appetite, find another job.")

5. *People in conflict will often be much more concerned with their own interests than with the good of the family, organization, or society.* A married couple in conflict might disregard the welfare of their children. An employee in the shipping department who is in conflict with his supervisor might neglect to ship an order. And a gang in conflict with another might leave a park or beach strewn with broken glass.

6. *An extreme, negative consequence of workplace conflict is that disgruntled employees return to the work site determined on violence.* They may attempt to get even by shooting former co-workers and supervisors. The number of violent incidents at work causing death or serious injury has risen dramatically in the last decade. Most of these assassinations are attributed to former employees who were enraged over being dismissed.[10]

DEALING WITH ANGER

Conflict typically leads to **frustration,** a blocking of need or motive satisfaction. People experience frustration when something stands between them and the goal they want to achieve. Frustration, in turn, leads to anger. Even if you did not experience frustration when in conflict, you would still feel some anger. Other common causes of anger are envy and jealousy. The anger component helps explain why envy and jealousy are such intense states of mind, and so difficult to shake.

THE NATURE OF ANGER

Anger is a feeling of extreme hostility, indignation, or exasperation. The feeling of anger triggers a stress reaction, including physiological changes as described in Chapter 4. One noticeable physical indicator of anger is that the pupils may enlarge, causing the wide-eyed look typical of people in a rage. Charles Darwin's description of anger published in 1872 is still accurate:

> The face reddens or becomes purple, with the veins on the forehead and neck distended. The chest heaves, the dilated nostrils quiver, the limbs become rigid, the mouth severely closed with firmness, showing fixed determination, and the teeth are clenched or ground together.[11]

Sound like anybody you know?

An unfortunate by-product of anger is that one's judgment may become clouded. People often act impulsively and violently when experiencing anger or rage. One punch or invective hurled at a supervisor can do serious damage to a person's career.

HOW BEST TO HANDLE ANGER

Experts go back and forth on how much free expression should be given to anger. Mental health professionals have always agreed that anger and frustration should not be entirely suppressed. Bottled emotions are said to be harmful—they can lead to psychosomatic disorders and sudden bursts of uncontrollable emotion. During the permissive 1960s people were urged to "tell it like it is" and "let it all hang out." Some psychotherapists even suggested that venting all anger would get rid of it. Managers and employees were urged to be candid in expressing anger toward each other.

In recent years, more emphasis has been placed on controlling anger so that it does not lead to destructive consequences. For example, a research report for executives recommends, "Avoid anger. Getting angry is a waste of time. If there is an open display of hostility between junior and senior, the junior staff member always loses."[12]

Despite these conflicting views about expressing anger, here are several suggestions that may prove helpful in managing anger in work and social situations:

1. *Recognize that anger is an energizer, and is therefore potentially useful.* When angry, for example, it is a good time to get through laborious tasks that do not require heavy judgment and concentration. Use the energy derived from anger to clean out your files, wash and wax a car, clean out a basement, or conduct an inventory. But stay away from operating potentially dangerous machinery such as power tools or automobiles.

2. *Use anger to remind you to share your feelings with an important person in your life.* You might say to a close friend, "I'm angry that you didn't invite me to that dinner party." On the job you might say, "I'm angry that I was passed over for promotion to supervisor. I wanted the job and I think I deserve it." (Notice that you have not flown into a rage by making these statements.)

3. *When angry at another person, first express those feelings to yourself and then share the less destructive feelings with him or her.* The old idea of counting to ten when angry has merit.[13] Or you can write down all your angry feelings and then sort out the useful ideas in your anger letter. Assume your instructor gave you a D on a paper you thought deserved an A. Compose a letter to yourself explaining how angry you are at the instructor. Then return to the instructor with your legitimate concerns and rational feelings.

4. *Don't carry grudges.* A **grudge** is the unresolved or unrepressed anger we feel against someone whom we believe has wronged us. (A grudge is much like the stone wall described previously.) A psychotherapist warns us that "Consistent grudges can lead to stress, and everything from backaches to chest pains. And they can be very damaging with friends, family, and at work . . ."[14] Exhibit 7-2 presents some useful ideas on how to get rid of grudges.

CONFLICT-MANAGEMENT STYLES

The information presented so far is designed to help you understand the nature of conflict. Such background information is useful for resolving conflict because it helps you understand what is happening in a conflict situation. The next two sections offer more specific information about managing and resolving conflict. Before describing specific methods of resolving conflict, it is useful to understand five general styles, or orientations, of handling conflict. As shown in Figure 7-1, Kenneth Thomas identified five major styles of conflict management: competitive, accommodative, sharing, collaborative, and avoidance. Each style is based on a combination of satisfying one's own concerns (assertiveness) and satisfying the concerns of others (cooperativeness).[15]

EXHIBIT 7-2

HOW TO EXORCISE A GRUDGE

Do you often carry a grudge? Since you recognize the problem, you have already taken an important step toward overcoming grudges. In addition to recognizing the problem, choose from among these suggestions:

- Express your hurt, disappointment, or anger to the person you believe has slighted you. You must communicate in order to clear the air.

- See the situation from the other person's perspective. There may be a very good reason for his or her behavior.

- Weigh the seriousness of the offense.

- Consider your options. List even the ridiculous ones to help you vent your anger.

- Confront the person you have a grudge against in a way that minimizes the consequences.

- Express your anger in a letter you never send if the risks are too great. This is a good way to vent anger against people who are no longer present, including an ex-spouse or a deceased parent.

- Work on acceptance. Let the anger go, and move on to positive life events.

SOURCE: Adapted with permission from Karen S. Peterson, "Holding Grudges Can Hold You Back," *USA Weekend,* October 18–20, 1985, p. 29.

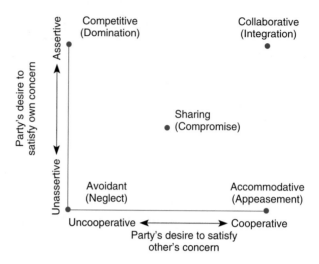

Figure 7-1   Conflict-Handling Styles According to Degree of Cooperation and Assertiveness

SOURCE: Kenneth W. Thomas, "Organizational Conflict," in Steven Kerr, ed., *Organizational Behavior* (Columbus, Ohio: Grid Publishing, 1979), p. 156.

Competitive.   The competitive style is a desire to win one's own concerns at the expense of the other party, or to dominate. A person with a competitive orientation is likely to engage in power struggles where one side wins and the other loses.

Accommodative.   The accommodative style favors appeasement, or satisfying the other's concerns without taking care of one's own. People with this orientation may be generous or self-sacrificing just to maintain a relationship. An irate customer might be accommodated with a full refund, "just to shut him (or her) up." The intent of such accommodation might also be to retain the customer's loyalty.

Sharing.   The sharing style is halfway between domination and appeasement. Sharers prefer moderate but incomplete satisfaction for both parties, which results in a compromise. The term "splitting the difference" reflects this orientation, and is commonly used in such activities as purchasing a house or car.

Collaborative.   In contrast to the other styles, the collaborative style reflects a desire to fully satisfy the desires of both parties. It is based on an underlying philosophy of **win-win,** the belief that after conflict has been resolved both sides should gain something of value. The user of win-win approaches is genuinely concerned about arriving at a settlement that meets the needs of both parties, or at least does not badly damage the welfare of the other side. When collaborative approaches to resolving conflict are used, the relationships among the parties are built on and improved.

Here is an example of a win-win approach to resolving conflict. A manager granted an employee a few hours off on an occasional Friday afternoon if she were willing to be on call for emergency work on an occasional weekend. Both parties were satisfied with the outcome and both accomplished their goals.

Avoidant. The avoider is a combination of uncooperative and unassertive. He or she is indifferent to the concerns of either party. The person may actually be withdrawing from the conflict or be relying upon fate. The avoidant style is sometimes used by a manager who stays out of a conflict between two team members who are left to resolve their own differences.

In the following description of specific techniques for resolving conflict, you should be able to relate most of them to these five key styles. For example, you will see that the confrontation and problem-solving technique reflects the collaborative style.

Techniques for Resolving Conflicts with Others

Because of the inevitability of conflict, a successful and happy person must learn effective ways of resolving conflict. Here we concentrate on methods of conflict resolution that you can use on your own. Most of them emphasize a win-win philosophy. Several of the negotiating and bargaining tactics to be described may be close to the competitive orientation.

Confrontation and Problem Solving

The most highly recommended way of resolving conflict is **confrontation and problem solving.** It is a method of identifying the true source of conflict and resolving it systematically. The confrontation in this approach is gentle and tactful rather than combative and abusive. Reasonableness is important because the person who takes the initiative in resolving the conflict wants to maintain a harmonious working relationship with the other party.

Assume that Jason, the person working at the desk next to you, whistles loudly while he works. You find the whistling to be distracting and annoying; you think Jason is a noise polluter. If you don't bring the problem to Jason's attention, it will probably grow in proportion with time. Yet you are hesitant to enter into an argument about something a person might regard as a civil liberty (the right to whistle in a public place).

An effective alternative is for you to approach Jason directly in this manner:

> **You:** Jason, there is something bothering me that I would like to discuss with you.
>
> **Jason:** Go ahead, I don't mind listening to other people's problems.
>
> **You:** My problem concerns something you are doing that makes it difficult for me to concentrate on my work. When you whistle it distracts me and grates on my nerves. It may be my hang-up, but the whistling does bother me.
>
> **Jason:** I guess I could stop whistling when you're working next to me. It's probably just a nervous habit.

An important advantage of confrontation and problem solving is that you deal directly with a sensitive problem without jeopardizing the chances of forming a constructive working relationship in the future. One reason that the method works so effectively is that the focus is on the problem at hand, and not upon the individual's personality.

DISARM THE OPPOSITION

The armament your criticizer has is valid negative criticism of you. The criticizer is figuratively clobbering you with knowledge of what you did wrong. If you deny that you have made a mistake, the criticism intensifies. A simple technique has been developed to help you deal with this type of manipulative criticism. **Disarm the opposition** is a method of conflict resolution in which you disarm the criticizer by agreeing with his or her criticism of you. The technique assumes that you have done something wrong.

Disarm the opposition capitalizes on the same principle that children often use in handling conflict or potential conflict with their parents. A child might say, "I spilled my drink on the sofa by mistake. Go ahead and punish me. I deserve it." Disarm the opposition works more effectively than counterattacking a person with whom you are in conflict.

Agreeing with criticism made of you by a superior is effective because by doing so you are then in a position to ask for that superior's help in improving your performance. Most managers realize that it is their responsibility to help employees overcome problems, not merely to criticize them. Imagine that you have been chronically late in submitting reports during the last six months. It is time for a performance review and you know you will be reprimanded for your tardiness. You also hope that your boss will not downgrade all other aspects of your performance because of your tardy reports. Here is how disarming the situation would work in this situation:

Your Boss: Have a seat. It's time for your performance review and we have a lot to talk about. I'm concerned about some things.

You: So am I. It appears that I'm having a difficult time getting my reports in on time. I wonder if I'm being a perfectionist. Do you have any suggestions?

Your Boss: I like your attitude. I think you can improve on getting your reports in on time. Maybe you are trying to make your reports perfect before you turn them in. Try not to figure out everything to four decimal places. We need thoroughness around here, but we don't want to overdo it.

APPEAL TO A THIRD PARTY

Now and then you may be placed in a conflict situation in which the other party either holds most of the power or simply won't budge. Perhaps you have tried techniques such as confrontation and problem solving or disarming the opposition, yet you cannot resolve your conflict. In these situations you may have to enlist the help of a third party with power—more power than you or your adversary has. Among such third parties are your common boss, union stewards, or personnel managers. Taking your opponent to court is another application of the third party technique.

In some situations, just implying that you will bring in a third party to help resolve the conflict situation is sufficient for you to gain advantage. One woman felt she was repeatedly passed over for promotion because of her sex. She hinted that if she were not given fairer consideration she would speak to the Equal Employment Opportunity Commission (EEOC). She was given a small promotion shortly thereafter.

NEGOTIATION AND BARGAINING TACTICS

Conflicts can be considered situations calling for **negotiating and bargaining,** conferring with another person to resolve a problem. When you are trying to negotiate a fair price for an automobile, you are also trying to resolve a conflict. At first the demands of both parties seem incompatible. After haggling for a while, you will probably reach a price that is satisfactory to both sides.

Negotiation has many applications in the workplace, including buying, selling, arriving at a starting salary or raise, and deciding on a relocation allowance. Negotiation may also take place with co-workers when you need their assistance. For example, you might need to strike a bargain with a co-worker to handle some of your responsibilities if you are faced with a temporary overload.

A sampling of negotiating tactics to help you resolve conflict successfully is presented next. As with the other techniques of resolving conflict already presented, choose the ones which best fit your style and the situation.

Create a Positive Negotiating Climate

Negotiation proceeds much more swiftly if a positive tone surrounds the session. So it is helpful to initiate a positive outlook about the negotiation meeting. A good opening line in a negotiating session is, "Thanks for fitting this meeting into your hectic schedule." Nonverbal communication such as smiling and making friendly gestures helps create a positive climate.

In negotiating with co-workers for assistance, a positive climate can often be achieved by phrasing demands as a request for help. Most people will be more accommodating if you say to them, "I have a problem that I wonder if you could help me with." The problem might be that you need the person's time and mental energy. By giving that person a choice of offering you help, you have established a much more positive climate than by demanding assistance.[16]

Allow Room for Compromise

The basic strategy of negotiation is to begin with a demand that allows you room for compromise and concession. Anyone who has ever negotiated the price of an automobile, bicycle, house, or used furniture recognizes this vital strategy. If you are a buyer, begin with a low bid. (You say, "I'll give you $35 for that painting" when you are prepared to pay $70.) If you are the seller, begin with a high demand. (You say, "You can have this painting for $100" when you are ready to sell it for as low as $70.) As negotiations proceed, the two of you will probably arrive at a mutually satisfactory price. This negotiating strategy can also be used for such purposes as obtaining a higher starting salary or dividing property after a divorce or legal separation.

Begin with a Plausible Demand or Offer

Common sense propels many negotiators to allow *too much* room for compromise. They begin negotiations by asking way beyond what they expect to receive, or offering far less than they expect to give. As a result of these implausible demands, the other side may become hostile, antagonistic, or walk away from the negotiations. Assume you spotted a VCR that you really wanted in a retail store. The asking price was $298.95. In an attempt to negotiate the price, you offered the store manager $98.95 for the VCR. Most likely the store owner would move on to the next customer. However, if you began with a plausible offer such as $240, the store manager would take you seriously.

Raise Your Level of Expectation

Set a high goal for yourself in resolving conflict, stick firmly to your demands, and you will fare well. People who set low goals for themselves in a negotiating or bargaining session do not fare as well. Part of the underlying psychology is that by setting such high goals (but not preposterous ones) for yourself, you project an air of self-confidence. And the other side is usually impressed by a self-confident individual.

Focus on Interests, Not Positions

Rather than clinging to specific negotiating points, keep your overall interests in mind and try to satisfy them. A negotiating point might be a certain amount of money or a concession that you must have. Remember that the true object of negotiation is to satisfy the underlying interests of both sides. For example, instead of negotiating for a particular starting salary, your true interests might be to afford a certain lifestyle. If the company pays all your medical and dental coverage, for example, you can get by with a lower salary. Or your cost of living might be much lower in one city than in another. You can therefore accept a lower starting salary in Gary, Indiana, than in Honolulu, Hawaii.

Make a Last and Final Offer

In many circumstances, presenting a final offer will break a deadlock. You might frame your message something like this, "All I can possibly pay for your guitar is $250. You have my number. Call me when it is available at that price." Sometimes the strategy will be countered by a last and final offer from the other side: "Thanks for your interest. My absolute minimum price for this guitar is $300. Call us if that should seem OK to you." One of you will probably give in and accept the other person's last and final offer.

Allow for Face-Saving

We have saved one of the most important negotiating and conflict resolution strategies for last. Negotiating does not mean that you should try to squash the other side. You try to create circumstances that will enable you to continue working with that person if it is necessary. People prefer to avoid looking weak, foolish, or incompetent during negotiation or when the process is completed. If you do not give your opponent an opportunity to save face, you will probably create a long-term enemy.

A real estate agent in Dallas, Texas, uses the following face-saving technique. If a client pays much more for a house than originally intended, the agent says: "I recognize that you invested a little more money up front than you planned. But just think. As we sit here the value of your property is already climbing. You have just made one of the surest investments of your life. You might double your money in six years." The agent is concerned about face-saving because she wants referral business.

DEVELOPING ASSERTIVENESS

Several of the techniques for resolving conflict require assertiveness. Without being forthright, confrontation and problem solving could not be achieved. Effective negotiation would also be difficult because assertiveness is required to carefully explain one's demands. Learning to express your feelings and make your demands known is also an important aspect of becoming an effective individual in general. Expressing your feelings

THANKS FOR THE OFFER. THE ASSISTANT MANAGER POSITION DOES INTEREST ME. MY MINIMUM REQUIREMENTS ARE $100,000 PER YEAR AND 4 WEEKS ANNUAL VACATION.

COMMON SENSE PROPELS MANY NEGOTIATORS TO ALLOW **TOO MUCH** ROOM FOR COMPROMISE helps you establish good relationships with people. If you aren't sharing your feelings and attitudes with other people, you will never get close to them.

Another benefit from being emotionally expressive, and therefore assertive, is that you get more of what you want in life. If you are too passive, people will neglect giving you what you want. Often it is necessary to ask someone when you want a raise, promotion, date, or better deal on a bank loan. Successful people usually make their demands known, yet do not throw tantrums and are rarely bullies. (Exceptions to this general principle include some flamboyant trial lawyers and athletic coaches.)

Let's examine the nature of assertiveness in some detail, and then examine several techniques for building assertiveness.

Assertive, Nonassertive, and Aggressive Behavior

As implied above, **assertive** people state clearly what they want or how they feel in a given situation without being abusive, abrasive, or obnoxious. People who are assertive are open, honest, and "up-front" because they believe that all people have an equal right to express themselves honestly. Fred Pryor describes the type of assertiveness individual particularly needed in today's workplace:

> These pleasantly assertive workers are not intimidated by age or power or tradition. They have a calm, cool steadiness. They are their own persons. They don't wait to be asked for alternatives to "the way we do things here." They speak out when they think they have something to say that will benefit the organization and will add luster to the bottom line.[17]

Assertive behavior can be more fully understood by comparing it to that shown by two other types of people. **Nonassertive** people let things happen to them without letting their feelings be known. **Aggressive** people are obnoxious and overbearing. They push for what they want with almost no regard for the feelings of others. Take Self-Examination Exercise 7-1.

Another way of explaining these differences is to say that the nonassertive person is stepped on and the aggressive person steps on others, while the assertive person deals with a problem in a mature and direct manner. Suppose a stranger invites you to a party and you do not wish to go with that person. Here are the three ways of responding according to the three-way classification under discussion:

Assertive: Thank you for the invitation but I prefer not to go.

Nonassertive: I'm not sure, I might be busy. Could you call me again? Maybe I'll know for sure by then.

Aggressive: I'd like to go to a party, but not with you. Don't bother me again.

Gestures as well as words can communicate whether the person is being assertive, nonassertive, or aggressive. Exhibit 7-3 illustrates these differences.

SELF-EXAMINATION EXERCISE 7-1

Are You Nonassertive, Assertive, or Aggressive?

The following questionnaire is designed to give you tentative insight into your current tendencies toward submissiveness, assertiveness, or aggressiveness. As with other questionnaires presented in this book, the Assertiveness Scale is primarily a self-examination and discussion device. Answer each question Mostly True or Mostly False, as it applies to you.

	Mostly True	*Mostly False*
1. It is extremely difficult for me to turn down a sales representative when that individual is a nice person.	_____	_____
2. I express criticism freely.	_____	_____
3. If another person were being very unfair, I would bring it to that person's attention.	_____	_____
4. Work is no place to let your feelings show.	_____	_____
5. No use asking for favors; people get what they deserve on the job.	_____	_____
6. Business is not the place for tact; say what you think.	_____	_____
7. If a person looked as if he or she were in a hurry, I would let that person go in front of me in a supermarket line.	_____	_____
8. A weakness of mine is that I'm too nice a person.	_____	_____
9. If my restaurant bill is even 25¢ more than it should be, I demand that the mistake be corrected.	_____	_____
10. I have laughed out loud in public more than once.	_____	_____
11. I've been described as too outspoken by several people.	_____	_____
12. I am quite willing to have the store take back a piece of furniture that contains a scratch.	_____	_____
13. I dread having to express anger toward a co-worker.	_____	_____
14. People often say that I'm too reserved and emotionally controlled.	_____	_____
15. Nice guys and gals finish last in business.	_____	_____
16. I fight for my rights down to the last detail.	_____	_____
17. I have no misgivings about returning an overcoat to the store if it doesn't fit me properly.	_____	_____
18. If I have had an argument with a person, I try to avoid him or her.	_____	_____
19. I insist on my spouse (or roommate or partner) doing his or her fair share of undesirable chores.	_____	_____
20. It is difficult for me to look directly at another person when the two of us are in disagreement.	_____	_____

(Continued)

21. I have cried among friends more than once.   _____ _____

22. If someone near me at a movie kept up a conversation with
another person, I would ask him or her to stop.   _____ _____

23. I am able to turn down social engagements with people
I do not particularly care for.   _____ _____

24. It is in poor taste to express what you really feel about
another individual.   _____ _____

25. I sometimes show my anger by swearing at or belittling
another person.   _____ _____

26. I am reluctant to speak up in a meeting.   _____ _____

27. I find it relatively easy to ask friends for small favors such
as giving me a lift to work when my car is being repaired.   _____ _____

28. If another person were talking very loudly in a restaurant
and it bothered me, I would inform that person.   _____ _____

29. I often finish other people's sentences for them.   _____ _____

30. It is relatively easy for me to express love and affection
toward another person.   _____ _____

Scoring and Interpretation: Give yourself plus 1 for each of your answers that agrees with the scoring key. If your score is 15 or less, it is probable that you are currently a nonassertive individual. A score of 16 through 24 suggests that you are an assertive individual. A score of 25 or higher suggests that you are an aggressive individual. Retake this score about 30 days from now to give yourself some indication of the stability of your answers. You might also discuss your answers with a close friend to determine if that person has a similar perception of your assertiveness. Here is the scoring key.

1. Mostly False	11. Mostly True	21. Mostly True
2. Mostly True	12. Mostly True	22. Mostly True
3. Mostly True	13. Mostly False	23. Mostly True
4. Mostly False	14. Mostly False	24. Mostly False
5. Mostly False	15. Mostly True	25. Mostly True
6. Mostly True	16. Mostly True	26. Mostly False
7. Mostly False	17. Mostly True	27. Mostly True
8. Mostly False	18. Mostly False	28. Mostly True
9. Mostly True	19. Mostly True	29. Mostly True
10. Mostly True	20. Mostly False	30. Mostly True

BECOMING MORE ASSERTIVE AND LESS SHY

There are a number of everyday actions a person can take to overcome shyness and lack of assertiveness. Even if the ones described here do not elevate your social skills, they will not backfire and cause you pain. After reading the following techniques, you might be able to think of others that will work for you.[18]

Set a Goal.   Clearly establish in your mind how you want to behave differently. Do you want to date more often? Speak out more in meetings? Be able to express dissatisfaction to co-workers? You can only overcome shyness by behaving differently; feeling differently is not enough.

Appear Warm and Friendly.   Shy people often communicate to others through their body language that they are not interested in reaching out to others. To overcome this impression, smile, lean forward, uncross your arms and legs, and unfold your hands.

Legitimate Telephone Calls to Strangers. Telephone conversations with strangers that have a legitimate purpose can help you start expressing yourself to people you do not know well. You might call numbers listed in classified ads to inquire about articles listed for sale. Try a positive approach: "Hello, my name is _____. I'd like to know about the condition of that piano you have for sale." Call the gas and electric company to inquire about a problem with your bill. Make telephone inquiries about employment opportunities in a firm of your choice. Call the library with reference questions. Call the federal government bureau in your town with questions about laws and regulations.

With practice, you will probably become more adept at speaking to strangers. You will then be ready for a more challenging self-improvement task.

Anonymous Conversations. Try starting a conversation with strangers in a safe setting such as a political rally, the waiting room of a medical office, a waiting line at the post office, or in a laundromat. Begin the conversation with the common experience you are sharing at the time. Among them might be:

"I wonder if there will be any tickets left by the time we get to the box office?"

"How long does it usually take before you get to see the doctor?"

"Where did you get that laundry basket? I've never seen one so sturdy before."

Greeting Strangers. For the next week or so, greet every person you pass. Smile and make a neutral comment such as "How ya doing?" "Great

---

EXHIBIT 7-3

ASSERTIVE, NONASSERTIVE, AND AGGRESSIVE GESTURES

Assertive	Nonassertive	Aggresive
Well-balanced	Covering mouth with hand	Pounding fists
Straight posture	Excessive head nodding	Stiff and rigid posture
Hand gestures, emphasizing key words	Tinkering with clothing or jewelry	Finger waving or pointing
	Constant shifting of weight	Shaking head as if other person isn't to be believed
	Scratching or rubbing head or other parts of body	Hands on hips
	Wooden body posture	

SOURCE: Donna E. Ledgerwood, "Workplace Relationships in the Federal Sector: Implications of Employees' Perceptions of Behavior," presentation for Employees of Dallas Region United States Office of Personnel Management, 1989.

day, isn't it." Since most people are unaccustomed to being greeted by a stranger, you may get a few quizzical looks. Many other people may smile and return your greeting. A few of these greetings may turn into conversations. A few conversations may even turn into friendships. Even if the return on your investment in greetings is only a few pleasant responses, it will boost your confidence.

Broken Record.   The assertion skill called *broken record* teaches you to persist until you get your way. **Broken-record technique** consists of calmly repeating your position over and over again without showing signs of anger or irritation. The person trying to persuade you will usually give up after a few minutes of hearing your "broken record." Acquiring this skill can help a shy person learn to say no, and not to give up after hearing the first no from another person.

Imagine this scenario. It is Sunday afternoon and you are busily preparing a report that is due Monday morning. A neighbor of yours, Tammy, rings your doorbell. After you open the door she says, "The whole gang is going to play volleyball this afternoon. We need you to join us. Could you be ready in fifteen minutes?" You decide that working on your report is more important than playing volleyball this afternoon. The broken-record technique might proceed in this manner:

You: Thanks anyway, but I'll have to decline your offer. I'm working on an important report this afternoon.

Tammy: You must be kidding. It's too nice a day to stay inside and work on a report.

You: No, I'm not kidding. I'll have to decline your offer.

Tammy: How about taking a two-hour break? I promise you that the game will be over in two hours.

You: No, I'll have to decline your offer.

Tammy: What kind of a neighbor are you? The whole gang will be disappointed. Can't you please join us?

You: No, I'll have to decline your offer.

Tammy: Thanks, anyway. Maybe we can catch you next time.

You: Sounds good. Have a nice day.

In the example just cited, your nonverbal behavior must correspond to your verbal statements. For example, your facial expressions and the tone of your voice must communicate the thought that you really do not want to be disturbed from your work. Sounding like a broken record may not be part of your self-image. However, it is preferable to being manipulated into doing something you prefer not to do.

Negative Inquiry.   Shy people have difficulty managing criticism. The technique of negative inquiry helps you deal with criticism. **Negative inquiry** is the active encouragement of criticism in order to elicit helpful information or exhaust manipulative criticism. At the same time, you prompt your critic to be more assertive and less manipulative. Negative inquiry involves asking a series of questions to get at the true nature of the criticism.

Assume that Pedro, a co-worker of yours, expresses displeasure with your performance in a recent department meeting. You find his criticism uncomfortable and undeserved. Here is how negative inquiry might be used:

Pedro: That was a pretty bad show you put on in yesterday's meeting.

You: What was bad about it?

Pedro: You took up too much of the meeting pushing your own ideas.

You: Whose ideas was I supposed to push?

Pedro: I'm not sure. I just know that you pushed too many of your own ideas.

You: What is it that you disliked about my pushing my own ideas?

Pedro: I guess I wanted you to tell the boss about some of the great ideas I had. I wanted some credit too.

You: Now I see why you're upset with me.

Negative inquiry, as illustrated above, helped you discover the true nature of Pedro's problem. Since the truth is out, Pedro can no longer manipulate you by making you feel bad about actively contributing to the meeting.

SUMMARY

Conflict occurs when two sets of demands, goals, or motives are incompatible. Such differences often lead to a hostile or antagonistic relationship between people. A conflict can also be considered a dispute, feud, or controversy.

Among the reasons for widespread conflict are (1) competition for limited resources, (2) personal differences and personality clashes, (3) differences in goals, (4) the building of stone walls, (5) sexual harassment, (6) competing work and family demands. Sexual harassment is of two types: quid pro quo (a demand for sexual favors in exchange for job benefits), and creating a hostile environment.

The benefits of conflict include the emergence of talents and abilities, constructive innovation and change, and increased unity after the conflict is settled. Among the detrimental consequences of conflict are physical and mental health problems, wasted resources, the promotion of self-interest, and workplace violence.

Conflict typically leads to frustration and anger. Frustration is a blocking of need or motive satisfaction. Anger is a feeling of extreme hostility, indignation, or exasperation that leads to stress. Anger and frustration should be expressed, but not so that they lead to destructive consequences. Suggestions for handling anger include: (1) use it as an energizer; (2) use it to remind you to share your feelings with an important person; (3)

express it to yourself and then share the less destructive feelings with another person; (4) don't carry grudges.

Five major styles of conflict management have been identified: competitive, accommodative, sharing, collaborative, and avoidant. Each style is based on a combination of satisfying one's own concerns (assertiveness) and satisfying the concerns of others (cooperativeness). The collaborative style is effective because it leads to win-win solutions to conflict.

Techniques for resolving conflicts with others include:

1. Confrontation and problem solving—get to the root of the problem and resolve it systematically.

2. Disarm the opposition—agree with the criticizer and enlist his or her help.

3. Appeal to a third party.

4. Use negotiation and bargaining tactics.

Negotiation and bargaining tactics include: (1) create a positive negotiating climate; (2) allow room for compromise; (3) begin with a plausible demand or offer; (4) raise your level of expectation; (5) focus on interests, not positions; (6) make a last and final offer; and (7) allow for face-saving.

Several of the techniques for resolving conflict require assertiveness, or stating clearly what one wants and how one feels in a given situation. Being assertive also helps you develop good relationships with people and get more of what you want in life.

People can become more assertive and less shy by using techniques such as:

1. Set a goal in relation to assertiveness.

2. Appear warm and friendly.

3. Make legitimate telephone calls to strangers.

4. Conduct anonymous conversations.

5. Greet strangers.

6. Use the broken-record technique (keep repeating your position without getting upset).

7. Use negative inquiry (press for details about why you are being criticized).

Questions and Activities

1. Why are conflict resolution skills considered so important in a culturally diverse workplace?

2. What differences in goals might management and workers have that would lead to conflict?

3. A manager invites a subordinate to dinner. The subordinate declines the offer, yet the manager repeats the invitation every week for five weeks. Is this persistent asking a form of sexual harassment? Explain.

4. Why are assertion skills useful in dealing with anger?

5. Suppose you are caught speeding by a police officer. Which conflict-resolution method do you think would be best suited to handling the conflict with the officer? Explain.

6. Identify several occupations in which conflict-resolution skills are especially important.

7. Some people contend that if you "make enough noise" you will get your way in a dispute. How does this belief fit any of the tactics described in this chapter?

8. Some people with very successful careers are apparently aggressive, even to the point of being obnoxious. Why, then, is there an emphasis on being assertive on the job?

9. How might negative inquiry be used to help a person learn from his or her mistakes?

10. Ask a successful person how much conflict he or she experiences in balancing the demands of work and personal life. Be prepared to report your findings in class.

REFERENCES

[1]Carl Rogers, "Dealing with Psychological Tensions," *Journal of Applied Behavioral Science,* no. 1, 1956, pp. 12–13.

[2]Quoted in Sybil Evans, "Conflict Can Be Positive," *HRMagazine,* May 1992, p. 50.

[3]Richard J. Mayer, *Conflict Management: The Courage to Confront* (Columbus, Ohio: Batelle Press, 1990).

[4]"High Court to Clarify Hostile Environment," *HRfocus,* May 1993, p. 22.

[5]Robert F. Prorok, "Employer Liability Extends to Customers, Clients, and Vendors," *HRfocus,* November 1993, p. 4.

[6]"The Role of the Manager in the Work/Family Dynamic," *Human Resources Forum,* November 1989, p. 1; "Work/Family Benefits on the Rise," *HRfocus,* January 1992, p. 22.

[7]"Work/Family Benefits on the Rise," p. 22.

[9]John D. Arnold, *When Sparks Fly: Resolving Conflicts in Your Organization* (New York: McGraw-Hill, 1993).

[10]"Workplace Violence: You're Not Immune," *Supervisory Management,* September 1993, pp. 1–2.

A HUMAN RELATIONS CASE PROBLEM: MARKETING VERSUS ENGINEERING*

Wayne Adams, a product development engineer at an electronics firm, was working on a new product with a tight schedule. The product incorporated a large number of high-tech features. Part of the plan was to release the product in different stages. At the early stage, the product would have some of the new features. The final product would have all of the advanced features.

The primary objective of the marketing department was to place the product with suitable customers as soon as possible. Engineering, however, was more concerned about meeting the long-range schedule of a final product that incorporated all the new features.

In the early stages of the project, the marketing team worked closely with the engineering team in trying to evaluate customer needs. The engineering team tried to respond to the requests made by marketing in order to make the product attractive to potential customers. At first the demands were small, and changes were fit into the existing schedule. However, as more marketing people were added to the product, the demands for changes escalated. Each representative had potential customers whose needs could be met with different features. The sales representatives were dependent upon such sales in order to earn commissions, and thus placed pressure on engineering to add features to the product.

One day Wayne received a telephone call from Terry Lemieux, a sales rep in Los Angeles who had been aggressively seeking new features. "We have a customer who's ready to sign for 200 machines, if you can deliver the ultrasound feature," said Terry.

"The ultrasound feature?" replied Wayne in disbelief. "You guys told us that no one would ever use that feature. The ultrasound is not slated until next year. In order to incorporate ultrasound, we would have to have an entire new subsystem. There's no way you can get it until next year."

Terry replied, "Look, we already told the customer we could deliver the product with the ultrasound. There could be some legal problems if you can't come through for us."

"Sorry Terry," replied Wayne. "There's just no way. Even if we dropped everything else from the schedule and started today, we wouldn't finish until late in the year.

Wayne reported the incident about Terry's demands to the lead engineer. The next day the lead engineer received a phone call from the Vice President of Marketing complaining about the engineers' lack of responsiveness to customer needs.

(Continued)

In the following several months, relations between engineering and marketing became even more strained. So much time was spent arguing about whether or not customer demands could or should be met that the project slipped further behind.

Marketing claimed that its representatives were losing confidence in engineering's ability to deliver the new product. As a backup plan, the sales representatives began to push other products. Marketing also claimed that customers were losing confidence in the new product because they had not received the features they were promised.

Engineering responded that the sales representatives were concerned only with earning commissions rather than the long-term success of the product. As the lead engineer said, "If marketing would wait for the finished product, they would really have something worthwhile to sell."

QUESTIONS

1. How would you characterize the nature of the conflict faced by marketing and engineering?

2. What should the company do next about resolving this conflict?

3. How could this conflict have been prevented?

*Case researched by Tamara Randall, Rochester Institute of Technology.

A HUMAN RELATIONS ROLE PLAY: MARKETING VERSUS ENGINEERING

Using the above case history as background information, two students play the roles of marketing representatives of the electronics firm. Two other students play the role of representatives from the engineering department. Conduct a role play in which the representatives from marketing and engineering attempt to resolve their conflict. Prepare by anticipating which specific conflict-resolution technique is likely to work in this situation.

[11]Charles Darwin, *The Expressions of Emotions in Man and Animals* (publisher unknown, 1872).

[12]"How to Buck Your Boss," *Research Institute Personal Report for the Executive,* March 1, 1986, p. 1.

[13]Carol Tarvis, *Anger: The Misunderstood Emotion* (New York: Simon & Schuster, 1990); Nancy Marx Better, "Learning to Handle Anger at Work," *Self,* June 1992, pp. 94–97.

[14]Quoted in Karen S. Peterson, "Holding Grudges Can Hold You Back," *USA Weekend,* October 18–20, 1985, p. 28.

[15]Kenneth Thomas, "Conflict and Conflict Management," in Marvin D. Dunnette (ed.), *Handbook of Industrial and Organizational Psychology* (Chicago: Rand McNally College Publishing, 1976), pp. 900–902.

[16]Joseph D'O'Brian, "Negotiating with Peers: Consensus, Not Power," *Supervisory Management,* January 1992, p. 4.

[17]Adapted from Fred Pryor, "Become 'Pleasantly Assertive,'" *The Pryor Report,* January 1992, p. 3.

[18]Philip Zimbardo, *Shyness: What It Is, What to Do About It* (Reading, Mass.: Addison-Wesley, 1977), pp. 220–26; Kevin Shyne, "Shyness: Breaking Through the Invisible Barrier to Achievement," *Success,* July 1982, pp. 14–16, 36–37, 51.

ADDITIONAL READING

Bisno, Herb. *Managing Conflict.* Newbury Park, Calif.: Sage Publications, 1990.

Bresler, Samuel J., and Thacker, Rebecca. "Four-Point Plan Helps Solve Harassment Problems." *HRMagazine,* May 1993, pp. 117–124.

Karras, Gary. *Negotiate to Close.* New York: Fireside/Simon & Schuster, 1993.

Magid, Renee. *The Work and Family Challenge.* New York: AMA Management Briefing, 1990.

Phillips, Deanne G., Cooke, Jerry A., and Anderson, Amy E. "A Surefire Resolution to Workplace Conflicts." *Personnel Journal,* May 1992, pp. 111–114.

Pinkley, Robin L., and Northcraft, Gregory B. "Conflict Frames of Reference: Implications for Dispute Processes and Outcomes." *Academy of Management Journal,* February 1994, pp. 193–205.

Smith, Bob. "Cease Fire! Preventing Workplace Violence." *HRfocus,* February 1994, pp. 1, 6.

Solomon, Charlene Marmer. "Sexual Harassment after the Thomas Hearings," *Personnel Journal,* December 1991, pp. 32–37.

Terpstra, David E. "Outcomes of Federal Court Decisions on Sexual Harassment." *Academy of Management Journal,* March 1992, pp. 181–90.

Tjosvold, Dean. *Learning to Manage Conflict: Getting People to Work Together Productively.* New York: Lexington Books, 1993.

CHAPTER 8

GETTING ALONG WITH YOUR MANAGER

Learning Objectives

After reading the information and doing the exercises in this chapter you should be able to:

- Recognize the impact your manager has on your future.

- Select several tactics for creating a favorable impression on your present or future manager.

- Select several tactics for dealing with your manager in a constructive manner.

- Prepare to deal effectively with a manager whom you perceive as being intolerable.

*I*mpressing your manager is the most basic strategy of getting ahead in your career. If you cannot gain favor with the boss, it will be difficult to advance to higher positions or earn much more money. Should you clash with one particular manager, you can sometimes be gracefully transferred to another department. Or you can first find a job with another firm and then quit. You will then have another chance to impress the person who recommends you for a salary increase and evaluates your work per-

formance. The principle remains the same—you have to be seen by your immediate superior as a competent person. Your boss is always the person who is contacted first when someone wants to determine what kind of employee you are. Usually this information is sought when you are being considered for transfer, promotion, or for a position with another firm.

In this chapter we present a variety of strategies and tactics that lead to constructive relationships with an immediate superior. The strategies and tactics are grouped for convenience into three categories: creating a favorable impression on your boss, dealing with your boss directly, and coping with an intolerable boss. Some of these tactics might seem like "office politics." Many are political tactics, but of a positive, sensible nature. We are decidedly *not* recommending any underhanded tricks that might prevent your boss or the company from accomplishing work.

Before reading further, do Self-Examination Exercise 8-1. It will sensitize you to the importance of getting along with the boss, even if you do not currently have a boss.

CREATING A FAVORABLE IMPRESSION ON YOUR MANAGER

The strategies and tactics in this section all help you create a favorable impression on the boss. The term *impression* refers to a true impression, not a false one. Following these straightforward suggestions helps you deserve a positive reputation.

SELF-EXAMINATION EXERCISE 8-1:

Are You In with the Boss or Out?

Whether you are part of your boss's in-group or in the out-group can determine the effectiveness of your working relationship. As a member of the in-group, you are given responsibility and support. As an outsider, you miss out on opportunities.

The following questions, taken from a survey developed by George Graen, should give you an indication of where you stand:

1. Do I know if my boss is satisfied with my work?

2. Would my boss bail me out of a jam?

3. Do I feel that our relationship is an effective one?

4. Am I willing to defend my boss when he or she is absent?

5. Does my boss recognize all of my potential?

6. Am I asked for my opinions and advice on work-related issues?

7. Could I influence my boss to take a particular course of action?

If most of your answers are "yes," you are in with the boss. If not, you will need to make an effort to become more cooperative for the sake of effectiveness.

SOURCE: *Research Institute Personal Report for the Executive,* March 1, 1987, p. 6.

DISPLAY GOOD JOB PERFORMANCE

Good performance remains the most vital strategy for impressing your manager. Some bosses seem to be more interested in praise than performance from employees. Nevertheless, the praise—and other forms of office politics—won't do you much good if you do not back it up with job accomplishment. When any rational superior evaluates a subordinate's performance, the first question asked is: "Is this employee getting the job done?" And you cannot get the job done if you are not competent.

Many factors contribute to whether you can become a competent performer. Among them are your education, training, personality characteristics, job experience, and special skills, such as being able to solve problems, resolve conflict, and organize your work. Much of this book discusses skills, techniques, and strategies that are designed to contribute to job competence.

DISPLAY A STRONG WORK ETHIC

A major factor contributing to good job performance is a strong **work ethic,** a firm belief in the dignity and value of work. People with a strong work ethic have strong internal motivation. An employee with a strong work ethic will sometimes be excused if his or her performance is not yet exceptional. This is true because the manager assumes that a strong work ethic will elevate performance eventually. A strong work ethic is more in demand today than ever because organizations are thinly staffed. With fewer people performing the same amount of work, everybody has to work harder. The best overall way to display a strong work ethic is to work hard and enjoy the task. Five specific suggestions follow for demonstrating a strong work ethic.

1. *Demonstrate competence even on minor tasks.* Attack each assignment with the recognition that each task performed well, however minor, is one more career credit. A minor task performed well paves the way for your being given more consequential tasks.

2. *Assume personal responsibility for problems.* An employee with a problem will often approach the manager and say, "We have a tough problem to deal with." The connotation is that the manager should be helping the employee with the problem. A better impression is created when the employee says, "I have a tough problem to deal with, and I would like your advice." This statement implies that you are willing to assume responsibility for the problem and for any mistake you may have made that led to the problem.

3. *Assume responsibility for free-floating problems.* A natural way to display a strong work ethic is to assume responsibility for free-floating (nonassigned) problems. Taking on even a minor task, such as ordering lunch for a meeting that is running late, can enhance the impression one makes on a manager.

4. *Get your projects completed promptly.* A by-product of a strong work ethic is an eagerness to get projects completed promptly. People with a strong work ethic respect deadlines imposed by others. Furthermore, they typically set deadlines of their own more tightly than those imposed by their boss.

5. *Accept undesirable assignments willingly.* Another way of expressing a strong work ethic is to accept undesirable assignments willingly. Look for ways to express the attitude, "Whether or not this assignment is glamorous and fun is a secondary issue. What counts is that it is something that needs doing for the good of the company."

BE DEPENDABLE AND HONEST

Dependability is a critical employee virtue. If an employee can be counted on to deliver as promised, and to be at work regularly, that employee has gone a long way toward impressing the boss. A boss is uncomfortable not knowing whether an important assignment will be accomplished on time. If you are not dependable, you will probably not get your share of important assignments. Honesty is tied to dependability because a dependable employee is honest about when he or she will have an assignment completed.

Dependability and honesty are important at all job levels. One of the highest compliments a manager can pay an employee is to describe the employee as dependable. Conversely, it is considered derogatory to call any employee undependable. As one company president put it when describing a subordinate: "When he's great, he's terrific, but I can't depend on him. I'd rather he be more consistent even if he delivered fewer peak successes—at least I could rely on him."[1]

BE LOYAL

A basic way to impress your manager is to be loyal. Loyalty can be expressed to the supervisor, the department, the division, or the entire firm. In whatever form it is expressed, loyalty tends to foster a good relationship with your immediate superior. A subordinate can express loyalty in many ways other than heaping flattery upon the manager and the department. Loyalty can be expressed through staying with the company, attending company picnics and other functions, using the company's products, or even wearing the company insignia.

An important characteristic of a loyal subordinate is defending the manager when the latter is under attack by people from other departments. Defending your boss under such circumstances does not necessarily mean that you think your boss is entirely correct. You can defend what deserves credit without agreeing with the boss's entire position. Assume your manager was under attack from another department for being late with the processing of materials needed by them. Your manager contends that delays in shipments by suppliers have created the problem. You realize that inefficiencies in the department are also a contributing factor. You might publicly agree with your boss that supplier delays have created problems. In private, you might make suggestions to your boss for improving department efficiency.

APPRECIATE YOUR MANAGER'S STRENGTHS

You may not admire every boss you work for, particularly early in your career. Your young boss might be inexperienced and therefore less than ideal. Older managers you work for early in your career tend to be people who have been passed over for promotion many times. In other words, the company recognizes they are not the strongest supervisors. But they are usually competent enough to perform their jobs satisfactorily.

If you focus only on the weaknesses of your boss, you will probably communicate many negative nonverbal messages to that individual. For instance, when your boss is making general suggestions, you might display a bored expression on your face. Instead of thinking primarily about your boss's weakness, look for strengths. Look for answers to such questions as, "What knowledge does he or she have that can help me advance my career?" "What good points about my boss led to his or her promotion?" or "What do some of my co-workers see as my boss's strengths?"

A case in point is Bruce, a young sales representative. Having recently graduated from business school, Bruce was fired up with modern techniques of selling, such as identifying the customer's most pressing problems. He was somewhat perplexed about why his boss, Arlie, was considered such an outstanding sales manager. He displayed few of the management techniques that Bruce had studied in school. Bruce then spoke to an aunt who worked in another department of the same company. "How come old Arlie is so highly regarded? He doesn't seem to know much about sales techniques or management." Bruce's aunt replied, "You could be right, Bruce. But Arlie knows how to read people and how to form good relationships. He's what is known as a good personal salesman."

From that point on Bruce began to look for techniques of forming good relationships with people that Arlie used. As he showed a sincere interest in learning more from Arlie, their relationship improved.

SHOW AN INTEREST IN YOUR FIRM'S PRODUCTS OR SERVICES

Showing a genuine interest in your company and its products or services impresses superiors in both profit and nonprofit firms. This tactic works because so many workers do not identify with their employers. Many employees are not even familiar with what their organization is trying to accomplish. A natural opportunity for showing interest in your firm's products and services is to promote them. Find a way to promote your company's products or services and you will endear yourself to top management. The next step is to casually mention that you are actively using the product. As an administrative assistant working for a printer manufacturer told a vice president:

> My husband and I bought one of our desktop color printers two years ago. We've become the neighborhood print shop whenever somebody wants to prepare a fancy graphic. So far, the printer has never been back for service. Our neighbors are so impressed with the printer that two of them plan to buy one of their own.

STEP OUTSIDE YOUR JOB DESCRIPTION

Job descriptions are characteristic of a well-organized firm. If everybody knows what he or she is supposed to be doing there will be much less confusion, and goals will be achieved. This logic sounds impressive, but job descriptions have a major downside. If people engage only in work included in their job description, an "It's not my job" mentality pervades. An effective way to impress your manager is therefore to demonstrate that you are not constrained by a job description. If something needs doing, you will get it done whether or not it is your formal responsibility. Such was the case with a computer programmer in an insurance company.

> Pierre, a computer programmer, volunteered to research how the company's personal computers could be made more accessible to the visually handicapped. As part of his research, Pierre contacted several computer manufacturers. One of the devices uncovered was a system that converted printed information into synthesized voice. The programmer's immediate superior and the vice president of information systems sent him a joint letter congratulating his initiative.

ANTICIPATE PROBLEMS

A highly alert worker anticipates problems even when the manager had not planned to work on them. Anticipating problems is characteristic of a resourceful person who exercises initiative. Instead of working exclusively on problems that have been handed to him or her, the worker has the insight to look for future problems. (This tactic is thus a variation of stepping outside one's job description.) Anticipating problems impresses most managers because it reflects an entrepreneurial, take-charge attitude.

DEALING DIRECTLY WITH YOUR MANAGER

To develop a good relationship with your manager you need to create a favorable impression, as already described. You also need to focus directly on your relationship with your manager in terms of your work transactions with him or her. In this section we emphasize techniques geared more toward transactions with the boss than focusing on the impression you create. (Do not be concerned about overlap in the categories.)

UNDERSTAND YOUR MANAGER

A crucial aspect of developing a good working relationship with the boss is to understand the boss, including the environment in which the boss works. An important starting point in understanding your manager is to recognize his or her style. A **style** is a person's way of doing things. Walter St. John identifies some questions that need to be answered to understand one's manager.[2]

1. What is your manager's position in the company hierarchy? What are his or her relationships with his or her manager?

2. What are your manager's blind spots, prejudices, pet peeves, and sore spots? What constitute positive and negative words to your manager?

3. Does you manager understand better as a reader (should you send a memo) or as a listener (should you tell him or her in person)?

4. Is you manager a morning or evening person? When is the best time of the day to approach your manager?

5. What is your manager's preference for getting things done?

6. What is most important to your manager?

7. What nonverbal signals does your manager communicate to you?

Finding answers to these questions, including understanding your manager's style, may involve discussions with co-workers as well as with the boss directly. Concentrate on "how" questions, such as "This is my first report for Julie. How does she like it done? Does she want a one-page summary at the beginning of the report or at the end?" Speaking to co-workers can also reveal what kinds of attitudes your boss expects you to have. For example, does the boss really believe that the customer is always right? Your question may also reveal that your manager is jumping to please a demanding superior. If this is true, you may be expected to do the same.[3]

FIND OUT WHAT YOUR MANAGER EXPECTS OF YOU

You have little chance of doing a good job and impressing your manager unless you know what you are trying to accomplish.[4] Understanding your immediate superior's goals and the priorities attached to these goals is a good starting point. Working toward a goal, such as "Set up an information system for our warehouse by the end of the month," will help keep you on track.

Unfortunately not every boss uses goal setting. Nor does every boss give you a clear statement of performance standards for your job. A **performance standard** is a statement of what constitutes acceptable performance. To get around this dilemma, career specialist Shirley Sloan Fader offers this advice: "Your boss, like most human beings, won't always spell out precisely what is expected of you. It's up to you to determine this."[5]

The answer to what is expected of you can be surprising. Jeremy took a position as a management trainee in a bank. Wanting to do a good job, Jeremy actively campaigned among people in his network to transfer their checking accounts to the bank. Jeremy asked his manager, "I take it an important part of my job is to bring new accounts to the bank. That's what I've been doing with good results so far." The manager replied, "No, Jeremy, we actually lose money on most small checking accounts. If you are going to attract new business to the bank, make sure it's individuals who maintain large balances. Business accounts are even better."

RESPECT YOUR MANAGER'S AUTHORITY

A common complaint about modern society is that respect for authority is decreasing. According to this sentiment, people in positions of authority such as police workers, physicians, lawyers, politicians, teachers, and managers are not treated with as much respect today as they were in the past. Many of these people would appreciate receiving more respect for their authority. You can use this factor to help develop a good relationship with your manager. By showing appropriate respect for his or her authority, you can win points.

Here are a few statements that might appeal to a manager's sense of authority without making you appear unduly status conscious:

"Yes, sir, that sounds like a good idea."

"Yes, ma'am, that sounds like a good idea."

"Okay, coach, what do I do now?"

"As the head of this department, what do you think we should do about this?"

"In your experience, what is the best way to go about handling this problem?"

Another authority-related issue is whether to address your manager by his or her first name. In almost every place of work outside of medical settings, some colleges and schools, a few conservative banks, and some retail stores, subordinates are encouraged to call superiors by their first names. Local custom, of course, will prevail. You might also ask your boss how he or she prefers to be addressed. Nevertheless, you are probably safe in using a title and last name to address your boss when visitors are around. Titles such as Mr., Miss, Ms., Sir, Madam, Doctor, Professor, Chief, Coach, and Captain send out the message that you respect your manager's authority. Most superiors will be pleased by that attitude.

SHARE YOUR ACCOMPLISHMENTS WITH YOUR MANAGER

Most higher-level jobs are team efforts. If you make a contribution, it is usually a shared one. A person who successfully completes a big project, such as formulating a proposal for reducing the company's health care costs, has received help from many people. Input and encouragement from the boss are usually part of the help received. Upon successful completion of the project, share credit for the accomplishment with your manager. The credit sharing reflects good courtesy on your part, and will help you cement the relationship.

Listen to Your Manager's Problems and Suggestions

A straightforward method of supporting your manager is to be a patient listener. Active listening to your boss can take several forms: listening to personal problems; asking for suggestions and then following them; nodding with enthusiasm and smiling when the boss speaks; and taking notes during a meeting.

Listening to your manager's problems can be very productive. A sympathetic subordinate is sometimes just the person the boss needs for thinking through a problem. To indicate that you might be a good listener, stop talking about your own problems, and ask one or two open-ended questions such as:

"How is your work going?"

"How have all these cutbacks in the firm affected your work?"

"How are you doing in selling your own house?"

Another way of displaying a willingness to listen is to show an interest whenever the boss begins to discuss work or even personal problems. If your manager says, "Those people in the home office are driving a hard bargain," you might say, "A hard bargain?" Most of the listening tips discussed in Chapter 6 would apply to relationships with the immediate superior.

Bring Forth Solutions as Well as Problems

An advanced tactic for developing a good working relationship with your immediate superior is to bring to your boss's attention solutions, not just problems. Too often, subordinates ask to see their bosses only when they have problems requiring help. A boss under pressure may thus anticipate additional pressure when a subordinate asks for an appointment. The subordinate who comes forth with a solved problem is thus regarded as a welcome relief. In short, you can ease your manager's suffering by walking into his or her office and saying, "Here's what I did about that mess that was plaguing us yesterday. Everything is under control now."

Minimize Complaints

In the previous chapter we extolled the virtues of being open and honest in expressing your feelings and opinions. Nevertheless, this type of behavior when carried to excess could earn you a reputation as a whiner. Few managers want to have a group member around who constantly complains about working conditions, co-workers, working hours, pay, and so forth. An employee who complains too loudly and frequently quickly becomes labeled a pill or a pest.

Another important reason a boss usually dislikes having a subordinate who complains too much is that listening to these complaints takes up considerable time. Most managers spend a disproportionate amount of time listening to the problems of a small number of ineffective or complaining employees. Consciously or unconsciously, a manager who has to listen to many of your complaints may find a way to seek revenge.

> Diane was the supervisor of a small group of computer programmers working for an insurance company. Her biggest employee problem was Henry, a programmer with four years of job experience. Henry loudly complained about matters such as the computers owned by the company, the wages, the food in the cafeteria, the music piped into the office, and his rate of advancement. As part of a productivity campaign, the company decided to run the computer operations twenty-four hours a day, instead of twelve. In this way, they could get by with fewer computer employees. Diane placed Henry's name at the top of the list for assignment to the midnight to eight o'clock shift. Henry complained bitterly to Diane about his new assignment. She retorted calmly, "Go complain to your new boss, the night supervisor. But I doubt it will do you much good. He doesn't care for that shift either."

How then does an employee make valid complaints to the manager? The answer is to complain only when justified. And when you do offer a complaint, back it up with a recommended solution. Anyone can take potshots at something. The valuable employee is the person who backs up these complaints with a constructive action plan. Following are two examples of complaints, backed up by action plans for remedying the complaint:

1. "I've noticed that several of us get very tired feet by the end of the working day. Maybe we could perform this work just as well if we sat on high stools."

2. "We have a difficult time handling emergency requests when you are away from the department. I would suggest that when you will be away for more than one or two hours, one of us can serve as the acting supervisor. It could be done on a rotating basis to give each of us some supervisory experience."

TAKE CRITICISM GRACEFULLY

Many managers feel uncomfortable criticizing employees, and therefore prefer to reserve criticism for when it is urgently needed. A group member who rebels against criticism makes the boss's job all the more difficult. Accepting valid criticism is thus another way of showing support for your boss. A marketing director said, "I dread performance reviews with people who won't learn from them. I'm telling them what doesn't work, and they sit there defending their actions instead of taking it to heart."[6]

AVOID BYPASSING YOUR MANAGER

A good way to embarrass and sometimes infuriate your manager is to repeatedly go to his or her superior with your problems, conflicts, and complaints. Such bypasses have at least two strongly negative connotations. One is that you don't believe your boss has the power to take care of your problem. Another is that you distrust his or her judgment in the matter at hand. A third is that you are secretly launching a complaint against your manager.

The boss bypass is looked upon so negatively that most experienced managers will not listen to your problem unless you have already discussed it with your immediate superior.[7] There *are* times, however, when running around your manager is necessary; for example, when you have been unable to resolve a conflict directly with him or her (see the following section). But even under these circumstances, you should politely inform your manager that you are going to take up your problem with the next level of management.

In short, if you want to keep on the good side of your manager, bring all problems directly to him or her. If your boss is unable or unwilling to take care of the problem, you might consider contacting your boss's superior. Nonetheless, considerable tact and diplomacy are needed. Do not imply that your manager is incompetent, but merely that you would like another opinion about the issues at stake.

KEEP YOUR MANAGER INFORMED

An effective way of sustaining a good relationship with your manager is to assume responsibility for keeping him or her informed about all aspects of your job. This would include information concerning tasks that were completed successfully and those that were not. Keeping a manager informed does not have to be time-consuming. All a worker needs to do is to say, for example: "Yesterday you asked me to ship the Cleveland order by noon today and report back. Well, I just thought you would like to know that it left on the truck this morning at 8:30."

Successes should be communicated to the manager to minimize the chances of having one's performance judged as "meets expectations." At promotion and raise time there is a big difference between being judged average and above average. Reporting on unsuccessful tasks is important because the boss may misinterpret why things went wrong. He or she may attach too much blame to you if a logical alternative explanation for the problem is not presented.[8]

STAY IN TOUCH

A surprising aspect of many jobs today is the amount of freedom from supervision they offer. If you have a busy manager who is frequently off to meetings in other parts of the firm or out of town, you might see that person infrequently. Also, many supervisors become so preoccupied with their own paperwork or electronic work they neglect to spend enough time with subordinates. The employee who prefers to avoid being supervised closely would enjoy circumstances such as those just described.

Despite this absence of close supervision, it is still important to have some contact with your manager if you want to maintain a good superior–subordinate relationship. Many employees who are aware of the importance of cultivating the boss develop a reason for seeing their boss, even if an urgent reason does not exist. Their tactics include getting a reaction to a routine memo or asking for clarification of a problem. However, a risk exists of being seen as a pest or an indecisive person if you overdo the principle of staying in touch.

What valid reasons can you think of for asking to see your boss?

USE DISCRETION IN SOCIALIZING WITH YOUR MANAGER

A constant dilemma facing employees is how much and what type of socializing with the manager is appropriate. Advocates of socializing contend that off-the-job friendships lead to more natural work relationships. Opponents of socializing with the boss say that it leads to **role confusion** (being uncertain about what role you are carrying out). For example, how can your manager make an objective decision about your salary increase on Monday morning when he or she had dinner with you on Sunday? To avoid cries of favoritism, you might be recommended for a below-average increase.

One guideline to consider is to have cordial social relationships with the manager of the same kind shared by most employees. "Cordial" socializing includes activities such as company-sponsored parties, group invitations to the boss's home, and business lunches. Individual social activities, such as camping with the boss, double-dating, and so forth, are more likely to lead to role confusion.

Socializing should not include a casual romantic involvement. Romantic involvements between a superior and a subordinate are disruptive to work and morale. Co-workers usually suspect that the manager's special friend is getting special treatment and resent the favoritism.

What should you do if you and your boss seem suited for a long-term commitment? Why walk away from Mr. or Ms. Right? My suggestion is that if you do become romantically involved, one of you should request a transfer to another department. Many office romances do lead to happy marriages and other long-term relationships. At the start of the relationship, however, use considerable discretion. Engaging in personal conversation during work time, or holding hands in the company cafeteria, is unprofessional and taboo.

TAKE THE INITIATIVE IN GETTING TO KNOW A NEW MANAGER

A special challenge faces those who want to build a good relationship with a superior in the current business environment. Organization structures (charts of who reports to whom) change so rapidly that you may have a series of new managers. The boss you have worked hard to build a relationship with suddenly moves on. You now have to start all over again.

A recommended approach here is to request a "get acquainted" meeting with your new manager. Discuss what you are currently doing in your job, and what new responsibilities you think you should be assuming. The new manager may decide that much of what you are now doing is less important than assignments he or she has in mind.[9] As a result, you will now be working on tasks that will enhance your reputation in your organizational unit.

Resolve Competing Demands of Two Bosses

A substantial change in the modern workplace is that many workers report to more than one manager. A typical arrangement is for a person to report to a manager in his or her regular or *home* department. At the same time the person also reports to the head of a project or task force. Many people like this arrangement because it adds variety and excitement to the workday. An unfortunate consequence of having two bosses, however, is that one might be caught in conflict. One boss might make a demand that is incompatible with a demand made by the other boss. You might be asked to attend two meetings at the same time, or told by both bosses that some task has to be done immediately.

A recommendation for resolving the competing demands of two managers is to assemble a list of possible solutions that you can sell to both parties. After you have prepared your solutions, explain to both managers the pros and cons of each solution. Recommend which one you think would work best, and describe how it would be implemented. Get a reaction from each manager. After you have taken the steps just indicated, you and the two bosses might have a three-way discussion to resolve the issue.[10] The three of you might decide, for example, that the only way you can get both their projects done immediately is to hire an office temporary for the duration of the project.

Engage in Favorable Interactions with Your Manager

The many techniques described above support the goal of engaging in favorable interactions with your manager. A study of interactions between bank employees and their supervisors showed that purposely trying to create a positive impression on the supervisor led to better performance ratings.[11] Although the finding is not surprising, it is reassuring to know that it is backed by quantitative evidence. Self-Examination Exercise 8-2 contains a listing of behaviors used by employees in the study to create positive interactions with their supervisors.

 # COPING WITH A PROBLEM MANAGER

Up to this point we have prescribed tactics for dealing with a reasonably rational boss. At some point in their careers many people face the situation of dealing with a problem manager—one who makes it difficult for the subordinate to get the job done. The problem is sometimes attributed to the boss's personality or incompetence. At other times, differences in values or goals could be creating the problem. Our concern here is with constructive approaches to dealing with the delicate situation of working for a problem manager.

SELF-EXAMINATION EXERCISE 8-2:

Supervisor Interaction Checklist

Use the following behaviors as a checklist for achieving favorable interactions with your present manager or a future one. The more of these actions you are engaged in, the higher the probability that you are building a favorable relationship with your manager.

1. Agree with your supervisor's major opinions outwardly even when you disagree inwardly.   _____

2. Take an immediate interest in your supervisor's personal life.   _____

3. Praise your supervisor on his or her accomplishments.   _____

4. Do personal favors for your supervisor.   _____

5. Do something as a personal favor for your supervisor even though you are not required to do it.   _____

6. Volunteer to help your supervisor on a task.   _____

7. Compliment your supervisor on his or her dress or appearance.   _____

8. Present yourself to your supervisor as being a friendly person.   _____

9. Agree with your supervisor's major ideas.   _____

10. Present yourself to your supervisor as being a polite person.   _____

SOURCE: Adapted from Sandy J. Wayne and Gerald R. Ferris, "Influence Tactics, Affect, and Exchange Quality in Supervisor-Subordinate Interactions: A Laboratory Experiment and Field Study," *Journal of Applied Psychology*, October 1990, p. 494.

REEVALUATE YOUR MANAGER

As noted by J. Kenneth Matejka and Richard J. Dunsing, some problem managers are not really a problem. Instead, they have been misperceived by one or more group members. Some employees think they have problem managers when those bosses simply have major role, goal, or value differences. (A role in this context is the expectations of the job.) The problem might also lie in conflicting personalities, such as being outgoing or shy. Another problem is conflicting perspectives, such as being detail-oriented as opposed to taking an overall perspective.

The differences just noted can be good or bad, depending on how they are viewed and used. For example, a combination of a detail-oriented group member with an "overall perspective" boss can be a winning combination.[12]

LEARN FROM YOUR MANAGER'S MISTAKES

Just as you can learn from watching your manager do things right, you can also learn from watching him or her do things wrong. In the first instance, we are talking about using your manager as a positive model. "Modeling" of this type is an important source of learning on the job. Using a superior as a negative model can also be of some benefit. As an elementary example, if your manager criticized you in public, and you felt humiliated, you would have learned a good lesson in effective supervision: Never criticize a subordinate publicly. By serving as a negative example your manager has taught you a valuable lesson.

An unfortunate mistake some workers make is to yell at their manager when he or she has made a mistake (such as yelling at *you* in public).

WHAT TO DO WHEN YOUR MANAGER IGNORES YOUR SUGGESTIONS

One subtype of a problem manager is the one who ignores suggestions because he or she prefers to maintain the status quo. These managers see their jobs as simply running a smooth operation, and they perceive employees who continue to bring forth suggestions as troublemakers. The problem with not bringing forth innovative ideas is that you will never earn the reputation of being imaginative and ambitious.

A management research report offers several suggestions for coping with this form of problem manager. One approach is to implement your idea without his or her approval. If your idea works out well, your manager may embrace your suggestion. Another tactic is to cultivate your boss's superior. Tactfully tell your boss's boss about your innovative idea. He or she might support your idea and give you the green light to implement it.[13]

A real problem with cultivating your boss's boss is that a boss bypass is generally frowned upon. However, so long as you do not say or imply anything negative about your manager, it could be worth a try. You might say to his or her superior, "I have brought this to McHendry's [your boss] attention, but she's too busy with other projects now to dig into my proposal."

WHAT TO DO WHEN YOUR MANAGER TAKES CREDIT FOR YOUR ACCOMPLISHMENTS

Imagine that you have been assigned the job of making the arrangements for a company meeting. Everything runs so smoothly that at the banquet your manager is praised for his or her fine job of arranging the meeting. You smolder while he or she accepts all the praise without mentioning that you did all the work. How should you handle a problem manager of this type—one who takes credit for your accomplishments?

Remember, first, that in one sense your manager does deserve much of the credit. Managers are responsible for the accomplishments and failures of their subordinates. Your boss had the good sense to delegate the task to the right person. Nevertheless, a self-confident manager would share the credit with you. To get the credit you deserve for your ideas and accomplishments, try these suggestions:

1. *Supply the pieces, but let others fit them together.* Suppose, for example, you were talking to your boss's boss at the company meeting mentioned above. You might state, "I'm happy that people enjoyed this meeting. I enjoyed being given so much responsibility for helping our department arrange this meeting." Your boss's boss may get the point without your disputing what your manager said.

2. *Try a discreet confrontation.* The manager who is taking credit for your accomplishments may not realize that you are being slighted. A quiet conversation about the issue could prevent recurrences. You might gently ask, for example, "At what point do I get recognition for doing an assigned task well? I noticed that my name was not mentioned when our department received credit for setting up a new billing system." (It was you who did 95 percent of the work on the system.)

3. *Take preventive measures.* A sensible way to receive credit for your accomplishments is to let others know of your efforts *while* you are doing the work. This is more effective than looking for recognition after your manager has already taken credit for your accomplishments. Casually let others know what you are doing, including your boss's boss and other key people. In this way you will not sound immodest or aggressive—you are only talking about your work.

4. *Present a valid reason for seeking recognition.* By explaining why you want recognition, you will not seem unduly ambitious or pushy to your manager. You might say "I am trying to succeed in this company. It would help me to document my performance. Would it therefore be possible for my name to also appear on the report of the new billing system?"[14]

How to Work with a Disorganized Boss

Many well-organized people report to disorganized managers, creating the opportunity for tension and personality clashes. Under these circumstances, the well-organized subordinate faces the challenge of creating a good working relationship. In contrast, a well-organized boss is unlikely to put up with a disorganized subordinate for long. Given that the well-organized group member cannot readily fire the boss, he or she faces the task of forever compensating for the boss's disorganization. For example, many assistants have to spend time searching for the misplaced files of their boss—both hard-copy and disk files.

According to management consultant Deborah Zeigler, you can take several steps to facilitate a good working relationship with a disorganized manager.[15] Begin by identifying goals and priorities. Find out what the organization and department are attempting to accomplish, and what your boss expects of you. This basic information can be used as a wedge to encourage your boss to be better organized.

The second step is to communicate your concerns to your manager about how his or her work habits could be interfering with goal attainment. Tact and diplomacy are essential. You might say, for example, "I want to prepare a chart explaining our need for more salespeople, but I can't do it without the figures you promised me last week."

Third, rely on co-workers and others throughout the company to supplement your boss as an information source. When your manager is unavailable (disorganized people are often difficult to find), or does not have the information you need, network members might be able to help. In the example above, maybe somebody else can provide the figures you need.

A fourth step is to become familiar with your boss's primary problems in organization. If you know your manager has difficulty getting projects completed on time, step in well before the deadline to offer encouragement and assistance. You might present a chart to your boss estimating how close the project should be to completion. If you offer help, rather than criticism, your contribution will be valued.

How to Gently Get Away from Your Manager

Perhaps you have tried long and hard to develop a better working relationship with your manager but the situation is still intolerable. Three alternatives remain: You can wait for your manager to leave; you can leave the company; or you can look for a job in the same firm. It generally makes the most sense to pursue the last course of action, particularly if you are satisfied with the firm.

The major strategy for getting away from your supervisor is to market yourself to other key managers in the company.[16] Make others aware of your accomplishments through such means as volunteering for committee work or getting your name in the company newsletter. Another method is to make personal contacts through such means as joining company teams or clubs.

While you are developing your contacts, speak to your manager about a transfer. Point out that although you are satisfied with your job, you value broad experience at this point in your career. Unfortunately, weak managers generally are reluctant to recommend subordinates for transfer.

Another recommended approach is to speak directly to the human resources department about your dilemma. Point out quietly that you want to be considered a candidate for transfer to another department. Suggest that you could make a bigger contribution if you worked for a manager who gave you more responsibility. However, never say anything derogatory about your present manager. Such a practice is strictly taboo.

SUMMARY

Developing a favorable relationship with your manager is the most basic strategy of getting ahead in your career. Your manager influences your future because he or she is often asked by other prospective superiors to present an opinion about your capabilities.

A general strategy for developing a good relationship with your manager is to create a favorable impression. Specific tactics of this type include:

1. Display good job performance.
2. Display a strong work ethic.
3. Be dependable and honest.
4. Be loyal.
5. Appreciate your manager's strengths.
6. Show an interest in your firm's products or services.
7. Step outside your job description.
8. Anticipate problems.

Many tactics for developing a good relationship with your manager require that you deal directly with him or her, including:

1. Understand your manager.
2. Find out what your manager expects of you.
3. Respect your manager's authority.
4. Share your accomplishments with your manager.
5. Listen to your manager's problems and suggestions.
6. Bring forth solutions as well as problems.
7. Minimize complaints.
8. Take criticism gracefully.
9. Avoid bypassing your boss.
10. Keep your manager informed.
11. Stay in touch with your manager.
12. Use discretion in socializing with your manager.
13. Take the initiative in getting to know a new manager.
14. Resolve competing demands of two bosses.
15. Engage in favorable interactions with your manager.

Coping with a manager you perceive to be a problem is part of getting along with him or her. Reevaluate your boss to make sure you have not misperceived him or her. One approach to handling the problem manager is to learn from his or her mistakes. When your boss ignores your suggestions you may have to take steps such as implementing your idea without approval. If your idea works, your manager might embrace your suggestions.

When your manager takes credit for your accomplishments, consider these tactics: Give enough information to others so they can figure out what you have done, discreetly confront your manager, take preventive measures by keeping others informed of work in progress, and present a valid reason for seeking recognition.

Working with a disorganized manager can lead to tension and a personality clash. Under these circumstances, tactfully explain how your manager's work habits create problems in attaining work goals. Rely on others to help you attain the information you need to accomplish work for your boss. Also, recognize your boss's biggest problems in organization and offer direct assistance.

When your relationship with your manager does not improve it may be necessary to seek a transfer. The best method is to market yourself to other key managers in the company. This may involve establishing a network of contacts. Also, speak to your manager about a transfer without speaking of dissatisfaction, and present your case to the human resources department.

Questions and Activities

1. Suppose your manager reads this chapter. How might this influence the effectiveness of your using the strategies and tactics described here?

2. Identify three of the tactics described in this chapter that you are most likely to use. Explain.

3. Identify three of the tactics described in this chapter that you are the least likely to use. Explain.

4. If it appeared to you that you were "out" with the boss, what could you do to get "in"?

5. Is this chapter simply about "kissing up to the boss"? Explain.

6. How can a person be graceful about apparently unjustified criticism from the manager?

7. Describe a situation in which you think it would be justifiable to bypass your manager.

8. How do policies about sexual harassment influence socializing between managers and group members?

9. Suppose you and a co-worker are best friends. Your friend gets promoted and becomes your manager. What should be your policy about socializing with this person?

10. Interview an experienced manager. Ask his or her opinion about what an employee can do to create a favorable impression.

A HUMAN RELATIONS CASE PROBLEM: THE BOSS BYPASS[17]

Fred was a hard-working supervisor whose demonstrated ability gave him a strong shot at a middle-management position. One morning Fred was reviewing next year's budget. He was distressed when he discovered that his budget was being cut and that he was losing one person in his department. "Sorry, things are tight and there's nothing we can do," said his manager, Ruth. Later, Fred found out that Phil, another supervisor (whose division was doing poorly), was getting a budget increase. Fred became furious and said to himself, "Of course Phil gets what he wants. He's always so buddy-buddy with Ruth."

Phil did take time to chat with Ruth. He would ask about her grandchild, and offer to have lunch together. Fred had a cordial relationship with Ruth, but he mostly kept to himself and tended to his job.

Fred thought over who in the company might be able to help him work out his dispute with Ruth. He remembered that he and the president had struck up an acquaintance when they met at a music concert several months ago. "Maybe if I talk to him," Fred thought, "I can get my budget restored."

Fred sent an E-mail message to the president's office justifying why he wanted his budget and group member restored. The president thought Fred's points were sound, and he requested that Ruth reverse her decision. Although miffed, Ruth complied with the president's request.

Fred was relieved at first, but Ruth started making life miserable for him. Working over the problem in his head, Fred thought there might be one way Ruth would change her attitude toward him. "Maybe a well-placed memo asking why Ruth was never available until eleven in the morning, or saying that I can't ever talk with her because she's always showing Phil photos of her grandchild, might work."

Fred sent another electronic message to his "friend" the president, sending a copy to Ruth. He didn't hear from the president, but he did hear from Ruth. "I'm putting you on notice," she said, "for gross insubordination."

Fred said calmly, "We'll see about that." He then returned to his office and put a call through to the president, who was in a day-long meeting. Finally, at 3:00 P.M. the president called and asked him to come to his office. "Ah, sweet revenge," thought Fred.

"I understand you're not happy here, Fred," said the president.

"But . . ." Fred tried to protest.

(Continued)

"You know we would hate to lose someone as competent as you, but I do have some connections in other companies. I strongly suggest you let me help you find a suitable position elsewhere."

QUESTIONS

1. What errors in boss relationships did Fred commit?

2. How might Fred have attempted to improve his relationship with Ruth?

3. How should Fred respond to the president's suggestion about looking for another job elsewhere?

A HUMAN RELATIONS ROLE PLAY: DISCUSSING A SENSITIVE ISSUE WITH YOUR MANAGER

Assume Fred decided to work directly with Ruth rather than go the president with the budget controversy. Assume also Fred did learn about Phil receiving a budget increase. One student plays the role of Fred who is trying to get back in good graces with Ruth. Another student plays the role of Ruth, who has granted Fred an appointment to further discuss the budget issue. The person who plays the role of Fred should work diligently at creating a favorable impression on Ruth.

REFERENCES

[1]William A. Cohen and Nuritt Cohen, "Get Promoted Fast," *Success,* July/August 1985, p. 6.

[2]Walter D. St. John, "Successful Communications Between Supervisors and Employees," *Personnel Journal,* January 1983, p. 76.

[3]John J. Gabarro and John P. Kotter, "Managing Your Boss," *Harvard Business Review,* May–June 1993, p. 152. (*HBR Classic* reprint of article originally published in January–February 1980.)

[4]Marilyn Moats Kennedy, "How to Manage Your New Boss," *Business Week Careers,* March–April 1987, p. 93.

[5]Shirley Sloan Fader, "What Your Boss Wants You to Know," *Business Week's Guide to Careers,* October 1985, p. 3.

[6]Judith Meyers, "Corporate Star Quality: How to Shine Better than Your Competition," *Woman's Day,* March 5, 1987, p. 162.

[7]Jay T. Knippen and Thad B. Green, "Why Keeping Your Boss Informed Benefits You," *Supervisory Management,* January 1990, pp. 10–11. The quote in this section is also from the same article.

[8]"Not-So-Dangerous Liaisons," *Executive Strategies,* February 6, 1990, p. 90; Kathleen Neville, *Corporate Attractions* (Washington, D.C.: Acropolis Books, 1990).

[9]"New Boss? Avoid the Negative," *Executive Communications,* September 1988, p. 8.

[10]Jay T. Knippen, Thad B. Green, and Kurt M. Sutton, "How to Handle Problems with Two Bosses," *Supervisory Management,* August 1991, p. 7.

[11]Sandy J. Wayne and Gerald R. Ferris, "Influence Tactics, Affect, and Exchange Quality in Supervisor—Subordinate Interactions: A Laboratory Experiment and Field Study," *Journal of Applied Psychology,* October 1990, pp. 487–99.

[12]J. Kenneth Matejka and Richard Dunsing, "Managing the Baffling Boss," *Personnel,* February 1989, p. 50.

[13]Ibid.

[14]*How to Win at Organizational Politics—Without Being Unethical or Sacrificing Your Self-Respect* (New York: The Research Institute of America, January 1985), pp. 7–8.

[15]"How to Work with a Disorganized Boss," *The Office Professional,* January 1994, pp. 1, 3–4.

[16]D. Keith Denton, "Survival Tactics: Coping with Incompetent Bosses," *Personnel Journal,* April 1985, p. 68.

[17]Adapted from George Milite, "Office Politics: It's Still Out There," *Supervisory Management,* July 1992, pp. 6–7.

ADDITIONAL READING

DuBrin, Andrew J. *Stand Out!: 330 Ways to Gain the Edge with Bosses, Subordinates, Co-Workers, Subordinates and Customers.* Englewood Cliffs, N.J.: Prentice Hall, 1993.

Eigen, Barry. *How to Think Like a Boss and Get Ahead at Work.* New York: Lyle Stuart, 1990.

Germer, Jim G. *How to Make Your Boss Work for You: More than 200 Hard-Hitting Strategies, Tips and Tactics to Keep Your Career on the Fast Track.* Burr Ridge, Ill.: Business One Irwin, 1992.

Grothe, Mardy, and Wylie, Peter. *Problem Bosses.* New York: Facts on File Publications, 1987.

Pfeffer, Jeffrey. *Managing with Power: Politics and Influence in Organizations.* Boston, Mass.: Harvard Business School Press, 1992.

CHAPTER 9

GETTING ALONG WITH CO-WORKERS AND CUSTOMERS

Learning Objectives

After studying the information and doing the exercises in this chapter you should be able to:

- Increase your awareness of the importance of establishing good co-worker relationships.

- Describe methods of taking the initiative to get along with co-workers.

- Know how to become a team player.

- Describe methods of reacting constructively to the behavior of co-workers.

- Describe methods of building good relationships with customers.

- Enhance your understanding of how to appreciate diversity among co-workers and customers.

*A*nyone with work experience is aware of the importance of getting along with co-workers and customers (including clients and patients). If you are unable to work cooperatively with others in the workplace, it will be difficult for you to do your job. You need their cooperation and they need yours. Furthermore, the leading reason employees are terminated is not poor technical skill but inability or unwillingness to form satisfactory relationships with others on the job.

In this chapter we describe a variety of strategies and tactics to help you gain favor or avoid disfavor with co-workers and customers. For convenience these approaches are divided into taking the initiative with co-workers, responding to co-workers, customer relationships, and appreciating diversity among co-workers and customers.

TAKING THE INITIATIVE IN CO-WORKER RELATIONSHIPS

The methods and tactics in this section have one common thread—they all require you to take the initiative in establishing good relationships with co-workers. Instead of reacting to the behavior of a co-worker, you launch an offensive of goodwill. Expressed another way, you are *proactive* instead of *reactive*. Later we deal with reactive methods of getting along with co-workers. Remember, however, that several of the tactics and methods could fit into either category.

DEVELOP ALLIES THROUGH GOOD FEELINGS

People who are courteous, kind, cooperative and cheerful develop allies and friends in the workplace. Storing up this reservoir of good feeling involves practicing basic good manners such as being pleasant and friendly. It also involves not snooping, spreading malicious gossip, or weaseling out of group presents such as shower or retirement gifts. In addition, it is important to be available to co-workers who want your advice as well as your help in times of crisis.[1]

Everyone knows that you gain more allies by being optimistic and positive than by being pessimistic and negative. Nevertheless, many people ignore this simple strategy for getting along well with others. Co-workers are more likely to solicit your opinion or offer you help when you are perceived to be a cheerful person.

From the supervisor's standpoint, an optimistic and positive employee is a greater asset than an employee with the opposite disposition. People who chronically complain are a drag on the morale of other employees in the office. People with a positive attitude tend to be asked first to try out new techniques and procedures. The reason is that they are more willing to accept change than are people with a negative outlook.

Another way of creating good feelings is to keep a large deposit in the "favor bank." This tactic is based on the idea that if you make deposits in the favor bank, other people owe you favors. Ways of making deposits include building goodwill and looking for favors you can do. You should also take credit discreetly for your favors.[2] For example, if you handled a customer complaint for a co-worker who was on break, let him or her know but do not inform the manager.

MAKE OTHER PEOPLE FEEL IMPORTANT

A fundamental principle of fostering good relationships with co-workers and others is to make them feel important. Sheila Murray Bethela advises us to make use of the Please-Make-Me-Feel-Important concept. Visualize that every one in the workplace is wearing a small sign around the neck that says, "Please make me feel important."[3] Although the leader has primary responsibility for satisfying this recognition need, co-workers also play a key role. One approach to making a co-worker feel important would

SELF-AWARENESS EXERCISE 9-1:

How Important Do I Make People Feel?

Indicate on a one-to-five scale how frequently you act (or would act if the situation presented itself) in the ways indicated below: very infrequently (VI); infrequently (I); sometimes (S); frequently (F); very frequently (VF). Circle the number underneath the column that best fits your answer.

	VI	I	S	F	VF
1. I do my best to correctly pronounce a co-worker's name.	1	2	3	4	5
2. I avoid letting other people's egos get too big.	5	4	3	2	1
3. I brag to others about the accomplishments of my co-workers.	1	2	3	4	5
4. I recognize the birthdays of friends in a tangible way.	1	2	3	4	5
5. It makes me anxious to listen to others brag about their accomplishments.	5	4	3	2	1
6. After hearing that a friend has done something outstanding, I shake his or her hand.	1	2	3	4	5
7. If a friend or co-worker recently received a degree or certificate, I would offer my congratulations.	1	2	3	4	5
8. If a friend or co-worker finished second in a contest, I would inquire why he or she did not finish first.	5	4	3	2	1
9. If a co-worker showed me how to do something, I would compliment that person's skill.	1	2	3	4	5
10. When a co-worker starts bragging about a family member's accomplishments, I do not respond.	5	4	3	2	1

Scoring and Interpretation: Total the numbers corresponding to your answers. Scoring 40 to 50 points suggests that you typically make people feel important; 16 to 39 points suggests that you have a moderate tendency toward making others feel important; 0 to 15 points suggests that you need to develop skill in making others feel important. Study this chapter carefully.

be to bring a notable accomplishment of his or hers to the attention of the rest of the group. Self-Awareness Exercise 9-1 gives you an opportunity to think through your tendencies to make others feel important.

MAINTAIN HONEST AND OPEN RELATIONSHIPS

In human relations we attach considerable importance to maintaining honest and open relationships with other people. Giving co-workers frank, but tactful, answers to their requests for your opinion is one useful way of developing open relationships. Assume that a co-worker asks your opinion about a memo that he intends to send to his boss. As you read it, you find it somewhat incoherent and filled with spelling and grammatical errors. An honest response to this letter might be: "I think your idea is a good one. But I think your memo needs more work before that idea comes across clearly."

As described in Chapter 7, accurately expressing your feelings also leads to constructive relationships. If you arrive at work upset over a personal problem and appearing obviously fatigued, you can expect some reaction. A peer might say, "What seems to be the problem? Is everything all right?" A dishonest reply would be, "Everything is fine. What makes you think something is wrong?" In addition to making an obviously untrue statement, you would also be perceived as rejecting the person who asked the question.

If you prefer not to discuss your problem, an honest response on your part would be, "Thanks for your interest. I am facing some problems today. But I think things will work out." Such an answer would not involve you in a discussion of your personal problems. Also, you would not be perceived as rejecting your co-worker. The same principle applies equally well to personal relationships.

BE A TEAM PLAYER

An essential strategy for developing good relationships with co-workers is to be a team player. A **team player** is one who emphasizes group accomplishment and cooperation rather than individual achievement and not helping others. Team play has surged in importance because of the current emphasis on having teams of workers decide how to improve productivity and quality. You will also have to be a team player if you reach the pinnacle of power in your organization. Executives are expected to be good team players as well as individual decision makers.

An opinion survey of high-level workers about effective tactics for getting things accomplished underscores the importance of team play. Forty-nine percent of men and 42 percent of women surveyed agreed that being a team player is an effective method of getting things accomplished on the job.[4]

Here we describe a representative group of behaviors that contribute to team play. In addition, engaging in such behavior helps one be perceived as a team player.

Share Credit with Co-workers

A direct method of promoting team play is to share credit for good deeds with other team members. Instead of focusing on yourself as the person responsible for a work achievement, point out that the achievement was the product of a team effort. Frank is a good example of a promoter of the team concept:

> "We won, team, we won," said Frank excitedly to his four lunchmates. "The world's largest manufacturer of air conditioners is going to use our new electronic switch in every one of their units. I just received the good news today. Thanks to all of you for giving me so darn many good suggestions for explaining the merits of our switch. I know that the big boss will be thrilled with our sales department."

Display a Helpful, Cooperative Attitude

Working cooperatively with others is virtually synonymous with team play. Cooperation translates into such activities as helping another worker with a computer problem, covering for a teammate when he or she is absent, and making sure a co-worker has the input required from you on time. A general approach to cooperation is to exchange favors with teammates. A person's job, for example, might occasionally require that a large number of photocopies be made in a hurry. If the person in charge of making large batches of photocopies goes out of the way to take care of such a request, the person is owed a favor. A worker in the accounting department might be able to help the photocopy specialists get a tuition-assistance refund processed in a hurry.

Exchanging favors as a method of building cooperation and teamwork remains effective only if these favors balance out in the long run. Can you think of any way in which an exchange of favors might be applied to a past or present job of yours?

Cooperation is so important to the smooth functioning in the workplace that it is often included as a factor in evaluating performance. Showing good cooperation with others contributes to a positive performance evaluation.

Give Information and Opinions to Co-workers

Teamwork is facilitated when group members share information and opinions. This is true because one of the benefits of group effort is that members can share ideas. The result is often a better solution to problems than would have been possible if people worked alone. The group thus achieves **synergy**—a product of group effort whereby the output of the group exceeds the output possible if the members worked alone.

Touch Base on Important Issues

Team play is also fostered when co-workers are informed about plans you have that could affect them. One example is to inform your peers about a suggestion you are planning to make to management. In this way, if your proposal is accepted, you are more likely to gain the support of your co-workers in implementing your idea than if it had been a big surprise.

Sharon, a computer repair specialist, worked for a computer store. Both she and her co-workers made occasional visits to customers to service their equipment. Sharon thought that if the store purchased a colorful van with the name of the store imprinted on it, the store would attract more business. Before bringing this idea to store management, Sharon discussed it with her teammates individually. One of them added the suggestion that the sign on the truck should read, "Repairs in your office or home." When management later discussed Sharon's ideas with the group, all of the repair technicians expressed enthusiasm. By touching base with her co-workers, Sharon won acceptance for her ideas.

Provide Emotional Support to Co-workers

Good team players offer each other emotional support. Such support can take the form of verbal encouragement for ideas expressed, listening to a group member's concerns, or complimenting achievements. An emotionally supportive comment to a co-worker who appears to be under stress might be: "This doesn't look like one of your better days. What can I do to help?"

Engage in Shared Laughter

Laughter is a natural team builder that enhances understanding and empathy, essential ingredients for team play.[5] The individual can trigger laughter by making humorous comments related to a situation at hand, or making in-group jokes.

> Tracy decided to enliven her work area by posting photographs of scantily clad males. (Part of her ploy was to retaliate against the men in the department who had posted photographs of women.) The manager complained about her photographs in a department meeting, stating that such behavior was unprofessional and might be regarded as sexual harassment. Tracy blurted out, "I don't understand where your *beef* is coming from." Her one-liner enhanced her reputation as a team member.

Attend Company-Sponsored Social Events

A worker's reputation as a team player is often judged both on the job and in company-related social events such as parties, picnics, and athletic teams. If you attend these events and participate fully, your reputation as a team player will be enhanced. In contrast, if you interact with teammates only in the office, your reputation as a team player could suffer. Company-sponsored social events are also important because they provide an opportunity to build rapport with co-workers. Rapport, in turn, facilitates teamwork.

When the company-sponsored event does not fit your capabilities or interests, innovative thinking can help. Lenny, a wheelchair user, felt that he might lose out on being part of the gang because he lacked all the physical skills necessary to play on the department softball team. His solution was to volunteer as official scorer. Lenny's role as the official scorer enabled him to interact with his teammates on the athletic field as well as in the office.

AVOID BACKSTABBING

A special category of disliked behavior is **backstabbing,** an attempt to discredit by underhanded means such as innuendo, accusation, or the like. A backstabber might drop hints to the boss, for example, that a co-worker performs poorly under pressure or is looking for a new job. Sometimes the backstabber assertively gathers information in order to backstab a co-worker. He or she might engage another worker in a derogatory discussion about the boss, and then report the co-worker's negative comments back to the boss.

Backstabbing tends to rise as the pressure for jobs increases. A career counselor noted that during a period of intense job competition, "People seem inclined to stab before they get stabbed themselves."[6] An implication to be drawn here is that when jobs and promotions are in short supply, a person might be more inclined to backstab. The practice is still unethical, and can backfire. A person who develops a reputation as a backstabber will receive poor cooperation from co-workers. The person might also be considered untrustworthy by management, thus retarding his or her own career.

REACTING CONSTRUCTIVELY TO THE BEHAVIOR OF CO-WORKERS

You are often forced to react to the actions and words of co-workers. How you react influences the quality of your relationship with them. In this section of the chapter we describe a number of time-tested ways of reacting constructively to the behavior of co-workers. (**Behavior** refers to the tangible acts or decisions of people, including both their actions and words.)

FOLLOW GROUP STANDARDS OF CONDUCT

The basic principle to follow in getting along with co-workers is to follow **group norms.** These refer to the unwritten set of expectations for group members—what people ought to do. Norms become a standard of what each person should do or not do within the group. Norms also provide general guidelines for reacting constructively to the behavior of co-workers. Norms are a major component of the organizational culture, or values and beliefs of the firm that guide people's actions. In one firm, the norms and culture may favor hard work and high quality. In another firm, the norms and culture may favor a weaker work ethic.

Group norms also influence the social aspects of behavior on the job. These aspects of behavior relate to such things as the people to have lunch with, getting together after work, joining a company team, and the type of clothing to wear to work.

Workers learn about norms both through observation and direct instruction from other group members. If you do not deviate too far from these norms, much of your behavior will be accepted by the group. If you deviate too far, you will be subject to much rejection and the feeling of being isolated. In some instances, you might even be subjected to verbal abuse if you make the other employees look bad.

Getting along too well with co-workers has its price as well. The risk of conforming too closely to group norms is that you lose your individuality. You become viewed by your superiors as "one of the office gang" rather than a person who aspires to move up in the organization.

EXPRESS AN INTEREST IN THE WORK OF OTHERS

Almost everyone is self-centered to some extent. Thus, topics that are favored are ones closely related to themselves, such as their children, friends, hobbies, work, or possessions. Sales representatives rely heavily on this fact in cultivating relationships with established customers. They routinely ask the customer about his or her hobbies, family members, and work activities. (Say, how's your coin collection going?) You can capitalize on this simple strategy by asking co-workers and friends questions such as these:

How is your work going? (*Highly recommended.*)

How are things going for you?

How did you gain the knowledge necessary for your job?

How does the company use the output from your department?

How does your present job fit in with your career plans?

How did Mitzie do in the county cat show?

A danger in asking questions about other people's work is that some questions may not be perceived as well intentioned. There is a fine line between honest curiosity and snooping. You must stay alert to this subtle distinction. A payroll specialist once asked an administrative assistant in her department, "What did you do today?" The administrative assistant interpreted the question as intimating that administrative assistants may not have a full day's work to perform.

BE A GOOD LISTENER

After you ask questions, you must be prepared to listen to the answers. The simplest technique of getting along with co-workers, friends, and acquaintances is to be a good listener. The topics you should be willing to listen to during working hours include job problems and miscellaneous complaints. Lunch breaks, coffee breaks, and after hours are better suited to listening to people talk about their personal lives, current events, sports, and the like.

Becoming an effective listener takes practice. As you practice your listening skills try the suggestions offered in Chapter 5. The payoff is that listening builds constructive relationships both on and off the job. Too often, people take turns talking rather than listening to each other. The result is that neither party feels better as a result of the conversation.

USE APPROPRIATE COMPLIMENTS

An effective way of developing good relationships with co-workers and friends is to compliment something with which they closely identify, such as their children, spouse, hobbies, or pets. Paying a compliment is a form of **positive reinforcement,** rewarding somebody for doing something right. The right response is therefore strengthened, or reinforced. A compliment is a useful multipurpose reward.

Another way of complimenting people is through recognition. The suggestions made earlier about making people feel important are a way of recognizing people, and therefore compliments. Investing a small amount of time in recognizing a co-worker can pay large dividends in terms of cultivating an ally. Recognition and compliments are more likely to create a favorable relationship when they are appropriate. *Appropriate* in this context means that the compliment fits the accomplishment. Praise that is too lavish may be interpreted as belittling and patronizing.

Let's look at the difference between an appropriate and an exaggerated compliment over the same issue. An executive secretary gets a fax machine operating that was temporarily not sending messages.

> *Appropriate compliment:* Nice job, Stephanie. Fixing the fax machine took considerable skill. We can now resume sending important fax messages.

> *Exaggerated compliment:* Stephanie, I'm overwhelmed. You're a world-class fax machine specialist. Are there no limits to your talents?

Observe that the appropriate compliment is thoughtful and is proportionate to what Stephanie accomplished. The exaggerated compliment is probably wasted because it is way out of proportion to the magnitude of the accomplishment.

DEAL EFFECTIVELY WITH DIFFICULT PEOPLE

A major challenge in getting along well with co-workers is to deal constructively with difficult people. A peer is classified as difficult if he or she is uncooperative, touchy, defensive, hostile, or even very unfriendly. Three widely applicable approaches to dealing with difficult people are (1) take problems professionally, not personally, (2) use tact and diplomacy, and (3) use humor.

Take Problems Professionally, Not Personally

A key principle in dealing with a variety of personalities is to take what they do professionally, not personally. Difficult people are not necessarily out to get you. You may just represent a stepping-stone for them to get what they want.[7] For example, if a co-worker insults you because you need his help Friday afternoon, he probably has nothing against you personally. He just prefers to become mentally disengaged from work that Friday afternoon. Your request distracts him from mentally phasing out of work as early as he would like.

Use Tact and Diplomacy in Dealing with Annoying Behavior

Co-workers who irritate you rarely do annoying things on purpose. Tactful actions on your part can sometimes take care of these annoyances without your having to confront the problem. Close your door, for example, if noisy co-workers are gathered outside. Or try one woman's method of getting rid of office pests: She keeps a file open on her computer screen and gestures to it apologetically when someone overstays a visit.

Sometimes subtlety doesn't work, and it may be necessary to diplomatically confront the co-worker who is annoying you. Jane Michaels suggests that you precede a criticism with a compliment. Here is an example of this approach: "You're one of the best people I've ever worked with, but one habit of yours drives me bananas. Do you think you could let me know when you're going to be late getting back to the office after lunch?"[8]

Use Humor in Dealing with Difficult People

Nonhostile humor can often be used to help a difficult person understand how his or her behavior is blocking others.[9] Also, the humor will help defuse conflict between you and that person. The humor should point to the person's unacceptable behavior, yet not belittle him or her. Assume that Kevin (who in your opinion is a difficult person) says that he will not sign off on your report because you used the decimal instead of the metric system. You need Kevin's approval, because the boss wants a consensus report from the group. You ask Kevin again the next day, and he still refuses to sign.

To gain Kevin's cooperation, you say: "I'm sorry we upset your scientific mind. But I swear on a stack of Bibles, one meter high, all future reports will use the metric system. Will you please affix your signature one centimeter below mine? By the way, did you see that 45.45-meter field goal the Ram kicker made in yesterday's game?" With a grin on his face, Kevin replies, "Okay, give me the report to sign." (The touch of humor here indicates that you respect Kevin's desire to convert to the metric system, but you also acknowledge that it can sometimes be impractical.)

FACE MATURELY THE CHALLENGE OF THE OFFICE ROMANCE

As described in the discussion about socializing with the boss (Chapter 8), office romances can be disruptive to morale and productivity. Co-worker romances are a more widespread potential problem, because more romances take place between co-workers on the same level than between superiors and subordinates. As more women have entered the work force in professional positions, and as professionals work longer hours, the office has become a frequent meeting place. Many companies have policies against managers dating people below them in the hierarchy, but few companies attempt to restrict same-level romantic involvements. Nevertheless, sensitivity is required to conduct an office romance that does not detract from one's professionalism.

Many companies are concerned about information leakage within their organization. If you date a person who has access to confidential information (such as trade secrets), management might be concerned that you are a security risk. You therefore might miss out on some opportunities for better assignments.

It is important not to abuse company tolerance of the co-worker romance. Do not invite the person you are dating to meals at company expense, take him or her on nonessential business trips, or create projects to work on jointly.[10]

Strive to keep the relationship confidential and restricted to after hours. Minimize talking to co-workers about the relationship. Such behavior as holding hands or kissing in public view is regarded as poor office etiquette.

Should your co-worker romance terminate, you face a special challenge. You must now work together cooperatively with a person toward whom you may have angry feelings. Few people have the emotional detachment necessary to work smoothly with a former romantic involvement. Extra effort will therefore be required on both your parts.

BUILDING GOOD RELATIONSHIPS WITH CUSTOMERS

Success on the job also requires building good relationships with both external and internal customers. *External customers* fit the traditional definition of customer that includes clients and guests. External customers can be classified as either retail or industrial. The latter represents one company buying from another, such as purchasing steel. *Internal customers* are the people you serve within the organization, or those who use the output from your job. For example, if you design computer graphics, the other people in the company who receive your graphics are your internal customers.

The information already presented about getting along with your manager (in Chapter 8) and co-workers dealt with internal customers. Here we emphasize providing good service (or delight) to external customers. As usual, categories overlap and some techniques for serving external customers would also work well with internal customers, and vice versa. Before reading the ten suggestions for high-level customer service presented next,[11] do Self-Examination Exercise 9-2. The exercise is designed to help you think through your present tendencies toward serving others.

1. *Establish customer satisfaction goals.*   Decide jointly with your manager how much you intend to help customers. Find answers to questions such as the following: Is your company attempting to satisfy every customer within ten minutes of his or her request? Are you striving to provide the finest customer service in your field? Is your goal zero defections to competitors? Your goals will dictate how much and the type of effort you put into pleasing customers.

2. *Understand your customer's needs.*   The most basic principle of selling is to identify and satisfy customer needs. Many customers may not be able to express their needs clearly. Also, they may not be certain of their needs. To help identify customer needs, you may have to probe for more

SELF-EXAMINATION EXERCISE 9-2:

Would You Buy from You?

One of the most effective ways to assess your effectiveness in handling customers is via the question: "If you were the customer, would you buy from yourself?" You would if you scored well on the following quiz. Answer each question by checking the appropriate blank. If you do not deal with external customers, take this quiz in relation to your handling of internal customers.

	Yes	No
1. Is your image one of honest and straightforward sincerity?	___	___
2. Based on your experience with customers over about the past year, *from the buyer's point of view,* would you be classified as reliable?	___	___
3. Could you say your customers obtained special benefits dealing with you they wouldn't have obtained from others?	___	___
4. Do you think you come off as an expert in the eyes of your customers?	___	___
5. Have you been effective helping to solve customer problems?	___	___
6. Wherever possible, would you say you handled customer complaints to the buyer's satisfaction?	___	___
7. Is *integrity* one of the most important words in your vocabulary?	___	___
8. Apart from your business dealings, do you think customers believe you have their personal welfare and well-being at heart?	___	___
9. Can you honestly say most of your company's customers believe you have their personal welfare and well-being at heart?	___	___
10. Do customers regard you as a good, reliable source of product and industry information?	___	___
11. Has doing business with you contributed positively to most of your customers' profit performance?	___	___
12. Would most of your company's customers continue dealing with you even if a competitor approached them with a price a little bit lower?	___	___
Total number of yes answers	___	___

Your Rating: Multiply the sum of your answers by 5. If you achieved a score of 55 or higher, it's a privilege to do business with you; 50 is well above average; and 40 to 45 is mediocre.

SOURCE: Adapted from "Making . . . Serving . . . Keeping . . . Customers," 1992. Reprinted with permission of Dartnell, 4660 N. Ravenswood Ave., Chicago, IL 60640, (800) 621-5463.

information. For example, the associate in a consumer electronics store may have to ask, "What uses do you have in mind for your television receiver aside from watching regular programs? Will you be using it to display electronic photographs? Will you be joining the electronic superhighway soon?" Knowing such information will help the store associate identify which television set will satisfy the customer's needs.

3. *Put customer needs first.* After you have identified customer needs, focus on satisfying them rather than doing what is convenient for you or your firm. Assume, for example, the customer says, "I would like to purchase nine reams of copier paper." The sales associate should not respond, "Sorry, the copying paper comes in boxes of ten, so it is not convenient to sell you nine reams." The associate might, however, offer a discount for the purchase of the full ten-ream box if such action fits company policy.

4. *Show care and concern.* During contacts with your customer, show concern for his or her welfare. Ask questions such as the following: "How have you enjoyed the television set you bought here a while back?" "How are you feeling today?" After asking the question, project a genuine interest in the answer.

5. *Communicate a positive attitude.* A positive attitude is conveyed by factors such as appearance, friendly gestures, a warm voice tone, and good telephone communication skills. If a customer seems apologetic about making a heavy demand, respond, "No need to apologize. My job is to please you. I'm here to serve."

6. *Make the buyer feel good.* A fundamental way of building a customer relationship is to make the buyer feel good about himself or herself. Also, make the buyer feel good because he or she has bought from you. Offer compliments about the customer's healthy glow, or a report that specified vendor requirements (for an industrial customer). An effective feel-good line is, "I enjoy doing business with you."

7. *Smile at every customer.* Smiling is a natural relationship builder and can help you bond with your customer. Smile several times during each customer contact, even if your customer is angry with your product or service. Yet guard against smiling constantly or inappropriately, because your smile then becomes meaningless.

8. *Follow up on requests.* The simple act of following up to see if your service is satisfactory is a powerful principle of good customer service. A telephone call to the requestor of your service is usually sufficient follow-up. A follow-up is effective because it completes the communication loop between two people.

9. *Display strong business ethics.* Ethical violations receive so much publicity that one can impress customers by being conspicuously ethical. Look for ways to show that you are so ethical that you would welcome making your sales tactics public knowledge. Also, treat the customer the same way you would treat a family member or a valued friend.

10. *Be helpful rather than defensive when a customer complains.* As described earlier, look at a complaint professionally rather than personally. Listen carefully and concentrate on being helpful. The upset customer cares primarily about having the problem resolved, and does not care whether or not you are at fault. Use a statement such as, "I understand that this mistake is a major inconvenience. I'll do what I can right now to solve the problem."

Exhibit 9-1 presents examples of the type of customer service spontaneously offered by workers employed by a firm that heavily emphasizes high-level customer service.

APPRECIATING DIVERSITY AMONG CO-WORKERS AND CUSTOMERS

The work force in the United States and Canada is becoming more culturally diverse. A frequent prediction is that by the year 2000, the majority of new workers will be women, African-Americans (and African-Canadians), Hispanics (or Latinos), and immigrants. Only one-third of the projected 140-million-person work force is predicted to be native-born white males.[12] Another key aspect of diversity is that more disabled people are joining the work force. Diversity among customers is also increasing, reflecting the mix in society.

One viewpoint in appreciating cultural diversity is that white males should be included in the diversity web. Many white males feel they are being omitted from concerns about diversity. Members of this same group believe they are excluded from some job opportunities because of sex and race.[13]

EXHIBIT 9-1

CUSTOMER DELIGHT AT GUEST QUARTERS SUITE HOTELS

John J. Weaver is vice president of human resources, Guest Quarters Suite Hotels, based in Boston, Massachusetts. Weaver is convinced that his hotel offers a superior level of customer service. He attributes much of this top-quality service to the fact that the hotel staff has the go-ahead to respond to customer needs in creative ways. Weaver presents two examples:

"When a guest at our Waltham, Massachusetts, hotel ripped a suit that the local dry cleaner couldn't repair overnight, Juan Gallego, a member of the bell staff, took the suit home with him. His mother repaired it and he delivered it in time for the executive to wear to a meeting the next morning.

"In the course of adopting a child, a couple made repeated visits to our hotel in Philadelphia. When they came to town to pick up the infant and bring her back to the hotel, they discovered that the hotel employees had turned their suite into a fully decorated nursery, complete with crib, balloons, a teddy bear personalized with the baby's name and a big greeting card signed by every member of the hotel staff."

SOURCE: John J. Weaver, "Want Customer Satisfaction? Satisfy Your Employees First," *HRMagazine*, February 1994, p. 112.

Succeeding in a diverse environment requires more than avoiding discriminatory behavior. Instead, success is facilitated by working comfortably with people of different sexes, races, ethnicity, values, sexual orientations, and physical capabilities. The job applicant who exhibits an ability to work effectively in a diverse environment is at a competitive advantage for many jobs.[14] Diversity skills can sometimes be displayed by descriptions of past work and school experiences with diverse people. Speaking a second language is also impressive.

The information already presented for dealing with co-workers and customers can be applied toward building relationships with diverse groups. In addition, it is important to develop an appreciation of cultural diversity in the workplace. Toward this end we will discuss recognizing diversity on the job and describe training for such purposes.

RECOGNIZING CULTURAL DIFFERENCES

Cultural diversity can be better understood if it is recognized that many apparent differences in personality actually arise from culture. For example, both white and black North Americans feel that authority should be challenged. However, Asians and Hispanics tend to respect and obey authority. Another notable difference is that Hispanic culture perceives music, family members, and food as appropriate for the workplace. Americans and Canadians reject these practices and may regard them as unprofessional.

Some forms of discrimination become more explainable, even if still unacceptable, when their cultural origins are recognized. For example, in many Asian countries few women hold executive positions in industry. It is therefore difficult for some Asian workers employed in North America to accept women as their administrative superiors.

The key principle to recognizing cultural differences is to be alert to these differences, and to be sensitive to how they could affect your dealings with people. Recognize that not everybody fits the same stereotype and adjust your assumptions accordingly. A furniture store manager who viewed the world with a *heterosexual bias* made the following mistake: A customer said he wished to return an end table because after he brought it home his partner said the table just didn't fit. The store manager responded, "What didn't your wife like about the table?" The customer replied angrily, "My partner is a man, and he said the design is atrocious." The customer then demanded a refund instead of a merchandise exchange.

DIVERSITY AWARENESS TRAINING

To help employees relate comfortably to people of different cultures and appreciate diversity, many companies conduct **diversity awareness training.** These programs provide an opportunity for employees to develop the skills necessary to deal effectively with each other and with customers in a diverse environment.[15]

A key component of these programs is to help workers recognize cultural differences, as described above. Another important part of diversity awareness training is to develop empathy for diverse viewpoints. To help training participants develop empathy, representatives of various groups explain their feelings related to workplace issues. In one segment of such a program, a minority group member was seated in the middle of a circle.[16] The other participants sat at the periphery of the circle. First, the co-workers listened to a Vietnamese woman explain how she felt excluded from the in-group composed of whites and African-Americans in her department. "I feel like you just tolerate me. You do not make me feel that I am somebody important."

The next person to sit in the middle of the circle was Muslim. He complained about people wishing him Merry Christmas. "I would much prefer that my co-workers would stop to think that I do not celebrate Christian holidays. I respect your religion, but it is not my religion."

Exhibit 9-2 describes a classroom exercise in diversity awareness training. The exercise has similarities to diversity training programs in business and industry.

EXHIBIT 9-2

GROUP IDENTITY AND STEREOTYPING

Working in small groups, students list the groups in which they feel they belong. Among these groups might be sex, age, family, race, community, social organization, education, and religion. Students do not have to justify why they perceive themselves as belonging to a particular group.

Students next examine the stereotypical beliefs about groups in which they do not belong. Working alone or in groups, students generate a list of stereotypes of the different groups identified above. To trigger your thinking on stereotypes, consider these several examples: "Women are more creative than men." "Hispanic people speak very rapidly." "Young African-American men are all good at basketball." "French men are romantic."

The next step is to examine the source of these perceptions and to discuss the dangers of such stereotyping. Students who believe the creative stereotype about women might explain how this perception came about. Keep in mind that *all* stereotypes are not inaccurate. To illustrate, in one group a woman said, "Jewish people value education and upward mobility." The rest of the group agreed that her stereotype was reasonably accurate, despite many exceptions.

SOURCE: Adapted from Arnola C. Ownby and Heidi R. Perreault, "Teaching Students to Understand and Value Diversity," *Business Education Forum*, February 1994, p. 28.

SUMMARY

Getting along with co-workers is important for performing your job satisfactorily or better. Methods and tactics that center around taking the initiative to establish good relationships include:

1. Develop allies through good feelings.

2. Make other people feel important.

3. Maintain honest and open relationships.

4. Be a team player (including sharing credit, being cooperative, giving out information and opinions, touching base on important issues, emotionally supporting co-workers, and engaging in shared laughter).

5. Attend company-sponsored social events.

6. Avoid backstabbing.

Methods and tactics of getting along with co-workers that center around reacting constructively to their behavior include:

1. Follow group standards of conduct.

2. Express an interest in the work of others.

3. Be a good listener.

4. Use appropriate compliments.

5. Deal effectively with difficult people (including taking problems professionally, using tact and diplomacy).

6. Face maturely the challenge of the office romance.

Success on the job also requires building good relationships with both internal and external customers. Representative techniques for building constructive customer relationships include: (1) establish customer-satisfaction goals, (2) understand customer needs, (3) put customer needs first, (4) show care and concern, (5) communicate a positive attitude, (6) make the buyer feel good, (7) smile at every customer, (8) follow up on requests, (9) display strong business ethics, and (10) be helpful rather than defensive in response to complaints.

The North American work force is becoming increasingly culturally diverse. Success on the job is facilitated by working comfortably with people of different sexes, races, religions, ethnicity, values, sexual orientations, and physical capabilities. To work comfortably with such groups it is important to recognize cultural differences. Being alert to cultural differences enhances understanding. Recognize that not everybody fits the same stereotype and adjust your assumptions accordingly. Diversity awareness training helps workers develop the skills necessary to deal effectively with each other and with customers in a diverse environment.

Questions and Activities

1. A critic of this chapter said, "A lot of ruthless people get ahead in business. So getting along with your co-workers may not really be that important." What do you think?

2. How does "making a deposit in your favor bank" relate to negotiating strategy?

3. Why is it important to make people feel important?

4. Make up an emotionally supportive statement to offer a co-worker whose wedding plans were canceled one week before the marriage date.

5. Should companies have a policy about backstabbing? Explain.

6. What are the advantages of meeting a potential mate in the office rather than through friends or in public places such as sports bars or dances?

7. Much has been written about satisfying customer needs. What obligation do you think customers have to satisfy the needs of their sales representatives?

8. In Japan, many middle managers are expected to regularly entertain customers until past 10 P.M. Explain whether you think this is going too far to satisfy customers.

9. What might you do to impress a job interviewer that you have good cultural diversity skills?

10. Ask an experienced worker what evidence he or she has that his or her employer has made progress in welcoming diversity. Compare notes with other classmates.

REFERENCES

[1]Jane Michaels, "You Gotta Get Along to Get Ahead," *Woman's Day,* April 3, 1984, p. 58.

[2]Robert L. Dilenschneider, *Power and Influence: Mastering the Art of Persuasion* (New York: Prentice Hall Press, 1990).

[3]Sheila Murray Bethel, *Making a Difference* (New York: G. P. Putman's Sons, 1989).

[4]Andrew J. DuBrin, "Sex Differences in the Endorsement of Influence Tactics and Political Behavior Tendencies," *Journal of Business and Psychology,* winter 1989, pp. 1–15.

[5]Paul S. George, "Teamwork Without Tears," *Personnel Journal,* November 1987, p. 124.

[6]Tony Lee, "Competition for Jobs Spawns Backstabbers and a Need for Armour," *The Wall Street Journal,* November 3, 1993, p. B1.

A HUMAN RELATIONS CASE PROBLEM: THE TIME-DEMANDING CUSTOMER

Gil McPherson worked as a field service technician for a manufacturer of numeric control machines. Machines of this type are used by other manufacturers to produce their products. Because customers are dependent on their numeric control machines to manufacture their products, they expect very little downtime. In addition, the line of numeric control machines produced by McPherson's company costs up to $500,000.

Gil's major job responsibilities are to repair customer machines. On rare occasions, Gil can instruct customers over the phone on how to fix a problem. Over 90 percent of the time, however, Gil must make an on-site visit to repair the machine. Sometimes he might spend two days on site when working with a complicated repair problem.

Another part of Gil's duties is to run acceptance tests on machinery. An acceptance test is a method of determining if a machine is running properly in the field. These tests are usually run over a thirty-day period during regular working hours. Traditionally, a representative from the customer and Gil's company had to be present to log and correct any errors that occurred during the tests.

A scheduling problem developed during a test at a bicycle manufacturer whose normal working hours for the first shift were 5:00 A.M. to 1:00 P.M. The bicycle management wanted the test run during the first shift because the machinery was placed under heavier pressure during that time period.

The bicycle manufacturer was located seventy-five miles from Gil's apartment. To be on location at 5:00 A.M. Gil estimated he would have to get up at 3:00 A.M. Gil also figured that getting up so early each morning would throw him off mentally for the evening, making it difficult to have an enjoyable time.

Gil also knew that his company discouraged customer visits at times that would necessitate overtime pay. Arriving at a customer site at 5:00 A.M. would entail overtime pay, because Gil would have to return to his office in the afternoon. Gil would therefore be drawing about ten days of overtime pay. (He would not have to be present for the full thirty days of the test runs.)

As Gil reviewed his voice mail, he found another message from the bicycle manufacturer. The company representative wanted an immediate answer on when Gil would be on their premises to make the test run. Gil thought to himself, "The customer is supposed to come first, but I'm in a bind. If I meet the customer's time schedule, I'll inconvenience myself. I also run the

(Continued)

risk of getting my boss angry because I've charged the company so much overtime.

"I've got to resolve this issue in thirty minutes."

QUESTIONS

1. Which principles of good customer service should Gil follow to resolve this problem?

2. How can Gil avoid conflict with his boss yet still meet the demands of his customer?

3. How serious is Gil's problem?

A HUMAN RELATIONS ROLE PLAY: GETTING ALONG WITH CO-WORKERS

The purpose of this role play is to practice a basic human relations technique for getting along well with co-workers by expressing an interest in their work. Three teams of co-workers enter into this role play. Observers will provide feedback about the effectiveness of the techniques displayed. With each pair of teams, one student takes the initiative to express interest in the work of the co-worker. One co-worker is a paralegal assistant, one is a telemarketing specialist (sales over the phone), and one is a store manager in a lingerie shop. In each situation, the two co-workers are on break together.

[7]Dru Scott, *Customer Satisfaction: The Other Half of Your Job* (Los Altos, Calif: Crisp Publications, 1991), p. 16.

[8]Michaels, "You Gotta Get Along," p. 60.

[9]Kaye Loraine, "Dealing with the Difficult Personality," *Supervision,* April 1989, pp. 6–8.

[10]"Not-So-Dangerous Liaisons," *Executive Strategies,* February 6, 1990, p. 8.

[11]Linda Thornburg, "Companies Benefit from Emphasis on Superior Customer Service," *HRMagazine,* October 1993, pp. 46–49; Andrew J. DuBrin, *Stand Out! How to Gain the Edge with Superiors, Subordinates, Co-workers and Customers* (Englewood Cliffs, N.J.: Prentice Hall, 1993), pp. 199–225; Karl Albrecht, *The Only Thing That Matters* (New York: Harper Collins, 1992).

[12]David Jamieson and Julie O'Mara, *Managing Workforce 2000: Gaining the Diversity Advantage* (San Francisco: Jossey-Bass, 1991), p. 1; Arnola C. Ownby and Heidi R. Perreault, "Teaching Students to Understand and Value Diversity," *Business Education Forum,* February 1994, p. 27.

[13]Charlene Marmer Solomon, "Are White Men Being Left Out?" *Personnel Journal,* November 1991, p. 88.

[14]Ownby and Perreault, "Teaching Students to Understand and Value Diversity," p. 27.

[15]Bill Leonard, "Ways to Make Diversity Programs Work," *HrMagazine,* April 1991, pp. 37–39, 98.

[16]Suzanne Elshult and James Little, "The Case for Valuing Diversity," *HRMagazine,* June 1990, pp. 50–51.

ADDITIONAL READING

Bell, Chip R., and Zemke, Ron. *Managing Knock-Your-Socks-Off Service.* New York: AMACOM, 1992.

Bray, Douglas W., (ed). *Diversity in the Workplace: Human Resources Initiatives.* New York: Guilford Publications, 1992.

Cohen, William A. *The Art of the Leader.* (Englewoods Cliff, N.J.: Prentice Hall, 1992).

Cox, Charles E. "18 Ways to Improve Customer Service." *HRMagazine,* March 1992, pp. 69–72.

Naum, Alan. *Adding Value for Customers.* Cincinnati: Thompson Executive Press, 1994.

Rosenbluth, Hal F., and Peters, Diane McFerrin. *The Customer Comes Second: And Other Secrets of Exceptional Customer Service.* New York: William Morrow and Co., 1992.

Tompkins, Neville C. "Employee Satisfaction Leads to Customer Service." *HRMagazine,* November 1992, pp. 93–95.

Ury, William. *Getting Past No: Negotiating with Difficult People.* New York: Bantam Books, 1991.

Walther, George R. *Power Talking: 50 Ways to Say What You Mean and Get What You Want.* New York: G. P. Putnam's Sons, 1992.

CHAPTER 10

CHOOSING A CAREER AND CAREER SWITCHING

Learning Objectives

After studying the information and doing the exercises in this chapter you should be able to:

- Make a tentative career choice if you have not already selected a first career.

- Appreciate the complexity of choosing a career.

- Identify current skills that could serve as the basis for your career.

- Identify several growth fields for the balance of the century.

- Know how to prepare for a career.

- Pinpoint major considerations in career switching.

*I*f you have not already chosen a career, or are beginning to tire of your present one, this chapter is especially important. If you are content with your career, this chapter can be read with the intention of learning more about that vital part of your life. What a person does for a living is one of the key influences on his or her life. Its impact rivals such things as your marital status, religion, or physical strength. Your career is

also a prime source of your self-esteem and your identity.

The next time you converse with a stranger at a social gathering, notice how quickly that person informs you of his or her occupation or main career interest. If you ask "What do you do?" you will almost always get a job-related answer such as "I'm a paralegal," or "I work at the Prudential." Few people will say, "I play my VCR," or "I eat dinner with my family regularly."

A **career** is a series of related job experiences that fit into a meaningful pattern. If you have a series of odd jobs all your working life, that is hardly a career. But if each job builds carefully on the previous one, we say you are "building a career." We assume that by making a sound initial choice of occupation, you will be on the first step toward building a real career. Chapters 11 through 14 provide information to help you advance in whatever career you have chosen.

The career chooser and job hunter face a favorable environment in the current decade. Because of the "birth dearth" after 1965, fewer younger workers will be available to take entry-level positions in almost all job categories. The number of workers age sixteen to twenty-four will drop by almost 8 percent by the end of the century. The ranks of teenagers began to grow again in the United States in 1992, after a fifteen-year decline.[1] Nevertheless, the combined forces of the Baby Bust and the trimming down of business firms in the early 1990s has created a favorable current job outlook. Employers will have to step up the recruitment of women and minorities—two key potential sources of talent.

The purpose of this chapter is to help you choose a career by describing systematic methods of career selection. For those who have already chosen a career field in general, this chapter may help you refine your career choice within your field. For example, a person entering the computer field might choose to emphasize those aspects of computers dealing heavily with people. People-contact work in the computer field includes computer sales. Another possibility is information systems, in which a specialist helps others make effective use of computers.

LEARN ABOUT YOURSELF FIRST

A general strategy for making a sound career choice is to understand first the inner you, including what you have to offer. You then match that information with opportunities in the outside world. The Self-Knowledge Questionnaire presented in Chapter 1 asks many questions that are relevant for making a career choice. Almost any of the information provided by candid answers to those questions could help you make a sound career choice. Several specific illustrations are in order.

Question 1 asks, "How far have I gone in school?" If you answered, "Three years of high school," or "Four years of high school and two years of business school," you will need additional education for many fields. Among them are management, teaching, counseling, or social work.

Question 9 asks, "What aspect of these jobs did I enjoy?" Suppose you answered, "Anytime I was left alone to do some figuring or report writing I was happy. Thinking made me happy." Your answer could mean that you should search for a field in which working with ideas and data is more important than working with people or things. What about investigating laboratory work or financial analysis?

Question 31 asks, "What gives me satisfaction in life?" Suppose you answered, "Playing with my children, going fishing, and getting involved with my friends almost every day." However good for your mental health this answer might be, it certainly does limit the level of responsibility you can aspire toward in most careers. A busy executive or professional person often comes out on the short end with respect to having ample time for family, fishing, and friends.

Some additional questions useful in clarifying the type of work you would prefer are presented in Exhibit 10-1.

The Importance of Skills in Choosing a Career

Exhibit 10-1 points to some aspects of self-understanding related to career selection. In addition, knowing which skills and abilities you possess—and enjoy performing—can be the basis for a successful career. A **skill** is a learned, specific ability such as writing a report, conducting a statistical analysis, or troubleshooting software problems. A vast number of skills exist that could be exercised in a career, including such things as calculating numbers, designing store displays, and resolving conflict. Identifying your skills is important both in choosing a career and in finding a job. Employers want to know what a job prospect can actually *do,* or what skills he or she possesses.

EXHIBIT 10-1

LEARNING MORE ABOUT YOURSELF

By candidly answering the questions that follow, you may be able to develop some new understanding about your career preferences. Try to write at least twenty-five words in response to each question, even if your answer is uncertain.

1. What kind of work would make me proud?
_____
_____

2. What would be a horrible way for me to make a living?
_____
_____

3. How important is a high income to me? Why?
_____
_____

4. How do I really feel about what other people think of the kind of work I do?
_____
_____

5. What kind of work would really be fun for me to do?
_____
_____

6. What kind of work would I be willing to do for ten consecutive years?
_____
_____

7. What kind of work would make me feel self-fulfilled?
_____
_____

8. What is my attitude toward doing the same thing every workday?
_____
_____

9. How do I really feel about being held responsible when things go wrong?
_____
_____

Your answers to these questions and the Self-Knowledge Questionnaire should be kept in mind as you read the section "Nine Clusters of Occupations," presented later in this chapter. Another suggestion is to discuss your answers with a counselor, instructor, or good friend.

EXHIBIT 10-2

SKILLS PROFILE

Directions

Review the following skills areas and specific skills. In the space provided, write down each one you believe is a strong skill for you. You can also add a specific skill that was not included in the skill area listed at the left.

Skill Area	Specific Skills	A Strong Skill for Me
Communication	writing, speaking, knowledge of foreign language, telephone skills, persuasiveness, listening	_____
Creative	originating ideas, thinking up novel solutions	_____
Interpersonal relations	ability to get along well with others, being a team player, diplomacy, conflict resolution, understanding others	_____
Management	ability to lead, organize, plan, motivate others, make decisions, manage time	_____
Manual and mechanical	mechanically inclined, build, operate, repair, assemble, install, drive vehicles	_____
Mathematics	math skills, computers, analyzing data, budgeting, using statistical techniques	_____
Office	keyboarding, filing, business math, bookkeeping, spread sheets, word processing, database management, record keeping	_____
Sales	persuading others, negotiating, promoting, dressing fashionably	_____
Scientific	investigating, researching, compiling, systematizing, diagnosing, evaluating	_____
Service of customers	serving customers, handling complaints, dealing with difficult people	_____
Service of patients	nurturing, diagnosing, treating, guiding, counseling, consoling, dealing with emergencies	_____
Other skill area:	_____	_____

SOURCE: Abridged and adapted from Julie Griffin Levitt, *Your Career: How to Make It Happen,* 2d ed. (Cincinnati, Ohio: South-Western Publishing Co., 1990), pp. 19–21.

Julie Griffin Levitt has developed a useful way of categorizing skills,[2] as outlined in Exhibit 10-2. Identifying which of these skills you possess, or are capable of developing, could be the basis for a satisfying and rewarding career.

Getting Help from a Career Counselor

In choosing a career or switching careers, an excellent method of learning more about yourself in relation to the world of work is to obtain help from a professional **career counselor.** A counselor usually relies on a wide variety of tests plus an interview to assist you in making a sound career choice. It is untrue that any single test will tell you what occupation you should enter. Tests are designed to provide useful clues, not to give you definite answers. Nor is it true that a career counselor will tell you what occupation you should enter. Using tests and human judgment, the counselor assists you to become more aware of yourself and the alternatives that might suit your circumstances. This chapter emphasizes choosing a career by yourself. It is recommended, however, that you seek the help of a guidance counselor, career counselor, or counseling psychologist.

Interest Testing to Identify Careers of Interest

Career counseling emphasizes finding a career that suits a person's interests. The most widely used instrument for matching a person's interests with careers is the **Strong Interest Inventory** (**SII**). The output of the SII is a computer-generated report that provides potentially useful information about making career choices.[3]

The Strong asks 325 questions about your preferences (likes, dislikes, or indifferences) concerning occupations, school subjects, activities, amusements, and types of people. Exhibit 10-3 presents a sampling of such questions. A person's answers to these questions are used to compute three sets of scores: (1) general occupational themes, (2) basic interest scales, and (3) occupational scales.

Scores on the Strong Interest Inventory

Each of the six occupational themes is associated with one or more basic interest scales as follows:

R Theme (Realistic): High scorers on this theme tend to be rugged, robust, practical individuals who are physically strong and frequently aggressive in outlook. The basic interest scales carrying the realistic theme are: Agriculture, Nature, Adventure Military Activities, and Mechanical Activities.

I Theme (Investigative): High scorers on this theme enjoy science and scientific activities, and are not particularly interested in working with others. They also enjoy solving abstract problems. The basic interest scale carrying the investigative theme are as follows: Science, Mathematics, Medical Science, and Medical Service.

EXHIBIT 10-3

TYPE OF TEST ITEMS FOUND ON THE STRONG INTEREST INVENTORY

1. Actor	L	I	D
2. Aviator	L	I	D
3. Architect	L	I	D
4. Astronomer	L	I	D
5. Athletic director	L	I	D
6. Auctioneer	L	I	D
7. Author of novel	L	I	D
8. Author of scientific book	L	I	D
9. Auto sales representative	L	I	D
10. Auto mechanic	L	I	D

NOTE: In this section of the test, the subject indicates whether he or she would like (L), dislike (D), or be indifferent to (I) working in each occupation.

A Theme (Artistic):   High scorers on these themes are artistically oriented and like to work in settings where self-expression is welcome. The associated interest scales are: Music/Dramatics, Art, and Writing.

S Theme (Social):   High scorers on this theme are sociable, responsible, humanistic, and concerned with the welfare of others. The associated interest scales are: Teaching, Social Service, Athletics, Domestic Arts, and Religious Activities.

E Theme (Enterprising):   High scorers on this theme are skillful with words and use this capability to sell, dominate, and lead. The associated interest scales are: Public Speaking, Law/Politics, Merchandising, Sales, and Business Management.

C Theme (Conventional):   High scorers on this theme prefer the ordered activities, both verbal and numerical, that characterize office work. They are comfortable following the rules and regulations of a large firm. The associated interest scale is Office Practices.

The Strong Interest Inventory has 119 occupational scales, divided among the six general occupational themes and basic interest scales. For example, the following occupations are among those associated with the conventional theme and the office practices scales: accountant, banker, credit manager, business education teacher, food service manager, nursing home administrator, and secretary.

Interpreting the Strong Profile

With the assistance of a counselor, a person looks for patterns of high and low scores. High scores indicate interests similar to people in occupational areas and occupations, whereas low scores suggest the opposite.

Assume that a person scores very high on the Office Practices Scale, and high on the occupations of banker and credit manager. The same person also scores very low on the Investigative theme, the Medical Service Interest Scale, and the medical technical and respiratory therapist Occupational Scales. We conclude that this person would be happier as an office manager than as an ambulance medic!

Note that interest is not the same as ability. Some people may not have the mental aptitude and skills to do well in the occupations they would enjoy. Interest is but one important factor contributing to successful performance. Being interested in your field makes its biggest contribution to keeping you motivated.

 ## MATCHING YOUR CAREER TO YOUR LIFESTYLE

Ideally, you should pursue a career that provides you with the right balance between work, leisure, and interaction with people. Some degree of compromise is usually necessary. If your preferred lifestyle is to take two-hour lunch breaks each workday, it would be difficult to attain a high level of responsibility. Executives, public relations specialists, and sales representatives who seem to spend considerable time at lunch are usually conducting business over their meal. They are not taking time out during the workday. If a cornerstone of your lifestyle is to remain in top physical and mental shape, you should probably avoid some of the high-pressure careers, such as ambulance paramedic or securities sales representative. On the other hand, you would want to avoid a career that provided too little challenge.

As just hinted, the term **lifestyle** can refer to many different key aspects of your life. In terms of making a career choice, it is helpful to regard lifestyle as the pattern by which a person invests energy into work and nonwork. Being the proverbial beach bum or ski bum is one lifestyle. So is being the ninety-hour-a-week government executive.

Today, an increasing number of people at different stages in their careers are making career choices that improve their chances of leading their preferred lifestyle. The general manager of a plant in a small town makes a revealing comment about modern lifestyles: "A number of years ago we couldn't get nearly the number of skilled people we needed to work here. The people who had a choice wanted to live in an area near a big city. Now we get loads of unsolicited résumés. It seems that a lot of people want access to camping and fishing. I think they're also worried about crime and pollution in the cities."

The move toward a healthy balance between work and nonwork might also be considered part of the movement toward a higher quality of life. For some people living in a $1,800-a-month studio apartment in New York or Washington, D.C., represents a high quality of life. Such city dwellers would, of course, have to aspire toward a very high-paying occupation in order to support their preference. How will your preferred lifestyle influence your career decision making?

Another key aspect of matching your career to your lifestyle is to choose a career that enables you to achieve the right balance between work and personal life. People vary widely in what they consider the right balance. Individuals who want to be home at regular hours and on weekends, with very little travel, will usually have to avoid industrial sales or managerial work. On the other hand, individuals who prefer the excitement of breakfast meetings, weekend meetings, and travel might choose the two occupations just mentioned.

FINDING OCCUPATIONAL FACTS

Whether or not you have already made a career choice, you should follow a fundamental rule of plotting your career—get the facts. Few people have valid information about careers they wish to pursue. A glaring example of occupational misinformation relates to the legal field. Many young people say, "I would like to be a lawyer. I'm good at convincing people. And I know I could sway a jury." Similarly, "I want to be a paralegal. I have the mind of a detective. I know I could break most of the tough cases given me to research."

In reality, the work of a lawyer or paralegal includes the processing of much nonglamorous information. One example is figuring out how much money a bankrupt bakery owes to twenty-seven different suppliers. Four general sources of occupational information are printed material, computer systems, spoken information, and firsthand experience. Without this information it is difficult to find a good fit between yourself and existing opportunities.

PRINTED INFORMATION

Most libraries and bookstores are well supplied with information on career opportunities. The most comprehensive source document of occupational information is the *Occupational Outlook Handbook,* published every two years by the U.S. Department of Labor. Each occupation listed is described in terms of (1) nature of the work, (2) places of employment, (3) training, (4) other qualifications and advancement, and (5) employment outlook.

Using the *Handbook,* one can find answers to such questions as "What do claims examiners do and how much do they earn?" The Bureau of Labor Statistics also publishes the *Occupational Outlook Quarterly,* which supplements the *Handbook* with articles on current occupational developments. Other useful general sourcebooks include:

Dictionary of Occupational Job Titles

Encyclopedia of Careers and Vocational Guidance

What Can I Be? A Guide to 525 Liberal Arts and Business Careers

A Guide to Careers Through College Majors

The Encyclopedia of Second Careers

COMPUTER-ASSISTED CAREER GUIDANCE

Several career-guidance information systems have been developed for access by computer. The information contained in these systems is designed to help users plan their careers. Guidance information systems go one step beyond printed information because you can ask questions of (interact with) the computer. For instance, when you are keyed in on a specific occupation, you can ask "What is the promotion outlook?" and "What effect will technology have?"

A widely used career-guidance information system is DISCOVER, available from The American College Testing Program (ACT).[4] Prior knowledge of computers is not required to use DISCOVER or other similar software. The system is intended for use by postsecondary students and by adults seeking a new career direction outside their current employment. DISCOVER has two approaches. The Information-Only approach allows quick access to information files in the system. For example, direct access is permitted to detailed information about 458 occupations included in the DISCOVER files. Another area of information provided is job-seeking skills.

The more comprehensive approach to DISCOVER is Guidance Information, containing nine major modules. It is designed to support users for the complex process of making career and educational decisions. The modules are as follows:

1. *Beginning the Career Journey.* Users investigate their current level of career decision-making maturity to determine which other modules will be the most useful.

2. *Learning about the World of Work.* Users learn how they fit into the world of work and find out about different programs of study or occupations.

3. *Learning about Yourself.* A series of on-line exercises are presented to help users become more aware of key aspects of their personal profile, including abilities, values, interests, and aptitudes.

4. *Finding Occupations.* This module generates lists of occupations for consideration and exploration by users. Contributors to making the right choice are job characteristics such as employment outlook, job pressures, travel, beginning income, and educational level required.

5. *Learning about Occupations.* Users may access detailed information about any of the 458 occupations, covering about 95 percent of employment opportunities in the United States.

6. *Making Educational Choices.* Users are helped to identify and plan for the type of educational experiences that will prepare them for their selected occupations. One step in this process is to identify pathways of training through which people typically enter their preferred occupations.

7. *Planning Next Steps.* This module contains detailed files of virtually every postsecondary occupational opportunity in the United States, including external degree and military programs.

8. *Planning Your Career.* Working through this module, users look at the roles they play (such as parent/spouse, friend), and plan their careers.

9. *Making Transitions.* Working through this module, users are given suggestions for handling the inevitable changes in their career and personal life, such as going back to school.

DISCOVER is comprehensive and complex, but so are the processes of finding a career and career planning in general.

SPEAKING TO PEOPLE

An invaluable supplement to reading about occupations is to speak to people engaged in them. No matter what occupation interests you, search out a person actually employed in that kind of work. Most people welcome the opportunity to talk about themselves and the type of work they do. If you do not know anyone engaged in the career field that interests you, do some digging. A few inquiries will usually lead to a person you can contact. It is best to interview that person in his or her actual work setting in order to obtain a sense of the working conditions people face in that field.

Remember, however, that many people will probably say that although they are very happy in their work, there are better ways to make a living. Ask your dentist, doctor, lawyer, or plumber about his or her field, and you will likely be told, "Don't believe all those stories about people in this field being wealthy. We work long and hard for our money. And there's always the problem of people not paying their bills. I don't recommend that you enter this field."

Suppose you want to learn about the field of total quality, yet you do not know anyone who knows any person doing this kind of work. Try the cold-canvas method. Call one or two large companies and ask to speak to some-one working with total quality. When you reach that department, indicate that you are trying to make a sound career choice and then proceed with your inquiry. The success ratio of this approach is remarkably high.

FIRSTHAND EXPERIENCE

If you want to explore an occupation in depth, it is important to obtain some firsthand experience in that occupation. Part-time and temporary employment is particularly useful. One man who is a self-employed land-scape consultant first tried out the field by working two summers for an established business. Some schools offer cooperative, or work-study, pro-grams. However modest your cooperative employment, it can provide you with much valuable information. For instance, it is surprisingly helpful to observe whether or not people engaged in that type of work ever smile or laugh. If not, the work might be intense and dreary. Exhibit 10-4 illus-

---

EXHIBIT 10-4

WORTH HER WEIGHT IN OIL

Petroleum engineer Shauna Freeman dismisses her reputation as an oil-patch whiz. Freeman saved her employers $2 million before she graduated from the University of Alberta. "That's what we're supposed to do," said the twenty-three-year-old engineer, who spent five years alternating between col-lege and co-op jobs.

Freeman received international recognition when named North America's Co-Operative Education Student of the Year. Her award places her as the top co-op student among 30,000 from sixty universities.

In talking about her accomplishments, Freeman says, "You're trying to pro-duce as much oil as you can for as little as possible." One time she was given the assignment of planning how to hook up a field of oil wells into a pipeline. Freeman recommended delaying the project until depressed oil prices rose to justify the expense. Another time, Freeman discovered an existing oil deposit was much larger than the original map indicated. Using that information, the energy firm earned an extra $1 million when it sold the property.

Freeman has received high praise from her placement supervisors. One noted, "I gave her the envelope of authority. She took it to the limits. And that's a compliment. We haven't had anybody around here with that kind of enthusiasm in a long time."

Freeman received job offers from the three firms she applied to. She chose to join Chevron's Edmonton office as an oil production engineer. Her new boss said, "She's coming with obviously high credentials. We're expecting good things from her and look forward to her joining the organization."

SOURCE: Adapted from "Top Co-op Student Is Oilpatch Whiz," *The Toronto Star,* March 20, 1993, p. C4.

trates an extreme case of how a co-op experience can shape and boost a person's career.

Temporary work in a field you might wish to enter could lead to a job offer. It is standard practice for employers to use part-time and temporary jobs as a way of screening prospective employees. A woman who is now a sales representative for a well-known business corporation presents this anecdote: "I took the most menial clerical position in the marketing department. My supervisor told her boss that I was a good worker—somebody who would give a fair shake to the company. Now I'm making more money and having more fun than I thought possible at my age."

CHOOSING A GROWTH OCCUPATION AND FIELD

An advantageous way of choosing a career is to pursue an occupation that appears to have growth potential. The career seeker searches for a match between his or her capabilities and interests and a growth occupation in a growth field. For instance, a person who likes dealing directly with people and computers might choose a career as a travel agent. The reasoning here is that travel agents deal with people, and they use computers to book travel and hotel reservations. Also, the travel agency business is a growth field.

Be aware that every position in a growth field is not a growth occupation. For instance, there is a decreasing demand for middle managers in both growth and declining fields. You can also be in a growth occupation in a declining field. A good example is a quality professional. Although manufacturing is declining in the United States and Canada, quality specialists (people who specialize in enhancing the quality of products) are also in strong demand. Computer specialists are also in demand in manufacturing, including robotics (the use of robots) specialists.

How does one identify growth fields? One way is to use the sources described in the section about finding career information. Exhibit 10-5 lists growth occupations based on such sources and other career information. The payoff from working in a growth field is that career advancement is likely to be more rapid than in a stable or declining field.

DATA, PEOPLE, OR THINGS

A helpful way of looking at career choices is to characterize jobs according to the amount of time devoted to data (or ideas), people, or things. The *Dictionary of Occupational Titles,* published by the Department of Labor, uses the data, people, or things categories in describing all the occupational titles.

1. *Data*   refers to working with facts, information, and ideas made from observations and interpretations. The activities involved in working with data are synthesizing, coordinating, analyzing, compiling, computing,

EXHIBIT 10-5

FAST-GROWING OCCUPATIONS IN BUSINESS AND RELATED FIELDS

Court Reporter: As the legal profession continues to expand, so will jobs for court reporters. Starting salary in 2000 will be $37,000. Two-year degree plus certification required.

Insurance Claim Examiner: About 172,000 insurance claim examiners and investigators will be needed by 2000, as more people are insuring more objects. Starting salary in 2000 will be about $33,000. Two-year degree required.

Insurance Underwriter: The growth of the insurance field will also create need for people to assess risk and to price insurance policies. Approximately 30,000 jobs will be added by 2000, with a starting salary of about $45,500. Two-year degree required.

Paralegal: The paralegal is one of the fastest-growing occupations, and is expected to add 62,000 jobs by 2000. Starting salary in 2000 will be about $40,000. Two-year degree plus certification required.

Real Estate Agent/Broker: About 72,000 more real estate agents and brokers will be needed by 2000, as more people qualify to become home owners. Average earnings (mostly commissions) in 2000 will be about $47,000. Two-year degree plus certification generally required; high-school diploma plus certification sometimes acceptable with business experience.

Real Estate Appraiser: As the real estate field grows, so will the need for people to evaluate the worth of properties. Starting salary in 2000 will be about $50,000. Two-year degree required.

Computer Service Technicians: The demand for servicing computers used in office and homes computers is growing rapidly. An additional 44,000 repairers will be needed by 2000, with a starting salary of $52,000. Two-year degree required.

Computer Operator: Despite the use of smaller computers, many specialists are needed to oversee the operation of large mainframe systems. An additional 92,000 computer operators will be needed by 2000, with a starting salary of about $38,000. Two-year degree required.

Accountant/Auditor: 340,000 new accounting and auditing jobs to be added by 2000; average starting salary by then will be $43,000. Four- or five-year degree required.

Bank Loan Officer: As banks expand their services, loan officer jobs may increase substantially. Starting salary in 2000 will be $40,000 to $65,000. Four-year degree required; sometimes an MBA.

Bank Marketer: As banks aggressively sell more of their services, the demand for workers to sell their services will expand. Starting salary in 2000 will exceed $50,000. Four-year degree required.

Financial Planner: As finances become more complex, the demand is increasing for people to set up savings and investment programs for individuals and corporations. Starting salary in 2000 will be $40,000. Four-year degree plus certification required.

SOURCE: Carol Kleiman, *The 100 Best Job$ for the 1990s & Beyond* (Chicago: Dearborn Financial Publishing, 1992), pp. 143–164, 179–196; U.S. Department of Labor, 1992.

copying, and comparing. Analyzing information by computers, for example, gives a person ample opportunity to work with data.

2. *People* refers to working with human beings, and also to working with animals as if they were human. The activities involved in working with people are mentoring, negotiating, instructing, supervising, diverting, persuading, speaking/signaling, serving, and taking instructions/helping. A customer service representative would have ample opportunity to work with people, as the representative regularly handles customer complaints.

3. *Things* refers to work with inanimate objects such as tools, equipment, and products. The activities involved in working with things are setting up, precision working, operating/controlling, driving/operating, manipulating, tending, feeding/offbearing, and handling. An office equipment repair technician would have ample opportunity to work with things while making service calls.

Most jobs involve a combination of dealing with data, people, and things. It is usually a question of the relative proportion of each dimension. Managers, for example, have high involvement with data and people and a low involvement with things. Registered nurses have an average involvement with all three.

Understanding one's preferences for working with data, people, and things sharpens a career choice. Job satisfaction is likely to increase when the individual engages in work that fits his or her relative interest in data, people, and things. A person with a balanced preference for all three would probably enjoy a position selling business equipment that also required substantial preparation of sales reports.

LEVELS OF RESPONSIBILITY

Another useful way of understanding occupations, and therefore helping to plan your career, is to think about the level of responsibility you are seeking. In general, the higher the level, the more education is required, and the harder you will have to work. But, the higher the level, the more the pay and personal satisfaction. Thus, if work is important to you, you will find greater fulfillment in performing high-level work. Work can be conveniently and logically divided into the following six levels.

1. *Unskilled work* is simple and routine, requiring little independent decision making or creativity. Beginners in the work force are usually assigned such jobs. Among them are floor sweeper, dishwashing machine attendant, and delivery person.

2. *Semiskilled jobs* require some skill and knowledge or a high degree of manual skill in a limited number of tasks. A general clerk in an office or a drill press operator in a factory fits here.

3. *Skilled occupations* require specialized skills, expert knowledge, and sound judgment in carrying out assigned tasks. Included here would be tool-and-die maker, administrative assistant, or X-ray machine technician.

4. *Semiprofessional and managerial positions* involve tasks requiring independent judgment and the making of nonprogrammed decisions. An insurance claims adjuster and a first-level supervisor both fit this category.

5. *Professional positions*   require considerable knowledge, judgment, and information that is carried from job to job. Computer scientists, accountants, and engineers fit here. Debate often exists as to whether a given occupation at this level belongs in the next-higher category.

6. *Higher professional and managerial positions*   require a high level of knowledge, judgment, and ability to work independently. Physicians, psychologists, research scientists, and business executives fit here.

The higher the occupational level, the higher the amount of formal education required. Level six usually requires a degree beyond a bachelor's degree such as an M.D., Ph.D., or M.B.A. Level 5 usually requires a college degree. Levels 3 and 4 usually demand high school, college, or other specialized training. Levels 1 and 2 can be attained with on-the-job training, or no training at all in many instances.

YOU NEED TO BE REALISTIC

In planning a career, you must realize that there are proportionally fewer positions available as you move up the occupational ladder. Each firm needs only a handful of top executives, and middle-manager jobs are becoming scarcer. In order to speed up decision making and decrease costs, many middle-manager positions have been eliminated. As a result, supervisors (first-level) managers are often given more responsibility.

Another aspect of realism in career planning is awareness that not everybody can earn an above-average income. Furthermore, many newcomers to the job market will not earn as much as their counterparts of the past. The economy is now generating fewer and fewer permanent jobs that pay middle-class wages, while churning out more and more lower-wage jobs. The reason is that service jobs, such as food service and child-care work, pay less than manufacturing jobs. A dominant trend in our economy is a decline in domestic manufacturing and an increase in services.

Despite the slight note of pessimism about career opportunities made above, keep two observations in mind. First, there are still plenty of good career opportunities as implied from the occupations outlined in Exhibit 10-5. Second, people with good technical and interpersonal skills are always in demand and thus find good opportunities.

Each person starting a first or later career should ponder this question: At what point will my demand for occupational status coincide with the demand for people of my talents and education? Or, "Considering who I am and what I can do, how low on the occupational ladder can I rest and still be happy?" Whoever can answer these questions will be on the road to job satisfaction.

NINE CLUSTERS OF OCCUPATIONS

The U.S. Department of Labor estimates that there are 24,000 different kinds of jobs. It is not surprising that many different methods have been used to organize these jobs into manageable categories or clusters.

These categories or clusters of occupations are useful in familiarizing people with career opportunities. The *Dictionary of Occupational Titles,* available in most libraries and career resource centers, divides occupations into nine clusters.

As you reach each job cluster, relate it to yourself. A question you should ask is, "Would I find satisfaction doing this kind of work?" The two numbers to the left of each occupation can be used to learn more about any occupation in the list of interest to you. Simply consult the *Dictionary of Occupational Titles,* and use the two-digit code to direct you to the right information.

A complete listing of the nine job clusters is presented in Exhibit 10-6. As you scan these occupations, circle those of highest interest to you. If you are attempting to identify a career, the occupations you spontaneously circle could provide a clue to the type of work best suited to your interests. Assume, for example, a person circles number 16, "Administrative Specializations," and "Printing," number 65. This person might be well suited to the field of printing management, such as operating a company document center.

CAREER SWITCHING

It is becoming increasingly common for people to switch careers (enter a new field after working in another). People switch careers for a variety of reasons, all centering around the idea that something is missing in their present one. A study revealed that the seven most frequent reasons a group of business managers switched careers were[5]:

- A quest for more meaningful work
- A desire for a better fit between values and work
- Changed values
- Looking for greater achievement
- A desire for more leisure time
- The hope for less stress on the job
- The desire for more variety on the job

Many people who make a career change later switch back to their original careers. Sometimes the change is not carefully thought through. Three important suggestions for the career switcher are: (1) be thorough; (2) build a new career gradually; and (3) consider self-employment.

BE THOROUGH

When you feel it is necessary to find a new career, go through the same kind of thinking and planning that is recommended for finding a first career. Everything said in this chapter about choosing a first career is also

---

EXHIBIT 10-6

TWO-DIGIT OCCUPATIONAL DIVISIONS

0/1	**PROFESSIONAL, TECHNICAL, AND MANAGERIAL OCCUPATIONS**
00/01	OCCUPATIONS IN ARCHITECTURE, ENGINEERING, AND SURVEYING
02	OCCUPATIONS IN MATHEMATICS AND PHYSICAL SCIENCES
03	COMPUTER-RELATED OCCUPATIONS
04	OCCUPATIONS IN LIFE SCIENCES
05	OCCUPATIONS IN SOCIAL SCIENCES
07	OCCUPATIONS IN MEDICINE AND HEALTH
09	OCCUPATIONS IN EDUCATION
10	OCCUPATIONS IN MUSEUM, LIBRARY, AND ARCHIVAL SCIENCES
11	OCCUPATIONS IN LAW AND JURISPRUDENCE
12	OCCUPATIONS IN RELIGION AND THEOLOGY
13	OCCUPATIONS IN WRITING
14	OCCUPATIONS IN ART
15	OCCUPATIONS IN ENTERTAINMENT AND RECREATION
16	OCCUPATIONS IN ADMINISTRATIVE SPECIALIZATIONS
18	MANAGERS AND OFFICIALS, N.E.C.
19	MISCELLANEOUS PROFESSIONAL, TECHNICAL, AND MANAGERIAL OCCUPATIONS
2	**CLERICAL AND SALES OCCUPATIONS**
20	STENOGRAPHY, TYPING, FILING, AND RELATED OCCUPATIONS
21	COMPUTING AND ACCOUNT-RECORDING OCCUPATIONS
22	PRODUCTION AND STOCK CLERKS AND RELATED OCCUPATIONS
23	INFORMATION AND MESSAGE DISTRIBUTION OCCUPATIONS
24	MISCELLANEOUS CLERICAL OCCUPATIONS
25	SALES OCCUPATIONS, SERVICES
26	SALES OCCUPATIONS, CONSUMABLE COMMODITIES
27	SALES OCCUPATIONS, COMMODITIES, N.E.C.
29	MISCELLANEOUS SALES OCCUPATIONS
3	**SERVICE OCCUPATIONS**
30	DOMESTIC SERVICE OCCUPATIONS
31	FOOD AND BEVERAGE PREPARATION AND SERVICE OCCUPATIONS
32	LODGING AND RELATED SERVICE OCCUPATIONS
33	BARBERING, COSMETOLOGY, AND RELATED SERVICE OCCUPATIONS
34	AMUSEMENT AND RECREATION SERVICE OCCUPATIONS
35	MISCELLANEOUS PERSONAL SERVICE OCCUPATIONS
36	APPAREL AND FURNISHINGS SERVICE OCCUPATIONS
37	PROTECTIVE SERVICE OCCUPATIONS
38	BUILDING AND RELATED SERVICE OCCUPATIONS
4	**AGRICULTURAL, FISHERY, FORESTRY, AND RELATED OCCUPATIONS**
40	PLANT FARMING OCCUPATIONS
41	ANIMAL FARMING OCCUPATIONS
42	MISCELLANEOUS AGRICULTURAL AND RELATED OCCUPATIONS
44	FISHERY AND RELATED OCCUPATIONS
45	FORESTRY OCCUPATIONS
46	HUNTING, TRAPPING, AND RELATED OCCUPATIONS

(Continued)

5   **PROCESSING OCCUPATIONS**
50   OCCUPATIONS IN PROCESSING OF METAL
51   ORE REFINING AND FOUNDRY OCCUPATIONS
52   OCCUPATIONS IN PROCESSING OF FOOD, TOBACCO, AND RELATED PRODUCTS
53   OCCUPATIONS IN PROCESSING OF PAPER AND RELATED MATERIALS
54   OCCUPATIONS IN PROCESSING OF PETROLEUM, COAL, NATURAL AND MANUFAC-
        TURED GAS, AND RELATED PRODUCTS
55   OCCUPATIONS IN PROCESSING OF CHEMICALS, PLASTICS, SYNTHETICS, RUBBER,
        PAINT, AND RELATED PRODUCTS
56   OCCUPATIONS IN PROCESSING OF WOOD AND WOOD PRODUCTS
57   OCCUPATIONS IN PROCESSING OF STONE, CLAY, GLASS, AND RELATED PRODUCTS
58   OCCUPATIONS IN PROCESSING OF LEATHER, TEXTILES, AND RELATED PRODUCTS
59   PROCESSING OCCUPATIONS, N.E.C. (not elsewhere classified)

6   **MACHINE TRADES OCCUPATIONS**
60   METAL MACHINING OCCUPATIONS
61   METALWORKING OCCUPATIONS, N.E.C.
62/63   MECHANICS AND MACHINERY REPAIRERS
64   PAPERWORKING OCCUPATIONS
65   PRINTING OCCUPATIONS
66   WOOD MACHINING OCCUPATIONS
67   OCCUPATIONS IN MACHINING STONE, CLAY, GLASS, AND RELATED MATERIALS
68   TEXTILE OCCUPATIONS
69   MACHINE TRADES OCCUPATIONS, N.E.C.

7   **BENCHWORK OCCUPATIONS**
70   OCCUPATIONS IN FABRICATION, ASSEMBLY, AND REPAIR OF METAL PRODUCTS,
        N.E.C.
71   OCCUPATIONS IN FABRICATION AND REPAIR OF SCIENTIFIC, MEDICAL, PHOTO-
        GRAPHIC, OPTICAL, HOROLOGICAL, AND RELATED PRODUCTS
72   OCCUPATIONS IN ASSEMBLY AND REPAIR OF ELECTRICAL EQUIPMENT
73   OCCUPATIONS IN FABRICATION AND REPAIR OF PRODUCTS MADE FROM
        ASSORTED MATERIALS
74   PAINTING, DECORATING, AND RELATED OCCUPATIONS
75   OCCUPATIONS IN FABRICATION AND REPAIR OF PLASTICS, SYNTHETICS, RUBBER,
        AND RELATED PRODUCTS
76   OCCUPATIONS IN FABRICATION AND REPAIR OF WOOD PRODUCTS
77   OCCUPATIONS IN FABRICATION AND REPAIR OF SAND, STONE, CLAY, AND
        GLASS PRODUCTS
78   OCCUPATIONS IN FABRICATION AND REPAIR OF TEXTILE, LEATHER, AND
        RELATED PRODUCTS
79   BENCHWORK OCCUPATIONS, N.E.C.

8   **STRUCTURAL WORK OCCUPATIONS**
80   OCCUPATIONS IN METAL FABRICATING, N.E.C.
81   WELDERS, CUTTERS, AND RELATED OCCUPATIONS
82   ELECTRICAL ASSEMBLING, INSTALLING, AND REPAIRING OCCUPATIONS
84   PAINTING, PLASTERING, WATERPROOFING, CEMENTING, AND RELATED
        OCCUPATIONS
85   EXCAVATING, GRADING, PAVING, AND RELATED OCCUPATIONS
86   CONSTRUCTION OCCUPATIONS, N.E.C.
89   STRUCTURAL WORK OCCUPATIONS, N.E.C.

(Continued)

relevant for choosing a later career. The advantage for the career switcher, however, is that the experienced person often has a better understanding of the type of work he or she does not want to do.

BUILD A NEW CAREER GRADUALLY

Few people are able to leave one career abruptly and step into another. For most people who switch careers successfully, the switch is more of a transition than an abrupt change. Business executives who become college professors are a case in point. During the last two decades a number of successful people in business and government have been able to find faculty or administrative positions for themselves at universities and colleges. Most of these career switchers taught courses part-time for several years in order to qualify for a full-time position. The lesson to be learned is to sample a new career part-time before making a complete switch. Eric, an industrial buyer, successfully applied this principle:

> I worked for the company as a buyer for close to ten years. No complaints. I had received three promotions and I was earning a good living. But somehow it wasn't enough for me. I wanted a little more excitement out of life than the company was providing me. A neighbor of mine owned a thriving, but small, car dealership. As we got to talking, he sensed that my big-company experience might help his dealership. So I began to help him out a little part-time. I helped him get some efficient new office procedures going. Then I sketched out a program of computerizing his car and parts inventory. Soon I got caught up in the excitement of making a major impact on an employer. Since my previous company had 85,000 employees, it was hard for me to believe that I was making a major impact. The punch line is that I became vice president of administration at the dealership. I took a 20 percent reduction in pay, but I would be participating in the profits of the dealership. If I helped them save money, I would be getting a piece of the action.

CONSIDER SELF-EMPLOYMENT

A major reason that many employees consider a new career is that they crave more independence. For those people a logical path to self-fulfillment is self-employment. A typical pattern is for a future entrepreneur (a person who founds and operates an innovative type of business) to first gain business experience as an employee. Soon that person develops an idea of the type of self-employment that would be sensible for him or her.

Despite all the glamour of self-employment, it has two well-documented problems. First of all, self-employed people work very hard and long; work weeks of sixty, eighty, or even one hundred hours are not uncommon. Second, about 50 percent of new businesses fail the first year. If you are skeptical, walk through a few shopping malls, take note of the small businesses there, and check back twelve months later. Or simply go through the yellow pages, calling a number of small businesses at random. You will receive many recorded messages saying "Sorry, the number you have dialed is no longer in service."

The prospective self-employed person needs to decide upon which particular business to enter. For those who lack specific plans of their own, prepackaged plans can be purchased. A sampling of these is listed in Exhibit 10-7. Another possibility is to purchase a franchise, thus lowering

---

EXHIBIT 10-7

A SAMPLING OF OPPORTUNITIES FOR SELF-EMPLOYMENT, AS SUGGESTED BY THE AMERICAN ENTREPRENEURS ASSOCIATION

Unusual-Type Business

Art-show promoting
Bartender trade school
Firewood dealer
Gold mining
Mobile locksmithing
Pet cemetery
Weight-control clinic

Automotive-Type Businesses

Auto painting shop
Auto valet parking
Propane conversion center
Sheepskin seat covers
Thirty-minute tune-up shop

Manufacturing-Type Businesses

Burglar alarm manufacturing
Customized rug making
Hot tub manufacturing
Sculptured candle manufacturing
Stained glass manufacturing

Food-Type Businesses

Churro snack shop
Gourmet coffee and tea shop
Health-food store
Low-calorie baker
No-alcohol bar

Tourist-Type Business

Antique photo shop
Balloon vending
Dive-for-a-pearl shop
Stuffed toy-animal vending

Service-Type Businesses

Chimney sweeps
Coin-op TVs
Dating service
Energy loss prevention
Roommate-finding service

Sports/Recreation-Type Businesses

Athletic-shoe store
Backpacking shop
Candid keychain photos
Physical fitness center
Windsurfing school

Retail-Type Businesses

Antique ceiling fan store
Day-care center
Do-it-yourself cosmetic shop
Intimate apparel shop
Vitamin store

the risk of a start-up business. A substantial cash investment is required to purchase a franchise. Start-up fees begin at about $6,000 for a newly formed franchise. Well-established national and international franchises such as Subway's or McDonalds can cost as much as $500,000. Part of these franchise fees can be financed providing the person has substantial assets. Currently, franchises account for about one-third of retail sales in the United States and Canada.

The franchise owner is self-employed, yet at the same time must abide by corporate rules and regulations. Have you ever seen a Domino's Pizza store with purple chairs, or one that served beer?

SEVEN SUGGESTIONS FOR CAREER PREPARATION

Preparing for a career is closely related to choosing a career. To prepare is to be ready to meet the challenges that lie ahead in whatever career you choose. Several of the points below[6] reinforce what you have already studied in this text, or will study in Chapter 12.

1. *Be flexible.*   You may have one career field in mind, such as business. Do not overlook the possibilities of applying your education and skills to a rapidly expanding field such as health care. Also, be flexible about the size of firm you hope to work for. Most of the job growth continues to take place in small and medium-size firms.

2. *Develop interpersonal skills.*   Good interpersonal skills, especially communication skills, are a foundation for many careers. Employers seek employees who speak and write well. Most jobs require contact with co-workers and customers, or working as part of a team—meaning that people skills are essential.

3. *Think globally.*   Many jobs are becoming international jobs even if they do not involve travel. An increasing amount of business is being conducted with customers and suppliers from other countries. To capitalize on the globalization of business, polish your skills in your second language. (Some people may have to learn a second language for the first time.) It is also important to study the culture associated with your second language.

4. *Develop your computer skills.*   Computers have become an integral part of most jobs, including people-oriented jobs such as sales. Have you noticed how many outside-sales representatives work with laptop computers? Lack of computer skills can be a career retardant.

5. *Get an edge.*   Although we may be on the verge of boom economic times, employers can still afford to be choosy. Any extra skill or knowledge can help distinguish you from other job applicants. Computer skills, foreign language skills, and another degree are assets for most fields.

6. *Keep learning after you have chosen a field.*   With technologies changing so rapidly, training has become a way of life in business and industry. Be prepared to take the initiative to acquire valuable new skills before the company offers you a training program.

7. *Take part in the quality revolution.*   A rapidly increasing number of employers are paying attention to quality-improvement programs and systems such as Total Quality Management. Whatever career field you choose, you are likely to encounter an employer intent on improving quality. Learn about quality from courses, books, magazine articles, and company training programs. Apply quality principles, such as "Get it right the first time" to your job.

SUMMARY

A career has a major influence upon one's life. Aside from being a way of earning a living, a career contributes to a person's level of self-esteem and identity. Career selection is therefore a major life activity.

A good starting point in career selection is self-understanding in terms of such things as values, preferences, and skills. Skill areas can be divided into: communication, creative, interpersonal relations, management, manual and mechanical, mathematics, office, sales, scientific, service of customers, and service of patients. Information about oneself can then be matched against career opportunities. Interest testing helps many people make the right career choice. Ideally, a person should choose a career that meshes with his or her preferred lifestyle.

A recommended strategy for making a sound career choice is to gather valid occupational facts. The four sources to be consulted are printed information, computer-assisted guidance, knowledgeable people, and firsthand experience. The last category covers information gained from visiting places of work or from part-time or temporary employment. An advantageous way of choosing a career is to pursue an occupation that appears to have growth potential. You search for a match between your capabilities and interests, and a growth occupation in a growth field.

A helpful way of looking at occupations is to characterize every job by the proportion of time you devote to working with data, people, or things. It is best to choose an occupation or field that fits your preferences in these three work dimensions.

Another useful way of planning your career is to consider the level of responsibility you are seeking. Occupations have been classified into six levels in terms of increasing responsibility (and sometimes income and prestige): unskilled work, semiskilled jobs, skilled occupations, semiprofessional, professional, and managerial positions. It is important to be realistic about the occupational level to which you aspire. Statistically, it is impossible for everyone to reach the top. Also, it helps to be candid about your true level of ambition.

Being aware of occupations that exist, and then seeking more information about those careers of potential interest, can help with career choice. For example, the *Dictionary of Occupational Titles* organizes occupations into the following nine clusters: (1) Professional, technical, and managerial; (2) Clerical and sales; (3) Service; (4) Agricultural, fishery, forestry, and related occupations; (5) Processing; (6) Machine trades; (7) Benchwork; (8) Structural work; (9) Miscellaneous.

Switching careers follows many of the same principles as choosing a first career. You must be thorough in investigating career possibilities. In addition, you might consider building a new career gradually and investigate self-employment.

At the same time you might be choosing a career, think of preparing for a career. Suggestions along these lines include: be flexible; develop interpersonal skills, think globally, develop computer skills, get an edge, keep learning, and learn about quality.

Questions and Activities

1. Now that you have read this chapter, what do you think you would do differently should you be choosing a career or career switching?

2. What are the major consequences of having made a poor career choice?

3. Which of the skills listed in Exhibit 10-2 do you think will take the longest time to develop? Why?

4. Why are scientific skills important for career people who are not entering a scientific field?

5. What occupations would you suggest for a person who scored very high on the Enterprising and Conventional themes on the Strong Interest Inventory?

6. How might attempting to match your career to your lifestyle block your career progress?

7. What flaw do you detect in the strategy of choosing a career based on whether the field you select is a growth field?

8. Identify an occupation you think requires a high level of skill with data, people, and things. Explain your reasoning.

9. How should the fact that jobs are not as secure as they were previously influence the importance of preparing for a career?

10. Speak to someone you think has a successful career to find out how that person made his or her career choice. Be ready to discuss your findings in class.

REFERENCES

[1]"Teens: Here Comes the Biggest Wave Yet," *Business Week,* April 11, 1994, p. 76; Robert W. Goddard, "Work Force 2000," *Personnel Journal,* February 1989, p. 67.

[2]Julie Griffin Levitt, *Your Career: How to Make It Happen,* 2d ed. (Cincinnati, Ohio: South-Western Publishing, 1990), pp. 11–21.

A HUMAN RELATIONS CASE PROBLEM: THE UNCERTAIN CAREER CHOICE

One year prior to entering college, Allison engaged her family, friends, and high-school guidance counselor in helping her make a good career decision. Allison was asked by her guidance counselor what activities in life she enjoyed the most. Allison's answer to this question provided her a strong clue to a possible career path.

Allison responded thoughtfully, "I've really enjoyed my vacations with my parents. I've always been impressed with the way hotels and cruise ships operate. The people in charge are so polite, well dressed, and well spoken. I would enjoy working with people in the hotel and travel field. I also like the atmosphere of hotels. It's kind of in my blood."

With this initial hunch about a career prospect, Allison next conducted serious research. She investigated programs of study in hotel and tourism. She also telephoned anybody she thought might know of someone working at a professional level in the hotel field.

Allison arranged interviews with two hotel managers and one assistant hotel manager. She also spoke to a friend's brother who had worked as a photographer on a few cruises. Based on these interviews and her own observations, Allison decided to major in hotel and tourism upon entering college.

Three weeks before the first fall semester at college, Allison asked to reserve dinnertime one Friday night for serious conversation. "What's on your mind, Allison," asked her dad.

Allison replied, "Mom and Dad, I'm not so sure I want to go into the hotel and tourism field. I think the work is great, but the sacrifice might be too big."

"What sacrifice?" asked her mother.

"The sacrifice," said Allison, "is that I couldn't lead a normal life. When my friends were off from work, I'd be working. When other people would be on vacation, I would be busier than ever. Another problem is that if you do a good job as a hotel manager, you're moved around from hotel to hotel.

"How could I ever lead a normal social life? How could I ever get married and raise children?"

Allison's dad commented, "Are you telling me that nobody in the hotel field has friends or family?"

"Maybe they have friends," said Allison, "but they must all be working at hotels or restaurants. These people are probably a culture of their own."

Allison's mom replied, "If you feel that strongly, pick another major. Just drop the whole idea. Find a field like office management where you could lead a normal life."

(Continued)

"It's not that simple," responded Allison. "I still want to enter the hotel and tourism field. I know I would love the work. It's just the work schedule that might ruin it.

"I'm going to have to give my career choice a lot more thought."

QUESTIONS

1. How serious is the career choice problem facing Allison?

2. In what way is Allison facing a conflict?

3. What advice can you give Allison for deciding whether to pursue a career in hotel and tourism?

A HUMAN RELATIONS ROLE PLAY: THE UNCERTAIN CAREER CHOICE

The above case serves as background information for this role play. One person plays the role of Allison who visits her guidance counselor to mull over her career choice dilemma. Allison has considerable emotion about making a career choice. Another student plays the role of the guidance counselor who wants to both ask Allison the right questions and give her concrete advice. Run the role play for ten to fifteen minutes.

[3]The description of the Strong Interest Inventory is based on James G. Clawson, John P. Kotter, Victor A. Faux, and Charles C. McArthur, *Self-Assessment and Career Development,* 3d ed. (Englewood Cliffs, N.J.: Prentice Hall, 1992), pp. 125–135.

[4]DISCOVER *for Colleges and Adults,* The American College Testing Program, updated regularly.

[5]O. C. Brenner and Marc G. Singer, "Career Repotters: To Know Them Could Be to Keep Them," *Personnel,* November 1988, p. 58.

[6]"Seven Tips for Career Preparation," *NBEA Keying In,* November 1993, p. 8; "Today's Critical Skills: Going Beyond the Basics," *Executive Strategies,* December 1993, p. 9.

ADDITIONAL READING

Allenbaugh, Eric. *Wake-Up Calls: You Don't Have to Sleepwalk Through Your Life.* Chicago: Discovery Publications, 1993.

Bolles, Richard N. *The Three Boxes of Life and How to Get Out of Them.* Berkeley, Calif.: Ten Speed Press, revised regularly.

Bolles, Richard N., *The 1994 What Color Is Your Parachute: A Practical Manual for Job Hunters and Career Changers.* Berkeley, Calif.: Ten Speed Press, 1994.

Hawkes, Gene R. *The Career Changer's Sourcebook.* New York: Facts on File, 1989.

McCormack, John and Legge, David. *Self-Made in America.* Reading, Mass.: Addison-Wesley, 1991.

Powers, Paul, and Russell, Deborah. *Love Your Job!* Sebastopol, Calif.: O'Reilly & Associates, 1993.

CHAPTER 11

FINDING A SUITABLE JOB

Learning Objectives

After studying the information and doing the exercises in this chapter you should be able to:

- Improve your chances of finding a suitable job.

- Identify the steps involved in conducting a job campaign.

- Prepare an effective cover letter, job résumé, and follow-up letter.

- Present yourself effectively in a job interview.

- Be aware of the types of employment tests an applicant is likely to take.

*P*eople need to find a job for many reasons. You may be starting your career; you may be tired of your present job; you may want to boost your career; and you might be laid off or fired. Finding a new job does not always mean that you will be leaving your present firm. People who work for large employers often seek new employment in another unit (division, department, agency, and so forth) within the same organization.

If you have already identified a field for yourself, the job-finding process will be somewhat narrowed—you will conduct your job campaign

for a position related to your primary field of interest. If you have not already selected a field, the job-finding process itself might help you identify a field. A twenty-seven-year-old hotel manager was asked how she got into the hotel management field. She replied, "Pure luck. I graduated from business school without any idea of what to do. I found out that a hotel chain was inter-viewing graduates from our school. After two interviews, I was offered a job as a management trainee. Here I am today, a real manager, and loving every minute of it."

The purpose of this chapter is to provide the basic information you need to conduct an effective job search. We also present a few fine points to help give you an edge over those who do the minimum necessary to find a suitable position.

 ## TARGETING YOUR JOB SEARCH

A job search begins with a reasonably flexible description of the type of job or jobs you are looking for. Flexibility is called for because with so many different jobs available, it is difficult to be too specific. A reasonable objective might be something of this nature: "I am searching for a job in the numerical field, with a large employer, located within thirty miles of here. I prefer accounting work. My minimum salary would be $475 per week."

Your chances of finding suitable employment are directly proportional to the number of positions that will satisfy your job objectives. One person with an interest in the literary field might be willing to accept a job only as a newspaper reporter—always a difficult position to find. Another person with the same background is seeking a job as (1) a newspaper reporter, (2) a magazine staff writer, (3) a copywriter in an advertising agency, (4) a communications specialist in a firm, or (5) a copywriter in a public relations firm. The second person has a better chance than the first of finding a job.

Closely tied in with the type of work you are seeking is the type of organization in which you would prefer to work. Unless you have had exposure to different types of organizations, you may have only tentative answers to this question. Questioning people who work at different places can provide you with some useful clues. Further, plant tours open to the public can provide valuable tips about what it is like to work in that particular firm. Visits to stores, restaurants, and government agencies will provide informal information about the general nature of working conditions in those places. As you begin your job search, ask yourself these questions to help you identify the type of organization that *might* be right for you:

- Would I feel more comfortable working in an office with hundreds of other people? Or would I prefer just a handful of co-workers?

- Would I prefer working in a place where people went out of their way to dress in a stylish manner? Or would I prefer an informal place where not so much emphasis was placed on appearance?

- Would I prefer to work in a small town or in a busy metropolitan area?

- How important is access to stores and restaurants?

- Would it be best for me to work where I could rely on public transportation?

- Would I really prefer an easygoing atmosphere or a highly competitive, "rat race" environment?

- How important are the social aspects of work to me? Would I be happy only in a place where I could meet prospective dates and make new friends?

A widely used approach in choosing an organization is to apply to a *good company*. What constitutes a good company is subjective. Robert Levering and Milton Moskowitz have collected subjective opinions about good employers for their book, *The 100 Best Companies to Work for in America*. The authors obtained nominees for these best companies from many sources: news articles and recommendations from friends, acquaintances, and from business writers. Some companies nominated themselves.

After receiving the nominations, Levering and Moscowitz collected information about all the nominated companies, and conducted on-site visits. Employees were asked how much they enjoyed working for the company and to explain their answers. The best companies showed up strong on six measures:

1. Good pay and benefits

2. Opportunities for training and promotion

3. Job security (a no-layoff policy even if it means that the company earns smaller profits)

4. Employees who have pride in work and the company

5. Openness/fairness (employees having freedom to speak to executives and having employee problems settled justly)

6. Camaraderie/friendliness (employees feeling they are part of a family, team, or special community)[1]

Exhibit 11-1 lists the top ten companies to work for, as perceived by the nominators and the authors. Recognize that these companies are not being ranked on profitability, yet most of the firms listed are financially successful.

QUALIFICATIONS SOUGHT BY EMPLOYERS

What you are looking for in an employer must be matched against what an employer is looking for in an employee. Job interviewers do not all agree on the qualifications they seek in employees. Nevertheless, a number of traits, characteristics, skills, and accomplishments are important to many employers.[2] Exhibit 11-2 summarizes these qualifications sought for in job applicants.

EXHIBIT 11-1

THE TOP TEN COMPANIES TO WORK FOR IN AMERICA AS PERCEIVED BY EMPLOYEES

1. Beth Israel Hospital Boston, Boston
2. Delta Air Lines, Atlanta
3. Donnelly (glass), Holland, Michigan
4. Federal Express, Memphis
5. Fel-Pro, Skokie, Illinois
6. Hallmark Cards, Kansas City, Missouri
7. Publix Super Markets, Lakeland, Florida
8. Rosenbluth International, Philadelphia
9. Southwest Airlines, Dallas
10. USAA (financial services), San Antonio

NOTE: The above employers are listed in alphabetical order.

SOURCE: Robert Levering and Milton Moskowitz, *The 100 Best Companies to Work for in America* (New York: Doubleday, 1993).

EXHIBIT 11-2

QUALIFICATIONS SOUGHT BY EMPLOYERS

Qualifications a substantial number of employment interviewers and hiring managers are looking for in job applicants include the following:

Appropriate Education and Satisfactory Grades. Your education should be a reasonable fit with the demands of the job. Satisfactory grades are important because they may be an indicator of intelligence and hard work. Large, successful employers place the most emphasis on grades.

Relevant Work Experience. Although a career beginner may have limited job experience, some job experience may be helpful. Part-time and temporary work related to your job objective may be sufficient. Co-op and internship experience is highly valued.

Communication and Interpersonal Skills. The ability to communicate with people and get along with different types of people are two of the most desirable qualities in job candidates. Job interviewers attempt to judge these qualities during the interview.

Motivation and Energy. Well-motivated and energetic employees are needed to increase productivity and keep employers profitable. Your past record of achievements will be used to judge your motivation and energy. It also helps to *look* energetic and well motivated. One way to do this is by speaking enthusiastically about the prospective job and employer.

Problem-Solving Ability. Employers seek bright employees except when hiring for routine, repetitive jobs. Your problem-solving ability is reflected in how you handled problems in the past, your grades, your interests, and how intelligently you respond to the interviewer's questions. The ability to analyze problems and arrive at solutions (analytical ability) is included in problem-solving ability.

Judgment and Common Sense. Good judgment and common sense are important supplements to job knowledge in every position. An applicant's description of how he or she handled problems in the past is often used to assess judgment and common sense. Behavior during the interview can also be an indicator. For example, if a phone call came through for the interviewer, good judgment would be to say, "Would you like me to step out of the room for a moment?"

Flexibility. Since job demands change so frequently, flexible employees are considered valuable. One indicator of flexibility is whether an applicant responds well to the prospects of taking a job different from the one originally planned.

Emotional Maturity. Maturity is valued because it helps an employee behave professionally and responsibly. What constitutes maturity is a subjective evaluation. However, a candidate who does such things as engage in excessive small talk, chew gum, ask for change to use the vending machine, or bring a friend to the waiting room will be considered immature.

(*Continued*)

Leadership.   Employers seeking potential supervisors and managers look for applicants to have past leadership accomplishments. Formal leadership positions, such as a team captain or club officer, are significant. So are experiences such as having organized a charity collection.

Teamwork skills.   The ability to work well in a team is required by most employers because so much work is organized into teams. Experience in working in teams, including project assignments in school and membership on an athletic team or band, is an asset. Applicants who enjoy working in teams are preferred over those who merely tolerate teamwork.

SOURCE: Based in part on Bob Weinstein, "What Employers Look For," *The Honda How to Get a Job Guide* (special edition of *Business Week's Guide to Careers*), 1985, pp. 10–13; updated and supported by survey of employers taken by the Central Placement Office, Rochester Institute of Technology, 1994; "What Personnel Offices Really Stress in Hiring," *The Wall Street Journal*, March 6, 1991.

Several important conclusions can be drawn from the list of qualifications in Exhibit 11-2. One is that these qualifications are success factors in most lines of work. For instance, to achieve success in most fields you must have the appropriate education, be a good problem solver, and be well motivated. Another conclusion is that most of these qualifications can be developed or acquired. To illustrate, if you have not yet demonstrated leadership ability, you can actively seek leadership experience.

A third implication of this list is that employers set high expectations when they fill job openings. As a human resources manager at a bank explained, "We see no sense in hiring an applicant who does not have a professional outlook. It does less damage to the bank to let a position go unfilled than to hire someone we are not proud to have as an employee."

JOB-FINDING METHODS

A cornerstone principle of conducting a job search is to use several methods. Some methods of job finding are better than others, but any technique will pay off now and then. A skilled job seeker will therefore pursue job-finding methods of high, medium, and low probability. To increase the probability of any job-finding method being successful, pursue jobs in a prospering field, industry, or geographic location. Many job seekers who cannot find a suitable job in their hometown fare better when they conduct a job search in a town with more economic expansion.

Job-finding techniques are divided here into six types: (1) networking, (2) mail campaign, (3) telesearch, (4) placement offices and employment agencies, (5) help wanted ads, and (6) support groups. Exhibit 11-3 will help you develop sensitivity to the many ways of finding a job.

NETWORKING (CONTACTS AND REFERRALS)

By far the most effective method of finding a job is through personal contacts. **Networking** is the process of establishing a group of contacts who can help you in your career. Networking is particularly helpful because it taps you into the "insider system" or "internal job market." The internal job market is the large array of jobs that haven't been advertised and are usually filled by word of mouth or through friends and acquaintances of employees.

About 85 percent of job openings are found in the hidden job market. The other 15 percent of jobs are advertised or registered with employment agencies and placement offices. The best way to reach the jobs in the hidden market is by getting someone to recommend you for one. When looking for a job it is therefore important to tell every potential contact of your job search. The more influential the person the better. Be specific about the type of job you are seeking.

To use networking effectively, it may be necessary to create contacts aside from those you already have. Potential sources of contacts include:

Friends

Parents and other family members

Parents of friends

Friends of parents

Work associates

Faculty and staff

Former or present employer (if you hold a temporary job)

EXHIBIT 11-3

CREATIVE JOB-FINDING TECHNIQUES

Job seekers often make the mistake of not exploring enough different methods for finding a job. After exploring a few conventional techniques, such as making a trip to the placement office, they sit back and wait for job offers to pour in. A better approach is to search for creative alternatives to finding a job. Think of every possibility, then sort out the workable from the unworkable later on. To accomplish this task, the class will be organized into brainstorming groups. The goal is to specify as large a number of job-finding techniques as possible. Follow the guidelines for brainstorming presented in Chapter 3, Exhibit 3-4.

After each group has assembled and edited its job-finding techniques, group leaders will present their findings to the rest of the class. Groups can then compare their job-finding suggestions.

Athletic team members and coaches

Religious and community groups

Trade and professional associations

Career and job fairs

To capitalize on these contacts, it is helpful to carry business cards. You do not have to be employed to use a business card. Simply place on your card a notation such as, "Alex Catalino, accounting specialist, Dallas, Texas." Also include your address and telephone number. An electronic-mail address on your business card adds flair.

Mary, who had just graduated from college, illustrates how contacts can be used innovatively. She combined her personal and her parents' holiday greeting card lists. Next she contacted each person on the list who lived in the city where she wanted to work. Mary then arranged a one-week visit to that city. She met with all the people she already contacted. In the process she eventually learned of several promising job leads, and accepted one of the offers she received.[3]

An important caution about networking: too many people are consuming too much of other people's time to help them with their job searches. Keep your request for assistance brief and pointed. Ask to reciprocate in any way you can. For example, you might prepare a chart or conduct research for a manager who gave you a job lead.

MAIL CAMPAIGN

Another way to tap the internal job market is to write dozens of letters to prospective employers. Although this method of finding a job is part of the insider system, it is unique enough to warrant a category of its own.

The plan is to come up with a master list of firms you might want to work for. The more comprehensive and thorough the list, the better your chances of finding employment. You make up the list according to the category or categories that make the most sense in your particular situation.

Central libraries have directories that provide such information. Two useful business directories are those published by Dun and Bradstreet and by Standard and Poor. Both provide full addresses and names of key people in the firms listed. The information is organized by such factors as size of the firm, location, or type of business (for example, banks or petroleum companies). Again, use a person's name—not Dear Sir, Madam, or Ms. Even if the person you write to is deceased or has moved, your letter will be referred to someone else who might be able to help you. It is helpful to verify names by telephoning the company.

Assume that you are intent on finding a job in the San Francisco Bay area. For you, geography is more important than the nature of the business. You might then purchase a business and industry list from the San Francisco Chamber of Commerce. Using a cover letter (described later in this chapter) you would write to specific individuals in as many firms as possible, including the federal, state, county, and city governments. Another term for this technique is the **unsolicited-letter campaign.** The approach often works well for a newcomer to the work force because that person is flexible and does not require the salary of a more experienced employee.

Another useful way of organizing your list is by type of enterprise. Suppose your long-term career goal is to become a bank executive. To get started in banking, write to as many banks in the areas of the country in which you would be willing to work.

How effective is the prospective employer list as a method of obtaining a job interview or a job? In general, think of writing about one hundred letters to get several interviews and one job. Your postage, stationery, and printing costs will be covered by your first two paychecks.

TELESEARCH

A related approach to the mail campaign is the **telesearch,** obtaining job leads by making unsolicited phone calls to prospective employers. The list of prospects can be assembled in the same manner as the mail campaign. Begin your inquiry into an organization by contacting the person who would be your boss if you landed the job you really want. A major goal of the telesearch is to establish direct contact with as many of these decision makers as you can.

John Truitt advises *not* to call an executive and ask if there are any openings. Such an inquiry invites a "no" response. Instead, use a brief presentation (about one minute) to attempt to arrange an interview:

> "Mr. Caldone, my name is Jack Paradise. I have three years of experience in your area of business and would like to drop by your office this week to discuss working for you. Would 3 P.M. on Thursday be convenient, or would 3 P.M. on Friday better fit your schedule?"[4]

This kind of approach is brief and direct, yet ends with a "choice of two," making it easier for the prospective employer to agree to an interview. If the person contacted has an opening or is interested in learning more about you, you will probably get the interview or be asked to mail in a résumé. Even if you fail to get an interview, you might be able to obtain a job lead from your contact. Inquire about who the person knows who might be interested in hiring someone with your experience.

The telesearch, like the unsolicited letter campaign, is used to make the prospective employer want to meet you. Use the interview to make him or her want to hire you. Although the prospective employer cannot see you, smile and speak with confidence and enthusiasm. Truitt estimates that approximately one hundred telephone calls will be needed to receive about five to ten interviews.[5]

Placement Offices and Employment Agencies

Your placement office is a primary avenue to finding a job. Even if you do not find a job through the placement office, you will still gain valuable experience. The job interviews you receive will help sharpen your job-finding skills. Placement offices also offer helpful suggestions for preparing résumés and cover letters.

The thought of using an employment agency crosses the mind of every job seeker. Employers use employment agencies to advertise jobs and screen applicants. Employment agencies are more valuable for people with about five to ten years of job experience than for newcomers. Not to be overlooked, however, is that many employment agencies specialize in temporary help. After working for the employer for about nine months, the temporary job might become permanent. (Employers are under contract with agencies not to hire temporary workers shortly after they begin.)

Employment agencies are worth exploring, especially if the employer pays the fee. If you pay the fee, it is still worthwhile if the agency helps you find an outstanding position. If the agency does not help you find the job you want, you are under no obligation.

Help Wanted Ads in Newspapers, Magazines, and Trade Journals

A thorough job search includes a careful scanning of the help wanted section of classified ads. Top-paying positions are more likely to be filled through other job-finding methods. Nevertheless, many people find good jobs through classified ads. Help wanted ads are found in local newspapers and national newspapers, such as the *Wall Street Journal,* the *New York Times,* and *USA Today.* Professional and trade magazines such as *Personnel Journal* often contain ads searching for workers in the field of interest covered by the publication.

Because so many people respond to ads listing attractive-sounding jobs, this method yields relatively few job interviews. Four types of want ads can be identified: (1) open ads, (2) blind ads, (3) employment agency ads, and (4) catch ads.[6]

1. *Open ads* disclose considerable information about the position opening, including the name of the employer, phone number, nature of the job and the company's business, and qualifications sought. Starting salary is sometimes mentioned. Consequently, open ads attract the largest number of applicants. An open ad is presented in Exhibit 11-4.

2. *Blind ads* conceal the organization in which the advertised position is available, but may contain other important information. The reader is requested to respond by sending a letter and résumé to a post office box or the newspaper. By placing a blind ad, the company does not have to deal with a large number of unqualified callers. Another reason the company uses a blind ad is to maintain secrecy with competitors and employees. One remote disadvantage of responding to a blind ad when currently employed is that the advertiser may be one's employer.

3. *Employment agency ads* are placed by agencies, and list one or more job openings for their employer clients. Agencies tend to advertise their more attractive openings. These positions may be filled quickly, but the agency may encourage the job hunter to examine other possibilities. One of the purposes of want ads placed by employment agencies is to enlarge their pool of qualified candidates.

4. *Catch ads* promise unusually high-paying job opportunities without requiring specific job qualifications. Frequently these jobs involve selling difficult-to-sell merchandise, strictly on commission or with a modest weekly draw against commission. Respondents often find that they are required to sell home siding, food supplements, or magazine subscriptions. Furthermore, you might be asked to purchase the merchandise, which you will then attempt to sell to customers. These jobs are best suited for high risk takers.

Another way of using classified ads to secure a job is to place a position wanted ad, describing the position you seek and your qualifications. Your ad must be creative and eye-catching because so many people self-advertise. Robert D. Lock cautions that most of the responses to these ads are from

---

EXHIBIT 11-4

AN OPEN AD

Sales

CAREER OPPORTUNITY

Medtronic, a *Fortune* 500 company and leading manufacturer in the medical industry, is seeking a Sales Rep for its tendon and muscle stimulator business through the Buffalo, N.Y. area. Successful candidate will have two years' proven sales experience, preferably with a medical sales background and a college degree or equivalent preferred. We offer competitive salary and benefits package, including commissions, car allowance, training, etc. Please send résumé and salary history to: Tom Miller, MEDTRONIC NORTECH, 9999 Sunset Blvd., Pittsburgh, PA 15255. Equal Opportunity Employer.

employment agencies and career advisers offering to help you conduct a job search.[7] Position wanted ads are thus a long shot, but could work.

Companies seeking to increase minority recruitment often advertise in minority-oriented publications, thus providing a good source of job leads for those who qualify. Among these publications are the *Black Collegian, Black Enterprise, Hispanic Business,* and *Vista.*

When should you begin looking for a job? The answer to this question depends somewhat on the type of job you are seeking. In general, the bigger the job, the longer the job campaign. Job-hunting advisers generally agree that it will take about six months to find a full-time position in your field. You will need this much time to prepare your résumé and cover letter, and to pursue all the methods described in this section. Another factor is that most prospective employers take at least thirty days to notify you of their employment decision.

SUPPORT GROUPS

People sometimes join forces to help each other find a job by forming a support group, especially when jobs are scarce. One such group is Forty Plus, a group of unemployed or underemployed managers and professionals age forty or over. (An underemployed person is overqualified for his or her job, such as a computer science graduate hired to operate a photocopying machine.) The organization provides members the use of office equipment such as word processors and fax machines, along with job-finding information. Members of Forty Plus encourage each other emotionally and sometimes share information about job opportunities. Support groups for job seekers can sometimes be found in churches and temples.

THE ATTENTION-GETTING COVER LETTER

A résumé is necessary but not sufficient for conducting an intelligent job campaign. You also need an attention-getting cover letter to accompany your résumé. The cover letter multiplies the effectiveness of the résumé because it enables you to prepare a tailor-made, individual approach to each job situation you are pursuing. The most important purpose of the cover letter is to explain why you are applying for the position in question. Simultaneously, you try to convince the prospective employer why you should be considered.

The cover letter is particularly suited to responding to a want ad or an announcement posted in a placement office, or when writing unsolicited job-seeking letters. Most job applicants use the conventional (and somewhat ineffective) approach of writing a letter attempting to impress the prospective employer with their background. A more effective approach is to capture the reader's attention with a direct statement of what you might be able to do for the firm in question. Keep this "what I can do for you" strategy paramount in your mind at every stage of finding a job. It works wonders in the job interview, as it will in the rest of your career.

After you have stated how you can help the employer, present a one-page summary of your education and highlights of your job and educational experience. A sample cover letter is presented in Exhibit 11-5. Notice that the opening line is an attention-getter: "Without a good service department, a new-car dealership is in big trouble."

You may not want to write an outrageous and flip cover letter, but it should have enough flair to attract the reader's attention. Avoid including only bland and conventional statements in your cover letter such as, "I am available for an interview at your convenience."

EXHIBIT 11-5

SAMPLE COVER LETTER

27 Buttercup Lane
Little Rock, AR 72203
Date

Mr. Bart Bertrand
President
South View Dodge
258 Princess Blvd.
Little Rock, AR 72201

Dear Mr. Bertrand:

Without a good service department, a new-car dealership is in big trouble. An efficiency-minded person like myself who loves autos, and likes to help customers, can do wonders for your service department. Give me a chance, and I will help you maintain the high quality of after-sales service demanded by your customers.

The position you advertised in the *Dispatch* is an ideal fit for my background. Shortly, I will be graduating from Pine Valley College with an associate's degree in automotive technology. In addition, I was an automotive mechanics major at Monroe Vocational High.

My job experience includes three years of part-time general work at Manny's Mobil Service, and two years of clerical work at Brandon's Chrysler-Plymouth. Besides this relevant experience, I'm the proud owner of a mint condition 1980 sports coupe I maintain myself.

I'm very stable in this community. A well-paying, secure job where I can make a contribution is important to me.

My enclosed résumé contains additional information about me. When might I have the opportunity to be interviewed?

Sincerely yours,

Rita Mae Jenkins

PREPARING AN EFFECTIVE JOB RÉSUMÉ

The purpose of a résumé is to help you obtain a job interview, not a job. A résumé is needed both as an outside candidate and often when seeking a transfer in a large firm. Very few people are hired without a personal interview. Effective résumés are straightforward, factual presentations of a person's experiences, education, skills, and accomplishments. Yet a résumé is much like art. People have different ideas about what constitutes an effective résumé. To add to the confusion, some people spell résumé with the acute accents (résumé is a French word), and some without. A challenge in preparing an effective résumé is to suit many different preferences.

Résumé length illustrates how employers hold different opinions about the best résumé format. A national survey of employers indicated that 24 percent said the résumé should be "no longer than one page"; 42 percent said "no longer than two pages," and 34 percent, "determined by information."[8]

A few general guidelines will be offered here which will help you avoid serious mistakes. An overall perspective to keep in mind is, "If your résumé is not a winner, it's a killer."[9] Done properly, a résumé can lead to an interview with a prospective employer. Done poorly, it will block you from further consideration.

THREE TYPES OF RÉSUMÉS

The three most commonly used résumé formats are the chronological, functional, and targeted. You might consider using one of these types, or a blend of them, based on the information about yourself you are trying to highlight. Whichever format you choose, you must include essential information.

The **chronological résumé** presents your work experience, education, and interests, along with your accomplishments, in reverse chronological order. A chronological résumé is basically the traditional résumé with the addition of accomplishments and achievements. Some people say the chronological résumé is too bland. However, it contains precisely the information that most employers demand, and it is easy to prepare.

The **functional résumé** organizes your skills and accomplishments into the functions or tasks that support the job you are seeking. A section of a functional résumé might read:

SUPERVISION: Organized the activities of five park employees to create a smooth-running recreation program. Trained and supervised four roofing specialists to help produce a successful roofing business.

The functional résumé is useful because it highlights the things you have accomplished and the skills you have developed. In this way, an ordinary work experience might seem more impressive. For instance, the tasks listed above under "supervision" may appear more impressive than listing the jobs "Playground supervisor" and "Roofing crew chief." One problem with the functional résumé is that it omits the factual information many employers demand.

The **targeted résumé** focuses on a specific job target or position and presents only information about you that supports that target. Using a target format, an applicant for a sales position would list only sales jobs. Under education, the applicant would focus on sales-related courses such as communication skills and marketing. A targeted résumé is helpful in dramatizing your suitability for the position you are seeking. However, this résumé format omits other relevant information about you, and a new résumé must be prepared for each target position.

Whichever résumé format you choose, it is best to place your most salable asset first.[10] If your work experience is limited, place education before work experience. If your skills are more impressive than your education or work experience, list them first.

A general-purpose résumé, following a chronological format, is presented in Exhibit 11-6. This person chose to place work experience before education. Although her résumé is chronological, it also allows room for accomplishments and skills. Many people have achieved good results with this format. However, do not restrict yourself. Investigate other résumé formats, including exploring software that provides the user a résumé outline.

HOW TO HANDLE THE JOB OBJECTIVE SECTION

On the résumé, a **job objective** is the position you are applying for now or intend to hold in the future. A job objective is also referred to as a *job target* or a *position objective*. Although stating a job objective seems easy, it is a trouble spot for many résumé writers. Early in their careers many people feel compelled to state their long-range career objectives in the job objective section. A twenty-one-year-old might state, "To become president of an international corporation." Certainly this is a worthy objective, but it is better to be more modest at the outset.

Employers will tend to interpret the job objective as a statement of your short-term plans. If you think your long-term objective should be stated, you might divide the section into "immediate objective" and "long-term objective." Current practice is to use the position under consideration as a job objective. Longer-term objectives can then be discussed during the job interview.

Another challenge with the job objective section is that your objective will often have to be tailored to the specific job under consideration. The job objective you have printed on your résumé may not fit exactly the job you are applying for. You might be considering a sales career. You find two good leads, one for selling an industrial product, and one for a consumer product. You would want your objective on one résumé to mention industrial sales, and on the other consumer sales.

One approach to this problem is to keep your résumé filed in a word processor. You can then modify the job objective section for a given job lead. Another approach is to omit the job objective section. Your cover letter can

EXHIBIT 11-6

A GENERAL-PURPOSE RÉSUMÉ

Rita Mae Jenkins
27 Buttercup Lane
Little Rock, AR 72203

Job Objective	Management position in service department of new-car dealership
Job Experience	
1994–present	Senior clerk, Brandon-Chrysler Plymouth, Little Rock. Responsible for receiving customer payments for service performed; preparing invoices; miscellaneous tasks as requested by service manager.
	• Set up database that saved space and reduced file-searching time.
1991–1994	Service station attendant, Manny's Mobil Service: Performed variety of light mechanical tasks such as assisting in brake relinings, installing mufflers and tail pipes, tune-ups, independent responsibility for lubrication and oil changes.
	• Increased sales of tires, batteries, and accessories by 18 percent during time periods on duty.
Formal Education	
1992–1994	Pine Valley College, Associate Degree, automotive technology, May 1994. Studied all phases auto repair including computerized diagnostics, service department management. Attended school while working about 30 hours per week. Grade Point Average, 3.25.
1988–1992	Harrison Vocational Technical High School, Little Rock. Graduated 10th in class of 137. Majored in automotive repair and maintenance. Also studied business education topics such as bookkeeping, business machines, and office systems and procedures.
Job-Related Skills	Word processing, spreadsheet analysis, development of databases. Can perform bookkeeping. Able to handle customer concerns and complaints in person or by phone. Know how to diagnose and repair wide range of automotive problems for domestic and imported vehicles.
Personal Interests and Hobbies	Enjoy automobile restoration and maintenance, Physical fitness enthusiast. Walt Disney movie buff. Read self-improvement books and current fiction; daily newspaper. Watch CNN and pro football on television.
References	On file with placement office at Pine Valley College. Permissible to contact present or former employer.

describe the link between you and the job under consideration. Notice how the cover letter in Exhibit 11-5 made this link. (The same person, however, did include a job objective on her résumé.)

How Do You Write a Résumé When Your Background Does Not Fit the Position?

Job seekers sometimes lack the type of experience expected to qualify them for a position they seek. This lack of direct fit may occur when the applicant is switching fields, or is entering the work force after a long absence. In both instances it is helpful to emphasize skills and experience that would contribute to success in the job under consideration.

Assume a person with five years of experience as a bookkeeper applies for a sales representative position at an office equipment company. The bookkeeper is advised to make these types of entries on his or her résumé: "Five years of experience in working directly with office equipment including computers, fax machines, and high-speed copiers." "Able to size up equipment needs of accountants and bookkeepers." "Accustomed to negotiating budgets with managers."

Assume a person has twenty years of experience managing a household, but has not worked outside the home. The candidate applies for an assistant manager position in a restaurant. The person should list relevant skills such as "Able to plan and prepare holiday meals and parties for large groups of people." The candidate is also advised to describe his or her volunteer work because such experience may be job-related. For example, "Coordinated church picnic for 250 people, including recruiting and supervising ten workers, and raising the necessary funds."

What About the Creative Style Résumé?

Since so many résumés are sent to employers, it is difficult to attract an employer's attention. The solution offered to this problem is a creatively prepared résumé. A **creative-style résumé** is one with a novel format and design. Do not confuse this idea with the "created résumé" in which one "creates" facts to make a favorable impression.

One creative approach is to print your résumé in the format of a menu. One job seeker went so far as calling his education the "appetizer," his work experience the "entrée," and his hobbies and interests the "dessert." Others try to make their résumés distinctive by printing them on tinted or oversized paper. A current trend is to present yourself in a video instead of using a written résumé. According to one job counselor, this approach is ill-advised for most people because few people appear impressive in a video.

If done in a way to attract positive attention to yourself, creative-style résumés have merit. The generally accepted approach, however, is for résumés to be conservative. In one study, 93 percent of college recruiters surveyed preferred white or ivory color for the résumé. For the entry-level job applicant, the conservative approach is the safest bet.[11] If you are applying for a position in which creative talent is a primary factor, the creative-style résumé is helpful. A more conventional job requires a more conventional résumé. Human resource managers often object to oversized résumés because they are difficult to fit into standard files.

Résumé Errors to Avoid

Another way to distinguish your résumé from others is to prepare one that is neat, well organized, and professional in appearance. The positive advice offered so far should help you attain this goal. Despite all the help available to job seekers, many applicants still mail out careless, poorly organized, and unprofessional-looking résumés. Avoid the following mistakes commonly found in résumés:

- No listing of accomplishments or skills

- Too lengthy, containing much useless information; or written in narrative, rather than short, punchy statements

- Disorganized, including the same type of information presented under different headings

- Poorly word-processed or typed, with narrow margins and writing in the margins, excessive spacing between lines and words, and typed or printed using a faded ribbon

- Skimpy or insufficient information (only dates, titles, and incomplete addresses)

- Excessive information, including general information (such as a listing of the product line of an employer like Procter and Gamble)

- Misspellings, typographical and input errors, errors corrected by pen, poor grammar, and frequent abbreviations

- Starting sentences with phrases such as "I did," "I was," "I am," instead of action verbs like initiated, created, supervised, managed, and so on

- Overly elaborate résumé; for example, using calligraphy, fancy typesetting, or plastic binder

- So much emphasis on a nontraditional résumé that basic facts are missing (if company officials cannot verify facts such as work experiences, addresses, or schools attended, or assess qualifications, the résumé is discarded)

- Too general, and therefore not targeted at all to the specific job opening

- Inflating experience or distorting information (if discovered when references are checked, this usually leads to immediate disqualification or, if the candidate has already been hired, to immediate dismissal)

COMPLETING THE JOB APPLICATION FORM

If your résumé is of interest to a prospective employer, you will most likely be invited for a job interview. Prior to the interview, you will be required to complete a job application form. Some employers conduct a brief screening interview. Candidates who appear promising are then requested to fill out an application form and take employment tests. If successful, the applicants are invited for a more comprehensive interview.

Although a completed application form duplicates much of the information in the résumé, there is an important difference. The résumé highlights information you want the employer to have. The job application form requests information the employer wants, and is more detailed. It is essential to answer all questions on the application form thoroughly. The Self-Knowledge Questionnaire presented in Chapter 1 contains most of the information needed to answer questions on the application form.

The application form requests information about a person's schooling, job experience, citizenship, special abilities, supervisory experience, and the like. Unlike résumés, job application forms are usually completed by the candidate without assistance from another party. As a result of fair employment legislation, companies are forbidden by law to ask questions about an applicant's age, race, sex, religion, ethnic background, marital status, disabilities, or sexual orientation.

Be aware that the application form serves more purposes than collecting factual information. How you complete the form might provide the employer with some clues to your intelligence, work habits, carefulness, and ability to manage time. An application form completed in a disorganized fashion (many crossouts, erasures, excessive writing in the margins) could suggest sloppy work habits. Many spelling errors could suggest poor language skills.

HAVING A SUCCESSFUL JOB INTERVIEW

A successful job campaign results in one or more employment interviews. Screening interviews are often conducted by telephone, particularly for customer-service positions requiring telephone skills. More extensive interviews are usually conducted in person. Becoming a skillful interviewee requires practice. You can acquire this practice as you go through the job-finding process. In addition, you can rehearse simulated job interviews with friends and other students. Practice answering the questions posed in Exhibit 11-7. You might also think of several questions you would not like to be asked, and develop answers for them.

Videotaping the practice interviews is especially helpful because it provides feedback on how you handled yourself. In watching the replay, pay particular attention to your spoken and nonverbal communication skills. Then make adjustments as needed.

Our discussion of a successful job interview is divided into how to perform well in an interview, and dealing with a stress interview.

EXHIBIT 11-7

QUESTIONS FREQUENTLY ASKED OF JOB CANDIDATES

The following questions are of the same basic type and content encountered in most employment interviews. Practice answering them in front of a friend, camcorder, or mirror.

1. Why did you apply for this job?
2. What are your short-term and long-term goals?
3. What do you expect to be doing five years from now?
4. How much money do you expect to be earning five years from now?
5. What are your strengths? Weaknesses?
6. Tell me about yourself.
7. How would other people describe you?
8. What did you think of school?
9. Why did you prepare for the career you did?
10. What makes you think you will be successful in business?
11. Why should we hire you?
12. If hired, how long will you be working for us?
13. Where else are you interviewing?
14. What has been your biggest accomplishment on the job?
15. What do you know about our firm?

Suggestions for Performing Well in the Interview

Present yourself favorably but accurately in the interview. Job hunters typically look upon the employment interview as a game in which they must outguess the interviewer. A sounder approach is to do your best to present a positive but accurate picture of yourself. The suggestions presented next will help you create a professional impact.

1. *Prepare in advance.* Be familiar with pertinent details about your background, including your employment history. Bring to the interview your social security number, driver's license, résumé, and the names of references.[12] Prepare a statement in your mind of your uniqueness—what differentiates you from other job candidates. Sometimes the uniqueness is not strictly job related, such as being a champion figure skater.

Do your homework regarding your potential employer. It is important to know some important facts about the firm in which you are seeking employment. Annual reports, brochures about the company, and sometimes newspaper and magazine articles should provide valuable information. A brief conversation with one or two current employees might provide some basic knowledge about the firm.

2. *Dress appropriately.* So much emphasis is placed on dressing well for job interviews that some people overdress. Instead of looking businesslike, they appear to be dressed for a wedding or a funeral. The safest tactic is to wear moderately conservative business attire when applying for most positions. Another important principle is to gear your dress somewhat to the type of prospective employer. If you have a job interview with an employer where sports attire is worn to the office regularly, dress more casually. Recognize also that dress standards have more latitude than in the past.

3. *Focus on important job factors.*   Inexperienced job candidates often ask questions about noncontroversial topics such as paid holidays, benefits, and company-sponsored social activities. All these topics may be important to you, but explore them after the basic issue—the nature of the job—has been discussed. In this way you will project a more professional image.

4. *Do not worry too much about hidden meanings.*   Few interview questions are as revealing as you might think. Respond in a straightforward and nondefensive way to even the most absurd-sounding question. If you believe that your privacy is being invaded or that the question is discriminatory, you may choose not to answer. (One extreme example, "Do you have to work, or is this job just for spending money?") Even professional interviewers do not necessarily have a wrong answer in mind to an unusual question. One such example is, "If you had to choose one, which animal would you prefer to be?" Any sane answer, given in a nondefensive way, will suffice. One woman impressed an interviewer with her answer to this question. She said, "An eagle, so I could soar to new heights in my career. And people would look up to me."

5. *Be ready for a frank discussion of your strengths and weaknesses.* Almost every personnel interviewer and many hiring supervisors will ask you to discuss your strengths and weaknesses. (Some other frequently asked questions are presented in Exhibit 11-7.) Everyone has weaknesses, or at least needs to improve in certain areas. To deny them is to appear uninsightful or defensive. However, you may not want to reveal weaknesses that are unrelated to the job (such as recurring nightmares or fear of swimming). A mildly evasive approach is to emphasize weaknesses that could be interpreted as strengths. A case in point: "Sometimes I'm too impatient to get things done."

A similar tactic is to turn a weakness into a strength. You admit the weakness, but also point out its beneficial side. For example, "One area for improvement I have is that I'm too methodical. However, by being methodical my work is of high quality."

6. *Do not knock former employers.*   To justify looking for a new position, or having left a position in the past, job candidates often make negative statements about former employers. Employer-bashing makes one appear unprofessional. Furthermore, it may suggest that one is likely to find fault with any employer.

7. *Ask a few good questions.*   An intelligent interviewee asks a few good questions. An employment specialist for managers said, "The best way to impress somebody on an interview is to ask intelligent questions."[13] Here are a few questions worth considering:

a. If hired, what kind of work would I actually be doing?

b. What would I have to accomplish on this job in order to be considered an outstanding performer?

c. What kind of advancement opportunities are there in your company for outstanding performers?

d. What personal characteristics are most important for success in this job?

8. *Discuss the total compensation package at a logical point in the interview.* It is generally best to let the interviewer introduce the topic of salary and benefits. Often the interviewer will specify the starting salary to the interviewee, allowing little room for questioning. If asked what starting salary you are looking for, mention a realistic salary range—one that makes you appear neither desperate nor greedy. Careful research, such as reading want ads or speaking to a member of the placement office, will help you identify a realistic salary range. If the interviewer does not mention salary, toward the end of the interview ask a question such as, "By the way, what is the starting salary for this position?"

9. *Smile and exhibit a positive attitude.* People who smile during job interviews are more likely to receive a job offer.[14] It is also important to express a positive attitude in other ways, such as agreeing with the interviewer and being impressed with facts about the company. If you want the job, toward the conclusion of the interview explain why you see a good fit between your qualifications and those demanded by the job. For example, "The way I see it, this job calls for somebody who is really devoted to improving customer service. That's me. I love to take good care of customers." Smiling also helps you appear relaxed.

10. *Show how you can help the employer.* To repeat, an effective job-getting strategy is to explain to a prospective employer what you think you can do to help the company. This gains more for you than telling the prospective employer of your good qualities and characteristics. If you were applying for the position of billing specialist in a small company that you knew was having trouble billing customers correctly, you might try this thrust: "Here is what I would do to work with experienced employees to help develop a billing system with as few bugs as possible: _____."

Another way to show how you can help the employer is to relate the employer problem to one you successfully resolved in the past. In the billing system example, you might state that your previous employer had a billing problem and than explain how you helped solve the problem.

11. *Ask for the job.* If you want the job in question, be assertive. Make a statement such as, "I'm really interested. What is the next step in the process?" "Is there any other information I could submit that would help you complete your evaluation of me?"

12. *Follow through.* Your responsibilities in job hunting do not end with the employment interview. The vital next step is to mail a courteous follow-up letter within three working days after the interview. Even if you decide not to take the job, a brief thank-you letter is advisable. You may conceivably have contact with that firm in the future.

If you want the position, state your attitudes toward the position and the company, and summarize any conclusions reached about your discussion. A follow-up letter is a tip-off that you are truly interested in the position. Sending such a letter may therefore give you an edge over other applicants for the position. A sample follow-up letter is shown in Exhibit 11-8.

Following through is essential, but draw the line between being persistent and becoming a pest. Bothering people in a human resources office can make you unpopular, so downplay the advice to keep on their cases until somebody hires you.[15]

DEALING WITH THE STRESS INTERVIEW

A **stress interview** is a deliberate method of placing a job applicant under considerable pressure and then observing his or her reactions. The purpose of the stress interview is to see how well the applicant handles pressure. It is difficult not to become defensive, distraught, or angry when the interviewer does such things as:

EXHIBIT 11-8

SAMPLE FOLLOW-UP LETTER

27 Buttercup Lane
Little Rock, AR 72203
Date

Mr. Bart Bertrand
President
South View Dodge
258 Princess Blvd.
Little Rock, AR 72201

Dear Mr. Bertrand:

Thank you for my recent chance to discuss the assistant service manager position with you and Mr. Ralph Alexander. It was illuminating to see what a busy, successful operation you have.

I was impressed with the amount of responsibility the assistant service manager would have at your dealership. The job sounds exciting and I would like to be part of the growth of the dealership. I realize the work would be hard and the hours would be long, but that's the kind of challenge I want and can handle.

My understanding is that my background is generally favorable for the position, but that you would prefer more direct experience in managing a service operation. Since the car repair and service business is in my blood, I know I will be a fast learner.

You said that about two weeks would be needed to interview additional candidates. Count on me to start work on July 1, should you extend me a job offer.

Sincerely yours,

Rita Mae Jenkins

Sits across from you and says nothing, waiting for you to begin talking about yourself.

Comments that "Most other people from your school have been a big disappointment to our firm. What's so special about you?"

Yawns when you describe your strengths.

Says, "I have the impression that others see you as kind of a punk."

Glares at you and says, "You've been lying to me and I know it."

Spills a glass of water on you, pretending it was an accident.

The best way to handle a stress interview is to try to relax, perhaps by exhaling or saying to yourself, "I won't let this get to me." After you have relaxed, answer the questions the best you can. Remember, there is really no one best answer to any of these off-the-wall questions. Also, there is no one best response to these off-the-wall comments and antics.

Another approach is to handle the pressure by expressing your feelings in an assertive manner. State how you feel but avoid being abrasive or hostile—even if such a response is deserved. Two possible comments are: "I feel as if I'm being placed under pressure. I don't mind because I work well under pressure." "Is this what is called a stress interview? It makes me tense, but I'm willing to cooperate." Expressing your feelings helps relieve tension and enables you to think more clearly.

Industrial psychologist Sandra Davis also recommends that you keep in mind anecdotes to illustrate your strengths.[16] In this way, if an interviewer tries to create stress for you by challenging your positive points, you can back up what you say. Suppose an interviewer says, "I doubt you can get your way with people," you respond by saying, "Let me give you an example of how I negotiated a better price on a tractor for our family farm."

EMPLOYMENT TESTING AND THE PHYSICAL EXAMINATION

Employment testing is another important challenge facing many job hunters who have made it through the interview. Employment (or personnel) tests can help both the employer and job candidate find a mutually satisfactory fit. The good fit is most likely to be found when the tests are accurate and fair, and the candidate answers them accurately. It is best to take these tests with a positive, relaxed attitude. Being physically and mentally well rested is the best preparation. Specialists who develop the test profiles of successful candidates are not expecting an incredible display of human attributes. Also, employment tests are but one factor in making employment decisions. Here we describe personnel and medical testing.

PERSONNEL AND PSYCHOLOGICAL TESTING

Five principal types of personnel and psychological tests are in current use: achievement, aptitude, personality, interest, and integrity tests. The fifth category is used particularly in the retail and financial services industry.

1. *Achievement tests*   sample and measure the applicant's knowledge and skills. They require applicants to demonstrate their competency on job tasks or related subjects. A person applying for a position as a paralegal might be given a test about real-estate and matrimonial law.

2. *Aptitude tests*   measure an applicant's capacity or potential for performing satisfactorily on the job, given sufficient training. Mental-ability tests are the best-known variety of aptitude test. They measure ability to solve problems and learn new material. Mental-ability tests measure such specific aptitudes as verbal reasoning, numerical reasoning, and spatial relations (visualizing three dimensions). Scores on mental-ability tests are related to success in most jobs in which problem-solving ability is important.

3. *Personality tests*   measure personal traits and characteristics that could be related to job performance. Among the many personal characteristics measured by these tests are dominance, self-confidence, energy, and emotional maturity. Personality tests have been the subject of heated controversy for many years. Critics are concerned that these tests invade privacy and are too imprecise to be useful. Nevertheless, personality factors have a profound influence on job performance.

4. *Interest tests*   measure preferences for engaging in certain activities such as mechanical, numerical, literary, or managerial work. They also measure a person's interest in specific occupations such as accountant, social worker, or sales representative. Interest tests are designed to indicate whether a person would enjoy a particular activity or occupation. They do not attempt, however, to measure a person's aptitude for that activity or occupation. The Strong Interest Inventory described in Chapter 10 is an interest test.

5. *Integrity tests*   are of two types: paper-and-pencil and polygraph tests (often referred to as lie-detector tests). Paper-and-pencil honesty tests ask people questions that directly or indirectly measure their tendency not to tell the truth. A direct question would be, "Should an employee be disciplined for stealing ten dollars worth of supplies from the company?" (A dishonest person would answer no.) An indirect question would be, "Do you read the editorial page of the local newspaper every day?" (Only a dishonest person would answer yes. Almost nobody can claim a perfect record in this regard.)[17]

Polygraphs record a person's internal physiological responses, such as heart rate and breathing rate, in response to questions. The level of emotional response to neutral questions is compared to responses to key questions. The federal Employee Polygraph Protection Act of 1988 severely limits the use of the polygraph for preemployment screening. Preemployment polygraphs can still be used by governments and government contractors engaged in national security activities. Applicants who will be working in security positions or those with direct access to drugs can still be administered polygraph tests. The devices also can still be used to investigate employee theft. Refusal to take the test cannot be used as the basis for dismissal.

The Physical Examination and Drug Testing

As part of the employee selection process, you will be required to take a physical examination. From the company's standpoint, this exam is important for two reasons. First, it gives some indication as to the applicant's ability to handle a particular job. A person with a back injury would have difficulty handling a job that required constant sitting. High absenteeism would be the result. Second, the physical exam provides a basis for later comparisons. This lessens the threat of an employee claiming that the job caused a particular injury or disease.

The physical examination has increased in importance since the passage of the American with Disabilities Act of 1991. An employer cannot deny a disabled individual a job because of increased insurance costs or the high cost of health benefits. However, the employer can deny employment to a disabled person if having the individual in the workplace poses a threat to his or her safety or the safety of others.[18]

Approximately one-half of employers test job applicants for the use of illegal drugs. You may therefore have to submit to drug testing for a job you want. Testing for substance abuse includes blood analysis, urinalysis, observation of eyes, and examination of the skin for punctures. Although employers have a legal right to screen applicants for substance abuse, some people are concerned that inaccurate drug testing may unfairly deny employment to worthy candidates. A strong argument in favor of drug testing is that employees who are drug abusers may create such problems as lowered productivity, lost time from work, and misappropriation of funds.[19]

MANAGING THE DOWNSIDE OF CONDUCTING A JOB SEARCH

For some people, finding a job is an easy task, particularly if they happen to be in a field in which the number of positions available is far greater than the number of job applicants. For many other people, the job search can be a mixed experience: some joy and some frustration. Much rejection can be expected. Few people are wanted by every employer. You have to learn to accept such rejection in stride, remembering that a good deal of personal chemistry is involved in being hired. Suppose the person doing the hiring likes you personally. You then have a much greater chance of being hired for the position than does another individual of comparable merit. If the interviewer dislikes you, the reverse is true.

Rejection and rudeness are frequently encountered in job hunting, which can easily create discouragement. Keep pressure on yourself to avoid slowing down because you are discouraged. Recent research documents the fact that assertive behaviors are associated with success in finding a job, even when the job hunter has average job qualifications.[20] Remember, you have to perform dozens of tasks to find a job. Many of them have already been described, such as preparing a statement of your job objective, a cover letter, and a résumé. You also have to line up your references and take care of every job lead that comes your way. When you do not have a job, almost no sensible lead should be ignored. Each lead processed takes you one step closer to finding a job. And all you are looking for is one job.

SUMMARY

Job-finding skills may be used at different stages in your career. The process of finding a job sometimes facilitates choosing a career. The job search begins with a reasonably flexible statement of the type of job you are seeking (your job objective). A job objective can also include the type of place where you would like to work.

Qualifications frequently sought by employers include: appropriate education and satisfactory grades, relevant work experience, communication and interpersonal skills, motivation, problem-solving ability, flexibility, emotional maturity, and teamwork skills.

A systematic job search uses many job-finding techniques including: networking (contacts and referrals), a mail campaign to prospective employers, a telephone campaign, placement offices and employment agencies, help wanted ads, and possibly support groups.

An attention-getting cover letter should accompany your job résumé. The letter should explain why you are applying for a particular position and should identify your potential contribution to the employer. Be positive and forceful without being brash.

An effective job résumé is the core of the job campaign. Most firms require a résumé before seriously considering an external or internal job candidate. There is no one best way to prepare a résumé. Effective résumés are straightforward, factual presentations of a person's experience, skills, and accomplishments.

The chronological résumé presents your work experience, education, and interests, along with your accomplishments, in reverse chronological order. The functional résumé organizes your skills and accomplishments into the functions or tasks that support the job you are seeking. The targeted résumé focuses on a specific job target or position, and presents only information that supports that target.

The job objective on your résumé should describe the position you are seeking now or in the short-term future. Creative-style résumés bring favorable attention to your credentials, but should be used with discretion.

A résumé should be neat, well organized, and professional in appearance. Common résumé mistakes to avoid include: excessive length, disorganization, poor typing or word processing, insufficient or excessive information, no listing of accomplishments, spelling and input errors, missing facts, and inflated facts.

The job application form should be completed thoroughly and accurately. How you complete the application form might reveal clues to your intelligence, work habits, carefulness, and ability to manage time.

Rehearse being interviewed, and then present yourself favorably but accurately in the interview. Specific interview tips include: (1) prepare in advance, (2) dress appropriately, (3) focus on important job factors, (4) do not worry too much about hidden meanings, (5) be ready to discuss your strengths and weaknesses, (6) do not knock former employers, (7) ask good questions, (8) discuss compensation at a logical time, (9) smile and exhibit a positive attitude, (10) show how you can help the employer, (11) ask for the job, and (12) follow through with a letter.

A stress interview is a deliberate method of placing a job applicant under considerable pressure and then observing his or her reactions. When placed under this type of pressure, use a relaxation technique or express your feelings. Also, be prepared for a stress interview by having anecdotes to support your statements.

Finding a job can be a demanding task with some joys and many frustrations. It is therefore important to keep pressure on yourself to perform the many chores required of a successful job-hunting campaign. Follow up on every lead, and try not to take rejection and rudeness personally.

Questions and Activities

1. Why get a job?

2. Does it seem that most employers have unrealistic expectations of job candidates? (Review Exhibit 11-1.)

3. Which job-hunting technique is used most frequently by people you know? What accounts for its popularity?

4. What do you see as the biggest drawback in attempting to find employment through the telesearch method?

5. Some job seekers send fax messages instead of postal mail when conducting an unsolicited letter campaign. Identify an advantage and disadvantage of using faxes for this purpose.

6. What do you think of the practice of sending a prospective employer an audiocassette with information about oneself, instead of using a résumé and cover letter?

7. What should you do if it appears that the job interviewer and you have poor rapport or negative chemistry?

8. Many employers use telephone screening interviews before inviting a candidate for an in-person interview. What special communication challenges does this present for the job hunter?

9. What can you do today to help you develop a contact that could someday lead to a job?

10. Ask an experienced career person what he or she thinks is the best method of finding a job. Be prepared to discuss your findings in class.

REFERENCES

[1] Robert Levering and Milton Moskowitz, *The 100 Best Companies to Work For* (New York: Doubleday, 1993).

[2] Based in part on Bob Weinstein, "What Employers Look For," in *The Honda How to Get a Job Guide* (*Business Week's Guide to Careers,* 1985), p. 24; Julie Griffin Levitt, *Your Career: How to Make It Happen* (Cincinnati, Ohio: South-Western, 1990), pp. 129–31.

[3] Karen O. Dowd, "Creative Job Search Strategies," in *The Honda How to Get a Job Guide* (*Business Week's Careers,* 1988), p. 28.

[4] Adapted from John Truitt, "7 Ways to Get a Job . . . Fast," *Business Week Careers,* October 1987, p. 4.

[5] Ibid.

[6] Robert D. Lock, *Job Search: Career Planning Guidebook, Book II* (Pacific Grove, Calif.: Brooks/Cole, 1988), pp. 34–35.

[7] Ibid.

[8] Mary Alice Griffin and Patricia Lynn Anderson, "Résumé Content," *Business Education Forum,* February 1994, p. 11.

[9] Peggy Schmidt, "When to Start Looking for a Job," *Business Week's Guide to Careers,* February 1986, p. 71.

[10] R. Neil Dortch, "Résumé Preparation," *Business Education Forum,* April 1994, pp. 47–48.

[11] Ibid., p. 47.

[12] Seth Godin, (ed.) *The 1994 Information Please Business Almanac & Desk Reference* (Boston: Houghton Mifflin, 1994), p. 354.

[13] "Talking with Lynn Bignell about Job Hunting," *Working Smart,* November 1991, p. 7.

[14] Susan Kleinman, "Is Your Attitude Killing Your Career?" *Cosmopolitan,* May 1994, p. 225.

[15] Barbara W. Durkin, "It Takes Know-How, but You Can Find a Job!" Rochester, New York *Democrat and Chronicle,* June 11, 1993.

[16] Sandra L. Davis, "How to Handle the Stress Interview," *Business Week's Guide to Careers,* March/April 1985, p. 29.

[17] Larry Reynolds, "Truth or Consequences," *Personnel,* January 1991, p. 5; Paul R. Sackett, Laura R. Burris, and Christine Callahan, "Integrity Testing for Personnel Selection: An Update," *Personnel Psychology,* Autumn 1989, p. 493.

[18] Gene Carmean, "The Medical Screening to the Job," *HRMagazine,* July 1992, p. 85.

[19] Rob Brookler, "Industry Standards in Workplace Drug Testing," *Personnel Journal,* April 1992, p. 128; "Drug and Literacy Testing Update," *The Fact Finder,* March 1994, p. 2.

A HUMAN RELATIONS CASE PROBLEM:
THE EAGER JOB APPLICANT

Paula Hayo waited anxiously outside the office of Charles Chadwick, the regional manager for Dem's, a chain of fast-food restaurants. Paula had already successfully gone through the preliminary screening interview and testing phases of the company's selection process. She believed strongly that if she could just get past this interview, she would be hired as the store manager for a Dem's opening in the area's newest shopping mall.

The receptionist motioned to Paula, and said: "Mr. Chadwick is ready to see you now." The door adjacent to the receptionist's desk opened. Out strode Charles Chadwick, a well-dressed man who looked to be in his mid-forties.

"Welcome," said Chadwick, "I've been looking forward to meeting you. Have a seat, and let's get started."

"Nice to meet you too, Chuck," said Paula. "I'm looking forward to managing the latest Dem's. It's located only two miles from my apartment. I could walk there on days when the climate is right."

"We'll get down to those details later," commented Chadwick. "I have carefully studied your résumé, but there are some areas I want to cover with you in person."

"I'll answer any question that isn't illegal, Chuck. This is your home court."

"Tell me, Paula, why should we hire you when there are so many other good people wanting to manage our stores?"

"I'll tell you why," replied Paula in an energetic tone. "I love the restaurant business. I'm a dynamo. Any of my references will verify that. Also, I need the job. I'm graduating next month, and my part-time job just doesn't pay enough to cover my bills. Also, I'm ready to start putting my skills to work so I can learn enough to become an executive in the restaurant business. Dem's would be a great starting point."

"How has your schooling prepared you for the job of a restaurant manager?"

"My schooling has been perfect training for this job. My accounting courses have shown me how to keep the books. My human relations and psychology courses have taught me how to deal with people. Being a student and a part-time worker has kept me so busy that I've been forced to eat in fast-food restaurants. In that way I've learned a lot about your business quite unintentionally."

"What did you learn about the fast-food restaurant business, Paula?" asked Chadwick.

"No offense, Chuck, but the key to your business is to feed them fast, feed them cheap, and make sure trash is kept off the floor and the tables."

"What are your most important strengths in relation to this job?" asked Chadwick in a somber tone.

"You asked for it, so I'll brag a little. As I mentioned before, I'm a dynamo. I get things done in a hurry. I'm also very good with people. I've received many compliments about my tactfulness. I'm a natural leader. I've organized many things for my friends such as parties and picnics. I was the president of the student marketing association."

"What are your weaknesses, or areas for improvement?"

"So far, I've had no problems. But you could say I'm a little intolerant of dull and uncooperative people. If somebody goofs off, I can throw a little tantrum. But it's really not too serious. People know I'm fair but firm.

(Continued)

"Also, I hate stupid questions," continued Paula.

"Could you give me an example of a stupid question?" asked Chadwick.

"I'll give you a good one that relates to your business. The other day I was at a McDonald's. An old man asked the manager if a Big Mac came with mustard and pickles. That was a ridiculous question. Anybody with half a brain knows that Big Macs come with mustard and pickles.

"If I were the manager, I would have told the man to buy a Big Mac and look inside. I was taught in psychology that the best kind of learning takes place when you make discoveries for yourself."

With a perplexed look on his face, Chadwick informed Hayo that the light was flashing on his telephone setup, signaling an emergency call. He asked Paula to please wait outside until he completed the call.

As Paula left, she said, "See you in a little bit. I'm enjoying our interview, and I have lots of questions to ask."

QUESTIONS

1. How is Paula Hayo doing so far in the interview?

2. Describe all the mistakes Paula has made in the interview.

3. Describe what Paula has done right.

4. How well is Charles handling the interview?

5. Based on the limited evidence you have, would you hire Paula Hayo as the manager of the new Dem's store?

A HUMAN RELATIONS ROLE PLAY: THE STRESSFUL AND THE SUPPORTIVE JOB INTERVIEWS

The interviewee role players in the following situation play themselves. The interviewee thus tries to act as he or she would under real circumstances. Your own work and educational background, attitudes, and preferences can be used as the basis for your answers. Both interviewees should assume that they want the job in question—a high-paying position as assistant to the marketing vice president of a major airline. As a fringe benefit, the person hired will have free air travel to many places in the world.

One person plays the role of the stress interviewer. After a pleasant warm-up, your intention is to place the interviewee under a good deal of pressure. You firmly believe that a person who cracks under pressure is unsuited for this job.

Another person plays the role of the supportive (warm and reassuring) interviewer. You want to encourage the person to talk freely and to feel respected.

Both interviewers should prepare some questions in advance. After the interview samples (about fifteen minutes) have been conducted, other class members will provide feedback on the behavior of both interviewer and interviewee.

[20]Mark J. Schmitt, Elise L. Amel, and Ann Marie Ryan, "Self-Reported Assertive Job-Seeking Behaviors of Minimally Educated Job Hunters," *Personnel Psychology,* Spring 1993, p. 119.

 ## ADDITIONAL READING

Barlow, Wayne, and Hane, Edward Z. "A Practical Guide to the Americans with Disabilities Act." *Personnel Journal,* June 1992, pp. 53–60.

Brookler, Rob. "Industry Standards in Workplace Drug Testing." *Personnel Journal,* April 1992, pp. 128–132.

Carter, C. J. *Getting the Job: Career Tips for Technical & Business Education Students* (Englewood Cliffs, N.J.: Prentice Hall, 1990).

Martin, Scott L., and Lehnen, Loren P. "Select the Right Employee Through Testing." *Personnel Journal,* June 1992, pp. 46–51.

Mayer, Jeffrey J. *Find the Job You've Always Wanted in Half the Time with Half the Effort: The Career Discovery System That Will Help You Land Your Dream Job in Weeks, Not Months.* Chicago: Mayer Enterprises, 1992.

Murphy, Kevin R., and Thornton, George C. III. "Characteristics of Employee Drug Testing Policies." *Journal of Business and Psychology,* spring 1992, pp. 295–309.

Smither, James W., et al. "Applicant Reactions to Selection Procedures." *Personnel Psychology,* spring 1993, pp. 49–76.

Stephens, Elvis C. "How Résumé Fraud Works As a Defense in EEO Case." *HRMagazine,* February 1994, pp. 91–95.

CHAPTER 12

DEVELOPING GOOD WORK HABITS

Learning Objectives

After studying the information and doing the exercises in this chapter you should be able to:

■ Appreciate the importance of good work habits and time management

■ Decrease any tendencies you might have toward procrastination

■ Develop attitudes and values that will help you become more productive

■ Develop skills and techniques that will help you become more productive

■ Overcome time-wasting practices

A person is more likely to be fired from a job or flunk out of school because of poor **work habits** rather than poor aptitude. Work habits refer to a person's characteristic approach to work, including such things as organization, priority setting, and handling of paper work. Poor work habits also interfere with social life because of such problems as canceled social appointments. In contrast, people with good work habits tend to achieve higher career success, and have more time to invest in their personal lives. They also enjoy their personal lives more because they are not preoccupied with unfinished tasks.

Effective work habits are also beneficial because they eliminate a major stressor—the feeling of having very little or no control over one's life. Being in control also leads to a relaxed, confident approach to work.

Good work habits and time management are more important than ever because of today's emphasis on **productivity,** the amount of quality work accomplished in relation to the resources consumed. Good work habits and time management lead to high personal productivity.

The goal of this chapter is to help you become a more productive person who is still flexible. Someone who develops good work habits is not someone who becomes so obsessed with time and so rigid that he or she makes other people feel uncomfortable. Ideally, a person should be well organized yet still flexible.

Information about becoming more productive is organized here into four related categories. One is overcoming procrastination, a problem that plagues almost everybody to some extent. The second is developing attitudes and values that foster productivity. The third category is the lengthiest: developing skills and techniques that lead to personal productivity. The fourth category is overcoming time wasters.

 ## DEALING WITH PROCRASTINATION

Procrastination is putting off doing a task for no valid reason. It is the major work-habit problem for most employees and students. Exhibit 12-1 will help you recognize when you are procrastinating. Unproductive

---

EXHIBIT 12-1

HOW DO YOU KNOW WHEN YOU ARE PROCRASTINATING?

Obviously, when you are not getting things done that should be done you are procrastinating. Procrastination can also be much more subtle. You might be procrastinating if one or more of the following symptoms apply to you:

- You overorganize a project by such rituals as sharpening every pencil, meticulously straightening up your desk, and discarding bent paper clips.

- You overresearch something before taking action, such as getting five different estimates on replacing a defective auto radiator.

- You keep waiting for the "right time" to do something, such as getting started on an important report.

- You underestimate the time needed to do a project, and say to yourself, "This won't take much time, so I can do it next week."

SOURCE: Based on information in "Procrastination Can Get in Your Way," *Research Institute Personal Report for the Executive,* December 24, 1985, pp. 3–4.

---

people are the biggest procrastinators, but even productive people have problems with procrastination. Think of all the people who fail to file their income tax reports on time even when the government owes them money.

WHY PEOPLE PROCRASTINATE

People procrastinate for many different reasons. One is that we perceive the task to be done (such as quitting a job) as unpleasant. Another reason we procrastinate is that we find the job facing us to be overwhelming, such as painting a house. Another major cause of procrastination is a fear of the consequences of our actions.[1]

One possible negative consequence is a negative evaluation of your work. For example, if you delay preparing a report for your boss or instructor, that person cannot criticize its quality. Bad news is another negative consequence that procrastination can sometimes delay. If you think your personal computer needs a new disk drive, delaying a trip to the computer store means you will not have to hear the diagnosis: "Your disk drive needs replacement. We can do the job for about $300."

Another reason some people procrastinate is that they **fear success.** People sometimes believe that if they succeed at an important task, they will be asked to take on more responsibility in the future. They dread this possibility. Some students have been known to procrastinate completing their degree requirements in order to avoid taking on the responsibility of a full-time position.

People frequently put off tasks that do not appear to offer a meaningful reward. Suppose you decide that your computer files need a thorough updating, including deleting inactive files. Even if you know this task should be done, the accomplishment of updated files might not be a particularly meaningful reward.

Finally, people often procrastinate as a way of rebelling against being controlled. Procrastination, used in this way, is a means of defying unwarranted authority.[2] Rather than submit to authority, a person might tell himself, "Nobody is going to tell me when I should get a report done. I'll do it when I'm good and ready."

TECHNIQUES FOR REDUCING PROCRASTINATION

To overcome, or at least minimize, procrastination we recommend a number of specific tactics. A general approach, however, is simply to be aware that procrastination is a major drain on productivity. Being aware of the problem will remind you to take corrective action in many situations. When your accomplishment level is low, you might ask yourself, "Am I procrastinating on anything of significance?"

Calculate the Cost of Procrastination.   You can reduce procrastination by calculating its cost.[3] One example is that you might lose out on obtaining a high-paying job you really want by not having your résumé and cover letter ready on time. Your cost of procrastination would include the difference in salary between the job you do find and the one you really wanted. Another cost would be the loss of potential job satisfaction.

Counterattack.   Forcing yourself to do something overwhelming, frightening, or uncomfortable helps to prove that the task was not as bad as initially perceived.[4] Assume that you have accepted a new position but have not yet resigned from your present one because resigning seems so uncomfortable. Set up a specific time to call your manager, or his or her assistant, to schedule an appointment. Force yourself further to show up for the resignation appointment. After you break the ice with the statement, "I have something important to tell you," the task will be much easier.

Create Some Momentum to Get You Moving.   One way to get momentum going on an unpleasant or overwhelming task is to set aside a specific time to work on it. If you have to write a report on a subject you dislike, you might set aside Saturday from 3 P.M. to 5 P.M. as your time to first attack the project. Another way to create some momentum is to find a leading task to perform. A **leading task** is an easy, warm-up activity.[5] If you were procrastinating about painting your apartment, you might purchase the paint and brush as a way of getting started.

Peck Away at an Overwhelming Task.   Assume that you have a major project to do that does not have to be accomplished in a hurry. A good way of minimizing procrastination is to peck away at the project in fifteen- to thirty-minute bits of time. Bit by bit the project will get down to manageable size and therefore not seem so overwhelming. "Pecking away" is also referred to as the **Swiss-cheese method** because you eat holes in the total task.

A related way of pecking away at an overwhelming task is to subdivide it into smaller units. For instance, you might break down moving into a series of tasks such as filing change-of-address notices, locating a mover, and packaging books. Pecking away can sometimes be achieved by setting aside as little as five minutes to work on a seemingly overwhelming task. When the five minutes are up, either work five more minutes on the task or reschedule the activity for sometime soon.

Motivate Yourself with Rewards and Punishments. Give yourself a pleasant reward soon after you accomplish a task you would ordinarily procrastinate about. You might, for example, jog through the woods after having completed a tough take-home exam. The second part of this tactic is to punish yourself if you have engaged in serious procrastination. How about eating only oatmeal for five days?

Make a Commitment to Other People. Put pressure on yourself to get something done on time by making it a commitment to one or more other people. You might announce to co-workers that you are going to get a project of mutual concern completed by a certain date. If you fail to meet this date you may feel embarrassed. One administrative assistant told his co-workers, "I will get the new coffee system in our office by March 31, or I will buy everybody's coffee for a week."

Use Subliminal Messages About Overcoming Procrastination. Software called *Mindset* flashes reinforcing messages across the menu bar on your computer. You can adjust the frequency and duration of the suggestions. The message can flash by subliminally (below the level of conscious awareness) or remain on the screen for a few seconds. The procrastination message is: "My goals are obtainable. I am confident in my abilities. I make and keep deadlines."[6]

DEVELOPING THE PROPER ATTITUDES AND VALUES

Developing good work habits and time-management practices is often a matter of developing proper attitudes toward work and time. For instance, if you think that your job is important and that time is valuable, you will be on your way toward developing good work habits. In this section we describe a group of attitudes and values that can help improve your productivity through better use of time and improved work habits.

BECOME A GOAL-ORIENTED PERSON AND VALUE YOUR TIME

Becoming goal-oriented is perhaps the first step in any serious program of improving work habits and time management. Being committed to a goal propels people toward good use of time. Imagine how efficient most employees would be if they were told, "Here is five days' worth of work facing you. If you get it finished in less than five days, you can have all that time saved to yourself." (One negative side effect, however, is that many employees might sacrifice quality for speed.)

As a consequence of being goal-oriented, successful people believe that their time is valuable. It is therefore difficult to engage them in idle conversation during working hours. As you proceed further into your career, the value of your time will usually increase.

VALUE GOOD ATTENDANCE AND PUNCTUALITY

On the job, in school, or in personal life, good attendance and punctuality are essential for developing a good reputation. Also, you cannot accomplish much if you are not present. Poor attendance and consistent lateness are the most frequent reasons for employee discipline.

Two important myths about attendance and punctuality should be challenged early in your career. One is that a certain number of sick days are owed an employee. Some employees who have not used up their sick days will find reasons to be sick at the end of the year. Another myth is that absence is preferred to lateness. Some employees believe, for example, that it is more honorable to be absent because of illness than late because of oversleeping. Consequently, the employee who oversleeps calls in sick rather than face the embarrassment of arriving at work late.

VALUE NEATNESS AND ORDERLINESS

An orderly desk, file cabinet, or work area does not inevitably signify an orderly mind. Yet orderliness does help most people become more productive. Less time is wasted and less energy is expended if you do not have to hunt for missing information. Knowing where information is and what information you have available is a way of being in control of your job. When your job gets out of control, you are probably working at less than peak efficiency. The best approach to maintaining a neat work area is to convince yourself that neatness is valuable.

Being neat and orderly helps you achieve good performance. Frequently breaking your concentration for such matters as finding a memo or a pen with ink remaining inhibits peak performance.

DEVELOP A TOTAL QUALITY MANAGEMENT (TQM) PHILOSOPHY

Total Quality Management (TQM) is a system of management in which all activities are directed toward satisfying external and internal customers. TQM involves painstaking attention to detail to ensure that all work activities are done right the first time. If your mental set is that of totally satisfying your customer, you will produce work of high quality based on pride. Knowing that getting things done on time pleases customers, you will also be prompt.

Despite the quest for excellent work in TQM, avoid the trap of perfectionism. You should strive for continuous improvement. However, if you never pass along your portion of a project until you are convinced no error can be found, your productivity will be low.

WORK SMARTER, NOT HARDER

People caught up in trying to accomplish a job often wind up working hard, but not in an imaginative way that leads to good results. Much time and energy are thus wasted. If you develop the attitude of seeking to work smarter rather than harder, your productivity and satisfaction will increase. Let's look at an example of the difference between working harder and working smarter.

A service technician checks his schedule to find that he has 35 service calls lined up for the week. If he takes the service calls in order of the time of their request, he will spend more than five full days crisscrossing his territory to visit customers. Taking the calls by time of request means that he will be working harder. In contrast, if he groups his calls according to proximity to each other, he can cover all customers in three and one-half days. The time savings comes from less travel time, thus allowing him to work smarter.[7]

BECOME SELF-EMPLOYED PSYCHOLOGICALLY

A distinguishing characteristic of many self-employed people is that they care deeply about what they accomplish each day.[8] Most of their job activities directly or indirectly affect their financial health. Additionally, many self-employed people enjoy high job satisfaction because they have chosen work that fits their interests. Because of the factors just mentioned, the self-employed person is compelled to make good use of time. Also, the high level of job satisfaction typical of many self-employed people leads them to enjoy being productive.

If a person working for an employer regards his or her area of responsibility as self-employment, productivity may increase. To help regard employment by others as self-employment, keep this thought in mind. Every employee is given some assets to manage to achieve a good return on investment. If you managed the printing and copying center for your company, you would be expected to manage that asset profitably.

APPRECIATE THE IMPORTANCE OF REST AND RELAXATION

A productive attitude to maintain is that overwork can be counterproductive and lead to negative stress and burnout. Proper physical rest contributes to mental alertness and improved ability to cope with frustration. Constant attention to work or study is often inefficient. It is a normal human requirement to take enough rest breaks to allow oneself to approach work or study with a fresh perspective. Each person has to establish the right balance between work and leisure within the bounds of freedom granted by the situation.

To help achieve rest and relaxation, some business people take *power naps*. You can train yourself to take these fifteen-minute naps to give you short bursts of energy and stretch your stamina over a long day. A few minutes' power nap in the late afternoon can keep you going for an overtime assignment.[9] Where to take these naps is left to your imagination, depending on your work situation. Some workers nap in their cars when the temperature is moderate.

 TIME-MANAGEMENT TECHNIQUES

So far we have discussed improving productivity from standpoints of dealing with procrastination and developing the right attitudes and values. Skills and techniques are also important for becoming more productive. Here we describe some well-established methods of work-habit improvement, along with several new ones.

PLAN YOUR ACTIVITIES

The primary principle of effective time management is **planning:** deciding what you want to accomplish and the actions needed to make it happen. The most elementary—and the most important—planning tool is a list of tasks that need doing. Almost every successful person works from a "to do" list. These lists are similar to the daily goals described in Chapter 2. Before you can compose a useful list, you need to set aside a few moments each day to sort out the tasks at hand. A list used by a working parent is presented in Exhibit 12-2.

Where Do You Put Your Lists?   Some people dislike having small "to do" lists stuck in different places. One reason is that these lists are readily lost among other papers. Many people therefore put lists on desk calendars or printed forms called *daily planners*. Software is also available to help you keep track of your activities.

Time-management consultants recommend another useful approach. Use a notebook (either spiral or loose-leaf) that is small enough to carry around with you. The notebook becomes your master list to keep track of errands, things to do or buy, and general notes to yourself about anything requiring action.

Setting Priorities.   Because everything on a "to do" list is not of equal importance, priorities should be attached to each item. A typical system is to use *A* to signify critical or essential items, *B* to signify important items,

---

EXHIBIT 12-2

A SAMPLE "TO DO" LIST

From the Desk of Jennifer Bartow

JOB
Make ten calls to prospects for new listings.
Have "For Sale" signs put outside Hanover Blvd. house.
Set up mortgage appointment at 1st Federal for the Calhouns.
Get old file cabinets replaced.
Order new memo pads.
Meet with the Goldsteins at 5 P.M.
Set up time to show house to the Bowens.

HOME
Buy running shoes for Todd.
Buy Jeans for Linda.
Get defroster fixed on freezer.
Write and send out monthly bills.
Clip cat's nails.
Check out problem with septic tank.
Make appt. with dentist to have chipped filling replaced.

FIRST REALTY CORPORATION
Jacksonville, Florida

and *C* for the least important ones. Although an item might be regarded as a *C* (for example, refilling your stapler), it still has a contribution to make to your productivity and sense of well-being. Many people report that they obtain a sense of satisfaction from crossing an item, however trivial, off their list. Second, if you are at all conscientious, small undone items will come back to interfere with concentration.

Schedule and Follow Through. To be effective, a "to do" list must be an action tool. To convert your list into action, prepare a schedule of when you are going to do each of the things on the list. Follow through by doing things according to your schedule, checking them off as you go along.

Get Off to a Good Start

Get off to a good beginning, and you are more likely to have a successful, productive day. Start poorly, and you will be behind most of the day. According to Douglass Merrill, people who get going early tend to be in the right place at the right time more often, thus seeming to be lucky. "When you start early, you are lucky enough to get a good parking spot. You are lucky enough to avoid traffic jams. You are lucky enough to finish your job by the end of the day.[10] To get off to a good start regularly, it is important to start the day with the conscious intention of starting strong.

An effective way of getting off to a good start is to tackle the toughest task first, because most people have their peak energy in the morning. With a major task already completed, you are off to a running start on a busy workday.

Make Good Use of Office Technology

Only in recent years have companies begun to achieve productivity increases from office automation. One reason office automation has not been as successful as hoped is that many office workers do not make extensive use of the technology available. Used properly, most high-tech devices in the office can improve productivity and quality. Among the most productivity-enhancing devices are word processors, electronic mail, spreadsheets, computer graphics, fax machines, voice mail, and photocopiers. How you use these devices is the key to increased productivity. Two examples follow[11]:

- A laptop computer can help you be much more productive during periods of potential downtime. While waiting in someone's office or in an airport or on the plane, you can spend your time answering correspondence.

- A fax machine has many productivity-enhancing applications. One manager frequently visits clients in the late afternoon. If there are important papers she must see before she leaves, she has them faxed to her office at home. Using this method, she saves a trip back to the office, but she can review the work in ten minutes during the evening.

CONCENTRATE ON ONE TASK AT A TIME

Effective people have a well-developed capacity to concentrate on the problem or person facing them, however surrounded they are with potential distractions. The best results from concentration are achieved when you are so absorbed in your work that you are aware of virtually nothing else at the moment. Another useful by-product of concentration is that it helps reduce absentmindedness. If you really concentrate on what you are doing, the chances that you will forget what you intended to do diminish.

Conscious effort and self-discipline can strengthen concentration skills. The best way to sharpen your concentration skills is to set aside fifteen minutes a day and focus on something repetitive, such as your breathing or a small word. This is the same approach that is used in meditation to relieve stress.

STREAMLINE YOUR WORK AND EMPHASIZE IMPORTANT TASKS

As companies continue to operate with fewer workers than in the past, more nonproductive work must be eliminated. Every employee is expected to get rid of work that does not contribute to productivity or help customers. Maybe you are sending forms and electronic messages to people who never read them. Perhaps you are sending receipts to customers that they do not need. If you get rid of work that is of little consequence, you will have more time to concentrate on value-contributing tasks.

Important (value-contributing) tasks are those in which superior performance could have a large payoff. No matter how quickly you took care of making sure that your store paid its bills on time, for example, this effort would not make your store an outstanding success. If, however, you concentrated your efforts on bringing unique and desirable merchandise into the store, this action could greatly affect your business success.

In following the *A-B-C* system, you should devote ample time to the essential tasks. You should not pay more attention than absolutely necessary to the *C* (trivial) items. Many people respond to this suggestion by saying, "I don't think concentrating on important tasks applies to me. My job is so filled with routine, I have no chance to work on the big breakthrough ideas." True, most jobs are filled with routine requirements. What a person can do is spend some time, perhaps even one hour a week, concentrating on tasks of potentially major significance.

TACKLE DISTASTEFUL TASKS FIRST

Another method of increasing productivity is to tackle distasteful tasks first. As explained earlier, a distasteful task often fosters procrastination. By gritting your teeth and directly attacking something unpleasant, you will free yourself to work on the more pleasant. Doing the relatively more enjoyable activities thus becomes a reward for having worked through the less attractive activities. Tackling distasteful tasks first is therefore a method of self-motivation.

The "distasteful first" principle can readily be applied to schoolwork. Tackle first the homework assignment you dislike the most. After the least favorite assignment is completed, you may find it relaxing and rewarding to work on an assignment of greater personal interest. In general, save the best for last and watch your productivity climb.

WORK AT A STEADY PACE

In most jobs, working at a steady clip pays dividends in efficiency. The spurt worker creates many problems for management. Some employees take pride in working rapidly, even when the result is a high error rate. At home, too, a steady pace is better than spurting. A spurt houseworker is one who goes into a flurry of activity every so often. An easier person to live with is someone who does his or her share of housework at an even pace throughout the year.

Another advantage of the steady-pace approach is that you accomplish much more than someone who puts out extra effort just once in a while. The completely steady worker would accomplish just as much the day before a holiday as on a given Monday. That extra hour or so of productivity adds up substantially by the end of the year. Despite the advantages of maintaining a steady pace, some peaks and valleys in your work may be inevitable. Tax accounting firms, for example, have busy seasons.

SCHEDULE SIMILAR TASKS TOGETHER

An efficient method of accomplishing small tasks is to group them together and perform them in one block of time. To illustrate, you might make most of your telephone calls in relation to your job from 11:00 to 11:30 each workday morning. Or you might reserve the last hour of every workday for correspondence. When you go downtown or to a shopping mall, think of all the errands that can be run while you are in that location. Over a period of time, you will save a large number of wasted trips.

By using this method you develop the necessary pace and mental set to go through chores in short order. In contrast, when you jump from one type of task to another, your efficiency may suffer.

CREATE SOME QUIET, UNINTERRUPTED TIME

Time-management specialist Merrill Douglass observes that most office workers find their days hectic, fragmented, and frustrating. Incessant interruptions make it difficult to get things done. The constant start-stop-restart pattern lengthens the time needed to get jobs done. Quiet time can reduce the type of productivity drain just described. To achieve quiet time, create an uninterrupted block of time enabling you to concentrate on your work. This could mean turning off the telephone and blocking drop-in visitors during certain times of the workday.

Quiet time is used for such essential activities as thinking, planning, getting organized, doing analytical work, writing reports, and doing creative tasks. One hour of quiet time might yield as much productive work as four hours of interrupted time.[12]

Quiet time is difficult to find in some jobs, such as those involving customer contact. An agreement has to be worked out with the manager about when and where quiet time can be taken. A buyer for office supplies in an insurance company worked out a sensible quiet-time arrangement. He reports, "I worked out a deal with my manager whereby every Thursday morning from 9 to 12, I could take my work into a vacant office adjacent to the boardroom. We agreed that I could be reached only in an emergency. It wasn't a way to goof off. Each month I had to write my boss a brief report of what I accomplished during my uninterrupted time."

MAKE USE OF BITS OF TIME

A truly productive person makes good use of miscellaneous bits of time, both on and off the job. While waiting in line at a post office, you might update your "to do" list; while waiting for an elevator, you might be able to read a brief report; and if you have finished your day's work ten minutes before quitting time, you can use that time to clean out a file. By the end of the year your productivity will have increased much more than if you had squandered these bits of time.

The craze referred to as "grazing" is a variation of making good use of bits of time. **Grazing** is eating meals on the run in order to make good use of time ordinarily spent on sitting down for meals. Many ambitious people today nibble at snacks rather than disrupt their work by visiting a restaurant. Grazing does have its disadvantages: You cannot network while grazing; eating while working can be bad for digestion; and it may deprive you of a needed rest break.

STAY IN CONTROL OF PAPERWORK AND E-MAIL

Paperwork essentially involves taking care of administrative details such as correspondence, expense account forms, and inventory forms. If the widespread use of copying machines and computers has increased rather than decreased paperwork in the office, then managing paperwork has actually become more important. Furthermore, responding to E-mail messages has created more administrative details that require handling even if they are actually *electronic work* rather than paperwork.

Unless you handle paperwork efficiently, you may lose control of your job or home life, which could lead to heavy stress. Ideally, a small amount of time should be invested in paperwork every day. Nonprime time (when you are at less than peak efficiency, but not overly fatigued) is the best time to take care of paperwork.

OVERCOMING TIME WASTERS

Another basic thrust to improved personal productivity is to minimize wasting time. Many of the techniques already described in this chapter help to save time. The tactics and strategies described next, however, are directly aimed at overcoming the problem of wasted time.

MINIMIZE DAY DREAMING

"Taking a field trip" while on the job is a major productivity drain. Daydreaming is triggered when the individual perceives the task to be boring—such as reviewing another person's work for errors. Brain research suggests that younger people are more predisposed to daydreaming than older people. Apparently, older people use neurons better to focus on tasks.[13]

Unresolved personal problems are an important source of daydreaming, thus blocking your productivity. This is especially true because effective time utilization requires good concentration. When you are preoccupied with a personal or business problem, it is difficult to give your full efforts to a task at hand.

The solution is to do something constructive about whatever problem is sapping your ability to concentrate (as discussed in Chapter 4 about wellness and stress.) Sometimes a relatively minor problem, such as driving with an expired operator's license, can impair your work concentration. At other times, a major problem, such as how best to take care of a parent who has suffered a stroke, interferes with work. In either situation, your concentration will suffer until you take appropriate action.

PREPARE A TIME LOG TO EVALUATE YOUR USE OF TIME

An advanced tool for becoming a more efficient time manager is to prepare a time log of how you are currently investing your time. For five full workdays, write down everything you do, including such activities as responding to mail and taking rest breaks. One of the most important outputs of a time log is to uncover time leaks. A **time leak** is anything you are doing or not doing that allows time to get away from you. Among them are spending too much time for lunch by collecting people before finally leaving, and walking to a co-worker's cubicle rather than telephoning.

A major time leak for many workers is **schmoozing,** or informal socializing on the job, including small talk and telephone conversations with friends. Schmoozing is useful in relieving tension and increasing job satisfaction, but too much of this activity is a major loss of productive time.

AVOID BEING A COMPUTER GOOF-OFF

We are all aware of the productivity improvements possible when computers are used in the office. An unproductive use of computers, however, is to tinker with them to the exclusion of useful work. Many people have become intrigued with computers to the point of diversion. They become almost addicted to creating new reports, exquisite graphics, and even playing computer games on company time. Some managers spend so much time with computers that they neglect leadership responsibilities, thus lowering their productivity. In short, avoid becoming a computer goof-off.

KEEP TRACK OF IMPORTANT NAMES, PLACES, AND THINGS

How much time have you wasted lately searching for such items as a telephone number you jotted down somewhere, your keys, or an appointment book? A supervisor suddenly realized he had forgotten to show up for a luncheon appointment. He wanted to call and apologize but was unable to locate the person's name and phone number! Standard solutions to overcoming these problems are to keep a wheel file (such as Rolodex) of people's names and companies. It is difficult to misplace such a file. Many managers and professionals store such information in a database or even in a word processing file. Such files are more difficult to misplace than a pocket directory.

Two steps are recommended for remembering where you put things. First, have a parking place for everything. This would include putting your keys and appointment book back in the same place after each use. Second, make visual associations. To have something register in your mind at the moment you are doing it, make up a visual association about that act. Thus, you might say, "Here I am putting my résumé in the back section of my attaché case."

SET A TIME LIMIT FOR CERTAIN TASKS AND PROJECTS

Spending too much time on a task or project wastes time. As a person becomes experienced with certain projects, he or she is able to make accurate estimates of how long a project will take to complete. A paralegal might say, "Getting this will drawn up for the lawyer's approval should take two hours." A good work habit to develop is to estimate how long a job should take and then proceed with strong determination to get that job completed within the estimated time period.

A productive version of this technique is to decide that some low- and medium-priority items are worth only so much of your time. Invest that much time in the project, but no more. Preparing a file on advertisements that come across your desk is one example.

BE DECISIVE AND FINISH THINGS

A subtle way of improving your personal productivity is to be decisive. Move quickly, but not impulsively, through the problem-solving and decision-making steps outlined in Chapter 3 when you are faced with a nonroutine decision. Once you have evaluated the alternatives to the problem, choose and implement one of them. Set a limit to how much time you will invest in arriving at a decision to a problem. Next, set a limit to the amount of time you will spend implementing your solution. If you are in charge of this year's office party committee, you might decide to hold the party at a particular party house. Decide next on approximately how much time you should invest in the project, and stick to your limit.

Another aspect of being decisive is to make the decision to finish tasks you have begun. Incompleted projects lower your productivity. Marge Baxter puts it this way: "It's better to complete a few things than to have seventeen things half done."[14] Another point to remember is that nobody gives you credit for an unfinished project.

Now that you have studied various ways to improve your personal productivity, see Self-Examination Exercise 12-1.

SELF-EXAMINATION EXERCISE 12-1:

The Personal Productivity Checklist

Class Project

Each class member will use the preceding checklist to identify the two biggest mistakes he or she is making in work habits and time management. The mistakes could apply to work, school, or personal life. In addition to identifying the problem, each student will develop a brief action plan about how to overcome it. For instance, "One of my biggest problems is that I tend to start a lot of projects but finish very few of them. Now that I am aware of this problem, I am going to post a sign over my desk that reads, 'St. Peter won't give me credit for things I never completed.'"

Students then present their problems and action plans to the class. After each student has made his or her presentation, a class discussion is held to reach conclusions and interpretations about the problems revealed. For instance, it might be that one or two time management problems are quite frequent.

	Especially applicable to me
Overcoming Procrastination	
1. Increase awareness of the problem.	_____
2. Calculate cost of procrastination.	_____
3. Counterattack by forcing self to do task.	_____
4. Create some momentum to get moving.	_____
5. Peck away at an overwhelming task.	_____
6. Motivate self with overwhelming task.	_____
7. Use subliminal messages about overcoming procrastination.	_____

(Continued)

	Especially applicable to me
Developing Proper Attitudes and Values	
1. Become a goal-oriented person and value your time.	_____
2. Value good attendance and punctuality.	_____
3. Value neatness and orderliness.	_____
4. Develop a total quality management (TQM) philosophy.	_____
5. Work harder, not smarter.	_____
6. Become self-employed psychologically.	_____
7. Appreciate the importance of rest and relaxation.	_____
Developing the Proper Skills and Techniques	
1. Plan your activities.	_____
2. Get off to a good start.	_____
3. Make good use of office technology.	_____
4. Concentrate on one task at a time.	_____
5. Streamline your work and emphasize important tasks.	_____
6. Tackle distasteful tasks first.	_____
7. Work at a steady pace.	_____
8. Schedule similar tasks together.	_____
9. Create some quiet, uninterrupted time.	_____
10. Make use of bits of time.	_____
11. Stay in control of paperwork and E-mail.	_____
Overcoming Time Wasters	
1. Minimize daydreaming.	_____
2. Prepare a time log to evaluate your use of time.	_____
3. Avoid being a computer goof-off.	_____
4. Keep track of important names, places, and things.	_____
5. Set a time limit for certain tasks and projects.	_____
6. Be decisive and finish things.	_____

SUMMARY

People with good work habits tend to be more successful in their careers than poorly organized individuals, and they tend to have more time to spend on personal life. Good work habits are more important than ever because of today's emphasis on productivity and quality.

Procrastination is the major work habit problem for most employees and students. People procrastinate for many reasons, including their perception that a task is unpleasant, overwhelming, or may lead to negative consequences. Fear of success can also lead to procrastination. Awareness of procrastination may lead to its control. Seven other techniques for reducing procrastination are: (1) calculate the cost of procrastination; (2) counterattack the burdensome task; (3) create some momentum to get you going; (4) peck away at an overwhelming task; (5) motivate yourself with rewards and punishments; (6) make a commitment to other people; and (7) use computerized subliminal messages.

Developing good work habits and time-management practices is often a matter of developing proper attitudes toward work and time. Seven such attitudes and values are: (1) become goal-oriented and value your time; (2) value good attendance and punctuality; (3) value neatness and orderliness; (4) develop a total quality management philosophy; (5) work harder, not smarter; (6) become self-employed psychologically; and (7) appreciate the value of rest and relaxation.

Eleven skills and techniques to help you become more productive are: (1) plan your activities; (2) get off to a good start; (3) make good use of office technology; (4) concentrate on one task at a time; (5) streamline your work and emphasize important tasks; (6) tackle distasteful tasks first; (7) work at a steady pace; (8) schedule similar tasks together; (9) create some quiet, uninterrupted time; (10) make use of bits of time; (11) stay in control of paperwork and E-mail.

Six suggestions for overcoming time wasting are: (1) minimize daydreaming; (2) prepare a time log to evaluate your use of time; (3) avoid being a computer goof off; (4) keep track of important names, places, and things; (5) set time limits for certain task and projects; and (6) be decisive and finish things.

Questions and Activities

1. How might the information in this chapter be used to increase company productivity?

2. How might the information in this chapter be used to improve a person's social life?

3. To what extent do athletes practice good work habits and time management during the game?

4. Some students contend that because they work best when they put things off until the last moment, procrastination probably

will not hurt them in their career. What is wrong with their reasoning?

5. Do you think an employer has the right to put subliminal messages on employee computer screens to get them to procrastinate less? Explain.

6. Some workers are concerned that if too much work streamlining goes on in the company, some workers will lose their jobs. What is your position?

7. Some professors, artists, and scientists have cluttered and disorganized offices. How can these people still be successful?

8. Identify five bits of time you could put to better use.

9. Complaints are mounting that the frequent use of E-mail is lowering productivity for many workers. What might be the problem?

10. Ask an experienced businessperson what steps he or she takes to stay well organized under pressure. Be prepared to discuss your findings in class.

A HUMAN RELATIONS CASE PROBLEM: THE BUSY OFFICE MANAGER

Mike Powers looked at clock on the electric range, and said to Ruth, his wife: "Oh no, it's 7:25. It's my morning to drop off Jason and Gloria at the child-care center. Jason hasn't finished breakfast, and Gloria is still in her pajamas. Can you get Gloria dressed for me?"

Ruth responded, "OK, I'll help Gloria. But today is your turn to take care of the children. And I have a client presentation at 8:30 this morning. I need to prepare for a few more minutes."

"Forget I asked," said Mike. "I'll take care of it. Once again I'll start my day in a frenzy, late for child care, and just barely making it to work on time."

"Why didn't you get up when the alarm rang the first time?" asked Ruth.

"Don't you remember, we talked until one this morning? It seems like we never get to talk to each other until midnight."

After getting Jason and Gloria settled at the childcare center, Mike dashed off to the public accounting firm where he worked as the office manager. After greeting several staff members, Mike turned on his computer to check his E-mail. Ann Gabrielli, one of the partners in the firm, left the following message: "See you today at 11:30 for the review of overhead expenses. Two other partners will be attending."

Mike quickly looked at his desk calendar. According to his calendar, the meeting was one week from today. Mike called Gabrielli immediately, and said, "Ann, my apologies. My schedule says that the meeting is one week from today at 11:30, not today. I'm just not ready with the figures for today's meeting."

"My calendar says the meeting is today," said Gabrielli harshly. I'm ready for the meeting and so are Craig and Gunther (the other partners). This isn't the first time you've gotten your weeks mixed up. The meeting will go on, however poorly you have to perform."

"I'll be there," said Mike. "It's just a question of reviewing some figures that I've already collected."

After placing down the phone, Mike calculated that he had about two hours and forty minutes in which to prepare a preliminary report on reducing overhead. He then glanced at his desk calendar to see what else he had scheduled this morning. The time looked clear except for one entry, "PA/LC."

"What is 'PA/LC' " thought Mike. "I can't imagine what these initials stand for. Wait a minute, now I know. The initials stand for performance appraisal with Lucy Cruthers, our head bookkeeper. I'm not ready for that session. And I can't do it this morning. Mike then sent Cruthers an E-mail message, suggesting that they meet the following week at the same time.

Cruthers answered back immediately. She wrote that she would not be able to meet the following week because that was the first day of her vacation. Mike sent her another note: "I'll get back to you later with another date. I don't have time now to make plans."

Next, Mike informed the department assistant, Lois Chavez, that he had to hurriedly prepare for the 11:30 meeting. Mike asked for her cooperation in keeping visitors away for the rest of the morning.

He then called up the directory on his hard drive to look for the file on overhead expenses he had begun last week. As he scanned through the directory, he found only three files that might be related to the topic: COST, EXPENSES, and TRIM. Mike reasoned that the file must be one of these three.

Mike retrieved the file, COST. It proved to be a summary of furniture expenses for the firm. Upon bringing EXPENSES up on the screen, Mike found that it was his expense account report for a business trip he took seven months ago. TRIM was found to be a list of cost estimates for lawn care services.

Agitated, and beginning to sweat profusely, Mike asked Chavez to help him. "I'm stuck," he pleaded. "I need to find my file for the overhead expense analysis I was doing for the partners. Do you recall what I named this file? Did I give it to you on disk?"

"Let me see if I can help," said Chavez. "We'll search your directory together." Chavez scanned about 100 files. "What a clutter," she sighed. "You ought to clean out your files sometime soon. Here's a possibility, PTR."

"I doubt it," said Mike. 'PTR' stands for partner. I'm looking for a file about overhead expenses."

"But you are preparing the file for the partners, aren't you?"

Lois proved to be right. The PTR file contained the information Mike sought. Within thirty minutes he completed the spreadsheet analysis he needed. He then prepared a brief memo on the word processor, explaining his findings. With twenty minutes left before the presentation, Mike asked Lucy if she could run off three copies in a hurry. Lucy explained that the department's photocopying machine was not operating. She said she would ask to use the photocopier in another department.

"Bring them into my meeting with the partners as soon as you can," said Mike. "I've run out of time."

On the way to the meeting, Mike exhaled a few times, and consciously relaxed his muscles to overcome the tension accumulated from preparing the report under so much pressure. Mike performed reasonably well during the meeting. The partners accepted his analysis of overhead expenses, and said they would study his findings further. As the meeting broke up at 12:30, the senior partner commented to Mike, "If you had gotten your weeks straight, I think you could have presented your analysis in more depth. Your report was useful, but I know you are capable of doing a more sophisticated analysis."

(Continued)

After returning from lunch, Mike reviewed his daily planner again. He noticed a Post-it™ note attached to the light on his desk. The entry on the slip of paper said, "Racquetball, monday night with Ziggy."

"Not again," Mike said to himself in a groan of agony. "Tonight I have to get Jason and Gloria to bed. Ruth has a makeup class scheduled for her course in Japanese. I'll have to call Ziggy now. I hope he's in his office."

Mike left an URGENT message on Ziggy's electronic mail, offering his apologies. He thought to himself, "I hope Ziggy won't be too annoyed. This is the second time this year I've had to reschedule a match at the last moment."

Mike returned from lunch at 2:00 P.M. He decided to finish the report on overhead he had prepared for the partners. By 4:00 P.M. Mike was ready to being the tasks outlined on his daily planner. At that point Lois Chavez walked into Mike's office, and announced: "There's a representative here from Account Temps. She said she was in the building, so she decided to drop in and talk about their temporary employment services."

"Might as well let her in," said Mike. "We will be hiring some temporary bookkeepers soon. Account Temps has a good reputation. It's getting too late to do much today anyway."

Mike made it to the child-care center by 5:45 and packed Jason and Gloria into the family minivan. Gloria, the oldest child, asked if the family could eat at Hardee's this evening. Mike said, "OK, but I'll have to stop at an ATM first. I don't have enough cash on hand to eat out. We'll stop at the ATM, stop by the house, and see if Mom wants to eat out tonight before class."

Mike and the children arrived home at 6:15 and asked Ruth if she would like to have a family dinner at Hardee's this evening.

"I have about one hour to spare before class," said Ruth. "Why not? By the way, how was your day?"

"My day?" asked Mike with a sigh. "I just fell one day deeper behind schedule. I'll have to do some paperwork after the children are asleep. Maybe we can watch the late night news together this evening. We should both be free by then."

Questions

1. What time-management mistakes does Mike appear to be making?

2. What does Mike appear to be doing right from the standpoint of managing time?

3. What suggestions can you offer Mike to help him get his schedule more under control?

A HUMAN RELATIONS ROLE PLAY: HELPING A BUSY OFFICE MANAGER

The above case presents background information for this role play. One person plays the role of Mike Powers who has decided to meet with a time-management counselor to discuss his problems. Mike feels that if he doesn't get help soon he will be doing serious damage to his career, and perhaps his marriage.

Another person plays the role of a time-management counselor who will listen to Mike and attempt to understand the root of his problem. The counselor will then make some recommendations. This particular counselor has a reputation for being a good listener, yet is known to give dogmatic recommendations.

REFERENCES

[1]Theodore Kurtz, "10 Reasons Why People Procrastinate," *Supervisory Management,* April 1990, pp. 1–2.

[2]Kurtz, "10 Reasons," p. 2.

[3]Alan Lakein, *How to Gain Control of Your Time and Your Life* (New York: Wyden Books, 1973), pp. 141–151.

[4]"Don't Procrastinate," *Practical Supervision,* January 1989, p. 3.

[5]Robert M. Meier and Susan Sheffler, "The Perils of Perfectionism," *Success!,* September 1984, p. 14.

[6]Michael Maren, "Program Yourself: Software for the Right Side of Your Brain," *Success,* October 1991, p. 58. (Software produced by Visionary Software, Portland, Oregon.)

[7]"Be Efficient—Get Organized," *Working Smart,* March 1994, p. 8.

[8]Raymond P. Rood and Brenda L. Meneley, "Serious Play at Work," *Personnel Journal,* January 1991, p. 90.

[9]"7 More Steps to More Control," *Working Smart,* May 1994, p. 8.

[10]Merrill Douglass, "Timely Time Tips: Ideas to Help You Manage Your Time," *Executive Management Forum,* September 1989, p. 4.

[11]"Save Time by Doing Two Things at Once," *Working Smart,* October 1991, p. 5.

[12]Douglas, "Timely Time Tips," p. 4.

[13]Paul Chance, "The Wondering Mind of Youth," *Psychology Today,* December 1988, p. 22.

[14]Quoted in Beth Brophy and Diane Cole, "10 Timely Tips," *USA Weekend,* October 25–27, 1985, p. 22.

ADDITIONAL READING

Bittel, Lester R. *Right on Time.* New York: McGraw-Hill, 1990.

Douglass, Merrill E., and Douglas, Donna N. *Time Management for Teams.* New York: AMACOM, 1993.

Fassle, Diane. *Working Ourselves to Death: The High Cost of Workaholism and the Rewards of Recovery.* New York: HarperCollins, 1990.

Fram, Eugene H. "Time Pressed Consumer." *Marketing Insights,* Summer 1991, pp. 34–39.

James, Dennis. "Simplify Your Life: Put First Things First." *Success,* September 1992, p. 48.

Mackenzie, Alec. *The Time Trap.* New York: AMACOM, 1990.

Mayer, Jeffrey J. *Winning the Fight Between You and Your Desk.* New York: HarperCollins, 1994.

CHAPTER 13

GETTING AHEAD IN YOUR CAREER

Learning Objectives

After studying the information and doing the exercises in this chapter you should be able to:

■ Select several strategies and tactics for getting ahead in your career by taking control of your own behavior.

■ Select several strategies and tactics for advancing your career by exerting control over your environment.

■ Recognize how to deal with the challenge of hidden barriers to career advancement.

A central theme of this book is that certain skills and behaviors will help you succeed in your career and personal life. In this chapter we focus on strategies, tactics, and attitudes that will help you achieve promotion or hold on to a position you enjoy. The same set of strategies, tactics, and attitudes will enable you to achieve **career portability,** the ability to move from one employer to another when necessary. Because many employers offer less job security than in past years, it is important for career-minded people to be able to move from one employer to another.

We have divided the vast information about career advancement into three sections. The first section deals with approaches to managing or taking control of your own behavior in order to advance or retain a good position. The second section deals with approaches to exerting control over your environment to improve your chances for success. A briefer section is also included on dealing with hidden barriers to career advancement.

Since the word *success* has many subjective meanings, it requires some clarification. **Success** as used here means attaining the twin goals of organizational rewards and personal satisfaction. Organizational rewards include such things as higher-ranking positions, more money, and challenging assignments. Personal satisfaction refers to enjoying, or liking, what you are doing. If your employer thinks you're terrific and therefore rewards you, and you're happy, you're a success from the viewpoint expressed here.

 ## TAKING CONTROL OF YOURSELF

The unifying theme to the strategies, tactics, and attitudes described in this section is that you must attempt to control your own behavior. You can advance your career by harnessing the forces under your control. Such a perspective is helpful because individuals have the primary responsibility for managing their own careers. The organization may help, but managing your career is your responsibility.

The following section concentrates on getting ahead by trying to control your external environment in some small way. Do not be concerned about overlap between the general categories of controlling yourself versus controlling the environment. Instead, be concerned about the meaning and application of the strategies and tactics.

DEVELOP OUTSTANDING INTERPERSONAL SKILLS

Getting ahead in business-related fields is exceedingly difficult unless you can relate effectively to other people. Workers are bypassed for promotion generally because someone thinks they cannot effectively be responsible for the work of others. Workers are more likely to be terminated for poor interpersonal skills than for poor technical skills.

Effective interpersonal or human relations skills refer to many specific practices. At a meeting, if you crack a joke that relieves tension and serves as an icebreaker, you are showing good interpersonal skill. If, as the team leader, you convince other team members to strive harder for quality, you are showing good interpersonal (and leadership) skill.

Chapters 6 through 9 of this book focus on important interpersonal skills such as communication, resolving conflict, being assertive, and listening to customers. Interpersonal skills also include other topics in this book, such as being self-confident and exerting leadership (Chapter 14).

DEVELOP EXPERTISE

A starting point in getting ahead is to develop a useful job skill. This tactic is obvious if you are working as a specialist, such as an insurance underwriter. Being skilled at the task performed by the group is also a requirement for being promoted to a supervisory position. After being promoted to a supervisor or another managerial job, expertise is still important for further advancement. It helps a manager's reputation to be skilled in such things as memo writing, computer applications, preparing a budget, and interviewing job candidates. Another important skill is **troubleshooting,** the knack for pinpointing and analyzing snags in your department's work flow as they arise.[1]

PERFORM WELL ON ALL YOUR ASSIGNMENTS

Common sense and research support the idea that you have to perform well on your present assignment in order to move ahead.[2] Good job performance is the bedrock of a person's career. In rare instances a person is promoted on the basis of favoritism alone. In all other situations an employee must have received a favorable performance appraisal in order to be promoted. Before an employee is promoted, the prospective new boss asks, "How well did this person perform for you?"

CREATE GOOD FIRST IMPRESSIONS

Every time you interact with a new person inside or outside your company, you create a first impression. Fair or not, these first impressions have a big impact on your career. If your first impression is favorable, you will often be invited back by an internal or external customer. Your first impression also creates a halo that may influence perceptions about the quality of your work in the future. If your first impression is negative, you will have to work extra hard to be perceived as competent later on.

Looking successful contributes to a positive first impression. Your clothing, your desk and office, and your speech should project the image of a successful, but not necessarily flamboyant, person. Your standard of dress should be appropriate to your particular career stage and work environment. Appropriate dress for an inventory specialist is not the same as for an outside salesperson dealing with industrial customers. Appearing physically fit is also part of the success image.

Projecting a sense of control is another key factor contributing to a positive first impression. Show that you are in control of yourself and the environment. Avoid letting your body language betray you—nonverbal messages are sent by fidgeting or rubbing your face. Make your gestures project self-assurance and purpose.[3] A verbal method of appearing in control is to make a positive assertion such as, "This is a demanding assignment and I welcome the challenge."

MAKE AN ACCURATE SELF-ANALYSIS

To effectively plan your career and to advance in it, you need an accurate picture of your strengths, areas for improvement, and preferences. The exercises in Chapters 1 and 2, combined with the job-finding material called for in Chapter 11, will provide much of the information needed for self-evaluation. In addition, listen attentively to feedback you receive from growth groups, superiors, and co-workers.

Here is an example of how this strategy might be used. Jimmy, an engineering technician, carefully fills out the Self-Knowledge Questionnaire. He notices that his self-evaluation is weakest in the area of dealing with people. Jimmy then requests a conference with his boss to discuss his development in this area. The verdict comes back, "Much improvement needed. You tend to be too abrupt with people, and you finish people's sentences for them." Jimmy then requests an assignment that emphasizes dealing with people. His boss is generous enough to allow Jimmy to risk a few mistakes in order to improve his human relations skills. While on this new assignment Jimmy concentrates on not being too abrupt with people. In addition, he plans some community activities that give him a chance to practice human relations skills, such as being toastmaster or assuming a leadership position in a technical society.

TAKE THE INITIATIVE TO DO WORK AT THE NEXT LEVEL

An assertive, yet constructive, approach to career advancement is to act as if you already have the job above you. You seize the initiative and perform some of the functions of the job you want. This tactic can often be implemented because many firms have looser job descriptions than in the past.[4] As team members, people are supposed to take more initiative. An example follows of taking the initiative to work at the next level:

Marilyn, a secretary at a bank, aspired to the position of executive assistant. She looked for an opportunity to show that she could carry out the type of leadership often required of executive assistants in her bank.

The bank initiated a program of *reengineering* whereby every department was supposed to study how it accomplishes its work, with an eye toward eliminating unnecessary steps. Training programs were established to orient many of the employees toward reengineering. Marilyn was one of the first people to volunteer for the training.

Marilyn began preparing *process maps* (flowcharts of work activity that are an essential part of reengineering) in her work area. When asked why she was preparing these maps, Marilyn explained that it was inevitable that they would soon be needed for the reengineering program. Several managers at the bank were impressed by Marilyn's contribution. She was chosen for the next open position as executive assistant. As part of her new job, Marilyn was given special responsibilities for coordinating part of the reengineering program.

DOCUMENT YOUR ACCOMPLISHMENTS

Keeping an accurate record of what you have accomplished on the job can be valuable when you are being considered for promotion or transfer. A record of this type is also useful when your performance is being evaluated. You can then show your boss what you have done for the organization lately. Here are two examples of documented accomplishments from different types of jobs:

1. As bank teller, suggested one side door be modified to accommodate customers in wheelchairs. Number of physically disabled customers jumped 324 percent in two years.

2. As maintenance supervisor decreased fuel costs in office by 27 percent in one year by installing ceiling fans.

After documenting your accomplishments, it pays to advertise. Let key people know in a tasteful way of your tangible accomplishments. You might request an opportunity to make a presentation to your boss to review the status of one of your successful projects, or use E-mail for the same purpose if it would be presumptuous for you to request a special meeting to discuss your accomplishments.

BE CONVENTIONAL IN YOUR BEHAVIOR

Although this book does not emphasize conformity to conventional norms of behavior, they are of value in getting ahead. More precisely, by flaunting tradition you could hurt your career. Areas in which conventional behavior is expected by most employers include good attendance and punctuality, careful grooming, courtesy to superiors, appropriate amount of smiling, good posture, adherence to company safety rules, and obeying authority. Employees who insist on being nonconformists in these areas do so at considerable risk to their career advancement. The chairman of the board of the world's largest manufacturer of photographic supplies once commented: "The biggest problem with young people today is that they spend so much time fighting the system. After about five years of fighting the system, some of them finally come around and are ready to work with the firm rather than against it. Those are the people we need." In what way do you fight the system?

Take a Creative Approach to Your Job

As emphasized in Chapter 3, being creative helps you get ahead in business. Your ideas must be backed up with concrete plans for their implementation. If you are associated with an innovative idea, and that idea pays dividends, your career might receive a big boost. By age twenty-seven, Garth was the regional manager of a chain of hotels. He explained his success in these terms:

> Several years ago I was working as the assistant manager at one of our big hotels. As I was reviewing the room rates one day, it hit me that the public really needed inexpensive, clean lodgings. There must be thousands of people who simply can't afford $100 a night and up for a room. If they don't want to pay that much, they often have to stay at third-rate places.
>
> My solution was to propose the construction of a no-frills motel on the outskirts of town in one sample location. We would use the least-expensive, safe construction available. The rooms would be clean but modest. Our prices would be about the lowest in the area except for really run-down hotels in the most undesirable section of town. Much to my surprise, the hotel executives agreed with my plan. From the beginning, we have had almost 100 percent occupancy at the first location. We're now looking for more locations where these inexpensive units can be built. I would never be where I am today in my career if it weren't for that one simple but important idea.

DISPLAY LOYALTY AND INTEGRITY

Being loyal and honest is a good way to impress your boss. It is also a good way to advance your career, or prevent your career from being short-circuited. Loyalty has many different meanings. On the job it means such things as keeping in mind the best interests of your boss, department, and firm. A loyal employee would not participate in a cafeteria gripe session about his or her boss, department, or firm. A loyal employee would emphasize the good aspects of his or her employer to people in the community. A loyal employee would also try to use products manufactured or sold by his or her employer. Also, loyal employees do what they can to attend company functions such as picnics and holiday parties.

Being loyal should not mean, however, that you surrender your ability to make constructive criticism about things that need change. An assistant buyer at a discount department store overheard a few customers talking about the incompetent help at her store. She brought this problem to the attention of the store management. After further investigation, they discovered that the complaints were not unfounded. A new training program for new employees was instituted that helped remedy the situation of employees having such limited ability to help customers.

KEEP GROWING THROUGH SELF-DEVELOPMENT

One of the major contributions of a formal education is that it equips you to keep on learning. You also have to help the process along by being willing to engage in self-development. Without a keen interest in self-development, you stand a good chance of being held back in your career. Although most firms offer courses of their own, or encourage you to take courses outside the company, self-development and self-improvement are still your responsibility. Self-development includes updating your technical and professional skills, such as learning to use new equipment. You should also keep in mind that much of the self-development you need to get ahead occurs outside of a formal course. Reading newspapers, books, and articles can be an important source of job-related self-development. Len describes how a simple form of self-development led to his promotion to supervisor:

> I knew we were having quality problems in our department. I heard a friend of mine talk about a great film showing how the Japanese have kept their manufacturing quality so high. I went to a library showing of this film. One segment described quality circles. This involves ordinary workers making suggestions for improving product quality. I then read an article on the same topic. The procedure is much like brainstorming. A group of employees and their supervisor, or a supervisor from another department, try to figure out how to improve the quality of a product. The employees take turns offering suggestions. Quality circles are based on the idea that the person who actually makes the product is in the best position to make suggestions for its improvement. Employees take pride in being able to make suggestions about improving the quality of the products made by the company.

Next, I wrote a memo to my boss suggesting that we try quality circles in our company. One thing led to another and I was appointed head of a quality circle project. It led logically to my being appointed supervisor of a small department.

Observe Proper Etiquette

Proper etiquette is important for career advancement because the pendulum has swing back toward a polite and mannerly business climate.[5] **Business etiquette** is a special code of behavior required in work situations. The term *manners* has an equivalent meaning. Both etiquette and manners refer to behaving in an acceptable and refined way.

Figuring out what constitutes proper etiquette and business manners requires investigation. One approach is to use successful career people as models of behavior or sources of information. Another approach is to consult a current book about business etiquette, such as *Letitia Baldrige's Complete Guide to Executive Manners.* Many of the suggestions offered in these books follow common sense, but many others would not be obvious to an inexperienced career person.

The overall principle of etiquette and business manners is to be considerate. Specific guidelines stem from this principle. Exhibit 13-1 presents examples of good business etiquette and manners.

EXHIBIT 13-1

BUSINESS ETIQUETTE AND MANNERS

Below are thirteen specific suggestions about office etiquette and business manners that should be considered in the context of a specific job situation. For example, the suggestion, "Shouting is out" would not apply to traders on the floor of the New York Stock Exchange, where shouting is routine.

1. *Be polite to people in person.*   Say "good morning" and "good night" to work associates at all job levels. Smile frequently. Offer to bring coffee or another beverage for a co-worker if you are going outside to get some for yourself.

2. *Write polite letters.*   An important occasion for practicing good etiquette is the writing of business and personal letters. Include the person's job title in the inside address, spell the person's name correctly. Use supportive rather than harsh statements. (For example, say "It would be helpful if you could" rather than "you must.") Avoid right margin justification because it is much harsher than indented lines.

3. *Practice good table manners.*   Avoid smacking your lips or sucking your fingers. If someone else is paying the bill do not order the most expensive item on the menu (such as a $150 bottle of Dom Pérignon champagne!). Offer to cut bread for the other person, and do not look at the check if the other person is paying.

4. *Names should be remembered.*   It is both good manners and good human relations to remember the names of work associates, even if you see them only occasionally.

(Continued)

5. *Males and females should receive equal treatment.*   Amenities extended to females by males in a social setting are minimized in business settings today. During a meeting, a male is not expected to hold a chair or a door for a woman, nor does he jump to walk on the outside when the two of them are walking down the street. Many women resent being treated differently from males with respect to minor social customs. In general, common courtesies should be extended by both sexes to one another.

6. *Shouting is out.*   Emotional control is an important way of impressing superiors. Following the same principle, shouting in most work situations is said to detract from your image.

7. *Coats can be removed in the office.*   Today it is considered appropriate to take off your coat, and keep it off, not only in your own work area, but when moving to other parts of the building.

8. *The host or hostess pays the bill.*   An area of considerable confusion about etiquette surrounds business lunches and who should pay the check—the man or the woman. The rule of etiquette is that the person who extends the invitation pays the bill. (Do you think this rule should be extended to social life?)

9. *Introduce the higher-ranking person to the lower-ranking person.*   Your boss's name will be mentioned before a co-worker's; you introduce the older person to the younger person; and a client is introduced first to co-workers.

10. *Address superiors and visitors in their preferred way.*   As the modern business world has become more informal, a natural tendency has developed to address people at all levels by their first names. It is safer to first address people by a title and their last name and then wait for them to correct you if they desire.

11. *Respect the chain of command.*   Organizations value the **chain of command,** the official statement of who reports to whom. It is therefore inadvisable for you to initiate contact with your boss's boss without your boss's permission.

12. *Make appointments with high-ranking people rather than dropping in.* Related to the above principle, it is taboo in most firms for lower-ranking employees to casually drop in to the office of an executive.

13. *Sexiness in the office should be muted.*   Women are strongly advised to avoid looking overly sexy or glamorous in the office. Thus waist-length hair should be avoided and so should dangling jewelry, four-inch-high heels, and heavy eye makeup. Men, too, should not appear too sexy, and thus tight pants and shirts are to be avoided.

Caution: Although all the above points could have some bearing on the image you project, violation of any one of them would not necessarily have a negative impact on your career. It is the overall image you project that counts the most. Therefore, the general principle of being considerate of work associates is much more important than any one act of etiquette or manners.

SOURCE: Based on information from George Mazzei, *The New Office Etiquette* (New York: Simon & Schuster, 1983); Annette Vincent and Melanie Meche, "It's Time to Teach Business Etiquette," *Business Education Forum,* October 1993, pp. 39–41.

TAKE SENSIBLE RISKS

An element of risk taking is necessary to advance very far in your career. Almost all successful people have taken at least one moderate risk in their careers. These risks include starting a new business with mostly borrowed money, joining a fledgling firm, or submitting a ground-breaking idea to management. Consultant Robert Wendover sizes up the importance of risk taking in this way: "Non-risk takers not only inhibit their careers, but may also impede the progress of an organization. Progress requires risks."[6]

LEARN TO MANAGE ADVERSITY

Some adversity is almost inevitable in an ambitious person's career. It is difficult to get through a career without at least once being laid off, fired, demoted, transferred to an undesirable assignment, or making a bad investment. Company mergers and takeovers also contribute to adversity because so many people are laid off in the process or assigned to lesser jobs.

Personal resilience—the capacity to bounce back from setback—is necessary to overcome adversity. A general-purpose way of handling adversity is to first get emotional support from a friend or family member, and then solve the problem systematically. You follow the decision-making steps described in Chapter 3. Laura, a computer sales representative, explains how she managed adversity:

> Three years ago I hit a low point in my life. The company I worked for was involved in a scandal about paying kickbacks to a few school and city administrators in exchange for several major contracts. I wasn't directly involved in offering the kickbacks, but I was the sales representative on one of the unethically handled accounts. As you can imagine, I got tarred with the same brush.
>
> At about the same time, my boyfriend was arrested for illegal stock trading. In a two-week period, I faced unemployment and the necessity to either help my boyfriend through his turmoil, or leave him. At first I thought the world was caving in on me. I cried on the shoulder of my girlfriend and my mother. After those conversations, I realized I was still a good person. I admit I should have been more perceptive about the wrongdoings of my firm and my boyfriend. Yet *I* had done nothing wrong.
>
> I had the self-confidence to face the world in a positive way. I told prospective employers that they could check out my story. I didn't offer kickbacks to anyone. My only error on the job was having had too much trust in my employer. Based on my good sales record, I did find a comparable job. I also decided to help my boyfriend through his rough times. So what if a few people thought I was too forgiving? I have enough confidence in myself to stick with my own inclinations.

DO WHAT YOU LOVE

A major strategy for attaining a successful career is to do work you love, and persist in doing it well. Work you love can be considered the ideal job. Most people have to work toward finding a job that approaches their personal ideal. Furthermore, many people have yet to discover their ideal job. Self-Examination Exercise 13-1 will help you identify an ideal job for yourself.

SELF-EXAMINATION EXERCISE 13-1:

Discovering Your Ideal Job

To develop insights into your ideal job, do the following:

1. Take a blank sheet of paper or computer file. On the top, write, "What I enjoy about my career." Underneath, record what you consider to be the most enjoyable aspects of a present or past job (full-time, part-time, or temporary). If your work experience is limited, think of a good job familiar to you.

2. On a second sheet of paper or another computer file, record the title, "My career standards." Below, list all the standards or values you have for your career. Include factors such as who you would like to work with, how much money you would like to earn, and the type of people you want to serve. To get started, complete the statement, "In my ideal career, I will . . . (earn, produce, create, etc.)." Strive for at least ten statements.

3. Now add the statements made in the first list to the second by converting them to statements relating to an ideal job. To illustrate, if a statement from the first list was "opportunity to help people," modify it to read, "In my ideal career, I will have the opportunity to help people."

   When you have completed the above, delete the word "standards" from the top of your page, and substitute the word "goals." Set priorities for statements by assigning a rank of 1 to the most important item, 2 the next important, and so on.

4. On a new sheet of paper or the next page on the computer file, key the new heading, "My career goals." List items 1 through 10 on your list. Later, after you have accomplished these ten goals, you can work on the others on your list.

   Make a photocopy of your list and place it where you will see it regularly—in your daily planner, on top of your desk, or on your kitchen bulletin board. From this point forward, take actions that will help you achieve these goals. Make them happen. If you enjoy helping others, take the initiative to help a work associate as soon as convenient.

   When you accomplish each item on your list—such as helping others solve problems—you should be moving toward creating a job that you love.

SOURCE: Adapted from Stuart Kamen, "Do What You Love," *Success Workshop*™, vol. 1, no. 1, 1994.

■ EXERTING CONTROL OVER THE OUTSIDE WORLD

Here we emphasize strategies and tactics requiring you to exert some control over the outside environment. If you do not fully control it, at least you can try to juggle it to your advantage. For instance, "Find a sponsor" suggests that you search out a powerful person who can help you advance in your career.

Develop a Career Path

Planning your career inevitably involves some form of goal setting. If your goals are laid out systematically to lead you to your ultimate career goal, you have established a career path. A **career path** is thus a sequence of positions necessary to achieve a goal.[7]

If a career path is laid out in one firm, it must be related to the present and future demands of that firm. If you aspire toward a high-level manufacturing job, it would be vital to know the future of manufacturing in that company. Many U.S. firms, for example, plan to conduct more of their manufacturing in the Far East or Mexico. If you were really determined, you might study the appropriate language and ready yourself for a global position. Computerization is another factor that should be considered in developing a career path. How much computer knowledge will you need in the future to be successful in your line of work?

While sketching out a career path you should list your personal goals. They should mesh with your work plans to help avoid major conflicts in your life. Some lifestyles, for example, are incompatible with some career paths. You might find it difficult to develop a stable home life (spouse, children, friends, community activities, garden) if you aspired toward holding field positions within the Central Intelligence Agency.

Your career path is a living document, and may need to be modified as your circumstances change.[8] Keep in mind changes in your company and industry. If becoming a branch manager is an important step in your career path, check to see if your company or industry still has branch managers. The changing preferences of your family can also influence your career path. A family that wanted to stay put may now be willing to relocate, which could open up new possibilities on your career path.

Contingency ("what if?") plans should also be incorporated into a well-designed career path. For instance, "If I don't become an agency supervisor by age thirty-five, I will seek employment in the private sector." Or, "If I am not promoted within two years, I will enroll in a business school program."

Lisa Irving, an ambitious twenty-year-old, formulated the following career path prior to receiving an associate's degree in business administration. After she presented her tentative career path to her classmates, several accused Lisa of shooting for the moon. Lisa's career goals are high, but she has established contingency plans. Presented as an example, not an ideal model, is Lisa's career plan path:

WORK

1. Purchasing trainee for two years

2. Assistant purchasing agent for three years

3. Purchasing agent for five years (will join Purchasing Managers Association)

4. Purchasing supervisor for five years

5. Purchasing manager for six years

6. Manager, materials handling for five years

7. Vice president, procurement, until retirement

PERSONAL LIFE

1. Rent own apartment after one year of working.

2. Attend college evenings until receive B.S. in business administration.

3. Marriage by age twenty-seven (plan only one marriage).

4. One child by age thirty.

5. Live in private home with husband and child by age thirty-three.

6. Volunteer work for Down's syndrome children.

7. Travel to India before age fifty.

Contingency Plans

1. Will seek new employment by stage 3 if not promoted to purchasing agent.

2. If not promoted to vice president by stage 6, will consider opening small retail business.

3. If I encounter sex discrimination at any stage, will look for employment with firm that has large government contracts (where discrimination is much less likely).

4. If develop stress disorder at any point, will seek nonsupervisory position in purchasing field.

Career paths can also be laid out graphically, as shown in Figure 13-1. One benefit of a career path laid out in chart form is that it gives a clear perception of climbing steps toward your target position. As each position is attained, the corresponding step can be shaded in color or cross-hatched.

Most of the goals just mentioned include a time element, which is crucial to sound career management. Your long-range goal might be clearly established in your mind (such as owner and operator of a health spa). At the same time you must establish short-range (get any kind of job in health spa) and intermediate-range (manager of a health spa by age thirty) goals. Goals set too far in the future that are not supported with more immediate goals may lose their motivational value.

The career path under discussion features a steady progression of promotions, yet a reasonable number of years in each position. Such planning is realistic because promotions often take a long time to achieve. A class exercise to help you obtain feedback on your career path is presented in Exhibit 13-2.

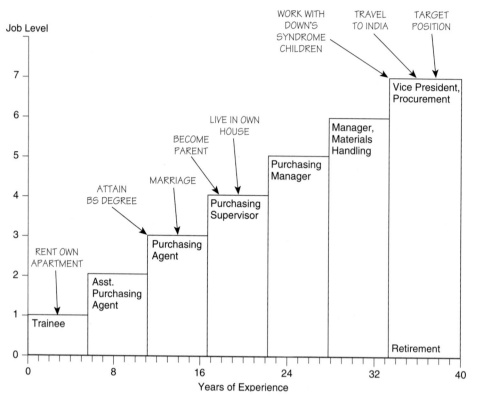

Figure 13-1   A Career Path

HAVE AN ACTION PLAN TO REACH YOUR GOALS

As described in Chapter 2, a useful goal is backed up by a logical plan for its attainment. A recommended practice is to supplement your career path with a description of your action plans. Lisa Irving, the woman who wants to succeed in the purchasing field, might have one or two action plans of this nature:

> In order to be promoted from purchasing agent to supervisor I will: (1) perform in an outstanding manner on my job, (2) have completed my B.S. degree, and (3) ask to attend company-sponsored supervisory training programs.
> In order to become manager of materials handling, I will need to: (1) perform in an outstanding manner as purchasing manager by such means as coordinating the billing system with the sales department, (2) engage in continuous self-study about the entire materials-handling field, (3) be active in the local purchasing association group, and (4) make sure that top management is aware of my talent and ambition.

Action plans can be drawn up in minute detail. As with any other aspect of career planning, however, avoid becoming too rigid in your thinking. Career paths and career plans are only tentative. A different path to your goal might fall right in your lap. Ten years from now, for instance, Lisa might receive a telephone call from an executive employment agency. The caller might say, "My client has engaged me to find a materials manager who is competent. Your name was given to us. Could you possibly meet me for lunch to discuss this exciting career opportunity?"

PRACTICE NETWORKING

Developing a network of contacts was recommended in Chapter 11 as a method of finding a job. Currently the most popular career-advancement tactic, networking has several purposes. The contacts you establish can help you find a better position, offer you a new position, become a customer, become a valuable supplier, or help you solve difficult problems. People in your network can also offer you emotional support during periods of adversity.

The starting point in networking is to obtain an ample supply of business cards. You then give a card to any person you meet who might be able to help you now or in the future. People in your network can include relatives; people you meet while traveling, camping, or attending trade shows; and classmates. Many cities have networking clubs that meet periodically after work at a cocktail lounge. In some clubs, only nonalcoholic beverages are served. Community activities and religious organizations can also be a source of contacts. Golf is still considered the number-one sport for networking because of the high-level contacts the sport generates.

EXHIBIT 13-2

CAREER PATHING

1. Each class member will develop a tentative career path, perhaps as an outside assignment. About six volunteers will then share their paths with the rest of the class. Feedback of any type will be welcomed. Class members studying the career paths of others should keep in mind such issues as:

   a. How logical does it appear?
   b. Is this something the person really wants or is it simply an exercise in putting down on paper what the ambitious person is supposed to want?
   c. How well do the individual's work plans mesh with personal plans?

2. Each class member will interview an experienced working person outside of class about his or her career path. Most of the people interviewed will have already completed a portion of their path. They will therefore have less flexibility (and perhaps less idealism) than people just getting started in their careers. The conclusions reached about these interviews will make a fruitful class discussion. Among the issues raised might be:

   a. How familiar were these people with the idea of a career path?
   b. How willing were they to talk about themselves?
   c. Were many actual "paths" discovered, or did a series of jobs simply come about by luck or "fate"?

A recent trend is for career-minded people to develop work and social contacts by computer networks. Every day and night, people are communicating by computer and modem with each other and information centers. (A modem is an instrument that allows computers to communicate over phone lines.) The essence of this form of networking is that people establish and develop contacts via E-mail.

Swim Against the Tide

Risk taking was mentioned previously as a strategy for taking control of your own behavior. A form of risk taking can also be applied to taking control of the environment. According to the tactic of **swim against the tide,** you advance your career by taking an unconventional path to career success. An unconventional path can be considered riskier. The key element to swim-against-the-tide is that you place yourself in an environment where the competition might not be so overwhelming.

Some men swim against the tide by entering nursing. Because a low percentage of nurses are male, male nurses are more readily noticed. Also, they are in strong demand in psychiatric nursing where upper body strength is often needed to manage patients. Some women swim against the tide by seeking managerial jobs in heavy industry.

Another way to swim against the tide is to capitalize on your personal characteristics. Suppose you are outgoing and personable. Many well-intended relatives and friends will say to you, "Go into sales. You're a natural." If you prefer to swim against the tide, enter the numerical or applied technology field. In this way, you can use your strong people skills to help you rise into management. You might have the edge over the many people in these fields who work better with data and things than with people.

A disadvantage of swimming against the tide is that you might place yourself in an environment in which your talents or credentials are not appreciated. Suppose you are seeking a career in business administration. You decide to work in the front office of a professional football team because so few people of your background have thought of this path. Ultimately, you find out that your background can take you only so far. The good jobs go to former football players, not to professionally trained administrators.

Achieve Broad Experience

Most people who land high-ranking positions are people of broad experience. Therefore, a widely accepted strategy for advancing in responsibility is to strengthen your credentials by broadening your experience. It is best to achieve this breadth early in your career. Since your salary demands are low at the early stages of your career, it is not so difficult to be transferred from one area of the business to another. Broadening can come about by performing a variety of jobs, or sometimes by performing essentially the same job in different organizations. You can also achieve breadth by working on committees and special assignments.

Transferring to a job at the same level and approximate salary as your present one is called a **lateral move.** An example would be a merchandising manager in a department store being transferred to director of store operations. As a result of this move, the person would be better prepared for promotion to a high-level retail position.

Broadening can come about by performing a variety of jobs in the same organization or by holding equivalent jobs at different organizations. Breadth can also be achieved by working on committees and special assignments.

PRACTICE SELF-NOMINATION

A more general strategy for achieving breadth is to practice self-nomination. Have the courage and assertiveness to ask for a promotion or a transfer. Your manager may not believe that you are actually seeking more responsibility. An effective method of convincing him or her is to volunteer yourself for specific job openings or for challenging assignments. A boss may need convincing, because many more people will be seeking advancement than who are actually willing to handle more responsibility.

BE VISIBLE

A big career booster for many people is to call favorable attention to themselves and their accomplishments. Ways of gaining visibility include: performing well on committee assignments, winning a suggestion award, performing well in a company-sponsored athletic event, getting an article published in a trade magazine, getting your name in the firm's newspaper, or distinguishing yourself in a community activity. Once you achieve visibility, you have a better chance of being noticed by an important person in the firm.

FIND A SPONSOR

A well-traveled route to career progress is to find someone at a high place in the firm who is impressed with your capabilities. A **sponsor** is a higher-ranking individual who is favorably impressed with you and therefore recommends you for promotion and choice assignments. A sponsor of this type can even be a relative by blood or by marriage. The major purpose of being visible is to find a sponsor. For example, many people who have been active in a company-sponsored activity such as the United Way have landed a sponsor and a promotion as a result.

FIND A MENTOR

Mentors are bosses who take subordinates under their wings and guide, teach, and coach them. Mentorship is an important development process in many occupations: master–apprentice, physician–intern, teacher–

student, and executive–junior executive.[9] An emotional tie exists between the less-experienced person (the protégé) and the mentor. The mentor therefore serves as a positive model. A relationship with a sponsor involves much less teaching, coaching, and formation of emotional ties. It is possible to have more than one mentor at a given point in one's career. Bob, a thirty-year-old sales manager, describes how finding a mentor helped him in his career:

> My career had its first big boost when I was noticed by Walt Brainbridge, our regional manager. He personally complimented me for my showing in a sales contest. From that point on he would ask to see me when he visited our office. He gave me lots of encouragement and told me what a good future I had with the firm. Without asking for credit, Walt was the one who assigned me to some of the best accounts. He set me up to succeed. He taught me a lot of good tricks, including how to fight the feeling of being rejected. I don't think I would have advanced nearly as far as I have today without Walt.

GRAB A SHOOTING STAR

Not everyone has ready access to a sponsor or mentor. There are only so many influential people around to take a personal interest in lower-ranking employees. Besides, if you are working at an entry-level position, it will be difficult for an executive to discover you (unless you do a superb job of being visible). It might be possible, however, to cultivate someone else who does have a sponsor or mentor.

Grabbing a shooting star involves finding someone who appears to be climbing the corporate ladder, and to develop a good relationship with that person. As the climber moves up the organization, you will follow. Val provides an apt illustration:

> I work for the city. In my department, the head of the internal audit section of the finance division was the protégé of the director of finance. An employee in the internal audit section became the protégé of the internal auditor because of family ties. When the position of assistant to the director of finance opened up, the internal auditor's protégé was chosen over five senior members of the department. A lot of people were surprised when this young man from another department was selected for the assistant position.

MANAGE LUCK

Few people do well in their careers without a good break along the way. Lucky events include your company suddenly expanding and therefore needing people to promote into key jobs; your boss quitting on short notice and you being asked to take over his or her job; or the business field in which you are working suddenly experiencing a boom, similar to the plastics recycling business today.

To be lucky, you first have to clarify what you want. Otherwise, you may not recognize an opportunity when it comes your way. Assume you know that you want to become an officer in your trade association.

Consequently, you will seize the opportunity when you hear that the group is looking for a new treasurer.

The strategy is not to simply wait for luck to come your way. Instead, manage luck to some extent by recognizing opportunities and taking advantage of them. The unlucky person is often the individual who, out of timidity, lets a good opportunity slip by. Suppose the boss says, "We need a volunteer to work on a special audit in the home office next month." The employee who manages luck will sense the opportunity to be noticed by influential people. The unlucky person will say, "Why bother doing all that extra work when there's no mention of extra money?"

Another way of capitalizing on luck is to be ready to take advantage of opportunities when they come along. If you maintain a record of excellent work performance, and you strive to complete your program of studies, you will position yourself to take advantage of opportunities.

Now that you have studied many strategies for advancing your career, look at Exhibit 13-3 to help you analyze the strategies you might choose to fit your personality and work situation.

DEALING WITH HIDDEN BARRIERS TO ADVANCEMENT

Concern exists that many white women as well as people of color of both sexes are held back from high-level promotions by a glass ceiling. A **glass ceiling** is an invisible but difficult-to-penetrate barrier to promotion based on subtle attitudes and prejudices. Fewer than 3 percent of senior executives in business are women, although women hold about 45 percent

---

EXHIBIT 13-3

SELECTING A SUITABLE CAREER-ADVANCEMENT STRATEGY

As with most suggestions for self-improvement, some of the suggestions in this chapter will have more relevance for you than will others. Among the factors influencing which strategy is best suited to you are your personality, the stage of your career, and the place you work. One person might say, "I think the tactic of displaying loyalty and integrity is a good one for me. I'm loyal by nature. I'm just getting started, so the company would look for those qualities. Also, our company generally promotes from the inside. They want to see loyalty before you get a big promotion."

Each class member will write down the two strategies described in this chapter that he or she will most probably put into action (or is already using), and provide a brief explanation of why this strategy is particularly relevant. Once these analyses are completed, each person will share his or her answers with the rest of the class.

It will be interesting to note if any strategy or tactic for getting ahead is mentioned by virtually all class members.

of managerial jobs in the United States.[10] White women, women of color, and men of color face few barriers to advancement for one or two promotions. After that point their promotional opportunities are often limited.

WHY THE GLASS CEILING EXISTS

An analysis of several factors contributing to the glass ceiling points to possible solutions to the problem employers can pursue. A dominant factor is tradition. Men often promote men, and white people often promote white people, because they are familiar with them. Another reason for the glass ceiling is a lack of acceptance of women and minorities in key positions by top-level managers.[11] The acceptance problem is higher in heavy industry than in service firms and consumer-oriented firms such as Levi Strauss and PepsiCo.

WHAT THE INDIVIDUAL CAN DO TO OVERCOME BARRIERS TO ADVANCEMENT

One strategy for overcoming the glass ceiling is to have patience. Barriers are lifting gradually in some companies and rapidly at others. As the work force continues to become more diverse, additional promotional opportunities are open to women and minorities. Within five years from now the glass ceiling may be shattered.

Individuals who have strong evidence that they are discrimination victims can lodge a formal complaint with the company, and then with an outside agency. Filing discrimination charges is more effective if a person is denied a first promotion. It is more difficult to prove discrimination took place when a person is not offered an executive position. The reason is that executives are chosen by difficult-to-pin-down factors such as broad thinking ability and personal appeal.

Another strategy for overcoming barriers to advancement is to enthusiastically apply all the other strategies and tactics in this chapter. A glass ceiling may exist for most people, but not for every woman and every member of selected minority groups. An outstanding performer who is also perceived as having superior leadership characteristics will often break through barriers to advancement. Chapter 14 presents details about the nature of leadership characteristics.

SUMMARY

Career success means that you attain organizational rewards and personal satisfaction. The strategies, tactics, and attitudes described here are generally accepted ways of advancing your career. One set of strategies and tactics for getting ahead can be classified as taking control of your own behavior. Included are the following:

1. Develop outstanding interpersonal skills.

2. Develop expertise.

3. Perform well on all your assignments.

4. Create good first impressions.

5. Make an accurate self-analysis.

6. Take the initiative to do work at the next level.

7. Document your accomplishments.

8. Be conventional in your behavior.

9. Take a creative approach to your job.

10. Display loyalty and integrity.

11. Keep growing through self-development.

12. Observe proper etiquette.

13. Take sensible risks.

14. Learn to manage adversity.

15. Do what you love.

Another set of strategies and tactics for getting ahead center around taking control of your environment, or at least adapting it to your advantage. Included are the following:

1. Develop a career path.

2. Have an action plan to reach your goals.

3. Practice networking.

4. Swim against the tide.

5. Achieve broad experience.

6. Practice self-nomination.

7. Be visible.

8. Find a sponsor.

9. Find a mentor.

10. Grab a shooting star.

11. Manage luck.

For some people, another part of managing their career is dealing with hidden barriers to advancement. These barriers take the form of a glass ceiling, an invisible but difficult-to-penetrate barrier to promotion based on subtle attitudes and prejudices. Diligently applying career-advancement strategies and tactics, including outstanding performance, can help overcome these barriers.

Questions and Activities

1. What are some of the organizational rewards that a successful person can hope to attain?

2. Why not simply do a good job and forget about all the other strategies and tactics described in this chapter?

3. To what extent do you think successful people make a deliberate attempt to use some of the strategies and tactics described in this chapter?

4. In the beginning of their careers job hunters often comment that employers are looking for specialists, not generalists. Which career advancement tactic does this comment support?

5. Why are career-advancement tactics and strategies more important than ever when corporations are trimming down?

6. What is the downside risk of "taking the initiative to do work at the next level"?

7. When men enter the secretarial field, are they making effective use of "swim against the tide"?

8. In a changing world, what good is a career path?

9. What is the theme of this chapter?

10. Speak to a successful person. Ask that person to identify the strategies and tactics in this chapter that he or she believes to be the most important for getting ahead. Be prepared to discuss your findings in class.

REFERENCES

[1]"Build a Reputation as an Expert Troubleshooter," *Personal Report for the Executive,* December 15, 1989, p. 7.

[2]Joseph A. Raelin, "First-Job Effects on Career Development," *Personnel Administrator,* August 1983, pp. 71–76; Julie Griffin Levitt, *Your Career: How to Make It Happen,* 2d ed. (Cincinnati, Ohio: South-Western Publishing, 1990), p. 294.

[3]"First Impressions: You Have to Make Them Count," *Executive Strategies,* December 1992, p. 10.

[4]"Moving Up: Play the Role and Get It," *Executive Strategies,* January 1994, p. 12.

[5]Robert Half, "Etiquette for Success," *New Accountant,* January 1990, p. 27; "Good Manners: Why They Matter in the Nineties," *Executive Strategies,* November 1992, p. 10.

[6]Robert Wendover, "The Importance of Risk Taking," *Business Week's Guide to Careers,* October 1985, p. 75.

A HUMAN RELATIONS CASE PROBLEM: THE BYPASSED CUSTOMER SERVICE REPRESENTATIVE

Helen Lee joined the phone company as a customer service representative. Her primary responsibilities were to answer by phone customer inquiries about billing and service problems. One reason Helen joined the company was to stay in northern California, the phone company location. She was also eager to join the company because it was expanding into new services such as wireless communication. Rumors circulated that the company might soon be involved in joint ventures with a cable television company to become part of the information superhighway.

Helen hoped that company expansion would translate into promotional opportunities for her. After a three-week training program, Helen was assigned her own cubicle as a full-fledged customer service representative. Determined to do an outstanding job, Helen listened intently to every customer problem. She attempted to show concern and sympathy for every customer problem she heard, yet not join a customer in blaming the company.

Feeling isolated working in a cubicle, Helen soon looked for ways to become acquainted with people outside her department. She began to rotate the location where she sat in the company cafeteria as a way of meeting new people. More often than not, the people sitting in a particular location simply nodded hello to Helen and then proceeded with their conversation.

Helen's next approach to developing acquaintances in the company was to join the company softball team. Although Helen was inexperienced at softball and had limited athletic ability, she showed up for practice regularly. After assessing her skills, Helen was assigned the position of substitute right fielder. She spent most of her time sitting on the bench, particularly after she struck out her first four times at bat. Helen noticed that most of the conversation was among the stronger players. Surmising that the softball team wasn't helping her develop meaningful contacts in the company, Helen quit the team.

Helen then decided that her best vehicle for becoming better known and developing contacts in the company was to get involved in assignments outside her area. She spoke to her boss, Kris Mogliani, about being available for special assignments. Mogliani told her that as a customer service representative, she would have precious little time to work outside the department, and explained that employees who were not working directly with customers had more time to spend on committees and projects.

Helen asked Mogliani's permission to write the human resources director, informing him of her availability for an occasional special assignment. Mogliani agreed, but again emphasized that Helen's primary job was to serve customers.

Two month's later, Mogliani called Helen into her office. She said to Helen, "Here's a break for you. Our department needs one representative to work about five hours per week on a customer-satisfaction project. I told the human resources department we could spare you for that amount of time."

Helen joined the customer-satisfaction team with enthusiasm. She told the team leader, "I want to help out very much. I wouldn't be a customer service representative if I weren't interested in improving customer service." Helen's efforts led to her receiving

(Continued)

the assignment of tabulating the results of several hundred customer-satisfaction surveys collected recently. Helen found the work tedious but did not complain. Six months later the committee disbanded and Helen was thanked for her contribution.

Helen thought to herself, "Six months of serving on a task force and doing a lot of the dirty work, and all I get is a thank you. This assignment wasn't a big help to me."

Helen continued in the customer service department, hoping to build a future in the company. At the end of both the first and second year, Helen received average performance evaluations. After the second evaluation, Helen asked Mogliani what she could do to receive an above-average evaluation. Mogliani suggested that perhaps Helen could handle a greater number of customer service calls per month.

To increase her number of calls, Helen worked toward shortening the average time per call by speaking more rapidly. She also focused her conversations more sharply, and attempted to prevent customers from talking about side issues. In addition, Helen cut both her morning and afternoon breaks by five minutes each. As a result of these efforts, Helen increase the number of customer service calls she handled per week by 15 percent. When Helen brought the improvement figures to Mogliani's attention her boss said she was pleased to see the progress.

Six months later, Mogliani announced that the department had expanded so rapidly that a new position of team leader would be created. The team leader would help with some of the administrative responsibilities Mogliani was now handling. Later that day, Helen sent an E-mail message to Mogliani, expressing her interest in the position. Mogliani sent back a message, "Thanks for your interest."

One week later Mogliani announced that Jack Muldoon, one of the customer service representatives, would be appointed as team leader. Disappointed that she did not receive the appointment, Helen asked Mogliani for an explanation. Mogliani told Helen, "Maybe your time will come in the future. For now we think Jack is best suited for the job. This doesn't mean that you don't have a future with the company. We would like to see you grow into an exceptional performer before we think of promoting you. Also, you've been with us for less than three years."

QUESTIONS

1. What advice can you give Helen to help her realize her hopes of advancing in the company?

2. Is Helen too preoccupied with getting ahead in the company?

3. Is the company treating Helen fairly?

4. Does Helen have an attitude problem?

A HUMAN RELATIONS EXERCISE: THE CAREER DEVELOPMENT INVENTORY

Career development activities inevitably include answering some penetrating questions about yourself. Following are twelve representative questions to be found on career development inventories. You may need several hours to do a competent job answering these questions. After individuals have answered these questions by them-

(Continued)

selves, it may be profitable to hold a class discussion about the relevance of the specific questions. A strongly recommended procedure is for you to date your completed inventory and put it away for safekeeping. Examine your answers in several years to see (1) how well you are doing in advancing your career and (2) how much you have changed.

Keep the following information in mind in answering this inventory: People are generous in their self-evaluation when they answer career development inventories. So you might want to discuss some of your answers with somebody else who knows you well.

1. How would you describe yourself as a person?

2. What are you best at doing? Worst?

3. What are your two biggest strengths or assets?

4. What are the two traits, characteristics, or behaviors of yours that need the most improvement?

5. What are your two biggest accomplishments?

6. Write your obituary as you would like it to appear upon your death.

7. What would be the ideal job for you?

8. Why aren't you richer and more famous?

9. What career advice can you give yourself?

10. Describe the two peak experiences in your life.

11. What are your five most important values (the things in life most important to you)?

12. What goals in life are you trying to achieve?

[7]Ray J. Friant, Jr., "Leadership Training for Long-Term Results," *Management Review,* July 1991, pp. 52–53.

[8]"Check Your Career Cadence," *Executive Strategies,* November 1993, pp. 7–8.

[9]Michael G. Zey, "Mentor Programs: Making the Right Moves," *Personnel Journal,* February 1985, p. 56.

[10]Andrew Harris, "Break the Glass Ceiling for Senior Executives," *HRfocus,* March 1994, pp. 1, 4–5; Julie Cohen Mason, "Knocking on the Glass Ceiling," *Management Review,* July 1993, p. 5.

[11]Barbara Ettorre, "Breaking the Glass . . . or Just Window Dressing?" *Management Review,* March 1992, pp. 16–22.

ADDITIONAL READING

Ettorre, Barbara. "A Brave New World: Managing International Careers." *Management Review,* April 1993, pp. 10–15.

Golzen, Godfrey and Garner, Andrew. *Smart Move: Successful Strategies and Tactics for Career Management.* London: Penguin Books Ltd., 1992.

Glassner, Barry. *Career Crash: The New Crisis and Who Survives.* New York: Simon & Schuster, 1994.

Greenhaus, Jeffrey H. *Career Management,* 2d ed. Chicago: The Dryden Press, 1994.

Gutteridge, Thomas G.; Leibowitz, Zandy B.; and Shore, Jane E. *Organizational Career Development: Benchmarks for Building a World Class Workforce.* San Francisco: Jossey Bass, 1993.

Haslett, Beth; Geis, Florence, L.; and Carter, Mae R. San Francisco: Ablex Publishing, 1992.

Levinson, Harry. *Career Mastery: Keys to Taking Charge of Your Career Throughout Your Work Life.* San Francisco: Berrett-Koehler Publishers, 1992.

Mainiero, Lisa A. "On Breaking the Glass Ceiling: The Political Seasoning of Powerful Women Executives." *Organizational Dynamics,* spring 1994, pp. 5–21.

Schwartz, Felice N. *Breaking with Tradition: Women and Work, the New Facts of Life.* New York: Warner Books, 1992.

CHAPTER 14

DEVELOPING SELF-CONFIDENCE AND BECOMING A LEADER

Learning Objectives

After studying the information and doing the exercises in this chapter you should be able to:

■ Develop a strategy for increasing your self-confidence if you think it is desirable to do so.

■ Understand the relationship of self-confidence to leadership.

■ Identify a number of personal traits and characteristics of effective leaders.

■ Identify a number of behaviors of effective leaders.

■ Map out a tentative program for developing your leadership potential and skills.

*I*f your efforts at developing career thrust are successful, you will eventually become a leader. Rising to leadership can happen when people come to respect your opinion and personal characteristics, and thus are influenced by you. Another way of becoming a leader is to be appointed to a formal position, such as supervisor or team leader, in which it is natural to exert leadership. Your greatest opportunity for exerting leadership, however, will come about from a combination of these methods of influence. As a result, an individual with appealing personal characteristics who is placed in a position of authority will find it relatively easy to exert leadership.

Before most people can exert personal or positional leadership, or both, they have to develop the right amount of self-confidence.

THE IMPORTANCE OF SELF-CONFIDENCE AND SELF-EFFICACY

Self-confidence is necessary for leadership because it helps assure group members that things are under control. Assume you are a manager in a company that is rumored to be facing bankruptcy. At a meeting you attend, the president sobs, "I'm sorry, I'm just no good in a crisis. I don't know what's going to happen to the company. I don't think I can get us out of this mess. Maybe one of you would like to try your hand at turning around a troubled company."

In this situation, company employees would feel insecure. Many would be so preoccupied with finding new employment that they couldn't concentrate on their work. You would want the president to behave in a confident, assured manner. Yet if the president were too arrogant about things, if he or she dismissed the problem too lightly, you might not feel secure, either.

In other leadership situations as well, the leader who functions best is self-confident enough to reassure others and to appear in control. But if the leader is so self-confident that he or she will not admit errors, listen to criticism, or ask for advice, that too creates a problem. Self-Examination

Exercise 14-1 provides some tentative insight into whether you have the right amount of self-confidence.

An appropriate amount of self-confidence is also important because it contributes to **self-efficacy,** the belief in one's capability to perform a task. Various studies have shown that people with a high sense of self-efficacy tend to have good job performance. They also set relatively high goals for themselves.[1] Self-efficacy is thus related to self-confidence, but is tied more directly into performing a task. A straightforward implication of self-efficacy is that people who think they can perform well on a task do better than those who think they will do poorly.

An encouraging note is that self-efficacy can be boosted through training. In an experiment, sixty-six unemployed people participated in a self-efficacy workshop. The group included bookkeepers, clerks, teachers, skilled mechanics, and technicians. The workshop featured watching video clips of successfully performing job-search behaviors, followed by encouragement from the trainer and peers. In contrast to unemployed people who did not attend the workshop, the people who were trained in self-efficacy became more involved in job searches.[2] Being involved in job searches included telephoning about a job and obtaining an interview.

Self-efficacy contributes to leadership effectiveness because a leader with high self-efficacy will usually believe that a task is doable. As a result, the leader can inspire others to carry out a difficult mission such as correcting a serious customer problem.

DEVELOPING SELF-CONFIDENCE

People who hope to become more self-confident have tried do-it-yourself, professional, and commercial approaches. Many people who do not feel confident enough to meet daily challenges have undergone psychotherapy or counseling—often with good results. Millions of people have achieved a boost in self-confidence from attending a Dale Carnegie training program. Also, an underlying reason that some people enter any kind of personal improvement program is to boost self-confidence.

Self-confidence is generally achieved by succeeding in a variety of situations. A confident sales representative may not be generally self-confident unless he or she also achieves success in activities such as taking exams, forming good personal relationships, operating a computer, composing a letter, and displaying athletic skills.

Although this general approach to self-confidence building makes sense, it does not work for everyone. Some people who seem to succeed at everything still have lingering self-doubt. Low self-confidence is so deeply ingrained in this type of personality that success in later life is not sufficient to change things. Following are some specific strategies and tactics for building and elevating self-confidence. They will generally work unless the person has deep-rooted feelings of inferiority. The tactics and strategies are arranged approximately in the order in which they should be tried to achieve best results.

SELF-EXAMINATION EXERCISE 14-1:

Just How Humble Are You?

A Purdue University social scientist has conducted a series of studies on the relationship of self-confidence to problem solving. One of his major findings is that people who do not have a particularly high level of self-confidence may do better at solving problems than people who are highly self-assured. The same finding about self-confidence also applies to leadership. Answer the questions below to obtain some tentative insight into your level of self-confidence (or humility).

Which category do you fit into? Do you have self-confidence to spare, a satisfactory level, a fair share of the characteristic, or do you score low in self-esteem? Take this quiz and find out (check the answers that best apply to you).

A. You are assigned a task involving an entire area that is unfamiliar to you. You would:
❏ 1. Delegate someone else to do it.
❏ 2. Get someone to help you do it.
❏ 3. Study the procedure carefully, and then do it yourself.
❏ 4. Plunge right into the work without giving it much thought.

B. You solicit the advice of others before making a decision:
❏ 1. Almost always.
❏ 2. Sometimes.
❏ 3. Rarely.
❏ 4. Never

C. You offer advice to others:
❏ 1. Never.
❏ 2. Hardly ever.
❏ 3. Willingly, if you are asked to do so.
❏ 4. Often (even when no one asks for it).

D. At business meetings, how often do you come up with ideas for projects?
❏ 1. Never.
❏ 2. Sometimes.
❏ 3. Frequently.
❏ 4. Always (to let the bosses know you've got a million ideas).

E. When meeting with your superiors, how often do you acknowledge the ideas you've received from others rather than passing them off as your own?
❏ 1. Never.
❏ 2. Rarely.
❏ 3. Often.
❏ 4. Always.

F. Your boss expresses an opinion that is contrary to your strong beliefs or convictions. You would:
❏ 1. Remain silent.
❏ 2. Attempt to disagree only if you felt it wouldn't jeopardize your job.
❏ 3. Explain your feelings about the issue.
❏ 4. Become incensed and speak up about your views.

G. If there were a job opening that you would like in a higher classification at work, you would:
❏ 1. Wait until a superior asked if you were interested in it.
❏ 2. Drop hints to your boss that you just might be interested in it.
❏ 3. Go through the regular channels to apply for it.
❏ 4. Do everything you can to persuade your boss that he or she should recommend you for the position.

(Continued)

H. How often do you feel your work is inadequate?
❏ 1. Always.
❏ 2. Frequently.
❏ 3. Hardly ever.
❏ 4. Never.

I. Do you feel that you deserve a position of leadership in an organization or in your job?
❏ 1. No.
❏ 2. Perhaps.
❏ 3. Yes (and hope others recognize your leadership qualities).
❏ 4. Without a doubt.

J. Do you believe you are brighter than many of your colleagues at work?
❏ 1. Never.
❏ 2. At times.
❏ 3. Usually.
❏ 4. Of course.

K. In response to criticism, you:
❏ 1. Feel devastated and say nothing to the person who made the comment.
❏ 2. Become angry at first but later try to analyze the criticism.
❏ 3. Discuss the matter with the person who made the comment and try to resolve it.
❏ 4. Tell the person to buzz off.

L. At a party, how often do you introduce yourself to people you don't know and begin conversations?
❏ 1. Never.
❏ 2. Hardly ever.
❏ 3. Usually.
❏ 4. Always.

M. In a restaurant, how often do you complain about improper service or bad food?
❏ 1. Never.
❏ 2. Sometimes.
❏ 3. Usually, and in a calm, constructive way.
❏ 4. Always and loudly.

N. While waiting in long line for a bus, at the movies, or in a supermarket:
❏ 1. You let others get ahead of you.
❏ 2. You wait patiently wherever you may be.
❏ 3. You try to speed up the line.
❏ 4. You push ahead of others.

O. When someone compliments you about something you've done:
❏ 1. You are embarrassed and don't know what to say.
❏ 2. You say, "Oh, it was nothing, really."
❏ 3. You smile and say, "Thank you."
❏ 4. You say, "Thanks," and add, "Yes, I know I'm talented and wonderful."

Score yourself by adding up the total of numbers you checked.

If you scored 16 to 29, you are eating too much humble pie.

If you scored 30 to 39, your SC (self-confidence) quotient is not low, but you could work a little on raising your self-esteem.

If you scored 40 to 54, you are brimming with self-confidence.

If you scored 55 to 60, you are overconfident and should give some thought to tempering your arrogance.

Take an Inventory of Personal Assets and Accomplishments

Many people suffer from low self-confidence because they do not appreciate their own good points. Therefore, a starting point in increasing your self-confidence is to take an inventory of personal assets and accomplishments. This same activity was offered in Chapter 1 as a method of developing self-esteem. Personal assets should be related to characteristics and behaviors, rather than tangible assets such as an inheritance. Accomplishments can be anything significant in which you played a key role in achieving the results. Try not to be modest in preparing your list of assets and accomplishments. You are looking for any confidence-booster you can find.

Two lists prepared by different people will suffice to give you an idea of the kinds of assets and accomplishments that might be included.

Lillian

Good listener; most people like me; good handwriting; good posture; inquisitive mind; good at solving problems; good sense of humor; patient with people who make mistakes; better-than-average appearance. Organized successful fund drive which raised $30,000 for church; graduated tenth in high-school class of 500; achieved first place in industrial bowling league; daughter has an excellent career.

Angelo

Good mechanical skills; work well under pressure; good dancer; friendly with strangers; strong as an ox; good cook; can laugh at my own mistakes; great-looking guy; humble and modest. Made award-winning suggestion that saved company $25,000; scored winning goal in college basketball tournament; dragged child out of burning building.

The value of these asset lists is that they add to your self-appreciation. Most people who lay out their good points on paper come away from the activity with at least a temporary boost in self-confidence. The temporary boost, combined with a few success experiences, may lead to a long-term gain in self-confidence.

An important supplement to listing your own assets is hearing the opinion of others on your good points. This tactic has to be used sparingly, however, and mainly with people who are personal-growth-minded. A good icebreaker is to tell your source of feedback that you have to prepare a list of your assets for a human relations exercise (the one you are reading about right now!). Since that person knows of your work on your capabilities, you hope that he or she can spare a few minutes for this important exercise.

For many people, positive feedback from others does more for building self-confidence than does feedback from oneself. The reason is that self-esteem depends to a large extent on what we think others think about us.

Consequently, if other people—whose judgment you trust—think highly of you, your self-image will be positive.

DEVELOP A SOLID KNOWLEDGE BASE

A bedrock for projecting self-confidence is to develop a base of knowledge that enables you to provide sensible alternative solutions to problems. Intuition is very important, but working from a base of facts helps you project a confident image. Formal education is an obvious and important source of information for your knowledge base. Day-by-day absorption of information directly and indirectly related to your career is equally important. A major purpose of formal education is to get you in the right frame of mind to continue your quest for knowledge.

In your quest for developing a solid knowledge base to project self-confidence, be sensitive to abusing this technique. If you bombard people with quotes, facts, and figures, you are likely to be perceived as an annoying know-it-all.

USE POSITIVE SELF-TALK

A basic method of building self-confidence is to engage in **positive self-talk,** saying positive things about oneself to oneself. As explained by Jay T. Knippen and Thad B. Green, the first step in using positive self-talk is to objectively state the incident that is casting doubt about self-worth.[3] The key word here is *objectively*. Terry, who is fearful of poorly executing a report-writing assignment, might say, "I've been asked to write a report for the company, and I'm not a good writer."

The next step is to objectively interpret what the incident *does not* mean. Terry might say, "Not being a skilled writer doesn't mean that I can't figure out a way to write a good report, or that I'm an ineffective employee."

Next, the person should objectively state what the incident *does* mean. In doing this, the person should avoid put-down labels such as "incompetent," "stupid," "dumb," "jerk," or "airhead." All these terms are forms of negative self-talk. Terry should state what the incident does mean: "I have a problem with one small aspect of this job, preparing professional-level reports. This means I need to improve my report-writing skill."

The fourth step is to objectively account for the cause of the incident. Terry would say, "I'm really worried about writing a good report because I have very little experience in writing along these lines."

The fifth step is to identify some positive ways to prevent the incident from happening again. Terry might say, "I'll get out my textbook on business communications and review the chapter on report-writing," or "I'll enroll in a course or seminar on business report-writing."

The final step is to use positive self-talk. Terry imagines his boss saying, "This report is really good. I'm proud of my decision to select you to prepare this important report."

Positive self-talk builds self-confidence and self-esteem because it programs the mind with positive messages.[4] Making frequent positive messages or affirmations about the self creates a more confident person. An example would be, "I know I can learn this new equipment rapidly enough to increase my productivity within five days." If you do make a mistake, your positive self-talk might be, "It's taken me more time than usual to learn how to use this new equipment. I know I'll have the problem licked in a few days."

Positive self-talk contributes to self-confidence in another important way. According to Douglas Bloch, a writer and lecturer, teaching children to think positively about themselves by practicing positive self-talk helps develop adult personalities capable of meeting life's challenges.[5]

AVOID NEGATIVE SELF-TALK

As mentioned above, you should minimize negative statements about yourself in order to bolster self-confidence. A lack of self-confidence is reflected in statements such as, "I may be stupid but . . . ," "Nobody asked my opinion," "I know I'm usually wrong, but . . . ," "I know I don't have as much education as some people, but . . ." Self-effacing statements like these serve to reinforce low self-confidence.

It is also important not to attribute to yourself negative, irreversible traits such as "idiotic," "ugly," "dull," "loser," and "hopeless."[6] Instead, look upon your weak points as areas for possible self-improvement. Negative self-labeling can do long-term damage to your self-confidence. If a person stops that practice today, his or her self-confidence may begin to increase.

USE POSITIVE VISUAL IMAGERY

Assume you have a situation in mind in which you would like to appear confident and in control. An example would be a meeting with a major customer who has told you over the telephone that he is considering switching suppliers. Your intuitive reaction is that if you cannot handle his objectives without fumbling or appearing desperate, you will lose the account. An important technique is this situation is **positive visual imagery,** or picturing a positive outcome in your mind. To apply this technique in this situation, imagine yourself engaging in a convincing argument about retaining your customer as the primary supplier. Imagine yourself talking in positive terms about the good service your company offers and how you can rectify any problems.

Visualize yourself listening patiently to your customer's concerns and then talking confidently about how your company can handle these concerns. As you rehearse this moment of truth, create a mental picture of you and the customer shaking hands over the fact that the account is still yours.

Positive visual imagery helps you appear self-confident because your mental rehearsal of the situation has helped you prepare for battle. If imagery works for you once, you will be even more effective in subsequent uses of the technique.

Strive for Peak Performance

A key strategy for projecting self-confidence is to display **peak performance.** The term refers to much more than attempting to do your best. To achieve peak performance you must be totally focused on what you are doing. When you are in the state of peak performance you are mentally calm and physically at ease. Intense concentration is required to achieve this state. You are so focused on the task at hand that you are not distracted by extraneous events or thoughts.

The mental state achieved during peak performance is akin to a person's sense of deep concentration when immersed in a sport or hobby. On days tennis players perform way above their usual game, they typically comment: "The ball looked so large today, I could read the label as I hit it." On the job, the focus and concentration allows the person to sense and respond to relevant information coming from both within the mind and from outside stimuli. When you are at your peak, you impress others by responding intelligently to their input.

Psychologist Charles Garfield says it is easy to detect those who have achieved or will achieve peak performance. Based on his study of more than 1,500 successful people, he concludes that peak performers have a mission in their work and lives. They have something they deeply care about to which they are fully committed.[7] Turning in peak performance helps you develop superior self-confidence, which projects through to others. Tony Alvarez, a quality manager in a hospital, explains how peak performance helped him project self-confidence:

> It was my day to make a presentation to the hospital administrators and medical chiefs about our new Total Quality Management program. I had done my homework, including researching the usual objections to this type of program in a hospital. I rehearsed my presentation alone three times in the conference room where it would take place. I had my multimedia presentation ready, and it was beautiful.
>
> I woke up on the morning of my presentation feeling great. My body tingled with excitement, and my vision and hearing were sharper than usual. I knew it was going to be a good day. The presentation went more smoothly than I could have imagined. I was on stage. It was my day. Both the administrators and the medical chiefs were nodding their heads in agreement. I knew my program was headed for approval. People congratulated me on my presentation. Two of them mentioned how confident and self-assured I was. I definitely think that exuding so much confidence helped my program get approved.

Attack Situations Assertively

If your self-confidence is at a low level, one way to elevate it is to start taking a positive, assertive approach to the problem situation. If you are demoted, and are upset and disappointed over this problem, plunge into your lesser responsibilities with aggressiveness and determination. As your positive approach begins to pay dividends, your self-confidence will inch back up to its former level.

The strategy of attacking situations assertively applies equally well to your social life. A loss in self-confidence often takes place after a person has been "dumped" by a boyfriend or girlfriend. After some of the initial hurt wears away, you can start to build confidence assertively by attacking the challenge of meeting new people. Among the positive techniques to use are joining clubs, asking for referrals from friends, taking up new recreational interests, and joining a singles group. As you begin to achieve some success in finding dates you enjoy, your self-confidence will elevate.

OBTAIN A FEW EASY VICTORIES FOLLOWED BY BIGGER CHALLENGES

Because self-confidence accumulates with a variety of successes, start with relatively easy tasks. Suppose you are studying business statistics, a subject that challenges your self-confidence. Before tackling a large, demanding assignment, conquer the easiest problems in the text. Solving the warm-up problems is likely to boost your self-confidence enough to help you cope with the demanding assignment. Similarly, a person who lacks self-confidence about learning to ski should stay on the easiest slopes until he or she has conquered them. After the beginner feels confident about handling the easiest slopes, he or she is ready to tackle an intermediate slope.

An extension of the easy-victory strategy is to place yourself in a less competitive environment when you find that you are over your head in your present environment. A less competitive environment might be just what you need to establish a satisfactory level of self-confidence.

After obtaining several easy victories, move on to bigger challenges. Lesser accomplishments are important because they pave the way toward being able to tackle more complex activities. A person who aspired to be a restaurant owner might first work as an assistant manager, then manager, of somebody else's restaurant. If you achieve something that stretches your capability, that achievement serves as objective evidence that you are a capable (and therefore confident) individual.

LEADERSHIP AND BEING A LEADER

So far we have emphasized the importance of developing self-confidence so that you are able to provide leadership to others. **Leadership** is the process of influencing others to achieve certain goals. Self-confidence makes a contribution to leadership because people tend to be influenced by a person of high—but not unreasonable—self-confidence.

The key word in understanding the concept of leadership is *influence*. If influence is not exerted, leadership, strictly speaking, has not been performed. A night manager of a hotel might work her designated five nights a week and perform her chores in a highly satisfactory manner. Guests, employees, and the hotel owner are all kept happy. Her boss checks with her from time to time to see how things are going, but the two of them have little contact with each other. The night manager performs well without the benefit of another's influence on her performance. She therefore does not require leadership. However, if the night manager's boss inspires her to achieve even greater heights of customer service, leadership has been exerted.

Effective leadership at the top of organizations is necessary for their prosperity, and even survival.[8] Effective leadership is also important throughout the organization, particularly in working with entry-level workers. Good supervision is needed to help employees deal with customer problems, carry out their usual tasks, and maintain high quality. The most rapidly growing form of leadership in the workplace is the team leader.

A **team leader** is a person who facilitates and guides the efforts of a small group which is given some authority to govern itself. Many firms use work teams instead of traditional departments to accomplish work. For example, a work team might take care of various aspects of issuing an insurance policy. Instead of having power over the group, the team leader works with teammates to help them achieve their goals. Much of quality improvement in organizations takes place in teams.

Before studying the personal qualities and behaviors of effective leaders, do Self-Examination Exercise 14-2. The exercise will help you understand how ready you are to assume a leadership role. Taking the quiz will also give you insight into the type of thinking that is characteristic of leaders.

TRAITS AND CHARACTERISTICS OF EFFECTIVE LEADERS

About 12,000 books and articles have been written about the characteristics that contribute to the leader's effectiveness. A frequent conclusion reached by these studies is that the answer depends on the situation. A supervisor in a meat-packing plant and one in a medical office will need different sets of personal characteristics. The situation includes such factors as the people being supervised, the job being performed, the company, and the cultural background of the employees.

Despite these differences in situations, there are certain inner qualities that contribute to leadership effectiveness in a wide variety of settings. **Effectiveness** in this situation means that the leader helps the group accomplish its objectives without neglecting satisfaction and morale. In the next several pages, we describe some of the more important traits and characteristics of leaders.

HUMAN RELATIONS SKILLS

An effective leader must work well with people. Working well with people does not necessarily mean a leader is particularly easygoing. It means that a leader relates to people in such a way as to capture their trust and cooperation. A leadership researcher observed that human relations skills involve:

- Accepting responsibility for your own ideas and feelings
- Being open to your own and other's sentiments

SELF-EXAMINATION EXERCISE 14-2:

Readiness for the Leadership Role

Instructions

Indicate the extent to which you agree with each of the following statements. Use a one-to-five scale: (1) disagree strongly; (2) disagree; (3) neutral; (4) agree; (5) agree strongly. If you do not have leadership experience, imagine how you might react to the questions if you were a leader.

1. It is enjoyable having people count on me for ideas and suggestions.   1 2 3 4 5
2. It would be accurate to say that I have inspired other people.   1 2 3 4 5
3. It's a good practice to ask people provocative questions about their work.   1 2 3 4 5
4. It's easy for me to compliment others.   1 2 3 4 5
5. I like to cheer up people even when my own spirits are down.   1 2 3 4 5
6. What my team accomplishes is more important than my personal glory.   1 2 3 4 5
7. Many people imitate my ideas.   1 2 3 4 5
8. Building team spirit is important to me.   1 2 3 4 5
9. I would enjoy coaching other members of the team.   1 2 3 4 5
10. It is important to me to recognize others for their accomplishments.   1 2 3 4 5
11. I would enjoy entertaining visitors to my firm even if it interfered with my completing a report.   1 2 3 4 5
12. It would be fun for me to represent my team at gatherings outside our department.   1 2 3 4 5
13. The problems of my teammates are my problems too.   1 2 3 4 5
14. Resolving conflict is an activity I enjoy.   1 2 3 4 5
15. I would cooperate with another unit in the organization even if I disagreed with the position taken by its members.   1 2 3 4 5
16. I am an idea generator on the job.   1 2 3 4 5
17. It's fun for me to bargain whenever I have the opportunity.   1 2 3 4 5
18. Team members listen to me when I speak.   1 2 3 4 5
19. People have asked to me to assume the leadership of an activity several times in my life.   1 2 3 4 5
20. I've always been a convincing person.   1 2 3 4 5

Total score: _____

(Continued)

Scoring and Interpretation: Calculate your total score by adding the numbers circled. A tentative interpretation of the scoring is as follows:

- 90–100   High readiness for the leadership role
- 60–89   Moderate readiness for the leadership role
- 40–59   Some uneasiness with the leadership role
- 39 or less Low readiness for carrying out the leadership role

If you are already a successful leader and you scored low on this questionnaire, ignore your score. If you scored surprisingly low and you are not yet a leader, or are currently performing poorly as a leader, study the statements carefully. Consider changing your attitude or your behavior so that you can legitimately answer more of the statements 4 or 5. Studying the rest of this chapter will give you additional insights into the leader's role that may be helpful in your development as a leader.

- Experimenting with new ideas and feelings

- Helping others accept, be open to, and experiment with their own ideas and attitudes[9]

- Being a warm person and projecting warmth, thus establishing better rapport with group members.

HONESTY, INTEGRITY, AND CREDIBILITY

Group members consistently believe that leaders must display honesty, integrity, and credibility. Leaders themselves believe that honesty and integrity make a difference in their effectiveness. Researchers and observers also share these views. Warren G. Bennis, a leadership authority, interviewed more than 100 corporate leaders and 50 private-sector leaders during a thirteen-year period. One of the common threads he found was the capacity of leaders to generate and sustain trust. He observed a consis-

KEEP UP YOUR SPIRITS. I SEE A DAY IN THE NOT-TOO-DISTANT FUTURE WHEN OUR FLY SWATTERS WILL BE RANKED NUMBER ONE IN THE WORLD.

tency among what leaders think, feel, and do. Bennis said it drives people crazy when bosses don't walk their talk.[10] How would you feel if you worked for a boss you couldn't trust?

INSIGHT INTO PEOPLE AND SITUATIONS

Good insight helps you develop human relations skills. **Insight** is a depth of understanding that requires considerable intuition and common sense. Insight into people and situations involving people is an essential leadership characteristic. A leader with good insight is able to make better work assignments and do a better job of training and developing subordinates.

An example of an insightful leader would be one who looks at the expression on subordinates' faces to see if they really understand a new procedure. If not, the leader would provide more explanation. An example of poor insight would be to hold a departmental meeting late in the afternoon before a major religious or national holiday. Why try to capture employees' attention when they are thinking about something else? An emergency meeting, however, would be an exception to this principle of poor insight.

SENSITIVITY TO PEOPLE AND EMPATHY

Having insight leads to **sensitivity**—taking people's needs and feelings into account when dealing with them. Sensitivity also implies that the leader minimizes hurting the feelings of people and frustrating their needs. Being sensitive to people is therefore needed for leadership effectiveness.

Insensitivity to others prevents many up-and-coming managers from realizing their full potential. In a study of executive leadership, psychologists compared "derailed" executives with those who had progressed to senior management positions. The leading category of fatal flaws was insensitivity to others, characterized by an abrasive, intimidating, bullying style.[11]

Achieving sensitivity to others requires **empathy,** the ability to place oneself in the other person's shoes. To empathize with another person you don't have to agree, but you do have to understand. As a team leader you might ask a team member to work late one Thursday. The team member says, "That's my night to play bingo. Working is out of the question." You can understand how important bingo is to that person, and express your understanding. Nevertheless, you emphasize the importance of the project.

ABILITY TO PERFORM THE GROUP TASK

The closer a leader is to the actual work of the group, the more skilled he or she must be with technical details. For example, the supervisor of internal auditing should be skilled at auditing. Being skilled in the actual work of the group can also be referred to as **technical competence.**

One widely held belief—that once you are a top-level leader you can leave technical details behind—is greatly exaggerated. Most successful people are still quite knowledgeable about the details of the field in which they found success. A recently appointed top executive of a major architectural and engineering firm had this to say about his new position: "I'm not going to be doing any design work on the boards and that's been true for a long time. But having a design sensibility is something you bring to the job every day, both in dealing with clients and in trying to help the people in the office do their work."[12]

STRONG WORK MOTIVATION AND HIGH ENERGY

Leadership positions tend to be both physically and mentally demanding. A successful leader must be willing to work hard and long in order to achieve success. Many leaders appear to be driven by a need for self-fulfillment. Another fundamental reason strong work motivation is required for effectiveness is that a person has to be willing to accept the heavy responsibility that being a supervisor entails. As one department manager said, "Whoever thought being a manager would mean that I would have to fire a single parent who has three children to feed and clothe?"

PROBLEM-SOLVING ABILITY AND OPENNESS TO EXPERIENCE

A current theory of leadership supports the view that effective leaders have good problem-solving ability. According to **cognitive resource theory,** the major source of the plans, decisions, and strategies that guide the group's actions are the leader's intellectual abilities.[13] Effective leaders anticipate problems before they occur and diligently stay with them until they are solved. By so doing, a leader demonstrates creative problem solving.

Practical intelligence is usually the most important type of problem-solving ability on the job. The president of a large company makes this comment about intelligence and leadership success:

> Sometimes less than a top IQ is an advantage because that person doesn't see all the problems. He or she sees the big problem and gets on and gets it solved. But the extremely bright person can see so many problems that he or she never gets around to any of them.[14]

Closely related to cognitive skills is the personality characteristic of **openness to experience,** a positive orientation toward learning. People who have considerable openness to experience have well-developed intellects. Traits commonly associated with this dimension of the intellect include being imaginative, cultured, curious, original, broad-minded, intelligent, and artistically sensitive.

SENSE OF HUMOR

Humor is a contributor to leadership effectiveness. Humor helps leaders influence people by reducing tension, relieving boredom, and defusing anger.[15] Another advantage is that an appropriate use of humor helps the leader appear warm and human.

The most effective form of humor by a leader is tied to the leadership situation. It is much less effective for the leader to tell rehearsed jokes. A key advantage of a witty, work-related comment is that it indicates mental alertness. A canned joke is much more likely to fall flat.

A sales manager was conducting a meeting about declining sales. He opened the meeting by saying, "Ladies and gentlemen, just yesterday I completed a computerized analysis of our declining sales. According to my spreadsheet analysis, if we continue our current trend, by the year 2001 we will have sales of negative $2,750,000. No company can support those figures. We've got to reverse the trend." The manager's humor helped dramatize the importance of reversing the sales decline.

THE ABILITY TO INSPIRE AND MOTIVATE OTHERS

An important quality for a high-level leader is **charisma,** a type of charm and magnetism that inspires others. Not every leader has to be charismatic, yet to be an effective leader you need some degree of this intangible personal quality.[16] A leader's charisma is determined by the subjective perception of him or her by other people. It is therefore impossible for even the most effective leaders to inspire and motivate everyone. Even popular business leaders are disliked by some of their employees.

VISION

Top-level leaders need a visual image of where the organization is headed, and how it can get there. The progress of the organization is dependent on the top executive having this vision. Effective leaders project ideas and images that excite people, and therefore inspire employees to do their best. Leadership positions of lesser responsibility also call for some vision. Each work group in a progressive company might be expected to form its own vision, such as "We will become the best accounts receivable group in the entire desk-manufacturing industry."

ENTHUSIASM AND EXCITEMENT

A psychoanalyst and Harvard Business School professor observes that leaders get excited about their work. Because of their contagious excitement, they stimulate group members.[17] Workers respond positively to enthusiasm, especially because enthusiasm may be perceived as a reward for good performance.

Enthusiasm is also effective because it helps build good relationships with group members. Verbal expression of enthusiasm include such statements as "Great job" and "I love it." The leader can express enthusiasm nonverbally through gestures, nonsexual touching, and so forth.

Enthusiasm has a positive effect on employees, while moodiness dampens the group spirit. Exhibit 14-1 describes observations about the negative consequences of a moody boss.

EXHIBIT 14-1

MANAGERS' MOODS MAY MIFF WORKERS

"Don't make your suggestion today," one employee counseled another. "I don't think he would even be receptive to a guaranteed cost-saving idea." The two employees were discussing their manager. They perceived, rightly or wrongly, that he was in a dark mood.

The manager's mood discouraged employees' suggestions, said Gerald Graham, the business school dean at Wichita State University. According to Graham, a lousy mood on the part of the manager can degrade both morale and performance. The impact is greater when a mood change surprises people.

"When managers glower and sulk or when they are pessimistic and gloomy, most subordinates would rather visit their dentist than their boss," said Graham. "Employees focus on avoiding contact with the leader rather than improving service or reducing costs."

Graham doesn't believe that managers should put a "good face" on everything. "In fact, it is better to express anger or disappointment than it is to suppress them. And both emotions can be expressed without creating a dour climate. Managers can be more effective by dealing with issues reasonably and leaving their unsuitable moods in the parking lot."

Symptoms of a boss with a "mood problem" are as follows (relate them to any manager you have worked for):

1. Sulks when team members disagree

2. Abruptly changes from approving to disapproving

3. Acts down and depressed frequently

4. Overly pessimistic

5. Changes moods unpredictably

6. Sees the worst in things

7. Worries excessively

8. Withdraws when things go poorly

9. Takes disagreements personally

10. Wears his/her feelings on his/her sleeve.

If three or more apply, it may suggest that the manager's moods negatively impact effectiveness. He or she also has an "enthusiasm problem."

SOURCE: Adapted from "Managers' Moods May Miff Workers," wire services, January 13, 1994.

The Entrepreneurial Spirit

An entrepreneurial leader assumes the risk of starting an innovative business. We ordinarily think of an entrepreneur as being self-employed because the person is a business owner. Yet the same entrepreneurial spirit can be applied as an employee. (This is much like the work habit technique of being self-employed psychologically.) A group leader with an entrepreneurial spirit would search for new activities for the group. The head of a manufacturing unit might say to the group, "Let's ask top management if we can take a shot at making this part that we now buy from a supplier."

The entrepreneurial spirit can also be expressed by reading trade publications and newspapers to keep up with what is happening in the industry. Talking with customers or others in the organization to keep aware of changing needs and requirements shows a spark of entrepreneurial thinking. The leader with an entrepreneurial spirit also visits other firms, attends professional meetings, and participates in educational programs.[18] All the activities just mentioned help the leader think of new activities for the group.

BEHAVIORS AND SKILLS OF EFFECTIVE LEADERS

The personal traits, skills, and characteristics just discussed help create the potential for effective leadership. A leader also has to *do* things that influence group members to achieve good performance. The behaviors or actions of leaders described next contribute to productivity and morale in most situations.

Develop Partnerships with People

Leadership is now regarded as a long-term relationship, or partnership, between leaders and group members. According to Peter Block, in a **partnership** the leader and group members are connected in such a way that the power between them is approximately balanced. To form a partnership, the leader has to allow the group members to share in decision making. Four conditions are necessary to form a true partnership between the leader and group members:

1. *Exchange of purpose.* The leader and team member should work together to build a vision.

2. *A right to say no.* In a partnership each side has the right to say no without fear of being punished.

3. *Joint accountability.* Each person takes responsibility for the success and failure of the group.

4. *Absolute honesty.* In a partnership, not telling the truth to each other is an act of betrayal. When group members recognize that

they have power, they are more likely to tell the truth because they feel less vulnerable to punishment.[19]

Help Group Members Reach Goals and Achieve Satisfaction

Effective leaders help subordinates in their efforts to achieve goals.[20] In a sense, they smooth out the path to reaching goals. One important way to do this is to provide the necessary resources to subordinates. An important aspect of a leader's job is to ensure that subordinates have the proper tools, equipment, and personnel to accomplish their objectives.

Another way of helping group members achieve goals is to reduce frustrating barriers to getting work accomplished. A leader who helps group members cut through minor rules and regulations would be engaging in such behavior. In a factory, a supervisory leader has a responsibility to replace faulty equipment, make sure unsafe conditions are corrected, and see that troublesome employees are either rehabilitated or replaced.

Another important general set of actions characteristic of an effective leader is looking out for the satisfaction of the group. Small things sometimes mean a lot in terms of personal satisfaction. One office manager fought for better coffee facilities for her subordinates. Her thoughtfulness contributed immensely to job satisfaction among them.

Provide Emotional Support and Consideration

Having good human relations skills of this nature is often more important for improving morale than for producing work. It is an important leadership behavior. An emotionally supportive leader would engage in activities such as listening to subordinates' problems and offering them encouragement and praise.

Make Expectations Known

People function better when they know what they have to do to achieve work goals. Each person needs to know what is expected of him or her in order to make a contribution to the mission of the department. The leader provides answers to such questions as "What am I as an individual supposed to do to help the company build this ocean liner?" or "What can I do to help get this budget completed today?"

Set High Expectations

In addition to making expectations clear, it is important for leaders to set high expectations for group members. If you as a leader expect others to succeed, they are likely to live up to your expectations. This mysterious phenomenon has been labeled the **Pygmalion effect.** According to Greek mythology, Pygmalion was a sculptor and king of Cyprus who carved an ivory statue of a maiden and fell in love with the statue. The statue was soon brought to life in response to his prayer.

The point of the Pygmalion effect is that the leader can elevate performance by the simple method of expecting others to perform well. The manager's high expectations become a self-fulfilling prophecy. Why high expectations lead to high performance could be linked to self-confidence. As the leader expresses faith in the group members' ability to perform well, they become more confident of their skills.

GIVE FREQUENT FEEDBACK ON PERFORMANCE

Effective leaders inform employees how they can improve and praise them for things done right. Less effective leaders, in contrast, often avoid confrontation and give limited positive feedback. An exception is that some ineffective leaders become involved in many confrontations—they are masters at reprimanding people!

MANAGE A CRISIS EFFECTIVELY

When a crisis strikes, that's the time to have an effective leader around. When things are running very smoothly, you may not always notice whether your leader is present. Effectively managing a crisis means giving reassurance to the group that things will soon be under control, specifying the alternative paths for getting out of the crisis, and choosing one of the paths.

Another aspect of managing a crisis is the ability to bounce back from adversity. Prominent leaders in any field are known for their ability to work their way out of difficult times. They are not discouraged by obstacles or turned aside by roadblocks. A telltale fact is that effective leaders rarely use the term "failure" in reference to things that did not go well. Instead, they prefer terms such as "bungle," "false start," and "setback."[21]

CULTIVATE STRONG CUSTOMER ORIENTATION

Effective leaders are strongly interested in satisfying the needs of customers, clients, or constituents. Such an orientation helps inspire employees to satisfy customers—a necessity for company survival. A customer-oriented leader makes statements to the group such as, "How would what you are proposing better satisfy our customers?" or "What have you done lately to keep our customers happy?"

DEVELOPING YOUR LEADERSHIP POTENTIAL

How to improve your potential for becoming a leader is a topic without limits. Almost anything you do to improve your individual effectiveness will have some impact on your ability to lead others. If you strengthen your self-confidence, improve your memory for names, study this book carefully, read studies about leadership, or improve your physical fitness, you stand a good chance of improving your leadership potential. Five general strategies might be kept in mind if you are seeking to improve your leadership potential:

1. *General education and specific training.* Almost any program of career training or education can be considered a program of leadership development. Courses in human relations, management, or applied psychology have obvious relevance for someone currently occupying or aspiring toward a leadership position. Many of today's leaders in profit and nonprofit organizations hold formal degrees in business. Specific training programs will also help you improve your leadership potential. Among them might be skill development programs in interviewing, employee selection, listening, assertiveness training, budgeting, planning, improving work habits, resolving conflict, and communication skills. After acquiring knowledge through study, you then put the knowledge into practice as a leader.

2. *Leadership development programs.* A focused way of improving your leadership potential is to attend development programs designed specifically to improve your ability to lead others and develop self-confidence. A popular type of leadership development program called *outdoor training* places people in a challenging outdoor environment for a weekend or up to ten days. Participants are required to accomplish physical feats such as climbing a mountain, white water canoeing, building a wall, or swinging between trees on a rope.[22]

Participants in these outdoor programs learn such important leadership skills and attitudes as teamwork, trusting others, and a confidence in their ability to accomplish the seemingly impossible. Exhibit 14-2 presents details about the type of leadership training under discussion.

3. *Leadership experience.* No program of leadership improvement can be a substitute for leadership experience. Because leadership effectiveness depends somewhat on the situation, a sound approach is to attempt to gain leadership experience in different settings. A person who wants to become an executive is well advised to gain supervisory experience in at least two different organizational functions (such as customer service and finance).

First-level supervisory jobs are an invaluable starting point for developing your leadership potential. It takes considerable skill to manage a fast-food restaurant effectively or to direct a public playground during the summer. A first-line supervisor frequently faces a situation in which subordinates are poorly trained, poorly paid, and not well motivated to achieve company objectives.

4. *Modeling effective leaders.* Are you committed to improving your leadership skill and potential? If so, carefully observe a capable leader in action and incorporate some of his or her approaches into your own behavior. You may not be able to or want to become that person's clone, but you can model (imitate) what the person does. For instance, most inexperienced leaders have a difficult time confronting others with bad news. Observe a good confronter handle the situation, and try that person's approach the next time you have some unfavorable news to deliver to another person.

EXHIBIT 14-2

ELECTRONIC COMPANY STAFF AT OUTWARD BOUND

The top executive at TCI West, Inc., an electronics firm, wanted key personnel to develop into a smooth team. He chose Outward Bound training because he hoped to break down communication barriers and put all participants on equal footing. The first TCI representatives were sent to a course on orienteering in the Nevada desert. Among these people were top managers, marketing directors, and five manager trainees. The group learned rappeling, rock climbing, and first aid. They hiked through hot desert days and awakened to temperatures of 5°F (–15°C). They cooked meals, pitched tents, rationed water, and taught each other outdoor techniques.

Another TCI group participated in an Outward Bound river program. One exercise that incorporates team building, leadership, and communication skills required participants to intentionally flip a raft over in deep water. Next, they had to return it to the upright position and then help each other back into the raft.

Developing trust is another critical aspect of Outward Bound. Participants must trust the commands that are shouted from the person leading the raft through swirling rapids. They must trust the lead person's sense of direction while hiking through the desert. Most of all, they must trust the person belaying the rappel that will save them from serious injury or death in case of a fall. (A *belay* is a mountain-climbing hold to secure the rope.)

Among the lessons learned are that getting help from others is not always a sign of weakness, that it's all right not to be perfect, and that most fears can be put in proper perspective.

SOURCE: Based on facts in Sally Howe, "TCI West Trains Outdoors," *Personnel Journal*, June 1991, pp. 58–59.

5. *Self-development of leadership characteristics and behavior.* Our final recommendation for enhancing your leadership potential is to study the leadership characteristics and behaviors described in this chapter. As a starting point, identify several attributes you think you could strengthen within yourself given some self-determination. For example, you might decide that with effort you could improve your enthusiasm. You might also believe that you could be more emotionally supportive of others. It is also helpful to obtain feedback from reliable sources about which traits and behaviors you particularly need to develop.

SUMMARY

Before most people can exert leadership, they need to develop an appropriate amount of self-confidence. Self-confidence is necessary for leadership because it helps assure group members that things are under control. A leader who is too self-confident, however, may not admit to errors, listen to criticism, or ask for advice. Also, you may appear insecure if you are too self-confident.

A general principle of boosting your self-confidence is to experience success (goal accomplishment) in a variety of situations. As you achieve one set of goals, you establish slightly more difficult goals, thus entering a success cycle. The specific strategies for building self-confidence described here are:

1. Develop a solid knowledge base.
2. Develop positive self-talk.
3. Avoid negative self-talk.
4. Use positive visual imagery.
5. Strive for peak performance.
6. Attack situations assertively.
7. Obtain a few easy victories followed by bigger challenges.

Leadership is the process of influencing others to achieve certain goals. Effective leadership is needed at the top of organizations, but supervisors and team leaders also need to provide effective leadership.

Although leadership is situational, certain traits and characteristics contribute to leadership effectiveness in many situations. Among them are: human relations skills; honesty, integrity, and credibility; insight into people and situations; sensitivity to people and empathy; ability to perform the group task; strong work motivation and high energy; problem-solving ability and openness to experience; sense of humor; the ability to inspire and motivate others; vision; enthusiasm and excitement; and the entrepreneurial spirit.

To be an effective leader (one who maintains high productivity and morale) you are advised to:

1. Develop partnerships with people (emphasizing power sharing).
2. Help group members reach goals and achieve satisfaction.
3. Provide emotional support and consideration.
4. Make expectations known.
5. Set high expectations.
6. Give frequent feedback on performance.
7. Manage a crisis effectively.
8. Develop a strong customer orientation.

Many activities in life can in some way contribute to the development of a person's leadership potential. Five recommended strategies for improving your leadership potential or leadership skills are: (1) general

*I*t is important to manage personal finances in such a way that money becomes a source of satisfaction rather than a major worry and concern. Financial problems lead to other problems. For example, poor concentration stemming from financial worries may lead to low job performance; many marital and family disputes stem from conflict about financial problems; worry about money can also drain energy that could be used to advance your career or enrich your personal life. The purpose of this chapter is to describe basic ideas that should enable you to start on the road to financial comfort and escape financial discomfort.

ESTABLISHING FINANCIAL GOALS

Personal finances is yet another area in which goal setting generally improves performance. A common approach to setting financial goals is to specify amounts of money you would like to earn at certain points in time. One individual might set yearly financial goals, adjusted for inflation. Many ambitious people in business hope to double their income every seven years. Although this goal sounds fanciful, it is realistic if you take into account inflation and the fact that your income increases are compounded. That is, the income base upon which you get a raise keeps increasing. One year you earn $30,000. The next year you receive a 10 percent increase, thus earning $33,000; the next year with another 10 percent increase, you will receive $36,300, and so forth.

Another common financial goal is to obtain enough money to cover a specific expense, such as making a down payment on a new car. These goals should include a target date, as shown in Exhibit 15-1. An important supplement to establishing these goals is an investment table which specifies the amount of money needed to be saved to achieve the goal (see Table 15-1). The chart assumes that deposits are made at the beginning of each month, and interest is compounded monthly. Monthly savings amounts are rounded to the nearest dollar.

Financial goals are sometimes more motivational when they point to the lifestyle one hopes to achieve with specific amounts of money. If financial goals are expressed in terms of what money can accomplish, they focus on ends rather than means. If the emphasis is on the ends money will

EXHIBIT 15-1

FINANCIAL GOAL SETTING

Goal	Target Date	Years to Goal	Dollars Needed
1. Pay off credit cards	June 1998	1½	$4,275
2. Pay for son's college	September 2015	18	$80,000
3. Down payment on home	June 2001	4½	$20,000

accomplish, financial goal setting may seem less crass. Here are two examples of financial goals expressed in terms of what money can accomplish:

By 2000, I want to earn enough money to have my own apartment and car, and buy nice gifts for my family and relatives.

By 2025, I want to earn enough money to have paid for my house, own a vacation home near a lake, and take a winter vacation each year.

DEVELOPING A SPENDING PLAN (BUDGET)

When most people hear the word *budget* they think of a low-priced item or of miserly spending habits. Their perception is only partly correct. A **budget** is a plan for spending money to improve your chances of using your money wisely and not spending more than your net income. The basic

TABLE 15-1

MONTHLY SAVINGS NEEDED TO REACH GOAL
(5% AFTER-TAX RATE OF RETURN)

	Dollar Goals				
Years	$5,000	$10,000	$20,000	$50,000	$100,000
2	198	395	791	1,977	3,954
4	94	188	376	939	1,878
6	59	119	238	594	1,189
8	42	85	169	423	846
10	32	64	128	321	641
20	12	24	48	121	242
30	6	12	24	60	120

idea is to estimate your expenses over a period of time and allocate the money you have available to cover those expenses. In addition, you set something aside for reserves or spending. Developing a spending plan can be divided into a series of logical steps. Exhibit 15-2 presents a worksheet helpful for carrying out the plan. Modify the specific items to suit your particular spending patterns. For instance, computer supplies and repairs might be such a big item in your spending plan that it deserves a separate category.

Step 1: Establishing goals. It is important to decide what you or your family really need and want. If you are establishing a family budget, it is best to involve the entire family. For the sake of simplicity, we will assume here that the reader is preparing an individual budget. Individual budgets can be combined to form the family budget. Goal setting should be done for the short, intermediate, and long term. A short-term goal might be "replace hot water heater this February." A long-term goal might be "accumulate enough money for a recreational vehicle within ten years."

Step 2: Estimating income. People whose entire income is derived from salary can readily estimate their income. Commissions, bonuses, and investment income are more variable. So is income from part-time work, inheritance, and prizes.

Step 3: Estimating expenses. After you have determined how much your income will be for the planning period, it is time for the difficult part—estimating your expenses. If you have any records of previous spending habits and patterns, such as a checkbook or old credit card bills, they can serve as a basis for your budget. For instance, "How much a month do I spend for newspapers, magazines, and books? How much for records and movies?" List the item of expense, followed by the actual or estimated amount you spend per month on that item. For most people a monthly budget makes the most sense, since so many expenses are once-a-month items. Included here are rent, mortgage payments, car payments, and credit card payments.

Use your records and your recollections to help you decide whether to continue your present pattern of spending or to make changes. For instance, estimating your expenses might reveal that you are spending far too much on gasoline. An antidote might be to consolidate errand-running trips or make some trips on foot or by bicycle.

An important part of estimating future expenditures is to plan for new situations and changing conditions. As a case in point, assume you will be joining a health club. Estimate your dues, cost of transportation, and extra meals out to accommodate the new demands on your time.

Try to plan your large expenses so they are spaced at intervals over several years. If you plan to purchase a car one year, plan to remodel your kitchen another year. If you buy an overcoat one season, you might have to delay buying a suit until the next year.

Step 4: Comparing expenses and income. Add the figures in your spending plan. Now compare the total with your estimate of income for the planning period. If the two figures balance, at least you are in neutral financial condition. If your income exceeds your estimate of expenses, you have made a profit. You may decide to satisfy more of your immediate

EXHIBIT 15-2

YOUR SPENDING PLAN

Monthly Expenses

Fixed:
Mortgage or rent ⎯⎯⎯
Property insurance ⎯⎯⎯
Health insurance ⎯⎯⎯
Auto insurance ⎯⎯⎯
Other insurance ⎯⎯⎯
Educational expenses ⎯⎯⎯
Child support
  payments ⎯⎯⎯
Taxes:
  Federal ⎯⎯⎯
  State or provincial ⎯⎯⎯
  Social security ⎯⎯⎯
  Local ⎯⎯⎯
  Property ⎯⎯⎯
Installment loans
  (auto and others) ⎯⎯⎯
Set aside for
  emergencies ⎯⎯⎯

Variable:
Food ⎯⎯⎯
Household supplies ⎯⎯⎯
Home maintenance
  and repairs ⎯⎯⎯
Medical and dental ⎯⎯⎯
Telephone ⎯⎯⎯
Clothing ⎯⎯⎯
Hair care and cosmetics ⎯⎯⎯
Transportation ⎯⎯⎯
Car maintenance ⎯⎯⎯
Travel and vacation ⎯⎯⎯
Clubs/organizations ⎯⎯⎯
Hobbies ⎯⎯⎯
Other ⎯⎯⎯

Total expenses ⎯⎯⎯

Monthly Income

Salary ⎯⎯⎯
Tips ⎯⎯⎯
Bonuses & commissions ⎯⎯⎯
Interest & dividends ⎯⎯⎯
Insurance benefits ⎯⎯⎯
Child support received ⎯⎯⎯
Other ⎯⎯⎯

Total income ⎯⎯⎯

Summary:
  Total income ⎯⎯⎯
  Less total expenses ⎯⎯⎯
  Balance for savings
    and investment ⎯⎯⎯

wants, set aside more money for future goals, or put the balance into savings or investment.

Remember that the true profit from your labor is the difference between your net income and your total expenses. Set-asides are considered an expense, since you will inevitably use up that money to meet future goals or pay for seasonal expenses. Without a miscellaneous category, many budgets will project a profit that never materializes. Any household budget has some miscellaneous or unpredictable items each month. After working with your budget several months you should be able to make an accurate estimate of miscellaneous expenses.

The key to lifelong financial security and peace of mind is to spend less money than you earn. By so doing you will avoid the stresses of being in debt and worrying about money.

If your income is below your estimated expenses, you will have to embark on a cost-cutting campaign in your household. If you brainstorm the problem by yourself or with friends, you will come up with dozens of valid expense-reducing suggestions.

Step 5: Carrying out the spending plan.   After you have done your best job of putting your spending plan on paper, try it out for one, two, or three months. See how close it comes to reality. Keep accurate records to find out where your money is being spent. It is helpful to make a notation of expenditures at the end of every day. Did you forget about that $23 you spent on party snacks Sunday afternoon? It is a good idea to keep all financial records together. You may find it helpful to set aside a desk drawer, a large box, or other convenient place to put your record book, bills, receipts, and other financial papers. Converting paper records into computerized files is strongly recommended for maintaining a spending plan.

Step 6: Evaluating the plan.   Compare what you spent with what you planned to spend for three consecutive months. If your spending was quite different from your plan, find out why. If your plan did not provide for your needs, it must be revised. You simply cannot live with a spending plan that allows for no food the last four days of the month. If the plan fitted your needs but you had trouble sticking to it, the solution to your problem may be to practice more self-discipline.

A budget usually needs reworking until it fits your needs. Each succeeding budget should work better. As circumstances change, your budget will need revision. A spending plan or budget is a changing, living document that serves as a guide to the proper management of your personal finances.

 ## BASIC INVESTMENT PRINCIPLES

After you have developed a spending plan that results in money left over for savings and investment, you can begin investing. To start developing an investment strategy, or refining your present one, consider the eight investment principles presented next. They are based on the collected wisdom of many financial planners and financially successful people.

1. *Invest early and steadily to capitalize upon the benefits of compounding.*   Investments made early in life grow substantially more than those made later. You will slowly and steadily accumulate wealth if you begin investing early in life and continue to invest regularly. Let's look at a straightforward example. Assume you invest $1,000 at the start of each year for five years. It earns 8 percent a year and the earnings are com-pounded. You would have $6,123 at the end of five years. If you invested $1,000 at the start of each year for twenty-five years you would have $79,252; at the end of 40 years you would have $290,917. To achieve these full results you would have to make tax-free investments (described in the section about retiring rich).

2. *Keep reinvesting dividends.*   As implied in the first principle, divi-dends and interest payments must be reinvested to fully benefit from early and regular investments. Here is an illustration based on stock dividends. Assume that $10,000 was invested in the Standard and Poor's 500 (a rep-resentative group of stocks) on December 31, 1961, and held for 30 years. The amount accumulated *without* reinvesting dividends is $71,793. *With* reinvestment of dividends, the total amount accumulated is $237,420. By allowing dividends to accumulate, the investor more than tripled the value of her or his investment.[1]

3. *Diversify your investments.*   A bedrock principle of successful investing is to spread your investments among stocks, bonds, and cash. (Home ownership can be considered a fourth basic type of investment.) Your specific allocation will depend on your tolerance for risk and your time frame. At the conclusion of the section on choosing your investments, we will describe several different investment allocations (or mixes).

4. *Maintain a disciplined, long-term approach.*   If you have an in-vestment plan suited to your needs, stick with it over time. The patient, long-term investor is likely to achieve substantial success. Investors who make investments based on hunches and hot tips, and sell in panic when the value of their investment drops, generally achieve poorer returns. Investing regularly often lowers the average cost of your investment pur-chases. (This technique is referred to as *dollar-cost averaging,* and is de-scribed later.)

5. *Practice contrary investing.*   If your purpose in making invest-ments is to become wealthy, follow the principle of **contrary investing**—buy investments when the demand for them is very low and sell when the demand is very high. When others are discouraged about purchasing real estate, and there are very few buyers around, invest heavily in real estate. When others are excited about real estate investing, sell quickly before prices fall again. In the words of the late billionaire J. Paul Getty, "Buy when everybody else is selling, and hold until everyone else is buying." This is not merely a catchy slogan. It is the very essence of successful investing."[2]

6. *Be willing to accept some risk.*   An unreasonable fear of risk is a major investment mistake. Small investors are frequently so afraid of los-ing their principal that they go to extremes in seeking safe investments. An investment executive explains: "If you put your money into something that *guarantees* you'll get your principal back, there's a good chance infla-tion will hurt that principal's buying power."[3]

7. *Invest globally as well as domestically.*   Diversifying your invest-ments among different countries is another contributor to financial suc-cess. Financial advisers regularly suggest international stocks and bonds as a diversification possibility. Overseas markets may offer investors values more promising than those provided domestically. As shown in Exhibit 15-3, the investment returns from foreign stock markets have outperformed those of the United States and Canada in recent years.

Be aware, however, that overseas investments have two substantial risks. The value of the overseas currency may go down rapidly, thus lowering your return should you sell your stocks or bonds. Another problem is that a politically unstable government can create havoc in the investment markets. One example is that a government might take over a private company and declare its stocks and bonds invalid.

8. *Pay off debt.* One of the best investment principles of all is the most straightforward. Paying off debt gives you an outstanding return on investment. A common scenario is a person paying about 18 percent on credit card debt, while earning 4 percent from an investment. Paying off the 18 percent debt with money from savings would thus yield a 14 percent profit. (We are excluding home equity loans from consideration because they carry tax-deductible interest.) Another way of looking at the cost of debt is this: You have to earn 13.9 percent a year on your money before taxes to pay off a 10 percent, four-year loan on a new car.

EXHIBIT 15-3

FOREIGN STOCK MARKETS COMPARED TO THE UNITED STATES AND CANADA

Since 1980, Most Foreign Markets Have Outperformed the U.S.

Hong Kong	24.84%
France	22.32%
Spain	20.75%
Japan	18.00%
U.K.	17.93%
Switzerland	16.23%
Australia	15.18%
Germany	15.13%
U.S.	14.11%
Canada	7.67%

Source: Morgan Stanley Capital International

As of March 31, 1993, as measured in U.S. dollars. Average annual total returns are based on changes in price and reinvestment of dividends (net of applicable foreign taxes) paid on the stocks in the indices.

CHOOSING YOUR INVESTMENTS

After understanding some basic principles of investing, you are ready to make choices among different investments. We describe investments here because they are an integral part of managing your personal finances. Investments can be categorized into two basic types: lending money or owning assets. Lending money is referred to as a *debt investment,* while owning an asset is an *equity investment.* For example, when you purchase a corporate bond you are lending money that will pay a fixed rate of return. When you purchase stocks you become an owner of an asset. Our discussion of choosing investments includes their relative risks, relative returns, different types, and selecting the right mix.

TYPES OF INVESTMENT RISKS

As illustrated in Exhibit 15-4, investments vary in the risk of losing the money you invested. Yet not even so-called *safe* investments are without risk. A sophisticated way of understanding risk is to recognize that

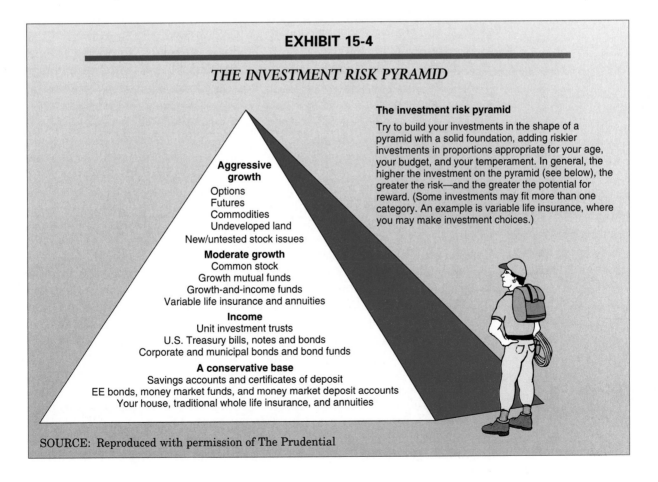

EXHIBIT 15-4

THE INVESTMENT RISK PYRAMID

Aggressive growth
Options
Futures
Commodities
Undeveloped land
New/untested stock issues

Moderate growth
Common stock
Growth mutual funds
Growth-and-income funds
Variable life insurance and annuities

Income
Unit investment trusts
U.S. Treasury bills, notes and bonds
Corporate and municipal bonds and bond funds

A conservative base
Savings accounts and certificates of deposit
EE bonds, money market funds, and money market deposit accounts
Your house, traditional whole life insurance, and annuities

The investment risk pyramid

Try to build your investments in the shape of a pyramid with a solid foundation, adding riskier investments in proportions appropriate for your age, your budget, and your temperament. In general, the higher the investment on the pyramid (see below), the greater the risk—and the greater the potential for reward. (Some investments may fit more than one category. An example is variable life insurance, where you may make investment choices.)

SOURCE: Reproduced with permission of The Prudential

there are four types.[4] *Investment risk* is the possibility of losing rather than gaining money (the conventional meaning of risk). People with extreme fears of investment risk might put their money in government-insured savings account or in a safe-deposit box.

Market risk means that the market for your type of investment can go up or down at any time. The market for stocks might go up, while you are heavily invested in bonds. Or you might be heavily invested in gold, and the market for gold plummets, but yields of bank certificates of deposit climb upward. People who fear market risk usually believe strongly in diversification.

Inflation risk is the risk that the cost of living will increase faster than the return on your investment. Assume that you have invested a $10,000 inheritance in a money market fund paying an average of 3.75 percent per year. At the same time, inflation proceeds at an average of 4.75 percent per year. Your $10,000 nest egg is losing purchasing power at the rate of 1 percent per year. The person concerned about inflation risk would do well to invest in stocks, bonds, and most money market investments because they typically have yields that outpace inflation.

Adequacy risk is the risk of not having accumulated enough money to reach your financial goals. One person might plan to retire from corporate life at age fifty so she can start a business of her own. She forecasts that she will need a lump of $250,000 to achieve her goal. In the meantime she suffers from adequacy risk because her investments are growing slowly. She may have to take some big investment risks, such as purchasing large amounts of stocks in start-up companies.

Relative Returns of Stocks and Bonds

Another key factor in choosing among investments is their relative returns in the past. The past may not guarantee future performance, but it serves as a reliable predictor. Since 1926, U.S. common stocks have returned about 10 percent annually, and corporate bonds about 5 percent. Intermediate government bonds have paid about 5 percent, and three-month treasury bills about 4 percent. Yet some stocks are poor investments despite generally good returns.

Throughout the 1980s and early 1990s, investment yields improved over the long-term historical pattern. In the 1980s the annual return averaged about 18 percent for stocks, 12 percent for corporate bonds, and 9 percent for treasury bills. In the early 1990s stocks and bonds yielded similar returns, while treasury bills averaged 4.5 percent as interest rates fell.[5] Highlights of this information are summarized in Table 15-2. In evaluating the rates of returns on stocks and bonds, recognize that the inflation rate for the last ten years has been 3.9 percent.

The rates of return just reported prompt financial specialists to urge every investor to include a minimum of 50 percent common stocks in his or her investment portfolio. Yet some investors resist such advice because they are upset by the fluctuations of the stock market. Instead, they invest in various types of bonds and save cash.

TABLE 15-2	
INVESTMENT PERFORMANCE COMPARISON, 1980S–1994	
Common stocks	18%
Corporate bonds	11%
Long-term government bonds	8%
Treasury bills	7%
Inflation	4%

DIFFERENT TYPES OF INVESTMENTS

Dozens of different savings plans and investments are available. They include everyday methods of savings as well as exotic investments such as buying into a lottery that gives the winners the rights to own an interactive television station. Here we summarize a variety of popular investments ranging from the most conservative to the more speculative.

1. *Interest-bearing checking accounts.* Keeping your monthly money in a checking account is necessary for most people. It allows for writing checks at a modest cost, or no charge if an average minimum balance of a specified amount (typically around $1,000) is maintained. Checks eliminate the risk of losing or being robbed of cash, and canceled checks are a reliable receipt. In recent years, the interest on bank checking accounts has been below the inflation rate.

2. *Passbook savings accounts.* With a passbook (or day-to-day) savings account the user can deposit or withdraw money as often as he or she wishes. This type of account pays slightly more than a regular checking account. Most sophisticated investors make little use of this type of savings account. Passbook savings accounts appeal to those who prefer the most traditional way of depositing money in a bank. Also, funds can be drawn immediately without any penalty.

3. *Certificates of deposit.* Banks and savings and loan associations offering certificates of deposit (CDs) require that you deposit a reasonably large sum of money for a specified time period. The time period can be anywhere from several months to ten years. CDs come in denominations such as $500, $5,000, and $10,000, paying a rate of return in excess of the rate of inflation.

If you have a considerable amount of cash and are not worried about having your money tied up for a fairly long time period, CDs are ideal. If you close one of these accounts before its due date, the amount of penalty lowers the interest rate to approximately that of an interest-bearing checking account.

4. *Money-market funds.* The fastest-growing savings and investment instrument recently has been money-market funds. Many people who formerly kept their money in banks have shifted their money to these high-yielding but uninsured funds. Paying well above the inflation rate, many of these funds can be used almost like checking accounts. Usually you need to invest an initial $2,500 in these funds. An important feature is that you have easy access to your money. Most funds allow you to write checks for amounts of $500 or more. The funds themselves charge a small, almost unnoticed, management fee. They invest your money in high-yield, short-term investments such as loans to the federal government or to top-quality business corporations.

5. *U.S. Treasury securities.* The U.S. government offers four types of secure investments to the public: treasury bills, treasury notes, treasury bonds, and United States savings bonds. In recent years the return on short-term treasury securities just about matched the inflation rate. Treasury bills are offered in denominations of $10,000 or more, and mature in twelve months or less. Treasury notes are sold in denominations of $1,000 or more, and mature in two to ten years. Treasury bonds have maturity dates of ten or more years, and pay high interest rates. United States savings bonds are the best known government security, and are often purchased out of patriotism.

6. *Corporate bonds.* Large corporations sell bonds to the public in order to raise money to further invest in their business. Many of these bonds are twenty- to thirty-year loans. They pay a fixed rate of return, such as 8 or 10 percent. If you want to cash in your bond early, you may not be able to sell it for the original value, especially if interest rates rise. You would thus take a loss. You can, however, purchase a bond for less than its face value. You might be able to buy a $1,000 bond for $920, collect interest on it, and eventually redeem it for its face value. Trading bonds—buying and selling them for speculation—is a risky activity that should be reserved for knowledgeable investors.

Junk bonds are bonds offering a high yield because they are rated as having a high risk. One reason could be that the firm offering them is facing financial trouble. Junk bonds are best suited to big investors, but some mutual funds invest in them, making them accessible to smaller investors.

7. *Common stocks.* Every reader of this book has heard of the stock market, a place where you can purchase shares of public corporations. On a given business day it is not unusual for over 300 million shares of stocks to be bought and sold on the American and Canadian stock exchanges. Common stocks are actually shares of ownership in the corporations issuing them. Stocks pay dividends, but the hope of most investors is that the stock will rise in value. The majority of buying and selling of stocks today is done by institutions rather than by small investors. These institutions include pension funds, banks, and mutual funds (described later).

Stock prices rise and fall over such tangible factors as the price of oil and fluctuations in interest rates. They also rise and fall over people's perception of events such as national elections. Good news elevates stock prices and bad news brings them down. To cope with these price fluctuations, investors are advised to use dollar-cost averaging. Using **dollar-cost averaging,** you invest the same amount of money in a stock or mutual fund at regular intervals over a long period of time. This eliminates the need for trying to time the highs and lows. Since you are investing a constant amount, you buy less when the price is high and more when the price is low. Over a long period of time, you pay a satisfactory price for your stock or mutual fund. Table 15-3 illustrates dollar-cost averaging.

8. *Mutual funds.*   Since most people lack the time, energy, and knowledge to manage their own stock portfolio, mutual funds are increasingly relied on. The concept of mutual funds is straightforward. For a modest management fee, a small group of professional money managers invest your money, along with that of thousands of other people, into a broad group of common stocks. Numerous mutual funds exist to suit many different purposes and risk-taking attitudes. You can find mutual funds that invest in conservative, low-risk stocks or flashy, high-risk stocks. The latter tend to have a larger payoff if the company succeeds. Some funds specialize in particular industries such as energy or food.

Mutual funding is no longer restricted to stocks. Some mutual funds invest only in corporate bonds, government securities, and municipal bonds. Municipal bonds are loans to state and local governments. Although they pay a lower interest rate than most other bonds, the interest from these bonds is exempt from federal income tax. Residents of the state in which a municipal bond is issued are also exempt from paying state income tax on the interest.

TABLE 15-3

HOW DOLLAR-COST AVERAGING WORKS

$500 Invested Regularly for 5 Periods
(Price trends chosen are for illustrative purposes only.
Different trends will result in different average costs.)

| | MARKET TREND | | | | | |
| | Down | | Up | | Mixed | |
Investment	Share Price	Shares Purchased	Share Price	Shares Purchased	Share Price	Shares Purchased
$ 500	$10	50	$10	50	$10	50
$ 500	9.25	54.05	10.50	47.62	11	45.46
$ 500	8.75	57.14	11.25	44.44	9	55.56
$ 500	8.25	60.61	11.75	42.55	11	45.46
$ 500	8	63.5	12	41.67	10	50
$2500	$44.25***	284.3	$55.50***	226.28	$51***	246.48

Avg. Cost: $8.79*	Avg. Cost: $11.95*	Avg. Cost: $10.14*
Avg. Price: $8.85**	Avg. Price: $11.10**	Avg. Price: $10.20**

*Average Cost is the total amount invested divided by shares purchases.
**Average Price is the sum of the prices paid divided by number of purchases.
***Cummulative total of share prices used by compute average price.

SOURCE: Courtesy, USAA Investment Management Company, San Antonio, Texas, 1994.

9. *Gold and silver.*   Gold and silver are widely recognized as sound investments, gold being the more favored. Financial experts note that gold and silver are helpful in fighting both depression and inflation. The most popular form of gold and silver ownership these days is gold coins. Despite all the amazing tales about wealth acquired through investment in gold and silver, these commodities have some disadvantages. Because it is risky to keep gold and silver at home, you have to pay to have them stored. Also, gold and silver pay no dividends. Your yield is zero until you convert them to cash.

10. *Coins, antiques, paintings, and other collectibles.*   An enjoyable way of investing is to purchase coins and objects of art that you think will escalate in value. Almost anything could become a collectible, including stamps, old advertising items, or even today's touch-tone telephone. You have to be both patient and lucky to cash in on collectibles. You should have a sound, diversified investment program before you invest your money in collectibles. If you are looking for an expensive hobby that might pay off financially, however, collectibles are ideal.

11. *Real estate investments.*   A natural starting point in making money in real estate is to purchase a single-family dwelling, maintain it carefully, and live in it for many years. Temporary downturns in the housing market should not deter the patient investor. In the long run, most homes increase in value faster than inflation. Homeowners receive many tax benefits, such as income tax deductions on mortgage interest, and interest paid for home equity loans (loans using one's house as collateral). Real estate taxes are fully tax-deductible. Furthermore, a homeowner who is at least fifty-five and who has lived in his or her house for three of the last five years pays no income tax on the first $125,000 of profit.

An investment that is really a form of business ownership is income property—real estate that you rent to tenants. The activities required of a landlord include collecting rent, resolving conflicts among tenants, and maintenance—fixing broken water pipes, painting rooms, etc. The highest returns from income property are derived from rehabilitating dilapidated property—if the owner does most of the physical work. Many people who own income property receive almost no operating profit from their work and investment in the early years. However, in the long run the property increases in value. Also, because the mortgage payments remain stable and rents keep increasing, monthly profits gradually appear.

12. *Life insurance as an investment.*   An investment plan should include life insurance for two reasons. First, the proceeds from life insurance protect dependents against the complete loss of income from the deceased provider. Second, most forms of life insurance accumulate cash, thus making the insurance a profitable investment. The one exception is term life insurance which is much like insurance on a house or car.

To figure out how much life insurance is necessary, calculate what would be required to support your family members until they can take care of themselves without your income. Take into account all assets in addition to life insurance. If you are single, consider the financial help you are providing loved ones.

CHOOSING THE RIGHT MIX OF INVESTMENTS

A major investment decision is how to allocate your investments among short-term interest-bearing accounts (including cash), stocks, and bonds. The best answer depends on such factors as your career stage, age, and tolerance for risk. In general, younger people are in a better position to take investment risks than those nearing retirement.

In selecting the right mix of investments, choose among three diversification strategies. A *capital preservation* strategy is for people who value holding on to their invested capital. A *moderate* strategy is a compromise between risk and growth potential. The *wealth-building* strategy is a long-range perspective combined with a toleration for risk. These three investment strategies are the basis for the broad guidelines presented in Exhibit 15-5.

MANAGING AND PREVENTING DEBT

Debt is inevitable for most people. Few people are wealthy enough, or have sufficient self-discipline, to avoid debt entirely. Major purchases such as a house, cooperative apartment, postsecondary education, or automobile usually require borrowing. Dealing with debt is therefore an important component of managing your personal finances. Here we describe three major aspects of managing and preventing debt: credit management, getting out of debt, and staying out of debt.

MANAGING CREDIT WISELY

Credit management is a problem for many people of all career stages. The number of people filing for bankruptcy in the United States has been climbing steadily, with close to 1 million people filing for bankruptcy annually.[6] Borrowing money, of course, is not inherently evil. Imagine what would happen to the banking industry and the economy if nobody borrowed money. Some borrowing in one's early career is desirable because without a credit record it is difficult to obtain automobile loans and home mortgages. Consider the following guidelines for the wise use of credit.[7]

1. Recognize the difference between good debt and bad debt. Good debt finances something that will benefit you in the future, such as a house, education, or self-development. Bad debt typically finances something that you consume almost immediately or that provides little real benefit. Borrowing for a trip to a gambling casino, including money for betting, might fall into this category.

2. Prepare a monthly spending plan as outlined previously to determine how much debt (if any) you can afford to assume. As a general rule, limit your total borrowing to 15 to 20 percent of monthly take-home pay, not including a house mortgage payment.

EXHIBIT 15-5

SELECTING THE RIGHT MIX OF INVESTMENTS

Capital Preservation Portfolio
For those with a shorter-term horizon, a substantial amount of personal debt, or low-risk tolerance, this portfolio seeks current income and capital preservation with modest growth potential to offset inflation.

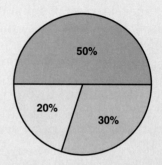

Moderate Portfolio
For those who do not have a high tolerance for risk, but still want reasonable growth potential for their investments, this portfolio seeks both income and capital appreciation.

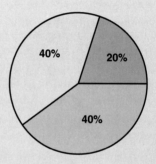

Wealth-Building (Aggressive) Portfolio
For long-range investors who are willing to assume more risk, a growth-oriented portfolio heavily weighted toward stocks is recommended.

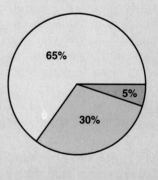

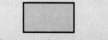 Short-term debt and cash   Stocks   Bonds

SOURCE: Based on information in "Allocate Your Assets with Our Fundmatch℠ Program," *Fidelity Focus,* winter 1993, p. 11; "Asset Allocation Matrix," *Retirement Focus,* April 1993, p. 2.

MANAGING AND PREVENTING DEBT **397**

3. Instead of filling your wallet or handbag with many credit cards, stick to one major credit card and your favorite department store's charge card.

4. Before accepting any new extension of credit, review your budget to see if you can handle it easily.

5. A homeowner with substantial equity accumulated should consider a home equity loan for financing a major purchase, such as an automobile, or educational expenses. The interest on home equity loans is fully tax-deductible.

6. Make monthly payments on your debts large enough to reduce the principal on your credit cards and other loans. Otherwise, you may be paying almost all interest and making small progress toward paying off the loan.

7. Even as you are paying off debts, set aside some savings each month. Attempt to increase your savings as little as $15 per month. Within two years you will be saving a substantial amount of money.

8. If you are unable to pay your bills, talk to your creditors immediately. Explain your situation and let them know you plan to somehow meet your debt obligations. Agree to a payment schedule you can meet. Never ignore bills.

9. Choose personal bankruptcy only as a last desperate option. A bankruptcy filing will remain on your credit record for seven to ten years. Creditors may look upon you as a bad risk even eleven years after filing bankruptcy. Future employers may be leery of hiring a person who was such a poor money manager. Of even greater significance, bankruptcy may result in a substantial blow to your self-esteem.

WORKING YOUR WAY OUT OF DEBT

Working your way out of debt is a major component of debt management. Heavy debt that forces you to postpone savings and investments can also create adverse amounts of stress. You must therefore assertively attack your debts to improve your general well-being. How do you know if you are too far in debt? Self-Examination Exercise 15-1 provides an answer[8]:

A recommended strategy of reducing debt is to **concentrate on one bill at a time.** According to this technique, you first pay off your smallest debt with a variable payment and then concentrate on your next-smallest variable-payment debt. You keep concentrating on one bill at a time until the last debt is eliminated. The technique is illustrated and described in Exhibit 15-6.

A financial specialist might rightfully contend that some loans are uneconomic to discharge more quickly than required. The interest rate you

SELF-EXAMINATION EXERCISE 15-1:

Are You Too Far in Debt?

1. Is an increasing percentage of your income being spent to pay debts?

2. Do you use credit to buy many of the things you bought in the past for cash?

3. Are you paying bills with money targeted for something else?

4. Have you taken out loans to consolidate your debts, or asked for extensions on existing loans to reduce monthly payments?

5. Does your checkbook balance get lower by the month?

6. Do you pay the minimum amount due on your charge accounts each month?

7. Do you get repeated dunning notices (letters demanding payments) from your creditors?

8. Are your threatened with repossession of your car or cancellation of your credit cards or with other legal action?

9. Have you been drawing on your savings to pay regular bills that you used to pay out of your paycheck?

10. Do you depend on extra income, such as overtime and part-time work, to get to the end of the month?

11. Do you take out new installment loans before old ones are paid off?

12. Is your total savings less than three months' take-home pay?

13. Is your total installment credit (not counting mortgage) more than 20 percent of your take-home pay?

14. Do you become horrorstruck when you look at your credit card bills?

If your answer is yes to two or more of the above questions, financial counselors would advise you to declare war on some of your debts.

pay on such loans might be less than the return you would earn by investing your extra payments elsewhere, such as in growth stocks. Although this is true from a financial standpoint, the biggest return on your investment from a mental health standpoint is getting out of debt.

STAYING OUT OF DEBT

Some people believe we are on the way to a cashless society. They contend that electronic transfer of funds, credit cards, and **bank debit cards** (ones that instantly transfer money from your bank account to the account of a merchant) will eliminate the need for cash. High technology may soon make the cashless society a reality. In the meantime, do not dismiss the value of cash in helping you recover from sloppy financial habits.

No one who bought things for cash only ever went bankrupt. Cash also refers to money orders and checks drawn against funds that you legitimately have on hand. If you buy only things that you can actually pay for at the moment of purchase, you may suffer some hardships. It is no fun riding the bus or walking until you save enough money to have another transmission put in your car. It would be agonizing if you needed dental treatment but had to wait until payday to have a broken tooth repaired. On balance, these are small miseries to endure in comparison with the misery of being overburdened with debt. For many people, preoccupation with debt interferes with work concentration and sleep.

Staying out of debt is often difficult because the debtor has deep-rooted problems that prompt him or her to use credit. For instance, the debtor may regard material objects as a way of gaining status. Exhibit 15-7 presents a psychological analysis of excessive borrowing.

PREPARING AN ANNUAL NET WORTH REPORT

A potentially uplifting strategy of managing your finances is to chart your yearly financial status. You can accomplish this by annually evaluating your **net worth,** the difference between your assets and liabilities. The uplift comes from discovering that you are making progress in the form of an improved net worth.

You include in your personal annual report only **liquid assets**—those you can convert into cash relatively quickly. Even if the equity in your home is not very liquid, it is worth including. Without house equity, most homeowners would have modest liquid assets.

Personal annual reports for two years are presented in Exhibit 15-8. The person who prepared both reports was in financial difficulty when the first report was prepared. Notice the progress this individual has made over the four-year period. In the first year, his liquid assets aside from his home equity and car resale value totaled $1,184. Including house and car, his assets were $22,784. Thanks in part to both self-discipline and modest inflation, his assets jumped to $44,195 four years later. Without the house equity and car resale value, his liquid assets were $4,395.

The liability picture is even more impressive. In the first year, the man had outstanding debts of $15,910. Four years later, his debts had shrunk to $4,058. His liability position had improved an enviable $11,852. Over the same period his asset picture had improved $11,411. Adding both improvements together, we are able to give the individual a financial improvement score of $23,263 for the four-year period. Recognize, however,

EXHIBIT 15-6

HEATH AND JUDY CONCENTRATE ON ONE BILL AT A TIME

After seventeen years of marriage, Heath and Judy had acquired an upsetting level of debt. Part of their problem was the debt they had accumulated in the process of acquiring two two-family houses that they used as income property. At the urging of a financial counselor, Heath and Judy scrutinized both their debts and their spending habits. Their debt picture looked like this:

Type of Loan	Balance on Loan	Approximate Monthly Payment
Auto	$ 2,850	$215
Home improvement	1,975	149
Visa	1,828	85
MasterCard	1,859	95
Furnaces for income properties	2,562	185
Tuition	800	90
Orthodontist	750	75
	$12,624	$894

In today's economy an indebtedness of $12,624 may not seem extreme. Nevertheless, in terms of their other living expenses, including the support of three children, $894 a month of debts was creating stress for Heath and Judy. The couple might have tried the traditional debt-reduction program of spreading out their monthly debt-reduction fund over all their bills. In so doing, they would have tried to make approximately equal payments to all creditors. Instead, Heath and Judy chose to reduce their debts by concentrating first on the variable-payment debt with the smallest balance. In other words, they concentrated first on the debt that they were capable of eliminating first.

Following this strategy, Heath and Judy began their debt-reduction program by first working down the Visa debt. Each month they would put as much money as they could spare into their Visa payment, even though they had previously paid only $85 monthly for that particular bill. The couple kept making minimum payments to MasterCard until their Visa balance was reduced to zero. Then came big progress when they were able to make two double payments. (The general principle is to eliminate, one by one, each of the loans for which variable—rather than fixed—payments are possible. In addition, take on new debts for emergency purposes only.)

The above case history indicates that an effective program of debt reduction involves both financial and emotional issues. Getting rid of debts one by one provides an important emotional boost to the debtor. As the debts are peeled off, tension is reduced. The one-debt-at-a-time strategy is also tied in with goal theory. You experience a feeling of accomplishment as each debt is eliminated. Simultaneously, you are motivated to tackle the next variable debt.

that the $10,000 growth in house equity was a major contributing factor to his financial improvement.

Personal computer software is available to help you prepare a yearly financial statement, along with monthly budgeting, check writing, check reconciliation and so forth. One such program is Quicken. It can memorize

---

EXHIBIT 15-7

CREDIT CARD SPLURGING IS A PSYCHOLOGICAL PROBLEM

When those credit card bills come pouring in, do you wonder how it all happened? Why *did* you buy three VCRs and a dozen pair of shoes you'll never use? Experts say your credit card splurging may be more than whimsical overindulgence. Psychiatrists and credit counselors are finding that credit card abuse often reflects deeper psychological problems and it is a growing problem in today's society. Credit card abuse is often associated with drug abuse, alcohol problems, delinquency, unconscious anger, revenge, or passivity.

More and more people are pushing their credit cards to the limit—and beyond. This is resulting in serious emotional and financial problems for the abusers and their families. One psychiatrist says, "The situation is explosive. The nation has gone crazy with credit, and it is a ticking plastic bomb." One problem is that this society emphasizes accumulation of material possessions as a mark of success. Credit card abuse cuts across all economic and social levels. Likely credit card offenders are found among[9]:

- People who suffer from generalized anxiety, have a history of marijuana and alcohol abuse, and often suffer from a binge eating disorder.

- A spouse in the middle of a bitter divorce. Credit cards offer a last chance to "get even."

- People who are depressed and think the cards can buy them a little happiness.

- People who have trouble dealing with rules and regulations. They feel life has shortchanged them and the cards give them a chance to catch up.

- Uncontrollable impulse buyers.

- People with a self-esteem problem who think that accumulation of possessions will make them feel better about themselves.

Once people realize that they have a borrowing problem, recovery comes slowly because underlying problems must also be solved. Credit card abuse is as difficult to discontinue as is smoking or fingernail biting. Treating the underlying problem is a slow process of learning to substitute more adaptive coping techniques and building self-esteem.

SOURCE: Marybeth Nibley, "Shopping 'Til You Drop Can Be a Crippling Addiction," Associated Press story, October 1 1989; Lisa Faye Kaplan, "Compulsive Shoppers Are More Likely to Suffer from Anxiety," Gannett News Service story, May 27, 1992.

recurring transactions such as monthly mortgage payments and phone bills. Instead of recreating the same check each month, you simply recall the memorized transaction, enter in the new amount if it has changed, and print the check.

 ## HOW TO RETIRE RICH

If you start investing early in your career, you can retire rich even without earning an astronomical salary or winning a lottery. The basic idea is to start a systematic savings and investment plan set aside for retirement only. The dividends and interest paid on these investments are

---

EXHIBIT 15-8

A PERSONAL ANNUAL REPORT

Assets	December 31, Year 1	December 31, Year 4
House equity (based on market value)	$28,000	$38,000
Cash in checking account	141	392
Cash on hand	75	315
Savings account	118	792
Mutual fund	—	896
Car resale value	3,600	1,800
Jewelry resale value	850	2,000
	$32,784	$44,195

Liabilities		
Auto payments	$3,500	—
Visa	1,215	$350
MasterCard	2,150	1400
American Express	850	80
Sears charge	1550	1128
Home improvement loan	3,975	—
Loan from uncle	895	—
Property tax due	850	350
School tax due	650	350
Plumber	275	400
	$15,910	$4,058

not taxed until retirement, and they keep compounding. As a result, you wind up with an extraordinary amount of money at the end of your career. Details about several of these retirement investment plans are presented next.

Whichever retirement plan you enter, remember to follow the key investment principle of asset allocation. Your retirement funds should be divided among stocks, bonds, and short-term notes and cash.

EMPLOYEE RETIREMENT PROGRAMS AND SOCIAL SECURITY

The foundation of most retirement plans is company pensions and social security. If you stay with one company long enough, you are likely to retire at about two-thirds of your final salary. However, not everybody stays with one employer for many years, and some companies go bankrupt or misuse pension funds, thus putting your retirement pay at risk. Social security is designed to supplement pensions and individual retirement plans, and pays approximately a minimum wage.

To retire rich, you will therefore need to supplement pension plans and social security with your own retirement investment program. All of the savings plans and investments described earlier in this chapter could become part of your retirement nest egg. In addition, many people have retirement accounts with built-in tax savings, as described next.

INDIVIDUAL RETIREMENT ACCOUNTS (IRAs) AND SIMPLIFIED EMPLOYEE PLANS (SEPs)

Retirement accounts held by individuals, rather than offered by employers, can be used to invest in most of the types of savings and investments described earlier. Both IRAs and SEPs are popular because they offer generous tax savings.

An **IRA** is a supplemental retirement account, fully funded by the individual, that qualifies for certain tax advantages. Anyone, including government employees with earned income, may open an IRA. Single workers may contribute up to $2,000 per year. One-paycheck couples may invest up to $2,250 annually. Two-paycheck couples may contribute up to $4,000 a year if both work and each earns at least $2,000. Distributions from your IRA may begin as early as age fifty-nine-and-a-half, but must begin by seventy-and-a-half. Early withdrawal incurs a 10 percent penalty plus payment of taxes on the amount withdrawn.

IRA contributions are tax deductible only at moderate income levels. Dividends and interest from an IRA are not taxed as long as they are not withdrawn. When you begin withdrawals, IRA distributions are taxed as ordinary income.

SEPs are retirement plans for individuals who are self-employed or for those who earn part of their income from self-employment. (Keogh plans are virtually the same as SEPs except for a complicated tax-reporting system.) SEPs and IRAs follow many of the same rules, with several exceptions. First, to qualify you must earn some self-employment income.

Second, you can invest up to 15 percent of your self-employment income in a SEP, up to a maximum of $30,000. An individual can hold an IRA and a SEP.

The dramatic financial returns from an IRA or SEP are shown in Table 15-4, which assumes that a person invested $2,000 each year. Much of the growth in funds is attributable to compound interest, and no withdrawals on which to pay taxes.

Annuities (Including Tax-Sheltered Annuities)

Annuities are long-term investments offered by insurance companies, with tax-deductible earnings. You can purchase an annuity in a large lump sum, or invest regularly in smaller amounts. A fixed annuity pays a specified fixed rate of return. A variable annuity pays a rate of return based on the success of the money invested. For both types of annuities, the money in the account compounds tax-free as long as it is not withdrawn. Penalty charges may be incurred for withdrawals made before age fifty-nine-and-a-half. Annuities may be withdrawn in a lump sum, or paid out monthly for many years.

The tax deferment feature of annuities is significant. A single-premium annuity purchased for $10,000 earning 8 percent per year would grow to $68,484 in twenty-five years. The same $10,000 invested without tax deferment by a person in the 28 percent tax bracket would grow to $40,554.

Tax-sheltered annuities (TSAs) are a special type of annuity for employees of educational institutions and certain other nonprofit institutions such as hospitals, churches, and scientific organizations. The TSA is a voluntary supplement to the retirement plans offered by the employer. Employees can deduct tax-free up to 20 percent of their income to a maximum of $9,500. TSAs, like other annuities, IRAs, and SEPs, earn tax-

	TABLE 15-4		
	How IRAs Can Grow		

| Years of Contribution | Rate of Return | | |
	8%	10%	12%
5	$ 11,733	$ 12,210	$ 12,705
10	$ 28,973	$ 31,875	$ 35,097
15	$ 54,304	$ 63,544	$ 74,559
20	$ 91,524	$114,550	$144,104
25	$146,212	$196,694	$266,667
30	$226,566	$328,998	$482,554
35	$344,634	$542,048	$863,326

NOTE: This chart assumes a $2,000 yearly contribution at year end, compound interest, and no tax payments.

deferred interest. Similar to the other investment programs described in this section, they will help you retire rich if you start early enough.

 ## SUMMARY

An important part of managing your personal life is to manage your personal finances in such a way that money is not a major source of worry and concern in your life. Financial problems often lead to marital problems, for example.

Setting financial goals is an important starting point in managing your personal finances. Such goals can be expressed in dollars, the type of things you would like to accomplish with money, or the type of lifestyle you would like to lead.

A vital aspect of financial management is to establish a spending plan or budget, which can be divided into six steps: (1) establishing goals, (2) estimating income, (3) estimating expenses, (4) comparing expenses and income, (5) carrying out the spending plan, and (6) evaluating the plan.

An effective spending plan allows room for investing. Basic investment principles include:

1. Invest early and steadily.

2. Keep reinvesting dividends.

3. Diversify your investments.

4. Maintain a disciplined, long-term approach.

5. Practice contrary investing (buy when the demand is low and sell when the demand is high).

6. Be willing to accept some risk.

7. Invest globally as well as domestically.

8. Pay off debt.

The two basic types of investments are lending money (debt) or owning assets (equity). All investments carry some risk, which can be divided into four types: investment risk, market risk, inflation risk, and adequacy risk (will the investment cover anticipated future expenses?). Investments with the highest investment risk also carry the highest potential rewards. Over time, stocks have yielded much higher returns than bonds.

Among the many ways of investing or saving money are the following: interest-bearing checking accounts; passbook savings accounts; certificates of deposit; money-market funds; U.S. Treasury securities; corporate bonds; common stocks; mutual funds; gold and silver; collectibles; real estate; and whole-life insurance.

A major investment decision is how to allocate your investments among short-term interest-bearing accounts, stocks, and bonds. To select the right mix, choose among three diversification strategies: capital preservation, moderate (or compromise), and wealth building.

Dealing with debt is an important component of managing personal finances. To use credit wisely, recognize the difference between good debt and bad debt. Limit your total borrowing to 15 to 20 percent of monthly take-home pay, not including a house mortgage payment. Using credit cards wisely includes such factors as restricting their use, selectively using a home equity loan, and making more than the minimum monthly payments on loans.

One way of working your way out of debt is to concentrate on one bill at a time—try to pay off first your variable payment with the smallest balance. To stay out of debt, pay for goods and services with cash or check and therefore stop borrowing money.

We recommend giving yourself a yearly financial checkup by preparing a list of your liquid assets and liabilities. Progress is measured in terms of the difference between assets and liabilities. The bigger the positive difference, the better your financial health.

People who start a retirement savings or investment program early in their careers may accumulate large sums of money by retirement. Employee retirement programs, social security, and regular investments are the foundation of retirement financial planning. People can also invest in retirement accounts that are partially or fully tax-deductible. Individual Retirement Accounts (IRAs) are available to people who already receive company pensions. Simplified Employee Plans (SEPs) and Keogh plans are retirement programs for people who are fully or partially self-employed. Annuities, including tax-sheltered annuities (TSAs), are retirement plans generally sold by insurance companies.

Questions and Activities

1. Is this chapter mostly for money-hungry, greedy people? Explain.

2. What types of problems do you think people can avoid by carefully managing their finances?

3. It has often been observed that the majority of people who file for bankruptcy have well-above-average incomes. How can this be true?

4. Why does preparing a spending plan sometimes help people reduce their worry about money?

5. How can a person resolve the conflict between investing money for the long range and buying things he or she wants right now, such as a personal computer with a CD-ROM capability or downhill skiing equipment?

6. What type of investment risk does a person face when keeping money in a safe for a long time?

7. If life insurance should be part of an investment plan, why are so many people unreceptive to solicitations from life insurance agents?

A HUMAN RELATIONS CASE PROBLEM:
THE PROBLEM SPENDING PLAN

The spending plan presented below was submitted by Greg Walters, a twenty-eight-year-old man with a good job. He says that owning a home and entertaining his friends are important parts of his lifestyle. Yet he also contends, "I'm committing slow-motion financial suicide. Each month I go further into debt. Right now I don't see a good way out unless I give up a lot of things that are important to me. You've got to have fun in life, don't you?"

Review Greg's budget and make some specific recommendations to him for improving his financial health. Also, what flaws do you find in his logic?

SPENDING PLAN FOR GREG WALTERS

Monthly Expenses

Fixed:

Mortgage or rent	$ 775
Property insurance	45
Health insurance	35
Auto insurance	45
Other insurance	35
Educational expenses	100
Child support payments	
Taxes:	
Federal	750
State or provincial	210
Social security	210
Local	
Property	175
Installment loans (auto and others)	300
Set aside for emergencies	0

Variable:

Food & beverage	250
Household supplies	40
Home maintenance and repairs	65
Medical and dental	40
Telephone	55
Clothing	110
Hair care and cosmetics	45
Transportation	75
Car maintenance	100
Travel and vacation	225
Clubs/organizations	145
Hobbies	35
Other (cable TV)	35

Total expenses	$ 3900

Monthly Income

Salary	$ 3500
Tips	
Bonuses & commissions	
Interest & dividends	
Insurance benefits	
Child support received	
Other	
Total income	$ 3500

Summary:

Total income	$ 3500
Less total expenses	3900
Balance for savings and investment	(400)

A HUMAN RELATIONS ROLE PLAY:
COUNSELING A CREDIT CARD JUNKIE

One person plays the role of a "credit card junkie." This person owns five credit cards and often uses cash advances from one to make minimum monthly payments on another. The person's boss observes that he or she is having difficulty concentrating on the job. The boss refers the employee to the company Employee Assistance Program which includes credit counseling for people in financial trouble. The employee shows up for the first appointment with the credit counselor, still thinking that extensive use of credit is a good idea. The employee contends that "our country runs on credit" and everyone "deserves a few luxuries in life."

The other person plays the role of the credit counselor who will try to get the credit card junkie to take constructive action about his or her problem. The counselor thinks he or she is committing slow-motion financial suicide.

8. What relevance does this chapter have for a full-time student?

9. If you think you will live at least one hundred years, how will this affect your savings and investment strategy?

10. Talk to a retired person and inquire what, if anything, he or she would do differently to plan financially for retirement. Be prepared to discuss your findings in class.

REFERENCES

[1]Example taken from "Looking at the Big Picture: The Income Stock Fund," *USAA Financial Spectrum,* June 1992, p. 6.

[2]Quoted in "The $3 Billion Man Shares His Secret," *Invest,* September 1993, p. 10.

[3]"The Four Most Common Mistakes Investors Make (and How to Avoid Them)," *USAA Financial Spectrum,* January 1990, pp. 1–2.

[4]"Making Smart Allocation Choices," *The Participant (Quarterly News for TIAA-Creff Participants),* November 1993, p. 3.

[5]Data from a Fidelity Investments newsletter, December 30, 1993.

[6]Data from Administrative Office of U.S. Courts, American Financial Services Association, 1994.

[7]"Managing Your Credit Wisely," a consumer information brochure written and produced by VISA USA, undated. "Taking Control of Debt," *Aide Magazine,* December 1993, pp. 17–28.

[8]"Debt-Danger Signal Quiz," *Aide Magazine,* December 1992, p. 26; Jane Bryant Quinn, "More People Facing Personal Credit Crisis," syndicated column, September 10, 1991.

[9]"Shopping 'Til You Drop Can Be a Crippling Addiction," Associated Press Story, October 1, 1989; "Money Management for Uncertain Times," *Aide Magazine,* December 1992, p. 26; "Taking Control of Debt," *Aide Magazine,* December 1993, pp. 17–28.

ADDITIONAL READING

Feinberg, Andrew. *Downsize Your Debt: How to Take Control of Your Personal Finances.* New York: Penguin Books, 1993.

Where to Invest in 1995. Business Week Yearend Double Issue, December 26, 1994/January 2, 1995. (See also current yearend issue.)

Lynch, Peter. *Beating the Street.* New York: Simon & Schuster, 1994.

Peterson, Ann Z. *Every Woman's Guide to Financial Security.* Washington, D.C.: Capital Publishing, 1994.

Pond, Jonathon D. *The New Century Family Money Book.* New York: Dell, 1993.

Quinn, Jane Bryant. *Making the Most of Your Money.* New York: Simon & Schuster, 1991.

CHAPTER 16

ENHANCING YOUR PERSONAL LIFE

Learning Objectives

After studying the information and doing the exercises in this chapter you should be able to:

■ Specify at least seven factors that contribute to personal happiness.

■ Develop a plan for meeting people (if you are in need of a new friend).

■ Pinpoint several principles for working through issues with a partner.

■ Identify strategies and tactics for making a dual-career couple work.

■ Choose among techniques for keeping a relationship of yours vibrant.

A satisfying and rewarding personal life is an important end in itself. It also contributes to a satisfying and rewarding career. If your personal life is miserable, you will have difficulty concentrating on your work. Also, a barren personal life leads one to question the meaning of one's work. As a lonely investment banker said to a bartender he had never met before, "What's this all about? Why am I working sixty-five hours a week, fifty weeks a year? I have no wife and no close friends. Nobody cares about me. What's my purpose?"

In this final chapter, we look at some of the major issues involved in leading an enriched personal life. In addition, we offer a number of concrete suggestions that may help some people enhance their personal lives. We begin by summarizing some modern ideas about happiness.

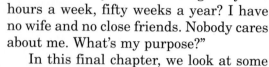

THE KEYS TO HAPPINESS

When asked what is the most important thing in life, most people respond, "happiness." Research and opinion on the topic indicate that people can take concrete steps to achieve happiness. Planning for happiness is possible because it appears to be somewhat under people's control. Unhappiness, in contrast, seems to be more predetermined by genes. Sadness appears to run in families.[1] The keys to happiness described below can also be regarded as simple but effective ways of improving your personal life.[2]

1. *Give high priority to the pursuit of happiness.*   Discover what makes you happy and make the time to pursue those activities. Spending time doing what you enjoy contributes directly to happiness.

2. *Experience love and friendship.*   A happy person is one who is successful in personal relationships, who exchanges care and concern with loved ones. Happy people are able to love and be loved. Hugging people you like, or being hugged by them, is an important part of having enjoyable personal relationships.

3. *Develop a sense of self-esteem.*   Self-love must precede love for others. High self-esteem enables one to love and be loved. Developing a good self-image leads to the self-esteem required for loving relationships. A feeling of self-worth is important because it helps prevent being overwhelmed by criticism. An important part of developing self-esteem is not wanting financial success more than other things. Insecure people seek society's approval in the form of purchasing consumer goods and accumulating investments.[3]

4. *Work hard at what you enjoy.*   Love may be the most important contributor to happiness, with staying involved in work you like coming in second. To achieve happiness, it is necessary to find a career inside or outside the home that fits your most intense interests.

5. *Seek accomplishments and the ability to enjoy them.*   A fundamental secret of happiness is accomplishing things and savoring what you have accomplished. A contributor to unhappiness is comparing one's successes, or lack of them, to those of other people. To be happy you must be happy with what *you* achieve.

6. *Develop an attitude of openness and trust.*   Trusting other people leads to happiness, and distrusting others leads to unhappiness. Happy people have open, warm, and friendly attitudes.

7. *Appreciate the joys of day-to-day living.*   Another key to happiness is the ability to live in the present without undue worrying about the future or dwelling on past mistakes. Be on guard against becoming so preoccupied with planning your life that you neglect to enjoy the happiness of the moment. The essence of being a happy person is to savor what you have right now.

8. *Be fair, kind, and helpful to others.*   The Golden Rule is a true contributor to happiness: "Do unto others as you would have them do unto you." It is also important to practice charity and forgiveness. Helping others brings personal happiness. Knowing that you are able to make a contribution to the welfare of others gives you a continuing sense of satisfaction and happiness.

9. *Have fun in your life.*   A happy life is characterized by fun, zest, joy, and delight. When you create a time for fun, you add an important element to your personal happiness. However, if you devote too much time to play, you will lose out on the fun of work accomplishments. In choosing fun activities, don't overplan. Because novelty contributes to happiness, be ready to pursue an unexpected opportunity or to try something different.

10. *Learn to cope with anxiety, stress, grief, and disappointment.*   To be happy one must learn how to face problems that occur in life without being overwhelmed or running away. Once you have had to cope with problems you will be more able to appreciate the day-to-day joys of life.

11. *Live with what you cannot change.*   Psychologist Martin Seligman says that attempting to change conditions unlikely to change sets us up for feeling depressed about failing. Weight loss is a prime example. Nineteen out of twenty people regain the weight they lost. It is therefore better to worry less about weight loss and concentrate on staying in good physical condition by engaging in moderate exercise. Good conditioning contributes much more to health than does achieving a weight standard set primarily to achieve an aesthetic standard.[4] You can then concentrate on being happy about your good physical condition instead of being unhappy about your weight.

12. *Energize yourself through physical fitness.*   Engage in regular physical activity, such as dancing or sports, that makes you aerobically fit. Whether it is the endorphins released by exercise, or just the relaxed muscles, physical fitness fosters happiness.

13. *Strive for a balanced emotional response to positive and negative experiences.* Emotional overintensity can be costly. People who reach the highest highs also tend to reach the lowest lows.

14. *Develop a philosophy or system of belief.* Another key contributor to happiness is to believe in something besides oneself. Happy people have some system of belief—whether it be religion, philosophy, or science—which comforts them and gives them a reason for being.

The balance of this chapter describes some challenges in personal life that need to be dealt with properly in order to accomplish the above ideal states. For example, you need to find a companion in order to have somebody to love.

A PLANNED APPROACH TO FINDING A RELATIONSHIP

How many people have you heard complain about a poor social life because of circumstances beyond their control? Such complaints take various forms: "The women in this school are all unappreciative," "The men at my school don't really respect women," "There's absolutely nobody to meet at work," or "This is the worst town for meeting people."

Some of the people expressing these attitudes are systematic when it comes to handling business or technology problems. Under those circumstances they use the problem-solving method. But when it comes to their social lives, they rely heavily on fate or chance.

The approach recommended here is to use your problem-solving skills to improve your personal life. Whatever the problem, try to attack it in a logical, step-by-step manner. We are not ruling out the influence of emotion and feeling in personal life. We are simply stating that personal life is too important to be left to fate alone. With good fortune you might form a relationship with a stranger you meet at a rapid-oil-change-and-lubrication center. Unfortunately, such good fortune is infrequent.

Too many people leave finding a new relationship to chance or to a few relatively ineffective alternatives. Too many unattached adults lament, "Either you go to a bar or you sit at home." In reality, both men and women can find dates in dozens of constructive ways. It is a matter of identifying some of these alternatives and trying out a few that fit your personality and preferences. See Exhibit 16-1 for more details.

EXHIBIT 16-1

IN SEARCH OF A DATE?

Every relationship begins with one person meeting another. In order to find one good relationship you may need to date more than a dozen people. Next is a sampling of potentially effective methods for making a social contact.

Highly Recommended

1. Participate in an activity that you do well and enjoy. For example, if you are a good frisbee player, use frisbee playing as a vehicle for meeting people.

2. Get involved in your work or another activity not logically related to dating. People of the opposite sex* naturally gravitate toward a busy, serious-minded person. Besides, the workplace has now become the number one, natural meeting place for singles.

3. Take courses in which the male-female ratio is in your favor, such as automotive technology for women and cooking for men.

4. Ask your friends for introductions and describe the type of person you are trying to meet—but don't be too restrictive.

5. Get involved in a community or political activity in which many single people participate. A good example is to become a political-party worker.

6. For men, join almost any formal singles group such as "Eastside Singles." The membership of these clubs is overwhelmingly female.

7. For women, join a national guard reserve unit. The membership of these units is overwhelmingly male.

8. Take advantage of every social invitation to a party, picnic, breakfast, or brunch. Social occasions are natural meeting places.

9. Place a personal ad in a local newspaper or magazine, stating the qualifications you are seeking in a companion and how you can be reached. Personal

(Continued)

ads have achieved such popularity that several national magazines now accept them. Personal ads are frequently integrated with voice mail. (You leave a voice message for the person who placed the ad.) Under many systems, your personal ad consists of a voice message to which people respond.

10. A rapidly growing number of people are meeting through computer networks whose primary purpose is to develop contacts with other people. (Such systems qualify as networking, both figuratively and literally.) After exchanging several electronic messages, the two people arrange for an in-person meeting. *Cyberdating* is a trendy term to describe this dating process.

11. Organize a singles party, and require each person invited to bring along an unattached person of the opposite sex—no regular couples allowed.

At Least Worth a Try

1. While networking for career purposes, also prospect for social companions.

2. Join a dating service, particularly one that offers videotapes. The videotapes give you valuable information about the prospective date's appearance, speech, and nonverbal behavior.

3. Shop at supermarkets from 11 P.M. to 2 A.M. You will frequently find other single people shopping at that time.

4. Spend a lot of time in laundromats.

5. Strike up a conversation while waiting in line for tickets at the movies or concerts.

6. Congregate, or float around, in large gatherings such as rallies for causes, registration for courses, or orientation programs.

7. Join special-promotion singles groups such as indoor tennis for singles or a singles ski weekend.

8. Find valid reasons for visiting other departments at your place of work. Chance meetings at photocopying machines, for example, have allegedly spawned thousands of romances.

*Although these suggestions are primarily geared toward meeting people of the opposite sex, the same principles will generally apply to meeting people and making friends of the same sex.

The steps to take after meeting someone are not always clear-cut. Susan Page, who runs singles workshops, recommends several actions to take after the initial meeting.[5] First, cast a wide net. "Most of your catches will be tossed back in the sea." Nevertheless, the more people you meet, the better the chances of one sharing your interests and values.

Second, limit the first date to about one or two hours. Mention that you have a prior commitment. The limited time frame guards against the unpleasantness of an uncomfortable first date. If the date is pleasant, you will look forward with strong anticipation to the next date. Third, screen for compatibility of what you are looking for in a relationship. Initial physical attraction is important, but also look for clues to the type of relationship the person is seeking. Talk about your own general opinions and desires in a relationship and see how your new prospective friend responds.

WHY PEOPLE ARE ATTRACTED TO ONE ANOTHER

As part of enriching social life, it is helpful to understand why people are attracted to each other. Understanding these forces may help in choosing a compatible person for a long-term relationship. Three different explanations of why two people develop a strong attraction to each other are balance theory, exchange theory, and the need for intimacy. All three of these explanations can apply in a given situation.

BALANCE THEORY OF ATTRACTION

According to **balance theory,** people prefer relationships that are consistent, or balanced. If we are very similar to another person, it makes sense (it is consistent or balanced) to like that person. We are also attracted to similar people because they reinforce our opinions and values. It is usually reassuring and rewarding to discover that another person agrees with you or has similar values.[6]

Balance theory explains why we are eager to stay in a relationship with some people, but it does not explain why opposites often attract each other. People sometimes get along best with those who possess complementary characteristics. A talkative and domineering person may prefer a partner who enjoys listening. The explanation is that a dominant person needs someone to dominate and therefore might be favorably disposed toward submissive people.

SOCIAL EXCHANGE THEORY OF ATTRACTION

A long-standing explanation of why two people become a couple is **social exchange theory,** the idea that human relationships are based mainly on self-interest. This research shows that people measure their social, physical, and other assets against a potential partner's. The closer the match, the more likely they are to develop a long-term relationship.

Exchange theory has been able to predict the permanence of a relationship based on the way each partner feels he or she stacks up against the other. One study of 537 dating men and women found that partners who thought they were getting far more in exchange for what they were giving felt guilty and insecure. In comparison, those who believed they gave more than they got were angry.

The giving was mostly psychological. It included such things as being more physically attractive than the partner, kinder, or more flexible. The greater the imbalance, the more likely the couple was to split up; the more equitable the partners believed the exchange to be, the more likely they were to remain partners. A researcher on the topic of love offered this explanation of the findings just presented:

> It's terribly corroding if one person feels taken advantage of. And it is just as disturbing to feel you can take advantage of your partner.[7]

NEED FOR INTIMACY

For some, the balance and exchange theories of mutual attraction are too mechanical and logical. Psychologist David McClelland proposes instead that love is an experience seated in the nonrational part of the brain (the right side). People who believe that they are in love have a strong **need for intimacy.** This craving for intimacy is revealed in the thoughts of people in love who are asked to make up stories about fictitious situations. Their stories reveal a preoccupation with harmony, responsibility, and commitment, and a preference for a relationship that includes warmth and intimacy.

McClelland and his associates say that these themes show up repeatedly in many guises in the stories told by people who say they are in love. The same stories are told by people in situations where love feelings run high, such as just having seen a romantic movie.[8]

The concept of love is part of the need for intimacy, as well as a key part of understanding personal relationships. Every reader has an idea of what love means to him or her. Harry Stack Sullivan, the famous psychiatrist, developed a particularly useful description of love, as follows:

> When the satisfaction or the security of another person becomes as significant to one as is one's own satisfaction or security, then the state of love exists. So far as I know, under no other circumstance is a state of love present, regardless of the popular usage of the word.

 ## WORKING OUT ISSUES WITHIN RELATIONSHIPS

People emotionally involved with each other often find themselves in conflict over a variety of issues, especially when they are emotionally dependent upon each other. Without conflict, relationships would be artificial. A study on male-female conflict was conducted among 600 people involved for different periods of time in a variety of relationships such as dating and marriage.[9]

The study found that both men and women were deeply upset by unfaithfulness and physical or verbal abuse. However, distinct differences were found between men and women in other behaviors that disturbed them. Sexual activity was one major area of difference. Women complained men were too sexually aggressive, while men complained that women too often declined sexual activity. A summary of the major areas of male-female conflict found in the study is presented in Exhibit 16-2.

Human relations specialists have formulated some ground rules for resolving the types of conflicts between partners listed in Exhibit 16-2.[10] These rules supplement the techniques for conflict resolution presented in Chapter 9.

1. *Good communications go both ways.*   Many conflicts intensify because the people involved never stop to listen carefully to what the other side is trying to say. After listening to your partner's point of view, express your *feelings* about the issue. Expressing your feelings leads to more understanding than expressing your judgments. It is therefore preferable to say, "I feel left out when you visit your mother" than to say "You're insensitive to my needs; look at the way you visit your mother all the time."

2. *Restate your partner's point of view.*   To help improve understanding, provide mutual feedback. Although you may disagree with your partner, communicate your understanding: "From your point of view it's frivolous of me to spend so much money on bowling. You would prefer that I invest that money in baby furniture."

3. *Define the real problem.*   What your partner or you grumble about at first may not be the real issue in the conflict. It will require mutual understanding combined with careful listening and sympathy to uncover the real problem. A man might be verbally attacking a woman's dress when he really means that she has gained more weight than he would like. Or a woman might verbally attack a man's beer drinking when her real complaint is that he should be out in the yard raking leaves instead of sitting inside playing video games.

4. *Stick to the issue.*   When two people who are emotionally involved become embroiled in a conflict, there is a natural tendency to bring old wounds into the argument. The two of you might be in conflict over financial matters, and one of you might say, "And I remember that weekend you were in Boston. You never called me." A good response here would be, "I'm sorry I did not take the time to call you, but it doesn't have anything to do with our problem today. Let's talk about *that* problem later."

5. *Don't hit below the belt.*   The expression "below the belt" refers to something that is unfair. Some issues are just plain unfair to bring up in a marital dispute. When you are intimate with another person, you are bound to know one or two vulnerable areas. Here are two below-the-belt comments:

> "You're lucky I married you. What other woman would have married a man who was so much of a loser that he had to declare bankruptcy."

> "Don't complain so much about being mistreated. Remember, when I married you, you were down on your luck and had no place to live."

Is anyone really as cruel as the above quotes would suggest? Yes, in the heat of a tiff between partners, many cruel, harsh things are said. If two people want to live harmoniously after the conflict, they should avoid below-the-belt comments.

EXHIBIT 16-2

COMMON CONFLICTS BETWEEN MEN AND WOMEN

Men Dislike Women Who Are:	*Women Dislike Men Who Are:*
Unfaithful	Sexually aggressive
Abusive	Unfaithful
Self-centered	Abusive
Condescending	Condescending
Sexually withholding	Emotionally constricted
Neglectful	Insulting about their appearance
Moody	Open admirers of another woman's appearance
Self-absorbed with appearance	Inconsiderate
Big spenders on clothes	Do not help much cleaning up the home
Overly concerned about how their face and hair look	

SOURCE: Table prepared from data in David M. Buss, "Conflict Between the Sexes: Strategic Interference and the Evocation of Anger and Upset," *Journal of Personality and Social Psychology,* May 1989, pp. 735–47.

6. *Be prepared to compromise.* For many issues compromise is possible. The compromise you reach should represent a willingness to meet the other person halfway, not just a temporary concession. On some issues the only compromise can be letting the other person have his or her way now, and waiting to have your turn later. Among such issues that cannot be split down the middle are whether to have children, whether to live in an apartment or a house, whether to go to Miami or London for a vacation, or whether to run a kosher or nonkosher household. Several of these issues should be settled before marriage or living together, since no real compromise on the basic issue is possible in these instances. The only solution is to reach some type of agreement:

> Okay, we'll have a nonkosher household, but we'll dine in a kosher restaurant twice a week.

7. *Minimize an accusatory tone.* You lessen the accusatory tone when you make "I" statements instead of "you" statements. The door to dialogue is opened when you make a statement such as, "I felt really disappointed when you did not call me to ask about how my promotion interview went." You shut off dialogue when you say, "You don't care about my happiness. You didn't even call to ask about how my promotion interview went."

8. *Avoid manipulative pressure.*   A common way of manipulating your partner is to grant him or her a little favor in order to win the conflict. One partner might buy the other an unexpected present or prepare a favorite meal. The originator of this list of rules warned, "Marriage partners usually see through manipulative techniques and end up feeling resentful, especially of those techniques that involve the withholding of love or approval."

9. *Be willing to go the extra mile.*   To keep a relationship vibrant, there are times when one side will have to make a major concession to the other. If your relationship is solid, in the long run these extra miles will balance out. A middle-aged woman suggested to her spouse that this year, instead of taking their annual vacation trip, the money be invested in her cosmetic surgery. At first the husband bristled, thinking that she was being too self-centered. After thinking through the problem, the man realized that she had a valid point. He agreed to the surgery and the result was an added closeness between the couple. Such closeness between partners after resolving conflict is a frequent occurrence.

MEETING THE CHALLENGES OF BEING A DUAL-CAREER COUPLE

The number of couples in which both partners have full-time jobs continues to increase. Today over 50 percent of households are two-income families.[11] Two critical factors influencing this steady growth are women's career aspirations and the high cost of living. Housing, in particular, costs more today than in the past. Many families need two incomes in order to own their own home.

It is challenging to run dual-career (or two-paycheck) households in a way that will enhance the couple's personal life. In Chapter 7 we presented information about using organizational support systems to help reduce work-family conflicts. Following are suggestions that couples themselves can implement to increase the chances of a dual-career couple or family running more smoothly.

1. *Establish priorities and manage time carefully.*   A major contributor to the success of a dual-career relationship is careful time management.[12] Each partner must establish priorities, such as ranking quality time together ahead of adding a community activity to the schedule. Or both partners might inform their employer of a certain date they would be taking as a vacation day to celebrate their wedding anniversary.

2. *Deal with feelings of competitiveness.*   Feelings of competitiveness between husband and wife about each other's career often exist even when both have a modern outlook. Competitive feelings are all the more likely to surface when both parties are engaged in approximately the same kind of work. One man became infuriated with his wife when she was offered a promotion before he was. They had both entered the same big company at the same time in almost identical jobs. In contrast, the working couple with traditional views is unlikely to have a problem when the husband outdistances his wife in career advancement.

The familiar remedy of discussing problems before they get out of hand is offered again here. One partner might confess to the other, "Everybody is making such a fuss over you since you won that suggestion award. It makes me feel somewhat left out and unimportant." A sympathetic spouse might reply, "I can understand your feelings. But don't take all this fuss too seriously. It doesn't take away from my feelings for you. Besides, two months from now maybe people will be making a fuss over you for something."

3. *Share big decisions equally.* A distinguishing characteristic of today's two-income families is that both partners share equally in making important decisions about the domestic side of life. Under such an arrangement, neither has exclusive decision-making prerogatives in any particular area. He may make a decision without consulting her over some minor matter (such as the selection of a plant for the living room). She may make the decision the next time a plant is to be selected for inside the house. But on major decisions—such as relocating to another town, starting a family, or investing in the stock market or real estate—husband and wife collaborate.

4. *Divide household tasks equitably.* Many women who work outside the home rightfully complain that they are responsible for too much of the housework. In the extreme, they have the equivalent of two full-time jobs. Under this arrangement, conflict at home is highly probable. The recommended solution is for the working couple to divide household tasks in some equitable manner. Equity could mean that tasks are divided according to preference or the amount of effort required. In one family, the husband might enjoy food shopping while the wife enjoys cleaning. Assignments could be made accordingly. Each couple should negotiate for themselves what constitutes an equitable division of household tasks.

5. *Take turns being inconvenienced.* In a very traditional family, the woman assumes the responsibility for managing inconvenient household tasks even if she, too, has a job outside the home. The underlying assumption may be that her work is less important than his work. For more modern couples, a more equitable solution is to take turns being inconvenienced. If Sue has to go to work late one day to be around for the plumber, Ted can go to work late when the dog has to be taken to the veterinarian. A working couple with children will frequently have to miss work because of a child's illness or accident, parent-teacher conferences, or school plays.

6. *Develop adequate systems for child care.* Any working couple with a young child or children will attest to the challenge of adequately balancing work and child demands. Imagine this scenario: Your spouse has already left for work, and you discover that your four-year-old child has a fever of 102°. The child-care center will not accept a sick child, nor will your neighbor who helps out occasionally. She fears contaminating her children. The logical solution is to stay home from work, but you have a crucial work meeting scheduled for 11 A.M.

One solution to dilemmas of this nature, and less serious problems, is to have a diverse support system. Make arrangements with at least three people, including relatives, who could help you out in an emergency.

Retired people, for example, often welcome the challenge of helping out in an emergency.

7. *Share parenting roles.*   A dual-career family functions best when both parents take an active interest in child-rearing. Mother and father have to regard spending extensive amounts of time with their child or children as an appropriate activity for their sex. A survey of 330 men and women who were part of a dual-career couple suggests that both partners are heavily involved in child-rearing. Nevertheless, women seem to be more concerned that they are not spending enough quality time with their children.[13]

8. *Decide who pays for what.*   Unfortunately, the problem of negotiating who pays for what arises for many two-income families. Many couples find that the additional expenses of a working couple prevent them from getting ahead financially. Child-care expenses are often involved; restaurant meals become more frequent; and a second car is usually a necessity outside of large metropolitan areas.

A division of income that minimizes conflict for many two-paycheck families is to allocate some money for common expenses (such as rent or mortgage payments) and some money for personal expenses. The specific allocation of the latter does not have to be discussed with the partner. For instance, one partner is free to buy a new CD player with his or her personal money. But an item like new draperies would be a joint expense and a joint decision. Another helpful practice is to have one joint checking account and two personal checking accounts.

KEEPING YOUR RELATIONSHIP VIBRANT

One of the major challenges in personal life is to keep a relationship with a partner alive, healthy, and vibrant. For many people, relationships that begin with enthusiasm, rapport, and compatibility end in a dull routine or in splitting up. The quiz in Self-Examination Exercise 16-1 pinpoints some of the symptoms of a relationship gone bad. Here we will look at some of the most important factors in achieving a mutually rewarding long-term relationship.

CHOOSE A PARTNER CAREFULLY

A principal problem in many poor relationships is that the couple used faulty judgment in choosing each other. Of course, it is difficult to be objective when choosing a partner. Your needs at the time may cloud your judgment. Many people have made drastic mistakes in choosing a spouse because they were lonely and depressed when they met the person they married. As one young man said, "I married her on the rebound. I was hurt by my previous girlfriend. My wife came along at the right time. We were married in six months. Three months after the marriage we both knew we had made a big mistake."

The problem of mate selection is indeed complicated. Do you marry for love, companionship, infatuation, or all three? It has been pointed out that the success rate of the arranged marriages still practiced in a few countries is about as good as that of nonarranged marriages. Since most people have only a limited amount of time to invest in finding the ideal mate, they are content to marry a good fit.

An in-depth study of 300 happy marriages provides a practical clue about mate selection. The most frequently mentioned reason for an enduring and happy marriage was having a generally positive attitude toward each other.[14] If you view your partner as your best friend and like him or her "as a person," you will probably be happy together. As obvious as it sounds, choose only a life partner whom you genuinely like. Some people deviate from this guideline by placing too much emphasis on infatuation.

A unique approach to mate selection would be to ask your family and best friends what they thought of your prospects for happiness with your prospective mate. Above all, recognize that when you are contemplating choosing a life partner you are facing one of life's major decisions. Put all of your creative resources into making a sound decision.

KEEP ROMANTIC LOVE IN PROPER PERSPECTIVE

A speaker told an audience that you can tell you are infatuated with your partner if your heart begins pounding at a chance meeting with him or her. An eighty-year-old in the audience responded, "I know just what you mean. The Mrs. and I have been married for fifty-five years, and that's exactly how I feel whenever I run into her downtown." This happy husband is an exception; although infatuation or romantic love is vital in getting a relationship started, it usually cools down within several years. When infatuation declines, instead of being disappointed, the couple should realize that the relationship has grown more mature and lasting.

A relationship counselor observes that as full of rapture and delight as the first phase of a relationship is, it is essentially a trick of nature designed to bring us together. Nature knows that without the illusion of perfection, we might not choose each other. After the emotional bond is secure, nature lifts the veil.[15] To avoid discouragement and disillusionment, it is important to keep romantic love in proper perspective. It helps launch a relationship, but does not have to be kept at its initial high intensity for a relationship to endure. However, the spark should not be *extinguished*.

STRIVE FOR INTIMACY, PASSION, AND COMMITMENT

True love requires intimacy, passion, and commitment, according to psychologist Robert Sternberg.[16] While a relationship can manage to survive with only one or two of these qualities, the fullest love requires all three. Passion is the quickest to develop, and the quickest to fade. Intimacy, a feeling of emotional closeness, develops more slowly. One requirement for intimacy is that the person has established his or her own identity. Commitment develops the most slowly. However, in the current era, commitment is highly sought after by both men and women. In addition, a recent value shift is that more men strive for intimacy now than

SELF-EXAMINATION EXERCISE 16-1:

The Relationship Quiz

Is romance slipping away from you and your spouse (or other long-term partner)? Has your relationship lost its spark? This quiz will help you determine if you are falling out of love.

Use this three-point scale to indicate the frequency of the following statements: 1—Seldom; 2—Sometimes; and 3—Often. (Partners might want to take this quiz separately and then discuss their answers.)

_____ When we go out for an evening together, at least one other person goes along with us.

_____ Our evenings at home are for the most part spent watching television.

_____ I am more comfortable talking about myself with friends than with my partner.

_____ My partner has trouble looking me directly in the eyes and telling me he or she loves me.

_____ There are things about me I think my partner doesn't understand.

_____ My partner thinks he/she is entitled to evenings out with the guys/girls.

_____ My partner pays more attention or is more affectionate with the children than with me.

_____ My partner talks more openly with friends or neighbors or both than with me—at least on some subjects.

_____ After intimate romantic moments, I lack feelings of satisfaction or fulfillment.

_____ I find myself wishing things between us were more like they were when we were first a couple.

Total up your points:

29 or 30 points: Professional relationship counseling may be appropriate.

15 to 28 points: You and your partner could use some help in making your relationship more fulfilling.

10 to 14 points: You and your partner have a satisfactory relationship; any steps to improve it will affirm and support values you already hold.

SOURCE: Worldwide Marriage Encounter, used with permission.

was previously the case. Monogamy is becoming the rule rather than the exception for an increasing number of couples of all ages—to which sex psychologist Ruth Westheimer says, "To think that being with one partner is now in fashion again is music to my ears."[17]

Intimacy between partners becomes more important as successful relationships mature. Both partners find it increasingly important to understand each others' wants and needs, to listen to and support each other, and to share values. Although passion peaks in the early phases of a relationship, it still matters to a long-term successful relationship. Happily married people usually regard their mates as physically attractive.

While a strong commitment is essential to a long-term relationship, it is not sufficient. Without passion and intimacy, commitment tends to be hollow.

HAVE COMMUNICATION SESSIONS

Good communication is vital for creating and maintaining a loving relationship. Therefore, one way to keep a relationship alive is to hold formal communication sessions in which you tell each other almost anything on your mind. The topics can be both positive and negative. A man may want to tell his partner of something she did that he appreciated very much. Or a woman may want to talk about the way her partner offended her in public. Or a couple may want to discuss concerns about finances, a child, in-law relations, or anything else.

One of many reasons that communication sessions are important is that many couples have different perceptions about what is good and bad in their relationship. The communication sessions help clear up misperceptions. A study of 119 couples conducted by James Deal revealed that partners with more similar perceptions of their marriage and family life were more satisfied with their relationship.[18]

A vital aspect of these sessions is that both facts and feelings are expressed. The statement "I am really afraid we are drifting apart" communicates much more than "You and I haven't been talking too much lately." The role play at the end of this chapter explores the type of communication that can keep a relationship thriving.

Communication sessions are also important because they can sometimes revive a failing relationship. This is true because communication breakdowns often lead to failed relationships. Typically, in the early stages of a relationship, the couple is keenly attuned to each other's thoughts and feelings. The partners look for small verbal and nonverbal signals of contentment and discontent in each other.

After the relationship seems secure, couples often replace the intense monitoring of the early stages with a nonrevealing style of communication. For example, the man and woman may mechanically say to each other, "How was your day?" or "Love ya." This shorthand style of communication obstructs the sending and receiving of messages that could indicate the relationship is in trouble.[19] Introducing communication sessions can make it possible for the couple to deal with subtle problems in the relationship.

AVOID STEADY BARRAGES OF CRITICISM

Honest communication is good for a relationship, but be judicious in the openness and frequency of your criticism. A steady barrage of criticism can weaken a marriage and gradually undermine the positive feelings that led to the marriage. Most people are sensitive to criticism and can be easily hurt. Openness is more palatable when what you say allows your partner some alternatives. For instance, Jerry had enough sense to tell his new girlfriend Courtney that he felt uncomfortable dancing—her favorite form of entertainment. Courtney then was aware of the alternatives facing her. She could (1) drop Jerry for a man who did enjoy dancing, (2) agree to some other mutually satisfying form of entertainment, (3) forget dancing for the present but hope that Jerry would decide to improve his dancing at a later date.

Openness also brings two people closer when feelings are expressed in a constructive rather than destructive way. Alex fell in love with Kathy. When he asked her if she loved him, Kathy replied honestly, "Alex, I consider you a fine person, but I have not fallen in love with you *yet.*" Alex could then decide for himself whether to continue expressing love to a woman when the feeling was not yet mutual.

Another helpful perspective on openness comes from the study of happily married couples mentioned above. Virtually all of these couples believed that intensely expressed anger can damage the relationship. A sales representative with a thirty-six-year marriage advised, "Discuss your problems in a normal voice. If a voice is raised, stop. Return after a short period of time. Start again. After a period of time both parties will be able to deal with their problems and not say things that they will be sorry about later."[20]

STRIVE FOR NOVELTY IN YOUR RELATIONSHIP

An unfortunate aspect of many relationships is that they drift toward a routine. A married couple might go to the same place for vacation, meeting the same family and friends for years on end. A man dating a woman might call her every night at the same time. Or a couple's sex life may turn into a routine. Many people have suggested that you try pleasant surprises to keep your relationship vibrant and fun. Make up a list of your own, but here are a few ideas to jog your thinking:

Ask your mate out for dinner on a *Monday* evening.

Write your partner a poem instead of sending a commercial greeting card.

Take up a new activity together in which you are both beginners (such as country dancing or scuba diving) and learn with each other.

MAINTAIN A NONPOSSESSIVE RELATIONSHIP

A **nonpossessive relationship** is one in which both partners maintain separate identities and strive for personal fulfillment, yet are still committed to each other. Such a relationship is based on interdependent love—love involving commitment with self-expression and personal growth.[21] A nonpossessive relationship does not mean that the partners have sexual relationships with other people.

A nonpossessive relationship is helpful because some people find the traditional form of marriage stifling. For example, many married people feel compelled to give up a hobby or interest because the partner does not share the interest. In a nonpossessive relationship, the couple can take many separate paths and pursue different interests and have friends of their own. Unfortunately, if couples pursue nonpossessive relationships too far, they wind up drifting away from each other. The reason is that happy partners spend considerable time with each other enjoying shared activities. Each couple must find the right balance between maintaining separate identities yet spending sufficient time together to remain close.

ATTEND RELATIONSHIP SEMINARS

A structured way of keeping a relationship vibrant is to attend enrichment seminars or workshops designed for that purpose. Among such seminars are Marriage Encounter and PAIRS. Most of the practices encouraged in these seminars follow closely the ideas presented so far about keeping a relationship vibrant.

The concept behind these programs is to bring couples together at a time and place where they can temporarily forget the hassles of home and career and focus on each other. During the seminar, couples are taught the tools needed for a thriving relationship. Among them are how to resolve conflict, establish agreements, and set priorities within the relationship. An important goal of relationship seminars is to help people learn to live with someone for a long time without getting bored or restless. Nina and Bill, a couple who attended a relationship seminar, made these comments about the experience[22]:

> "It was really important that Bill committed to do this with me," said Nina. "And the ironic thing is that, even though I realized we had a lot to learn, I didn't think I was going to do the learning. I thought it was going to be him. We'd learned from our own parents how to be angry and dump on each other. In the course, we learned that that's not OK, that we needed new rules for living together."

> "What we saw were couples struggling after two cars, camps for their kids, vacations and big houses, but still missing what it takes to really extend themselves to each other," said Bill.

CHALLENGES FACED BY SINGLE PARENTS AND BLENDED FAMILIES

Approximately one-half of households in the United States are single-parent families or blended families. About 18 percent of parents are raising their children alone, while 33 percent of families are classified as blended.[23] A **blended family** is one composed of adult partners and children from present and/or previous marriages. For a large segment of the population, part of enhancing personal life is therefore to adequately handle the challenges of single parenthood, or being part of a blended family.

SINGLE PARENTHOOD

Being a single parent usually involves both working outside the home and raising one or more children with only some or no help from another parent. As a single mother puts it, "I have one of the toughest roles in life. I'm trying to get ahead in my career as a tax accountant. At the same time, I have to give top priority to raising two preschool children. Their father lives out-of-town and sees them infrequently. He pays the minimum in child support. To add to the confusion, I'm trying to be a decent homemaker and have a social life of my own."

As implied in this woman's statements, the problems of single parenthood are lessened when the former partner contributes to parenting. The former partner is much more likely to take an active role in parenting and continue with child support payments when the couple is no longer warring. Children and parents involved in a divorce adjust best when one parent has physical custody, but both share legal custody.[24] Children who have to cope with a living arrangement such as switching living quarters each week have greater difficulty making plans with friends.

With shared legal custody, the noncustodial parent still has the right to contribute to major decisions affecting the child, such as education and medical treatment. Many of the advantages of shared (or joint) physical custody can be obtained when the child regularly sees the noncustodial parent. A good schedule would include one overnight stay per week at the noncustodial parent's house.

Whether joint physical or joint legal custody is best is controversial, but one conclusion is universally accepted. A child needs a warm, supportive relationship with both parents to minimize the trauma of family splitting. When the parents can minimize conflict, it is easier to establish a peaceful environment conducive to healthy child rearing.

Another challenge of single parenthood is to keep the child's role unambiguous. Instead of developing a new social life, some single parents attempt to use the child as a partner substitute. The child may be asked to attend social functions with the parent, accompany the parent on all vacations, and become a confidant. Although parent-child closeness is healthy, both parent and child also need an independent social life.

BLENDED FAMILIES

When single parents team up with a new partner, they become members of a blended family. Many of the challenges involved in being part of a blended family center around the stepparent role. Nearly one-half of second marriages fail. The reason most often cited for this high failure rate is problems with the partner's children. Stepparent issues to be faced include:

- How much authority does the stepparent have to discipline?

- Should the stepparent be regarded as a "real" mother or father?

- Should the stepparent be asked to contribute to their stepchildren's medical, educational, and automobile expenses?

Stepparents and stepchildren have to make an active contribution to create a harmonious blended family. According to Pearl Ketover Prilik, strategies used by successful stepparents include the following[25]:

1. *Remaining in the present.* Confident stepparents are not threatened by the past; they can accept the fact that their stepchildren were raised previously by another parent.

2. *Planning for the future.* Making plans, such as vacation trips or improving the house, projects a feeling of optimism to stepchildren.

3. *Commitment to stepchildren.* Confident stepparents commit themselves to caring for their stepchildren, even though they know their stepchildren did not choose them.

4. *Playing active roles in the blended family.* Successful stepparents function with energy and confidence. They take action rather than waiting for things to fall into place.

5. *Gracefully accepting the rewards of stepparenthood.* Successful stepparents enjoy blended family relationships that are founded upon commitment rather than biology. Powerful rewards can be found in relationships that are the product of mutual choice rather than obligation.

 SUMMARY

A satisfying and rewarding personal life is an important end in itself. It can also enhance your career or prevent a loss of concentration on the job.

Contributors or keys to happiness are somewhat under a person's control. They include: (1) giving priority to happiness, (2) love and friendship, (3) self-esteem, (4) working hard at things enjoyed, (5) accomplishment and the ability to enjoy it, (6) openness and trust, (7) appreciation of the joys of day-to-day living, (8) fairness, kindness, and helpfulness to others, (9) fun, (10) coping with anxiety, stress, grief, and disappointment, (11) living with what you cannot change, (12) energizing yourself through physical fitness, (13) balancing your emotional responses to extreme experiences, and (14) developing a philosophy or system of belief.

A good social life begins with finding the people you want to date. Such an important activity in life should not be left to chance or fate alone. Instead, use a planned approach that includes exploring many sensible alternatives.

Understanding why people are attracted to one another helps in choosing a compatible partner. The balance theory of attraction contends that people prefer relationships that are consistent or balanced, and therefore they are comfortable with people similar to themselves. According to social exchange theory, people seek relationships in which there is an even match of personal assets. A third explanation is that people are attracted to each other because their need for intimacy prompts them to fall in love.

To keep intimate relationships healthy, you should resolve issues as they arise. Suggestions for accomplishing this include: engage in two-way communication; restate your partner's point of view; define the real problem; stick to the issue; don't hit below the belt; minimize an accusatory tone; avoid manipulative pressure; and be willing to go the extra mile.

Dual-career couples are subject to unique pressures. To sustain a good relationship, a dual-career couple should consider these approaches: (1) establish priorities and manage time carefully; (2) deal directly with feelings of competitiveness; (3) share big decisions equally; (4) divide household tasks equitably; (5) take turns being inconvenienced; (6) develop adequate systems for childcare; (7) share parenting roles; and (8) decide who pays for what.

Keeping a relationship vibrant is a major challenge. Among the strategies proposed to meet this goal are: (1) choose a partner carefully; (2) keep romantic love in perspective; (3) strive for intimacy, passion, and commitment; (4) have communication sessions; (5) avoid steady barrages of criticism; (6) strive for novelty in your relationship; (7) maintain a non-possessive relationship; and (8) attend relationship seminars.

For a large segment of the population, part of enhancing personal life is to adequately handle the challenges of single parenthood or being part of a blended family. The problems of single parenting are lessened when both parents cooperate in providing a high-quality family environment for the child. For blended families to function smoothly, stepparents must make an active contribution by such means as being committed to stepchildren.

Questions and Activities

1. Identify at least three ideas from the previous chapters that might help you achieve any of the "keys to happiness."

2. Ask a happy older person what he or she thinks of the accuracy of the ten keys to happiness.

3. At what point in a relationship might it be appropriate to tell another person that you love him or her?

4. In this chapter you were told that the office has become the best place to meet a mate. In Chapter 9 you were cautioned about the hazards of an office romance. How do you integrate these two opinions?

5. How well do the balance and exchange theories of attraction explain the formation of friendships that do not involve romance?

6. To help select a mate more carefully, some people hire detectives or background investigation firms to dig up information on the prospective mate. What is your reaction?

7. How might a couple resolve the issue of one person being upset because the other person has little ambition?

8. Should the married partner who earns the most money have the most say in making decisions? Explain your position.

9. When one person in a dual-career couple loses a job, should that person be responsible for all the household errands?

10. Ask a friend with a stepparent what he or thinks are the biggest challenges a stepparent faces.

 REFERENCES

[1]Diane Swanbrow, "The Paradox of Happiness," *Psychology Today,* July/August 1989, p. 38.

[2]Maury M. Breecher, "C'mon Smile!" *Los Angeles Times,* October 3, 1982; Swanbrow, "The Paradox of Happiness"; Martin Seligman, *What You Can Change and What You Can't* (New York: Knopf, 1994).

A HUMAN RELATIONS CASE PROBLEM: THE UNHAPPY LADDER CLIMBER

After graduating with a major in business administration and marketing, Shin Lee took a position as a customer service specialist with the local gas and electric company. The core of Shin's job was to handle customer complaints and problems over the phone and in person. Most of the complaints dealt with billing problems, but Shin also handled disputes about cutting off service to nonpaying customers. Shin welcomed this demanding position; it was his first assignment in a job rotation program that prepared him for climbing the company ladder.

In addition to handling customer problems, Shin had to prepare reports summarizing his activities, attend department meetings, and study company manuals to learn more about the company's operations. On a typical workday, Shin would deal with customers and attend meetings from 8:30 A.M. until 5:30 P.M. He would then stay in the office for two more hours to take care of paperwork. When Shin left the office at 7:30 P.M., he would bring paperwork home. On nights he brought work home, Shin would work from approximately 9:30 until 10:30.

While attending a cousin's wedding, an aunt from his mother's side, Kim Chiang, asked Shin whether he had any wedding plans. "I'm further from marriage than the man in the moon," said Shin. "My social life is at rock bottom. As you can see, I'm here alone. I couldn't think of even one person to invite."

"Why didn't you have anybody to invite?" asked Kim. "You are an eligible young man with a good job and a great future. Besides that, you have many fine qualities."

(Continued)

"Thanks for the compliment, Aunt Kim, but it's my job that's killing my social life. I'm on the way up in the company, and it leaves very little time for social life. I'm beginning to hate all the nights and weekends alone. But I guess it's the sacrifice one has to make to achieve greatness."

"Shin, you have the wrong attitude, I'm worried about you being alone so much. It's no good for your mental outlook. I bet there are some eligible young ladies right here at this wedding. Let me see if I can introduce you to one. I'll be back shortly, after I speak to some people to find out which women are unattached."

"Don't bother, Aunt Kim. It just won't work. I've had introductions before. I've had a couple of dates since I joined the company. After a woman finds out I have very little time available for social life, she loses interest. Having a miserable social life is the price one pays for success.

"I may be lonely, but I'll survive. Maybe after I become promoted to customer service supervisor in a year or so, I can start building my social life."

QUESTIONS

1. What advice would you offer Shin Lee so he can achieve his career goals yet still lead a reasonable social life?

2. Should the company be blamed for Shin's loneliness? Or is it self-imposed?

3. How helpful is Aunt Kim's planned approach to improving Shin's social life?

4. How does this case relate to the major theme of this book?

A HUMAN RELATIONS ROLE PLAY: KEEPING YOUR RELATIONSHIP VIBRANT

The role-playing exercise described here will help you experience the type of communication and interaction required for keeping a relationship vibrant. As with any other role play, visualize yourself in the role briefly described. Try to develop the feel and the flavor of the person depicted.

The man in this relationship is becoming concerned that his wife does not enthusiastically participate in activities involving his family. He prefers that he and his wife spend their Sunday afternoons with his parents and other relatives. He thinks they are all loads of fun and cannot imagine why his wife is beginning to drag her heels about spending time with them. Twice in the last month she has come up with excuses for not going along with him to visit his folks on Sunday.

The woman in this relationship still loves her husband but thinks his preference for Sunday afternoons with his folks is unreasonable. She thinks that it is time for her to pursue her own interests on Sunday afternoons. She plans to confront her husband about the situation this evening.

Two people act out this role play for about fifteen to twenty minutes. Other members of the class can act as observers. Among the observation points will be: (1) How well did the couple get to the key issues? (2) How much feeling was expressed? (3) Do they appear headed toward a resolution of this problem?

[3]Based on research being conducted by Tim Kasser, department of psychology, the University of Rochester, 1994.

[4]Martin Seligman, "Don't Diet, Be Happy," *USA Weekend,* February 4–6, 1994, p. 12.

[5]Quoted in Gary Soulsman, "Looking for Love in All the Right Places," *The Wilmington News Journal,* syndicated story, May 4, 1991.

[6]John M. Darley, Sam Glucksberg, and Ronald A. Kinchla, *Psychology,* 4th ed. (Englewood Cliffs, N.J.: Prentice Hall, 1988), p. 681.

[7]Daniel Goleman, "Making a Science of Why We Love Isn't Easy," *The New York Times* syndicated story, July 23, 1986.

[8]Ibid.

[9]David M. Buss, "Conflict Between the Sexes: Strategic Interference and the Evocation of Anger and Upset," *Journal of Personality and Social Psychology,* May 1989, pp. 735–747.

[10]Adapted from Ann Ellenson, *Human Relations* (Englewood Cliffs, N.J.: Prentice Hall, 1973), p. 211; updated with information about fighting fair from Lori Gordon, *Love Knots* (New York: Dell, 1990).

[11]Renee Magid, *The Work and Family Challenge,* American Management Association Briefing (New York: American Management Association, 1990), pp. 37–38.

[12]Steven R. Covey, "Decide Your Priorities," *USA Weekend,* December 31, 1993–January 2, 1994, p. 9.

[13]Jack L. Simonetti, Nick Nykodym, and Janet M. Goralske, "Family Ties: A Guide for HR Managers," *Personnel,* January 1988, p. 39.

[14]Jeannette Lauer and Robert Lauer, "Marriages Made to Last," *Psychology Today,* June 1985, p. 24.

[15]Harville Hendrix, "Love and Marriage," *Family Circle* syndicated story, March 17, 1990.

[16]Robert J. Sternberg, *The Triangle of Love: Intimacy, Passion, and Commitment.* New York: Basic Books, 1988.

[17]Quoted in Elizabeth Mehren, "Love! Intimacy! Passion! New Books Say Even (Gasp!) Married Folks Can Have It All," *Los Angeles Times* syndicated story, February 5, 1994.

[18]Research reported in "Listen and Improve Relations," *The Pryor Report,* May 1994, p. 12.

[19]Diane Vaughan, "The Long Goodbye," *Psychology Today,* July 1987, p. 39.

[20]Lauer and Lauer, "Marriages Made to Last," p. 26.

[21]Francesca M. Cancian, *Love in America: Gender and Self-Development* (Cambridge, England: Cambridge University Press, 1987).

[22]Ellen Rosen, "Back in Touch," Rochester, New York *Democrat and Chronicle,* July 18, 1993, p. 4D.

[23]Lynn Smith and Bob Sipchen, "Workers Crave Time with Kids," *San Francisco Chronicle,* August 13, 1990, p. B3.

[24]Gina Kolata, "Child Splitting," *Psychology Today,* November 1988, p. 34.

[25]Pearl Ketover Prilik, *Step-Mothering: Another Kind of Love* (New York: Berkely Books, 1990), p. 5.

ADDITIONAL READING

Barbach, Lonnie, and Guisinger, David. *Going the Distance.*

Cate, Rodney M., and Lloyd, Sally A. *Courtship.* Newbury Park, Calif.: Sage, 1992.

Nardi, Peter M. (ed.). *Men's Friendships.* Newbury Park, Calif.: Sage, 1992.

Poduska, Bernard. *For Love & Money: A Guide to Finances and Relationships.* Pacific Grove, Calif.: Brooks/Cole, 1993.

Silberstein, Lisa R. *Dual-Career Marriages: A System in Transition.* Hillsdale, N.J.: Earlbaum, 1992.

Utterback, Betty. *Suddenly Single.* New York: Simon & Schuster, 1992.

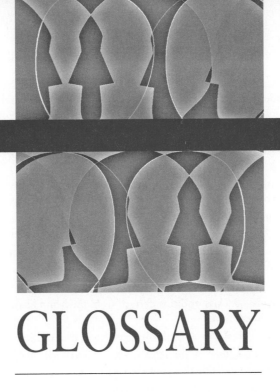

GLOSSARY

Achievement need   The need to accomplish something difficult, to win over others.

Action plan   A description of how a person is going to reach a goal.

Aggressive   Acting in an overbearing, pushy, obnoxious, and sometimes hostile manner.

Anger   A feeling of extreme hostility, indignation, or exasperation.

Annuity   A long-term investment offered by an insurance company, with tax-deductible earnings.

Assertive   To state clearly what one wants or how one feels in a given situation without being abusive, abrasive, or obnoxious.

Assertiveness training (AT)   A self-improvement program that teaches people to express their feelings and act with an appropriate degree of openness and assertiveness.

Backstabbing   An attempt to discredit by underhanded means such as innuendo, accusation, or the like.

Balance theory   An explanation of attraction stating that people prefer relationships that are consistent or balanced.

Bank debit card   A bank card that instantly transfers money from your bank account to the account of a merchant.

Behavior   The tangible acts or decisions of people, including both their actions and words.

Behavior modification (mod)   A system of motivating people that emphasizes rewarding them for doing the right things and punishing them for doing the wrong things.

Bias   A prejudgment toward another person or group based on something other than fact.

Blended family   A family composed of adult partners and children from current and/or previous marriages.

Body image   One's perception of one's body.

Brainstorming   A technique by which group members think of multiple solutions to a problem.

Brainwriting   (or solo brainstorming) Arriving at creative ideas by jotting them down yourself.

Broken-record technique   An assertive skill of calmly repeating your position over and over again without showing signs of anger or irritation.

Burnout   A condition of emotional, mental, and physical exhaustion along with cynicism in response to long-term job stressors.

Business etiquette   A special code of behavior required in work settings.

Cannabis   A class of drugs derived from the hemp plant that generally produce a state of mild euphoria.

Career   A series of related job experiences that fit into a meaningful pattern.

Career counselor   A specialist whose professional role is to provide counseling and guidance to individuals about their careers.

Career path   A sequence of positions necessary to achieve a goal.

Career portability   The ability to move from one employer to another when necessary.

Carpal tunnel syndrome   A condition that occurs when repetitive flexing and extension of the wrist causes the tendons to swell, thus trapping and pinching the median nerve.

Chain of command   In an organization, the official statement of who reports to whom.

Charisma   A type of charm and magnetism that inspires others.

Chronological résumé   A job résumé that presents work experience, education, and interests, along with accomplishments, in reverse chronological order.

Cognitive resource theory   An explanation of leadership stating that the major source of the plans, decisions, and strategies that guide the group's actions are the leader's intellectual abilities.

Communication   The sending and receiving of messages.

Competence   As part of wellness, the presence of both job skills and social skills, including the ability to solve problems and control anger.

Compulsiveness   A tendency to pay careful attention to detail and to be neat.

Concentrate on one bill at a time   A technique of debt reduction by which you pay off your smallest debt with a variable payment and then concentrate successively on your next smallest debts.

Conflict   A condition that exists when two sets of demands, goals, or motives are incompatible.

Confrontation and problem solving   A method of identifying the true source of conflict and resolving it systematically.

Contrary investing   The principle of buying investments when the demand for them is very low, and selling when the demand is very high.

Creative-style résumé   A job résumé with a novel format and design.

Creativity   The ability to develop good ideas that can be put into practice.

Database   A systematic way of storing files for future retrieval.

Decision making   Selecting one alternative from the various solutions or courses of action that can be pursued.

Decision-making software   Any computer program that helps the decision maker work through the problem-solving and decision-making steps.

Decoding   The process of the receiver interpreting the message and translating it into meaningful information.

Defensive communication   The tendency to receive messages in such a way that our self-esteem is protected.

Denial   The suppression of information by the person that he or she finds to be uncomfortable.

Depressant   A drug that slows down vital body processes.

Depression   A widespread emotional disorder in which the person has such difficulties as sadness, changes in appetite, sleeping difficulties, and a decrease in activities, interests, and energy.

Disarm the opposition   A method of conflict resolution in which you disarm the criticizer by agreeing with valid criticism directed toward you.

Diversity awareness training   A program that provides an opportunity for employees to develop the skills necessary to deal effectively with each other and with customers in a diverse environment.

Dollar-cost averaging   An investment technique in which you purchase the same amount of money in a stock or mutual fund at regular intervals over a long period of time.

Downsizing (or **rightsizing**)   A method of reducing the number of employees to save money and improve efficiency.

Effectiveness   In relation to leadership, a situation in which the leader helps the group accomplish its objectives without neglecting satisfaction and morale.

Empathy   Understanding another person's point of view, or placing oneself in another's shoes.

Encoding   The process of organizing ideas into a series of symbols, such as words and gestures, designed to communicate with the receiver.

Expectancy theory of motivation   An explanation of motivation stating that people will be motivated if they believe that their effort will lead to desired outcomes.

External locus of control   A belief that external forces control one's fate.

Fear of success   The belief that if one succeeds at an important task, he or she will be asked to take on more responsibility in the future.

Feedback   Information that tells you how well you have performed, and helps you make corrections where indicated.

Feeling-type individuals   People who have a need to conform and attempt to adapt to the wishes of others.

Fight-or-flight response   The body's battle against a stressor that helps one deal with emergencies.

Flow experience   Total absorption in one's work.

Frustration   A blocking of need or motive satisfaction, or blocking of a need, wish, or desire.

Functional résumé   A job résumé that organizes your skills and accomplishments into the functions or tasks that support the job you are seeking.

Galeta effect   Improving your performance through raising your own expectations.

Glass ceiling   An invisible but difficult-to-penetrate barrier to promotion based on subtle attitudes and prejudices.

Goal   An event, circumstance, object, condition, or purpose for which a person strives. Also, a conscious intention to do something.

Grazing Popular term for eating meals on the run in order to make use of time ordinarily spent sitting down for meals.

Group norms The unwritten set of expectations for group members—what people ought to do.

Grudge Unresolved or unrepressed anger felt toward someone whom we believe has wronged us.

Hallucinogens A class of drugs that in small doses produce visual effects similar to hallucinations.

Human relations The art of using systematic knowledge about human behavior to improve personal, job, and career effectiveness.

Information (or communication) overload A condition in which the individual is confronted with so much information to process that he or she becomes overwhelmed and therefore does a poor job of processing information.

Insight A depth of understanding that requires considerable intuition and common sense.

Internal locus of control A belief that one is the primary cause of events happening to oneself.

Interpersonal Anything relating to the interactions between and among people.

Intuition A method of arriving at a conclusion by a quick judgment or "gut feel."

Intuitive-type individuals People who prefer an overall perspective, or the big picture.

IRA (individual retirement account) A supplemental retirement account, fully funded by the individual, that qualifies for certain tax advantages.

Job objective The position one is applying for now or a job one intends to hold in the future.

Lateral move Transferring to a job at the same level and approximate salary as your present one.

Lateral thinking Thought process whereby an individual seeks out many alternative solutions to a problem. Lateral thinking is creative and broad-based, as opposed to *vertical thinking,* which zeros in on a single best solution.

Leadership The process of influencing others to achieve certain goals.

Leading task An easy, warm-up activity that helps you get started on a project that you might otherwise procrastinate doing.

Life-change units A scale of values assigned to the impact caused by certain life events, representing the average amount of social readjustment considered necessary to cope with a given change, such as death of a spouse. The higher the number of life-change units, the greater the stress.

Lifestyle A person's typical approach to living, including moral attitudes, clothing preferences, and ways of spending money.

Liquid assets Assets that can be converted into cash relatively quickly.

Maslow's need hierarchy A widely accepted theory of motivation emphasizing that people strive to fulfill needs. These needs are arranged in a hierarchy of importance—physiological, safety, belongingness, esteem, and self-actualization. People tend to strive for need satisfaction at one level only after satisfaction has been achieved at the previous one.

Mentors Bosses who take subordinates under their wings and guide, teach, and coach them.

Mirroring A form of nonverbal communication in which one person subtly imitates another, such as following the other person's breathing pattern.

Motive An inner drive that moves a person to do something.

Narcotic A drug that dulls the senses, facilitates sleep, and is addictive with long-term use.

Need   An internal striving or urge to do something. (Or a deficit within an individual that creates a craving for its satisfaction.)

Need for intimacy   An explanation of love centering on the idea that people crave intimacy.

Negative affectivity   A tendency to experience aversive (intensely disliked) emotional states.

Negative inquiry   The active encouragement of criticism in order to use helpful information or exhaust manipulative criticism.

Negotiation and bargaining   Conferring with another person to resolve a problem.

Networking   The process of establishing a group of contacts who can help you in your career.

Net worth   The difference between your assets and liabilities.

Neurobiological disorders   A quirk in the chemistry or anatomy of the brain that creates a disability.

Nonassertive   A passive type of behavior in which people let things happen to them without letting their feelings be known.

Nonpossessive relationship   A relationship in which both people maintain separate identities and strive for personal fulfillment.

Nonverbal communication   Sending messages other than by direct use of words, such as in writing and speaking with gestures.

Nonverbal feedback   The signs other than words that indicate whether or not the sender's message has been delivered.

Openness to experience   A positive orientation toward learning.

Participative leader   A person in charge who shares power and decision making with the group.

Peak performance   The mental state necessary for achieving maximum results from minimum effort.

Peer evaluations   A system in which co-workers contribute to an evaluation of a person's job performance.

Performance standard   A statement of what constitutes acceptable performance.

Personality clash   An antagonistic relationship between two people based on differences in personal attributes, preferences, interests, values, and styles.

Planning   Deciding what needs to be accomplished and the actions needed to make it happen.

Positive mental attitude   A strong belief that things will work in your favor.

Positive reinforcement   Rewarding somebody for doing something right.

Positive self-talk   Saying positive things about oneself to oneself in order to build self-confidence.

Positive visual imagery   Picturing a positive outcome in your mind.

Private self   The actual person that one may be.

Problem   A gap between what exists and what you want to exist.

Procrastination   Putting off a task for no valid reason.

Productivity   The amount of quality work accomplished in relation to the resources consumed.

Psychological hardiness   Describes an individual who tends to profit from stressful situations instead of developing negative symptoms.

Psychotherapy   A method of overcoming emotional problems through discussion with a mental health professional.

Public self   What the person is communicating about himself or herself, and what others actually perceive about the person.

Pygmalion effect   The mysterious phenomenon that occurs when group members succeed because their leader expects them to (i.e., a group tends to live up to the leader's expectations).

Realistic goal   One that represents the right amount of challenge for the person pursuing the goal.

Relaxation response   A bodily reaction in which the person experiences a slower respiration and heart rate, lowered blood pressure, and lowered metabolism.

Resilience   The ability to withstand pressure and emerge stronger for it.

Role ambiguity   A condition in which a job holder receives confusing or poorly defined expectations.

Role conflict   The state that occurs when a person has to choose between two competing demands or expectations.

Role confusion   Uncertainty about the role one is carrying out. For example, socializing with one's boss may create fuzzy demarcation lines at work.

Role overload   A burdensome work load that can lead to stress.

Role underload   Having too little to do. Can sometimes create stress similar to having too much to do (role overload).

Schmoozing   Informal socializing on the job.

Self   A person's total being or individuality.

Self-concept   What you think of yourself and who you think you are.

Self-defeating behavior   A behavior pattern in which the person intentionally or unintentionally engages in activities or harbors attitudes that work against his or her best interests.

Self-determining work   Work that allows the person performing the task some choice in initiating and regulating his or her own actions.

Self-disclosure   The process of revealing your inner self to others.

Self-efficacy   The belief in one's capability to perform a task.

Self-esteem   The sense of feeling worthwhile and the pride that comes from a sense of self-worth.

Self-understanding   Knowledge about oneself, particularly with respect to mental and emotional aspects.

Sensation-type individuals   People who prefer routine and order.

Sensitivity   Taking people's needs and feelings into account when dealing with them.

SEP (simplified employee pension)   Retirement plans for individuals who are self-employed or for those who earn part of their income from self-employment.

Sexual harassment   Behavior of a sexual nature in the workplace that is offensive to an individual and that interferes with a person's ability to perform the job.

Skill   A learned, specific ability to perform a task competently (for example, writing a report, conducting a statistical analysis, or troubleshooting software problems).

Social exchange theory   The idea that human relationships are based mainly on self-interest; therefore, people measure their social, physical, and other assets against a potential partner's.

Sponsor   A higher-ranking individual who is favorably impressed with you and therefore recommends you for promotion and choice assignments.

Stimulants   A class of drugs that produce feelings of optimism and high energy.

Stress   An internal reaction to any force that threatens to disturb a person's equilibrium.

Stress interview   A deliberate method of placing a job applicant under considerable pressure and then observing his or her reactions.

Stressor   The external or internal force that brings about the stress.

Strong Interest Inventory (SII)   The most widely used instrument for matching a person's interests with careers.

Substance abuse   The overuse of any substance that enters the bloodstream.

Success   Used in this book to mean attaining the twin goals of organizational rewards and personal satisfaction.

Support system   A group of people a person can rely on for encouragement and comfort.

Swim against the tide   Advancing your career by taking an unconventional path to career success.

Swiss-cheese method   A method of fighting procrastination whereby you "eat holes" in a large task until it is completed. You thus work on a task a little bit at a time.

Targeted résumé   A job résumé that focuses on a specific job target or position and presents only information about you that supports the target.

Tax-sheltered annuity (TSA)   A special type of annuity for employees of educational institutions and certain other nonprofit institutions, such as hospitals.

Team leader   A person who facilitates and guides the efforts of a small group which is given some authority to govern itself.

Team player   A person who emphasizes group accomplishment and cooperation rather than individual achievement and not helping others.

Technical competence   In leadership, being skilled in the actual work of the group.

Telesearch   Obtaining job leads by making unsolicited phone calls to prospective employers.

Thinking-type individuals   People who rely on reason and intellect to deal with problems.

Time leak   Anything you are doing or not doing that allows time to get away from you.

Total Quality Management (TQM)   A system of management in which all activities are directed toward satisfying external and internal customers.

Traditional mental set   A fixed way of thinking about objects and activities.

Transcendental meditation (TM)   A mental technique of establishing a physiological state of deep rest.

Troubleshooting   The knack for pinpointing and analyzing snags in work flow as they arise.

Type A behavior   A pattern of being aggressively involved in a chronic, incessant struggle to achieve more in less and less time.

Unsolicited-letter campaign   A job search method in which the job seeker sends letters to prospective employers without knowing if a job opening exists.

VDT stress   An adverse physical and psychological reaction to prolonged work at a video display terminal.

Vertical thinking   An analytical, logical thought process whereby an individual is seeking a single best solution to a problem. Narrower than *lateral thinking* because it results in fewer solutions.

Visualization   As a stress-management technique, picturing yourself doing something you would like to do. In general, a method of imagining yourself behaving in a particular way in order to achieve that behavior.

Wellness   A formalized approach to preventive health care.

Win-win   The belief that, after conflict has been resolved, both sides should gain something of value.

Work ethic   A firm belief in the dignity and value of work.

Work habits   A person's characteristic approach to work, including such things as organization, handling of paperwork, and the setting of priorities.

Worst-case scenario   The dreadful alternative in a decision-making situation.

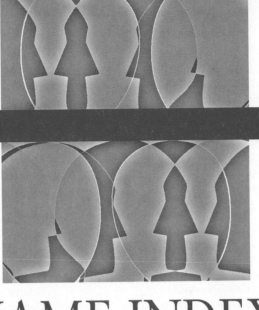

NAME INDEX

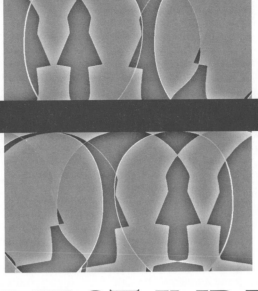

SUBJECT INDEX